ב"ה

Book Smart

—

AUTHOR
Rabbi Yanki Tauber

Cover Art: *Holy Books Four,*
David Baruch Wolk, oil on canvas, 2013.

Printed in the United States of America

718-221-6900
WWW.MYJLI.COM

Book Smart

Exploring Judaism's Most Important Titles, and the Authors Who Inscribed Them

STUDENT TEXTBOOK

The Rohr Jewish Learning Institute
gratefully acknowledges the pioneering
and ongoing support of

George and Pamela Rohr

Since its inception, the Rohr JLI has been a beneficiary of the vision, generosity, care, and concern of the Rohr family.

In the merit of the tens of thousands of hours of Torah study by JLI students worldwide, may they be blessed with health, *Yiddishe nachas* from all their loved ones, and extraordinary success in all their endeavors.

DEDICATED TO

Michael and Fiona Scharf

With deep appreciation for their friendship and partnership with JLI and their commitment to furthering Jewish continuity, education, and literacy worldwide.

May they go from strength to strength and enjoy good health, happiness, *nachas* from their loved ones, and success in all their endeavors.

Citation Types

SCRIPTURE

The icon for Scripture is based on the images of a scroll and a spiral. The scroll is a literal reference; the spiral symbolizes Scripture's role as the singular source from which all subsequent Torah knowledge emanates.

SCRIPTURAL COMMENTARY

Throughout the ages, Jews have scrutinized the Torah's text, generating many commentaries.

TALMUD AND MIDRASH

The Talmud and Midrash record the teachings of the sages—fundamental links in the unbroken chain of the Torah's transmission going back to Mount Sinai.

TALMUDIC COMMENTARY

The layers of Talmudic teaching have been rigorously excavated in each era, resulting in a library of insightful commentaries.

JEWISH MYSTICISM

The mystics explore the inner, esoteric depths. The icon for mystical texts reflects the "*sefirot* tree" commonly present in kabbalistic charts.

JEWISH PHILOSOPHY

Jewish philosophic texts shed light on life's big questions and demonstrate the relevance of Jewish teachings even as the sands of societal values continuously shift.

JEWISH LAW AND CUSTOM

The guidance that emerges from Scripture and the Talmud finds practical expression in Jewish law, known as *Halachah* ("the way"), alongside customs adopted by Jewish communities through the generations.

CHASIDUT

Chasidism's advent in the eighteenth century brought major, encouraging changes to Jewish life and outlook. Its teachings are akin to refreshing, life-sustaining waters from a continuously flowing well of the profoundest insights.

LITURGY

The texts of the Jewish prayer book burst with the full spectrum of human emotion, from joy to longing to contrition and to hope. They all share the authentic search for a meaningful encounter with G-d.

PERSPECTIVES

Personal, professional, and academic perspectives, expressed in essays, research papers, diaries, and other works, can often enhance appreciation for Torah ideas and the totality of the Jewish experience.

Contents

Foreword

Torah. Midrash. Talmud. Halachah. Musar. Kabbalah . . . Regardless of the degree of your engagement with Judaism and its teachings, you are most probably familiar with these terms. Chances are that you have encountered, in print or in conversation, statements preceded by, "The Midrash says . . .", "The Talmud discusses . . .", "According to Kabbalah . . ." etc.

What, exactly, is "the Torah"? When, how, why, and by whom was "the Talmud" written? What is in "Kabbalah"? What makes a particular teaching a "Midrash"? Each of these areas of Jewish learning has its own unique history, its own authors and heroes, its own library of classics and foundational works, its own methodologies and objectives, its own ecosystem and culture. Each is a world unto itself, even as they all collectively nourish the unceasing quest for wisdom and knowledge that has defined us as the "People of the Book" for thirty-eight centuries.

Book Smart is an immersive journey through this multiverse of Jewish learning. In the course of our journey, we will not only learn *about* these different fields of study but also experience them firsthand. We will familiarize ourselves with the twenty-four books of the Jewish Bible; analyze a Midrashic parable; engage in Talmudic *pilpul* and debate; trace a Halachic dilemma through centuries of codes, commentaries, and responsa; investigate ideas in Jewish philosophy and ethics; and decipher a mysterious Kabbalistic passage.

At the conclusion of our six-week journey, these various areas of Torah will no longer be abstract terms but familiar domains of the mind, providing us with the contexts for all of our future Jewish learning.

LESSON

1

THE TORAH

What's in the twenty-four books of the Jewish Bible? When and by whom were they transcribed? In this lesson, we review the contents of the Tanach—the Five Books of Moses, the eight books of the Prophets, and the eleven "Scriptural" books—and explore the relationship between the "Written Torah" and the many thousands of works of Jewish teaching that extend from it.

FOR OUT OF ZION SHALL GO FORTH THE TORAH I
Yossi Rosenstein, acrylic on canvas, Israel, 2021.

I. WHAT IS THE TORAH?

In this section, we introduce the aims and goals of this course. The vast body of Jewish learning includes many fields—Bible, Talmud, Midrash, Halachah, Kabbalah, Musar, Chakirah, and so on. Each of these "genres" includes works by hundreds or even thousands of different authors, composed over many centuries in every part of the world. Our goal is to understand the unique character and function of each genre of Torah, familiarize ourselves with its primary works and authors, and experience the "flavor" of learning it represents.

We begin with the basic question: What is the Torah? We learn that the term "the Torah" refers both to one specific book, as well as to the entire body of Jewish teaching. What is the nature of the relationship between the two "Torahs"? How did "Torah A" develop into "Torah B"?

What Is the Torah? **Rabbi Mendel Kaplan** explains: **myjli.com/booksmart**

FIGURE 1.1

Course Map—Genres of Torah

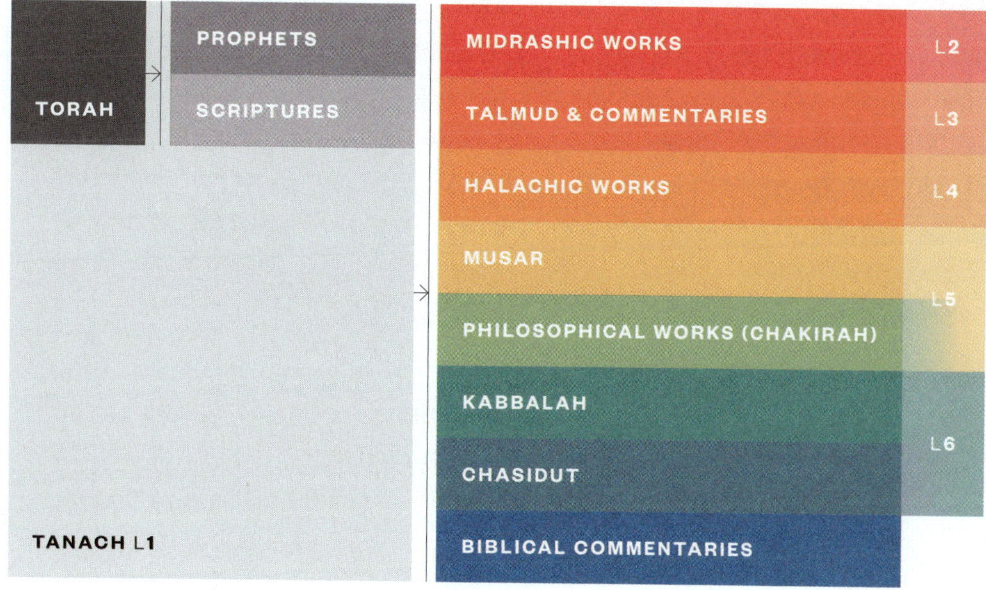

FIGURE 1.2

Two Definitions of Torah

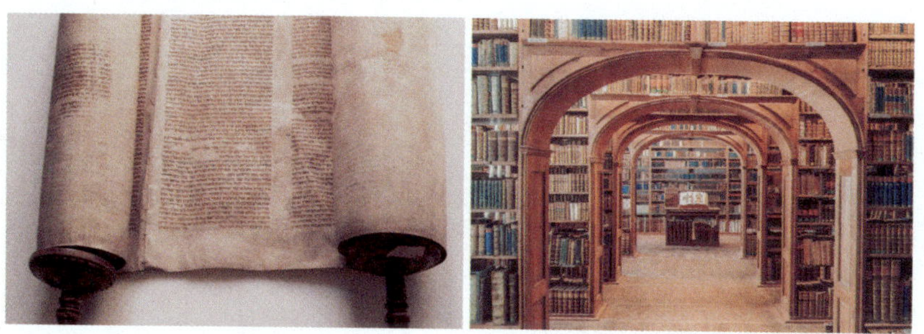

(A)
THE TORAH

(B)
THE TORAH

II. THE WRITTEN TORAH AND THE ORAL TORAH

The Torah comes in two forms: written and oral. Jewish tradition insists that the "Written Torah" be treated as an inviolable text—every word and letter is significant and must be meticulously preserved. In contrast, the "Oral Torah" must be preserved as an ongoing oral communication from teacher to disciple; for many centuries, it was even forbidden for it to be officially transcribed. This duality is integral to the nature of Torah.

TEXT 1

The Pen and the Mouth

Talmud, Gitin 60b

דְבָרִים שֶׁבִּכְתַב אִי אַתָּה רַשַּׁאי לְאוֹמְרָן עַל פֶּה.
דְבָרִים שֶׁבְּעַל פֶּה אִי אַתָּה רַשַּׁאי לְאוֹמְרָן בִּכְתָב.

The words that were given in writing—you are not allowed to communicate them orally. And the words that were taught orally—you are not allowed to communicate them in writing.

Frontispiece to the *Griselini Bible* depicting the binding of Isaac. Printed by the Bragadin printing office in Venice, this 1739 edition of the Tanach is most famous for its four engraved frontispieces. (Braginsky Collection 150)

BABYLONIAN TALMUD

A literary work of monumental proportions that draws upon the legal, spiritual, intellectual, ethical, and historical traditions of Judaism. The 37 tractates of the Babylonian Talmud contain the teachings of the Jewish sages from the period after the destruction of the 2nd Temple through the 5th century CE. It has served as the primary vehicle for the transmission of the Oral Law and the education of Jews over the centuries; it is the entry point for all subsequent legal, ethical, and theological Jewish scholarship.

QUESTION

Why is the Torah formulated as both a written text and an oral dialogue? What would be lacking if it were only a written document, or only an oral tradition?

Jewish Bookshop on Wentworth Street, Pearl Binder, in *The Real East End* by Thomas Burke (London, U.K.: Constable, 1932), lithograph.

III. THE TWENTY-FOUR BOOKS OF TANACH

In this section, we survey the twenty-four books of the Written Torah, which the world knows as "the Jewish Bible." We learn that these are divided into three categories—"Torah," "Prophets," and "Writings"—representing three levels of Divine revelation. We are introduced to the contents of each book, its author/transcriber, and its historical background. We also peruse selected texts (appearing in the "Additional Features" for this lesson) that highlight the variety of historical, legal, philosophical, mystical, and inspirational content in these books.

BOYS TIME
Alex Levin, oil on canvas.

FIGURE 1.3

The Jewish Bible

TORAH

PROPHETS

WRITINGS

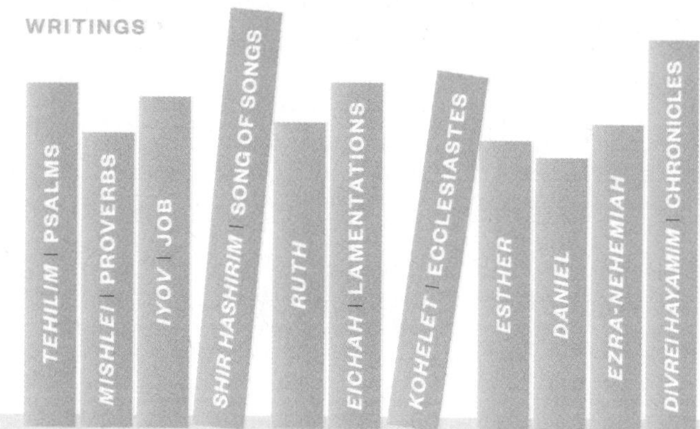

For a detailed chart, see the infographic "Contents of the Twenty-Four Books of the Tanach" on Side B of the pullout card provided with your Student Textbook.

TEXT 2

Encyclopedia of Life

Mishnah, Avot 5:21

הֲפָךְ בָּהּ וַהֲפָךְ בָּהּ, דְּכֹלָּא בָהּ.
וּבָהּ תֶּחֱזֵי, וְסִיב וּבְלֵה בָהּ, וּמִנָּהּ לֹא תָזוּעַ,
שֶׁאֵין לְךָ מִדָּה טוֹבָה הֵימֶנָּה.

Delve and delve into it, for all is in it; see with it; grow old and worn in it; do not budge from it, for there is nothing better.

AVOT *(ETHICS OF THE FATHERS; PIRKEI AVOT)*

A 6-chapter work on Jewish ethics that is studied widely by Jewish communities, especially during the summer. The first 5 chapters are from the Mishnah, tractate Avot. Avot differs from the rest of the Mishnah in that it does not focus on legal subjects; it is a collection of the sages' wisdom on topics related to character development, ethics, healthy living, piety, and the study of Torah.

FIGURE 1.4

Three Modes of Divine Communication

SECTION OF WRITTEN TORAH	MODE OF DIVINE COMMUNICATION
TORAH (FIVE BOOKS OF MOSES)	Direct Communication
NEVIIM—PROPHETS	Prophecy
KETUVIM—WRITINGS	*Ru'ach Hakodesh* ("Divine Spirit")

TEXT 3

Beyond Prophecy

Exodus 33:11 and Numbers 12:6–8

וְדִבֶּר ה' אֶל מֹשֶׁה פָּנִים אֶל פָּנִים,
כַּאֲשֶׁר יְדַבֵּר אִישׁ אֶל רֵעֵהוּ.

G-d[*] would speak to Moses face-to-face,
as a man speaks to his fellow.

אִם יִהְיֶה נְבִיאֲכֶם, ה' בַּמַּרְאָה אֵלָיו אֶתְוַדָּע, בַּחֲלוֹם אֲדַבֶּר בּוֹ. לֹא כֵן עַבְדִּי מֹשֶׁה, בְּכָל בֵּיתִי נֶאֱמָן הוּא. פֶּה אֶל פֶּה אֲדַבֶּר בּוֹ, וּמַרְאֶה וְלֹא בְחִידֹת, וּתְמֻנַת ה' יַבִּיט.

If there be a prophet among you, I, G-d, will make Myself known to them in a vision; I will speak to them in a dream. Not so is My servant Moses; in all My house he is trusted. Mouth to mouth I speak with him, in a vision and not in riddles; he gazes at the image of G-d.

[*] Throughout this book, "G-d" and "L-rd" are written with a hyphen instead of an "o" (both in our own translations and when quoting others). This is one way we accord reverence to the sacred Divine name. This also reminds us that, even as we seek G-d, He transcends any human effort to describe His reality.

TEXT 4

The Limits of Prophecy

Talmud, Megilah 14a

אַרְבָּעִים וּשְׁמוֹנָה נְבִיאִים וְשֶׁבַע נְבִיאוֹת נִתְנַבְּאוּ לָהֶם לְיִשְׂרָאֵל, וְלֹא פִּחֲתוּ וְלֹא הוֹתִירוּ עַל מַה שֶּׁכָּתוּב בַּתּוֹרָה.

Forty-eight prophets and seven prophetesses prophesied to the people of Israel, and they neither subtracted from nor added to what is written in the Torah.

TEXT 5

The Divine Spirit

Maimonides, *Guide for the Perplexed*, 2:45

שֶׁיִּמְצָא הָאָדָם כְּאִלּוּ עִנְיָן אֶחָד חָל עָלָיו, וְכֹחַ אַחֵר הִתְחַדֵּשׁ וַיְשִׂימֵהוּ לְדַבֵּר. וַיְּדַבֵּר בְּחָכְמוֹת אוֹ בְּתִשְׁבָּחוֹת אוֹ בְּדִבְרֵי הַזְהָרָה מוֹעִילִים אוֹ בְּעִנְיָנִים הַנְהָגִיִּים אוֹ אֱלוֹקִיִּים; וְזֶה כֻּלּוֹ בְּעֵת הַיְקִיצָה וְהִשְׁתַּמֵּשׁ הַחוּשִׁים עַל מִנְהֲגֵיהֶם. וְזֶהוּ אֲשֶׁר יֹאמַר עָלָיו שֶׁהוּא מְדַבֵּר בְּ'רוּחַ הַקֹּדֶשׁ'.

וּבְזֶה הַמִּין מֵ'רוּחַ הַקֹּדֶשׁ' חִבֵּר דָּוִד תְּהִלִּים, וְחִבֵּר שְׁלֹמֹה מִשְׁלֵי וְקֹהֶלֶת וְשִׁיר הַשִּׁירִים; וְכֵן דָּנִיֵּאל וְאִיּוֹב וְדִבְרֵי הַיָּמִים וּשְׁאָר הַ'כְּתוּבִים' בְּזֶה הַמִּין מֵ'רוּחַ הַקֹּדֶשׁ' חֻבְּרוּ . . . וְעַל כַּיּוֹצֵא בְּ'רוּחַ הַקֹּדֶשׁ' הַזֶּה אָמַר דָּוִד "רוּחַ ה' דִּבֶּר בִּי וּמִלָּתוֹ עַל לְשׁוֹנִי" - רְצוֹנוֹ לוֹמַר, שֶׁהִיא הֱבִיאַתְהוּ לְדַבֵּר בְּאֵלּוּ הַדְּבָרִים.

The person feels as if something has come upon them, and as if they have received a new power that drives them to speak. They speak words of wisdom, or compose hymns, or exhort their fellows with useful advice, or discourse on matters of communal leadership or theology; all this while they are awake and in the full possession of their senses. Such a person is said to speak by *ru'ach hakodesh*.

It was through this kind of Divine inspiration that David composed the Psalms, and Solomon composed the books of Proverbs, Ecclesiastes, and the Song of Songs; also Daniel, Job, Chronicles, and the rest of the "Writings" were written in this manner. . . . In reference to such *ru'ach hakodesh*, David says, "The spirit of G-d spoke in me, and His word is on my tongue" (II SAMUEL 23:2); i.e., the spirit of G-d caused him to speak these words.

RABBI MOSHE BEN MAIMON (MAIMONIDES, RAMBAM) 1135–1204

Halachist, philosopher, author, and physician. Maimonides was born in Córdoba, Spain. After the conquest of Córdoba by the Almohads, he fled Spain and eventually settled in Cairo, Egypt. There, he became the leader of the Jewish community and served as court physician to the vizier of Egypt. He is most noted for authoring the *Mishneh Torah*, an encyclopedic arrangement of Jewish law; and for his philosophical work, *Guide for the Perplexed*. His rulings on Jewish law are integral to the formation of Halachic consensus.

A PROPHET
Shoshanna Brombacher, India ink on colored paper, 2003.

IV. THE DIVINE AND THE HUMAN IN TORAH

If the Written Torah is the product of Divine revelation, what is the nature of the Oral Torah? Are the teachings of the Oral Torah also of Divine origin, given to Moses at Mount Sinai and transmitted from teacher to disciple, or are they the product of human minds, the innovations of many generations of Torah scholars? The Torah itself seems to contain mixed messages on this question.

TEXT 6

The Sinaitic Origin of Torah

Jerusalem Talmud, Pe'ah 2:4

מִקְרָא, מִשְׁנָה, תַּלְמוּד וְאַגָּדָה,
אֲפִלּוּ מָה שֶׁתַּלְמִיד וָתִיק עָתִיד לְחַדֵּשׁ,
כְּבָר נֶאֱמַר לְמֹשֶׁה בְּסִינַי.

Scripture, Mishnah, Talmud, and Agadah, even what a proficient student is destined to innovate, were already said to Moses at Sinai.

JERUSALEM TALMUD

A commentary to the Mishnah, compiled during the 4th and 5th centuries. The Jerusalem Talmud predates its Babylonian counterpart by 100 years and is written in both Hebrew and Aramaic. While the Babylonian Talmud is the most authoritative source for Jewish law, the Jerusalem Talmud remains an invaluable source for the spiritual, intellectual, ethical, historical, and legal traditions of Judaism.

Woodcut depiction of the giving of the Torah in a 1775 book of Jewish customs by Shimon Levy Ginsburg, printed by Gerard Johann Janson in the printing house of Israel Mondovi in Amsterdam. (Gross Family Collection, Tel Aviv)

Explore the development of the written and oral Torah with **Rabbi Chaim Block**: *The Written and Oral Torah, Explained*
myjli.com/booksmart

TEXT 7

The Torah Is Not in Heaven

Talmud, Bava Metzi'a 59a–b

בְּאוֹתוֹ הַיּוֹם הֵשִׁיב רַבִּי אֱלִיעֶזֶר כָּל תְּשׁוּבוֹת שֶׁבָּעוֹלָם וְלֹא קִבְּלוּ הֵימֶנּוּ. אָמַר לָהֶם: . . . "אִם הֲלָכָה כְּמוֹתִי, אַמַּת הַמַּיִם יוֹכִיחוּ!" חָזְרוּ אַמַּת הַמַּיִם לַאֲחוֹרֵיהֶם. אָמְרוּ לוֹ: "אֵין מְבִיאִין רְאָיָה מֵאַמַּת הַמַּיִם".

חָזַר וְאָמַר לָהֶם: "אִם הֲלָכָה כְּמוֹתִי, כָּתְלֵי בֵּית הַמִּדְרָשׁ יוֹכִיחוּ!" הִטּוּ כָּתְלֵי בֵּית הַמִּדְרָשׁ לִפֹּל. גָּעַר בָּהֶם רַבִּי יְהוֹשֻׁעַ, אָמַר לָהֶם: "אִם תַּלְמִידֵי חֲכָמִים מְנַצְּחִים זֶה אֶת זֶה בַּהֲלָכָה, אַתֶּם מָה טִיבְכֶם?" לֹא נָפְלוּ מִפְּנֵי כְּבוֹדוֹ שֶׁל רַבִּי יְהוֹשֻׁעַ, וְלֹא זָקְפוּ מִפְּנֵי כְּבוֹדוֹ שֶׁל רַבִּי אֱלִיעֶזֶר, וַעֲדַיִן מָטִין וְעוֹמְדִין.

חָזַר וְאָמַר לָהֶם: "אִם הֲלָכָה כְּמוֹתִי, מִן הַשָּׁמַיִם יוֹכִיחוּ!" יָצָאת בַּת קוֹל וְאָמְרָה: "מָה לָכֶם אֵצֶל רַבִּי אֱלִיעֶזֶר, שֶׁהֲלָכָה כְּמוֹתוֹ בְּכָל מָקוֹם!"

עָמַד רַבִּי יְהוֹשֻׁעַ עַל רַגְלָיו וְאָמַר: "לֹא בַּשָּׁמַיִם הִיא!" (דְּבָרִים ל, יב).

מַאי "לֹא בַּשָּׁמַיִם הִיא"? אָמַר רַבִּי יִרְמְיָה: שֶׁכְּבָר נִתְּנָה תּוֹרָה מֵהַר סִינַי, אֵין אָנוּ מַשְׁגִּיחִין בְּבַת קוֹל. שֶׁכְּבַר כָּתַבְתָּ בְּהַר סִינַי בַּתּוֹרָה, "אַחֲרֵי רַבִּים לְהַטּוֹת" (שְׁמוֹת כג, ב).

On that day, Rabbi Eliezer brought them all sorts of proofs, but they were rejected. So he said to them, . . . "If the law is as I say, this water channel will prove it." The water channel began flowing backward. Said they to him, "One does not cite Halachic proof from a water channel."

Rabbi Eliezer then said to them, "If the law is as I say, the walls of the study hall will prove it." The walls of the study hall leaned in and began to fall. Rabbi Yehoshua scolded the walls: "If Torah scholars are contending with each other in matters of Torah law, what is the nature of your involvement?" The walls did not fall, out of deference to Rabbi Yehoshua, and neither did they straighten, out of deference to Rabbi Eliezer; they still remain leaning.

Rabbi Eliezer then said to them, "If the law is as I say, let it be proven from Heaven!" There then issued a Heavenly voice, which proclaimed: "What do you want of Rabbi Eliezer—the law is as he says. . . ."

Rabbi Yehoshua stood on his feet and said: "[The Torah] is not in heaven!" (DEUTERONOMY 30:12).

What is the meaning of the statement, "It is not in heaven"? Said Rabbi Yirmiyah: "As the Torah has already been given at Mount Sinai, we take no notice of Heavenly voices. For You, G-d, have already written in the Torah at Mount Sinai, 'Follow the majority'" (EXODUS 23:2).

TEXT 8

Prophets vs. Sages

Maimonides, *Introduction to the Mishnah*

אֶלֶף נְבִיאִים, כֻּלָּם כְּאֵלִיָּהוּ וֶאֱלִישָׁע, יִהְיוּ סוֹבְרִים סְבָרָא אַחַת, וְאֶלֶף חֲכָמִים וְחָכָם סוֹבְרִים הֵפֶךְ הַסְּבָרָא הַהִיא, "אַחֲרֵי רַבִּים לְהַטּוֹת", וַהֲלָכָה כְּדִבְרֵי הָאֶלֶף חֲכָמִים וְחָכָם . . . וְכֵן אִם יָעִיד הַנָּבִיא שֶׁהַקָּדוֹשׁ בָּרוּךְ הוּא אָמַר אֵלָיו שֶׁהַדִּין בְּמִצְוָה פְּלוֹנִית כָּךְ, וְכִי סְבָרַת פְּלוֹנִי הִיא אֱמֶת . . . הוּא נְבִיא שֶׁקֶר . . . כְּמוֹ שֶׁנֶּאֱמַר: "לֹא בַשָּׁמַיִם הִיא". וְלֹא הִרְשָׁנוּ הַקָּדוֹשׁ בָּרוּךְ הוּא לִלְמֹד מִן הַנְּבִיאִים, אֶלָּא מִן הַחֲכָמִים, אַנְשֵׁי הַסְּבָרוֹת וְהַדֵּעוֹת.

If one thousand prophets, all on the level of Elijah and Elisha, have one opinion on a matter of Torah law, and one thousand and one sages have an opposite opinion, we must "follow the majority," and the ruling is according to the opinion of the sages. . . . Similarly, if a prophet testifies that G-d has revealed to him that the law regarding this commandment is such and such, or that the opinion of a certain sage is the correct one, . . . he is a false prophet, . . . as it is written, "It is not in heaven." G-d has not permitted us to learn Torah law from prophets, but from sages basing themselves on logical arguments and opinions.

TEXT 9

Moses Meets Rabbi Akiva

Talmud, Menachot 29b

בְּשָׁעָה שֶׁעָלָה מֹשֶׁה לַמָּרוֹם, מְצָאוֹ לְהַקָּדוֹשׁ בָּרוּךְ הוּא שֶׁיּוֹשֵׁב וְקוֹשֵׁר כְּתָרִים לְאוֹתִיּוֹת. אָמַר לְפָנָיו: "רִבּוֹנוֹ שֶׁל עוֹלָם, מִי מְעַכֵּב עַל יָדְךָ?"

אָמַר לוֹ: "אָדָם אֶחָד יֵשׁ שֶׁעָתִיד לִהְיוֹת בְּסוֹף כַּמָּה דוֹרוֹת, וַעֲקִיבָא בֶּן יוֹסֵף שְׁמוֹ, שֶׁעָתִיד לִדְרֹשׁ עַל כָּל קוֹץ וָקוֹץ תִּילִין תִּילִין שֶׁל הֲלָכוֹת".

אָמַר לְפָנָיו: "רִבּוֹנוֹ שֶׁל עוֹלָם, הַרְאֵהוּ לִי" . . .

הָלַךְ וְיָשַׁב בְּסוֹף שְׁמוֹנָה שׁוּרוֹת, וְלֹא הָיָה יוֹדֵעַ מָה הֵן אוֹמְרִים. תָּשַׁשׁ כֹּחוֹ. כֵּיוָן שֶׁהִגִּיעַ לְדָבָר אֶחָד, אָמְרוּ לוֹ תַּלְמִידָיו: "רַבִּי, מִנַּיִן לְךָ?"

אָמַר לָהֶן: "הֲלָכָה לְמֹשֶׁה מִסִּינַי". נִתְיַשְּׁבָה דַּעְתּוֹ.

When Moses ascended on high, he found G-d attaching coronets to the letters of the Torah. Said Moses to G-d: "Master of the world! Why have You need for these?"

Said G-d to him: "There will be a man some generations hence, whose name is Akiva the son of Joseph, and he will expound mounds upon mounds of laws from each and every tittle."

Said Moses: "Master of the world, show him to me." . . .

Moses was sitting behind eight rows [of Rabbi Akiva's disciples], but he did not understand what they were saying, and he became despondent. Until they reached one teaching, and Rabbi Akiva's disciples said to him, "Master, from where do you know this?"

Said Rabbi Akiva to them, "It is the law given to Moses at Sinai." And Moses's mind was eased.

Textual illustration in the *Ashkenazi Haggadah* depicting Rabbi Akiva discussing the story of Passover together with four other sages. Produced in Germany, c. 1460, this beautiful manuscript, decorated by Yoel ben Shimon Feibush, contains many miniatures and marginal drawings to accompany the Haggadah's text. (British Library, London)

V. A LIVING ORGANISM

One approach to resolving the paradox of Divine revelation and human innovation in Torah is with an analogy from the field of biology. A single cell, encoding everything that it will become, develops within the womb into a living organism. Similarly, the human mind is the "womb" in which the Divine truths communicated at Sinai gestate and develop into the life-wisdom and guidance of Torah.

In this section, we also answer the question (posed earlier in Section II) as to why Torah consists of both written and oral components. The Torah is a *partnership* of Divine revelation and human intellectual toil—a partnership that finds expression in the differences between the written and oral forms of Torah and the relationship between them.

FIGURE 1.5 The Torah as a Living Organism

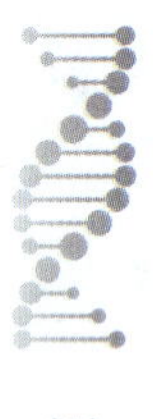

(A)

(B)

TEXT 10

The Baker and the Weaver

Midrash, *Tana Devei Eliyahu, Eliyahu Zuta* 2

פַּעַם אַחַת הָיִיתִי מְהַלֵּךְ בַּדֶּרֶךְ, מְצָאַנִי אָדָם אֶחָד . . . וְהָיָה בּוֹ מִקְרָא וְלֹא הָיָה בּוֹ מִשְׁנָה, וְאָמַר לִי: "רַבִּי, מִקְרָא נִתַּן לָנוּ מֵהַר סִינַי, מִשְׁנָה לֹא נִתַּן לָנוּ מֵהַר סִינַי". וְאָמַרְתִּי לוֹ: "בְּנִי, מִקְרָא וּמִשְׁנָה שְׁנֵיהֶם מִפִּי הַגְּבוּרָה נֶאֶמְרוּ. וּמָה בֵּין מִקְרָא לְמִשְׁנָה? אֶלָּא מָשְׁלוּ מָשָׁל:

לְמָה הַדָּבָר דּוֹמֶה? לְמֶלֶךְ בָּשָׂר וָדָם שֶׁהָיָה לוֹ שְׁנֵי עֲבָדִים, וְהָיָה אוֹהֲבָן אַהֲבָה גְדוֹלָה. וְנָתַן לָזֶה קַב חִטִּין, וְלָזֶה קַב חִטִּין, וּלְכָל אֶחָד מֵהֶן נָתַן גַּם כֵּן אֲגוּדָה שֶׁל פִּשְׁתָּן. הַפִּקֵּחַ שֶׁבָּהֶן נָטַל אֶת הַפִּשְׁתָּן וְאָרַג מַפָּה יָפָה, וְנָטַל אֶת הַחִטִּין וַעֲשָׂאָן סֹלֶת, וּבְרָרָהּ וְטָחֲנָהּ וְלָשָׁהּ וַאֲפָאָהּ, וְסִדְּרָהּ עַל הַשֻּׁלְחָן וּפָרַס עָלֶיהָ מַפָּה יָפָה, וְהִנִּיחוֹ עַד שֶׁבָּא הַמֶּלֶךְ. וְהַטִּפֵּשׁ שֶׁבָּהֶן לֹא עָשָׂה כְּלוּם.

לְיָמִים, בָּא הַמֶּלֶךְ לְתוֹךְ בֵּיתוֹ וְאָמַר לָהֶם לִשְׁנֵי עֲבָדָיו: 'בָּנַי, הָבִיאוּ לִי מָה שֶׁנָּתַתִּי לָכֶם'. אֶחָד מֵהֶן הוֹצִיא אֶת הַפַּת שֶׁל סֹלֶת עַל הַשֻּׁלְחָן וּמַפָּה הַיָּפָה פְּרוּסָה עָלָיו, וְאֶחָד מֵהֶן הוֹצִיא אֶת הַחִטִּין בְּקֻפָּה וַאֲגֻדָּה שֶׁל פִּשְׁתָּן עֲלֵיהֶם . . . אֵיזֶה מֵהֶן חָבִיב יוֹתֵר?

כְּשֶׁנָּתַן הַקָּדוֹשׁ בָּרוּךְ הוּא אֶת הַתּוֹרָה לְיִשְׂרָאֵל לֹא נְתָנָהּ לָהֶם אֶלָּא כְּחִטִּין לְהוֹצִיא מֵהֶן סֹלֶת, וּכְפִשְׁתָּן לֶאֱרֹג מֵהֶן בֶּגֶד . . . "

I was once traveling on the road when a person encountered me. . . . This person had Scripture,

TANA DEVEI ELIYAHU

A Midrashic work, sometimes referred to as *Seder Eliyahu*. Midrash is the designation of a particular genre of rabbinic literature usually forming a running commentary on specific books of the Bible. This work deals with the Divine precepts, their rationales, and the importance of knowledge of Torah, prayer, and repentance. The work is divided into 2 sections (*sedarim*): *Eliyahu Rabah* and *Eliyahu Zuta*.

but he did not have Mishnah. He said to me, "Master, Scripture was given to us at Mount Sinai; Mishnah was not given to us at Mount Sinai." I said to him, "My son, both Scripture and Mishnah issued from the mouth of the Almighty. What is the difference between them? The following parable was said to explain this:

"There was a king who had two beloved servants. He gave a measure of wheat to one of them, and a measure of wheat to the other. He also gave each a bundle of flax. The wise one among them took the flax and wove a beautiful cloth out of it; he took the wheat and made fine flour from it, sifting it, milling it, kneading it, and baking it. He arranged it on a table and spread the beautiful cloth over it, setting it aside for when the king would come. The foolish servant did nothing.

"Then the king arrived in his palace and said to his two servants: 'My children, present to me what I have gifted you.' The first one brought out the bread made of fine flour on a table with a beautiful cloth spread over it; the other brought out the wheat in a box with the bundle of flax on top of it. . . . Now, which of the servants is more precious [to the king] . . . ?

"When the Almighty gave the Torah to the people of Israel, He gave it as wheat from which to make fine flour, and as flax from which to weave a cloth. . . ."

TEXT 11

Wording vs. Understanding

The Rebbe, Rabbi Menachem Mendel Schneerson, *Likutei Sichot* 29, p. 176

בְּתוֹרָה שֶׁבִּכְתָב מַאכְט מֶען בִּרְכַּת הַתּוֹרָה בִּקְרִיאָתָהּ, וֶוען אֲפִלוּ לֹא יָדַע מַאי קָאָמַר. בְּלִמּוּד תּוֹרָה שֶׁבְּעַל פֶּה אָבֶּער, אִיז אוֹיבּ לֹא יָדַע מַאי קָאָמַר, קֶען מֶען קֵיין בִּרְכַּת הַתּוֹרָה נִיט מַאכְן. לִמּוּדָהּ אִיז פַארְבּוּנְדְן מִיט הֲבָנַת הָאָדָם.

With the Written Torah, a person says the blessing on the Torah when they read it, even if they don't understand what they are saying. With the Oral Torah, however, a person cannot say the blessing unless they understand what they are saying. For as regards the Oral Torah, "learning" entails human understanding.

RABBI MENACHEM MENDEL SCHNEERSON 1902–1994

The towering Jewish leader of the 20th century, known as "the Lubavitcher Rebbe," or simply as "the Rebbe." Born in southern Ukraine, the Rebbe escaped Nazi-occupied Europe, arriving in the U.S. in June 1941. The Rebbe inspired and guided the revival of traditional Judaism after the European devastation, impacting virtually every Jewish community the world over. The Rebbe often emphasized that the performance of just one additional good deed could usher in the era of Mashiach. The Rebbe's scholarly talks and writings have been printed in more than 200 volumes.

A scene from the *Darmstadt Haggadah*, a fifteenth-century manuscript, elaborately decorated by Israel ben Meir Heidelberg. Its most lavish pages show remarkable scenes of men and women passing open books and studying together, emphasizing the communal sharing of knowledge and Jewish unity. (Darmstadt University and State Library, Germany)

VI. THE MANY FACES OF TORAH

The twenty-four books of the Written Torah include every subject and style of learning: law and ethics, history and biography, poetry and philosophy, cosmology and psychology. These expand into the various "genres" that developed in the Oral Torah—Halachah, Agadah, Kabbalah, Musar, and so on—empowering us to discover the area of Torah that most resonates with us.

Indeed, the Written Torah is the "source code" for the whole of the Oral Torah. As the examples in this section illustrate—and as we will repeatedly discover in the next five lessons—every teaching of the Oral Torah can be traced back to a source text in the Written Torah.

TEXT 12

The Perpetual Voice

Rabbi Yeshayahu Halevi Horowitz,
Shenei Luchot Haberit, 1:25a–b

וְעִנְיָן "נוֹתֵן הַתּוֹרָה", בֶּאֱמֶת ה' יִתְבָּרֵךְ כְּבָר נְתָנָהּ, אֲבָל עֲדַיִן נוֹתֵן הַתּוֹרָה וְלֹא יִפְסֹק. וְדָבָר זֶה צָרִיךְ בֵּאוּר רָחָב.

הַפָּסוּק אוֹמֵר: (דְבָרִים ה, יט) "אֶת הַדְּבָרִים הָאֵלֶּה דִּבֶּר ה' אֶל כָּל קְהַלְכֶם בָּהָר . . . קוֹל גָּדוֹל וְלֹא יָסָף". פֵּרֵשׁ רַשִׁ"י: "וְלֹא יָסָף, מְתַרְגְּמִינָן "וְלֹא פְסַק", כִּי קוֹלוֹ חָזָק וְקַיָּם לְעוֹלָם. דָּבָר אַחֵר: וְלֹא יָסָף, לֹא הוֹסִיף לְהֵרָאוֹת בְּאוֹתוֹ פִּמְבִּי" עַד כָּאן לְשׁוֹנוֹ.

יֵשׁ בְּזֶה הָעִנְיָן סוֹד כָּמוּס, וְהַשְּׁנֵי פֵּרוּשִׁים כֻּלָּם הֵם אֱמֶת. עִנְיָן "לֹא יָסָף" - לֹא הוֹסִיף, הוּא מִצְוֹת דְּרַבָּנָן וַחֲבוּרָתָן הֵן וּסְיָגֵיהֶן עֲדַיִן לֹא נִצְטַווּ מִפִּי הַגְּבוּרָה. וְעִנְיָן "לֹא פְסַק" פֵּרוּשׁ שֶׁאַף זֶה לֹא פָּסַק מֵהַקּוֹל הַהוּא, כִּי

RABBI YESHAYAHU HALEVI HOROWITZ (*SHALAH*)
1565–1630

Kabbalist and author. Rabbi Horowitz was born in Prague and served as rabbi in several prominent Jewish communities, including Frankfurt am Main and his native Prague. After the passing of his wife in 1620, he moved to Israel. In Tiberias, he completed his *Shenei Luchot Haberit*, an encyclopedic compilation of kabbalistic ideas. He is buried in Tiberias, next to Maimonides.

הָיָה כָּלוּל בַּקּוֹל הַהוּא בְּכֹחַ, אֲבָל לְכָל זְמַן וָעֵת, לֹא הִגִּיעַ עֲדַיִן עֵת שֶׁיֵּצֵא מִכֹּחַ אֶל הַפֹּעַל, כִּי הָיָה הַדָּבָר תָּלוּי לְפִי הִתְעוֹרְרוּת הַתַּחְתּוֹנִים וּלְפִי מַהוּתָם וְאֵיכוּתָם, וּלְפִי מַדְרֵגוֹת נְשָׁמוֹת שֶׁבְּכָל דּוֹר וָדוֹר, וְאָז הוֹסִיפוּ הַחֲכָמִים לְהִתְעוֹרֵר הַכֹּחַ הָעֶלְיוֹן וְיָצָא לַפֹּעַל בִּזְמַנּוֹ וּבְעִתּוֹ, לֹא חַס וְשָׁלוֹם שֶׁחִדְּשׁוּ חֲכָמִים מִדַּעְתָּם, רַק כִּוְּנוּ דַּעַת עֶלְיוֹן.

[In the blessing recited before studying Torah, we say, "Blessed are you, G-d,] Who gives the Torah." In truth, G-d has already given us the Torah [at Mount Sinai]; yet He still "gives the Torah," perpetually. This matter requires some elaboration.

The Torah says (DEUTERONOMY 5:19): "These words G-d spoke to your entire assembly at the mountain . . . a great voice that did not cease." Rashi explains the meaning of the words "did not cease" (*velo yasaf*) in accordance with the translation by Unkelos—"it did not stop," for it is a powerful voice that endures forever. Rashi also offers a second interpretation of the words "*velo yasaf*"—"it did not anymore," i.e., that G-d did not again speak so openly and publicly as He did at Sinai.

There is a profound significance in these two interpretations, as they are simultaneously true. The Divine voice spoke the Torah at Sinai and "did not anymore," as all the subsequent laws and edicts instituted by the sages throughout the

The Four Layers of Secret Code in the Bible, Explained
myjli.com/booksmart

generations were not explicitly commanded by G-d at the time. At the same time, "it did not cease," for everything was included, in potential form, within that voice. It is only that "for everything there is a time and season" (ECCLESIASTES 3:1), and the time had not yet come for that potential to emerge into actuality, as that depends on the initiative of those down here below, in accordance with their nature and their abilities, and in accordance with the qualities of the souls of each generation. The sages of each generation were then roused to actualize from that potential in accordance with the time and season. Thus, the sages did not invent anything from their own minds, G-d forbid, but rather actualized the Divine intent.

TEXT 13

The Mitzvah of Shabbat

Exodus 20:8–10

זָכוֹר אֶת יוֹם הַשַּׁבָּת לְקַדְּשׁוֹ, שֵׁשֶׁת יָמִים תַּעֲבֹד וְעָשִׂיתָ
כָּל מְלַאכְתֶּךָ, וְיוֹם הַשְּׁבִיעִי שַׁבָּת לַה' אֱלֹקֶיךָ.

Remember the Shabbat day to sanctify it.
Six days you shall labor and do all your work.
And the seventh day is a rest-day unto G-d.

TEXT 14

The Resting Mind

Mechilta, Exodus 20:9

"שֵׁשֶׁת יָמִים תַּעֲבֹד":
וְכִי אֶפְשָׁר לוֹ לָאָדָם לַעֲשׂוֹת מְלַאכְתּוֹ בְּשֵׁשֶׁת יָמִים?
אֶלָּא שְׁבוֹת כְּאִלּוּ מְלַאכְתְּךָ עֲשׂוּיָה . . .
שְׁבוֹת מִמַּחְשֶׁבֶת עֲבוֹדָה.

"Six days you shall labor [and do all your work]": Is it possible for a person to do all their work in six days? But [the meaning of this verse is:] Rest [on Shabbat] as if all your work is done. . . . Rest from even thinking about work.

MECHILTA

A Halachic Midrash to Exodus. Midrash is the designation of a particular genre of rabbinic literature usually forming a running commentary on specific books of the Bible. The name *Mechilta* means "rule" and was given to this Midrash because its comments and explanations are based on fixed rules of exegesis. This work is often attributed to Rabbi Yishmael ben Elisha, a contemporary of Rabbi Akiva, though there are some references to later sages in this work.

TEXT 15

The Two Paths

Deuteronomy 30:15–19

רְאֵה נָתַתִּי לְפָנֶיךָ הַיּוֹם אֶת הַחַיִּים וְאֶת
הַטּוֹב, וְאֶת הַמָּוֶת וְאֶת הָרָע . . .

הַחַיִּים וְהַמָּוֶת נָתַתִּי לְפָנֶיךָ, הַבְּרָכָה וְהַקְּלָלָה,
וּבָחַרְתָּ בַּחַיִּים.

See, I have set before you this day,
life and good, and death and evil. . . .

Life and death I have set before you,
blessing and curse; and you shall choose life.

TEXT 16

The Basis of Morality

Maimonides, *Mishneh Torah*, Laws of Repentance 5:1–4

רְשׁוּת לְכָל אָדָם נְתוּנָה, אִם רָצָה לְהַטּוֹת עַצְמוֹ לְדֶרֶךְ טוֹבָה וְלִהְיוֹת צַדִּיק, הָרְשׁוּת בְּיָדוֹ, וְאִם רָצָה לְהַטּוֹת עַצְמוֹ לְדֶרֶךְ רָעָה וְלִהְיוֹת רָשָׁע, הָרְשׁוּת בְּיָדוֹ . . .

וְדָבָר זֶה עִקָּר גָּדוֹל הוּא, וְהוּא עַמּוּד הַתּוֹרָה וְהַמִּצְוָה, שֶׁנֶּאֱמַר: "רְאֵה נָתַתִּי לְפָנֶיךָ הַיּוֹם אֶת הַחַיִּים" . . . אִלּוּ הָקֵל הָיָה גּוֹזֵר עַל הָאָדָם לִהְיוֹת צַדִּיק אוֹ רָשָׁע, אוֹ אִלּוּ הָיָה שָׁם דָּבָר שֶׁמּוֹשֵׁךְ אֶת הָאָדָם בְּעִקַּר תּוֹלַדְתּוֹ לְדֶרֶךְ מִן הַדְּרָכִים, אוֹ לְמַדָּע מִן הַמַּדָּעוֹת, אוֹ לְדֵעָה מִן הַדֵּעוֹת, אוֹ לְמַעֲשֶׂה מִן הַמַּעֲשִׂים . . . הֵיאַךְ הָיָה מְצַוֶּה לָנוּ עַל יְדֵי הַנְּבִיאִים: עֲשֵׂה כָּךְ וְאַל תַּעֲשֶׂה כָּךְ . . . ? וּמָה מָקוֹם הָיָה לְכָל הַתּוֹרָה כֻּלָּהּ? וּבְאֵי זֶה דִּין וְאֵיזֶה מִשְׁפָּט נִפְרַע מִן הָרָשָׁע אוֹ מְשַׁלֵּם שָׂכָר לַצַּדִּיק . . . ?

Freedom of choice has been granted to every person. If a person wants to turn to the path of good and be righteous, the choice is theirs; and if a person wants to turn to the path of evil and be wicked, the choice is theirs. . . .

This truth is a fundamental principle and a pillar of the Torah and its commandments. As it is written, "See, I have set before you this day, life [and good, and death and evil]. . . ." Were G-d to decree that a person should be righteous or wicked, or if there were to exist something in the very essence of a person's nature that would compel them toward a particular path, a particular conviction, a particular character trait, or a particular deed, . . . how could G-d command us through the prophets "do this" and "do not do this". . . ? What place would the entire Torah have? And by what measure of justice would G-d punish the wicked and reward the righteous . . . ?

TEXT 17

The Divine Attributes

I Chronicles 29:11

לְךָ ה' הַגְּדֻלָּה וְהַגְּבוּרָה וְהַתִּפְאֶרֶת וְהַנֵּצַח וְהַהוֹד,
כִּי כֹל בַּשָּׁמַיִם וּבָאָרֶץ לְךָ ה' הַמַּמְלָכָה . . .

To You, G-d, is greatness, and power, and beauty, and victory, and splendor, as all that is in heaven and earth; to You, G-d, is kingship. . . .

Initial word panel to Maimonides's *Mishneh Torah*, Laws of *Teshuvah*, in an elaborate manuscript copied in Spain and decorated in Spain and Italy, c. 1400. (U.S. Library of Congress, Washington, D.C.)

CHRONICLES

Biblical book. The book of Chronicles (Divrei Hayamim), commonly divided into two parts, is the concluding book of the Writings (*Ketuvim*) section of the Tanach. Chronicles contains a genealogical list from Creation until the establishment of the first Kingdom of Israel, and then it briefly surveys the history of the Davidic dynasty until the destruction of the First Temple. The book was written by Ezra the Scribe in the fourth century BCE. The book has been artificially divided into I Chronicles and II Chronicles, but it is essentially one book.

KEY POINTS

1 *Two Meanings of Torah.* The term "Torah" has two primary meanings. In its more specific sense, it refers to the Five Books of Moses (the "*Chumash*") inscribed in the Torah scroll. In the broader sense of the term, "the Torah" is the entire body of Jewish teaching, consisting of numerous "genres"—Bible, Midrash, Talmud, Halachah (Torah law), Musar (ethics and self-improvement), Chakirah (philosophy), Kabbalah, etc.—composed by many thousands of authors over a period of more than 3,300 years. The two "Torahs" are two faces of the same coin, two articulations of the same truths.

2 *The Written Torah and the Oral Torah.* The Torah comes in two forms: written and oral. Jewish tradition insists that the "Written Torah" be treated as an inviolable text—every word and letter is significant and must be meticulously preserved. In contrast, the "Oral Torah" must be preserved as an ongoing oral communication from teacher to disciple; for many centuries, it was even forbidden that it be officially transcribed. This duality is integral to the nature of Torah.

3 *The Jewish Bible.* The twenty-four books of the Written Torah (also known as "the Jewish Bible") are divided into three categories—"Torah," "Prophets," and "Writings"—representing three different levels of Divine revelation. All 613 *mitzvot* (Divine commandments) are in the "Torah" section, while the books in the "Prophets" and "Writings" sections are the source for many of the historical, philosophical, moral, and inspirational teachings of the Torah.

4 *The Divine and the Human in Torah.* G-d desired that the Torah should embody a partnership between Him and us. The Torah therefore incorporates both Divine and human elements, involving a collaboration of Divine revelation and human intellectual toil. In the Written Torah, the Divine side of the partnership dominates, and is expressed in the precise wording of the text. In the Oral Torah, the human contribution is more pronounced, and finds expression in our analysis, exposition, and application of its content.

5 *The Source Code.* The letters and words of the Written Torah are the "source code" for the entire body of Jewish teaching. Thus, every subject, teaching, or law in the Oral Torah has its source in the Written Torah.

Selected Readings from Tanach

TORAH

GENESIS

The Beginning

GENESIS 1:1–5

בְּרֵאשִׁית בָּרָא אֱלֹקִים אֵת הַשָּׁמַיִם וְאֵת הָאָרֶץ.

וְהָאָרֶץ הָיְתָה תֹהוּ וָבֹהוּ וְחֹשֶׁךְ עַל פְּנֵי תְהוֹם
וְרוּחַ אֱלֹקִים מְרַחֶפֶת עַל פְּנֵי הַמָּיִם.

וַיֹּאמֶר אֱלֹקִים יְהִי אוֹר וַיְהִי אוֹר.

וַיַּרְא אֱלֹקִים אֶת הָאוֹר כִּי טוֹב וַיַּבְדֵּל
אֱלֹקִים בֵּין הָאוֹר וּבֵין הַחֹשֶׁךְ.

וַיִּקְרָא אֱלֹקִים לָאוֹר יוֹם וְלַחֹשֶׁךְ קָרָא לָיְלָה
וַיְהִי עֶרֶב וַיְהִי בֹקֶר יוֹם אֶחָד.

In the beginning G-d created the heavens and the earth.

And the world was desolate and void, and darkness on the face of the deep; and the spirit of G-d hovered upon the face of the water.

And G-d said, "There shall be light!" And there was light.

G-d saw the light that it is good; and G-d separated between the light and the darkness.

And G-d called the light "day," and the darkness he called "night"; and it was evening and it was morning, one day.

Good and Evil

Bereshit Rabah, 2:5

Said Rabbi Avahu: In the beginning of Creation, G-d beheld the deeds of the righteous and the deeds of the wicked. . . . "And the world was desolate and void"—these are the deeds of the wicked. "There shall be light"—these are the deeds of the righteous. But I still do not know which of these G-d desires. When it says, "G-d saw the light, that it is good," I know that G-d desires the deeds of the righteous, and does not desire the deeds of the wicked.

Tanya, Chapter 29

In truth, evil has no actual substance at all. This is why evil is compared to darkness, which has no actual substance, and therefore is automatically banished in the presence of light. So, too, the forces of evil, although they seem to possess much vitality, . . . are automatically nullified in the presence of holiness, as physical darkness is nullified in the presence of physical light.

Also see: Lesson 5, Texts 5, 6, 7, 8, and 9; Lesson 6, Text 5.

The Creation of the Human Being

GENESIS 1:26–28; 2:7–15

וַיֹּאמֶר אֱלֹקִים: "נַעֲשֶׂה אָדָם בְּצַלְמֵנוּ כִּדְמוּתֵנוּ. וְיִרְדּוּ בִדְגַת הַיָּם
וּבְעוֹף הַשָּׁמַיִם וּבַבְּהֵמָה וּבְכָל הָאָרֶץ וּבְכָל הָרֶמֶשׂ הָרֹמֵשׂ עַל הָאָרֶץ."

וַיִּבְרָא אֱלֹקִים אֶת הָאָדָם בְּצַלְמוֹ,
בְּצֶלֶם אֱלֹקִים בָּרָא אֹתוֹ; זָכָר וּנְקֵבָה בָּרָא אֹתָם.

וַיְבָרֶךְ אֹתָם אֱלֹקִים; וַיֹּאמֶר לָהֶם אֱלֹקִים,
"פְּרוּ וּרְבוּ וּמִלְאוּ אֶת הָאָרֶץ וְכִבְשֻׁהָ..."

וַיִּיצֶר ה' אֱלֹקִים אֶת הָאָדָם עָפָר מִן הָאֲדָמָה,
וַיִּפַּח בְּאַפָּיו נִשְׁמַת חַיִּים; וַיְהִי הָאָדָם לְנֶפֶשׁ חַיָּה...

וַיִּקַּח ה' אֱלֹקִים אֶת הָאָדָם; וַיַּנִּחֵהוּ בְגַן עֵדֶן לְעָבְדָהּ וּלְשָׁמְרָהּ.

G-d said: "Let us make a human being in our image, after our likeness. And they shall rule over the fish of the sea and the birds of the heavens, and the beasts, and all the earth, and every crawling thing that crawls upon the earth."

And G-d created the human in His image, in the Divine image He created him; male and female He created them.

G-d blessed them, and G-d said to them: "Be fruitful and multiply, and fill the earth and conquer it. . . ."

And G-d Almighty formed the human, dust from the earth, and He blew into his nostrils a breath of life; and the human became a living soul.

And G-d Almighty took the human; and He put him in the Garden of Eden, to work it and to keep it.

The Meaning of "Adam"

Shenei Luchot Haberit, Toldot Adam, 3a

The name *Adam* ("human") is the explanation of the story of humanity and of humanity's ultimate purpose. If a person connects themselves Above, and emulates G-d and follows in G-d's ways, then they are called by the name Adam in the sense of *edameh le'elyon*, "I resemble the Supernal One" (Isaiah 14:14). . . . But if a person separates from this Divine attachment, then they are Adam in the sense of the *adamah*, "soil" from which they were taken, as the human is dust, and to dust does the human return.

Also see: Lesson 2, Text 2; Lesson 6, Texts 12 and 13.

The First Jew

GENESIS 12:1-8

וַיֹּאמֶר ה' אֶל אַבְרָם: "לֶךְ לְךָ מֵאַרְצְךָ וּמִמּוֹלַדְתְּךָ
וּמִבֵּית אָבִיךָ אֶל הָאָרֶץ אֲשֶׁר אַרְאֶךָּ.

וְאֶעֶשְׂךָ לְגוֹי גָּדוֹל וַאֲבָרֶכְךָ וַאֲגַדְּלָה שְׁמֶךָ וֶהְיֵה בְּרָכָה.

וַאֲבָרֲכָה מְבָרְכֶיךָ וּמְקַלֶּלְךָ אָאֹר וְנִבְרְכוּ בְךָ כֹּל מִשְׁפְּחֹת הָאֲדָמָה".

וַיֵּלֶךְ אַבְרָם כַּאֲשֶׁר דִּבֶּר אֵלָיו ה', וַיֵּלֶךְ אִתּוֹ לוֹט;
וְאַבְרָם בֶּן חָמֵשׁ שָׁנִים וְשִׁבְעִים שָׁנָה בְּצֵאתוֹ מֵחָרָן.

וַיִּקַּח אַבְרָם אֶת שָׂרַי אִשְׁתּוֹ וְאֶת לוֹט בֶּן אָחִיו וְאֶת
כָּל רְכוּשָׁם אֲשֶׁר רָכָשׁוּ וְאֶת הַנֶּפֶשׁ אֲשֶׁר עָשׂוּ בְחָרָן;
וַיֵּצְאוּ לָלֶכֶת אַרְצָה כְּנַעַן, וַיָּבֹאוּ אַרְצָה כְּנָעַן.

וַיַּעֲבֹר אַבְרָם בָּאָרֶץ עַד מְקוֹם שְׁכֶם עַד אֵלוֹן מוֹרֶה; וְהַכְּנַעֲנִי אָז בָּאָרֶץ.

וַיֵּרָא ה' אֶל אַבְרָם וַיֹּאמֶר, "לְזַרְעֲךָ אֶתֵּן אֶת הָאָרֶץ הַזֹּאת";
וַיִּבֶן שָׁם מִזְבֵּחַ לַה' הַנִּרְאֶה אֵלָיו.

וַיַּעְתֵּק מִשָּׁם הָהָרָה מִקֶּדֶם לְבֵית אֵל וַיֵּט אָהֳלֹה;
בֵּית אֵל מִיָּם וְהָעַי מִקֶּדֶם, וַיִּבֶן שָׁם מִזְבֵּחַ לַה', וַיִּקְרָא בְּשֵׁם ה'.

G-d said to Abram: "Go you from your land, from your birthplace, and from your father's house; to the land that I will show you.

"I will make you into a great nation, and I will bless you, and I will make great your name; and you will be a blessing.

"I will bless those who bless you, and the one who curses you I will curse; and all the families of the earth will be blessed through you."

And Abram went, as G-d had spoken to him, and Lot went with him; and Abram was seventy-five years old when he went out from Haran.

Abram took his wife Sarai and his brother's son Lot, and all their possessions that they had acquired, and the souls they had made in Haran; and they went out to go to the land of Canaan, and they came into the land of Canaan.

Abram passed through the land, until the place of Shechem, until the plain of Moreh; and the Canaanites were then in the land.

And G-d appeared to Abram, and He said, "To your seed I will give this land"; and there he built an altar to G-d, who had appeared to him.

He removed from there to the mountain, east of Beth-El, and he pitched his tent; Beth-El was to the west and Ai was to the east, and there he built an altar to G-d, and he called in the name of G-d.

Unequivocal Choice

Rabbi Yehudah Loew of Prague, *Netzach Yisrael*, Chapter 11

We know that Abraham recognized the truth of G-d at a young age, and devoted many decades to teaching this truth to the world, to the point of self-sacrifice—all before G-d spoke to him to leave his land and birthplace and journey to the Holy Land. So why doesn't the Written Torah tell us anything about Abraham's righteousness and his achievements in the first 75 years of his life?

Because the Torah wishes to emphasize that G-d's choice to make a great nation of the descendants of Abraham was not a consequence of Abraham's particular merits. If that were the case, then the subsequent sins and failings of the Jewish people may arguably cause them to forfeit their chosenness. Rather, G-d's choice has no cause or reason, and is therefore eternal and immutable. In the words of the sages (Ethics of the Fathers 5:17): "A love that is dependent on something—when that thing ceases, the love ceases; but a love that is not dependent on any thing, never ceases."

Soul Makers

Shir Hashirim Rabah, 1:22

Regarding Abraham and Sarah it is written, "the souls that they made in Haran." Yet if the entire world would convene, they could not create a single flea! Rather, these are the converts whom Abraham and Sarah converted. Said R. Chunya: Abraham would convert the men, and Sarah would convert the women.

Abraham would invite them into his home, give them to eat and to drink, show them love and fellowship, and bring them under the wings of the Divine Presence. This teaches us that whoever brings a person close to the Almighty, it is considered as if they have created them.

The Burning Bush

EXODUS 3:1–17

וּמֹשֶׁה הָיָה רֹעֶה אֶת צֹאן יִתְרוֹ חֹתְנוֹ כֹּהֵן מִדְיָן; וַיִּנְהַג
אֶת הַצֹּאן אַחַר הַמִּדְבָּר, וַיָּבֹא אֶל הַר הָאֱלֹקִים חֹרֵבָה.

וַיֵּרָא מַלְאַךְ ה' אֵלָיו בְּלַבַּת אֵשׁ מִתּוֹךְ הַסְּנֶה;
וַיַּרְא, וְהִנֵּה הַסְּנֶה בֹּעֵר בָּאֵשׁ, וְהַסְּנֶה אֵינֶנּוּ אֻכָּל.

וַיֹּאמֶר מֹשֶׁה: אָסֻרָה נָּא וְאֶרְאֶה אֶת הַמַּרְאֶה
הַגָּדֹל הַזֶּה; מַדּוּעַ לֹא יִבְעַר הַסְּנֶה?

וַיַּרְא ה' כִּי סָר לִרְאוֹת; וַיִּקְרָא אֵלָיו אֱלֹקִים מִתּוֹךְ
הַסְּנֶה וַיֹּאמֶר, "מֹשֶׁה! מֹשֶׁה!" וַיֹּאמֶר, "הִנֵּנִי".

וַיֹּאמֶר, "אַל תִּקְרַב הֲלֹם; שַׁל נְעָלֶיךָ מֵעַל רַגְלֶיךָ, כִּי
הַמָּקוֹם אֲשֶׁר אַתָּה עוֹמֵד עָלָיו אַדְמַת קֹדֶשׁ הוּא".

וַיֹּאמֶר: "אָנֹכִי אֱלֹקֵי אָבִיךָ, אֱלֹקֵי אַבְרָהָם
אֱלֹקֵי יִצְחָק וֵאלֹקֵי יַעֲקֹב"; וַיַּסְתֵּר מֹשֶׁה
פָּנָיו, כִּי יָרֵא מֵהַבִּיט אֶל הָאֱלֹקִים.

וַיֹּאמֶר ה', "רָאֹה רָאִיתִי אֶת עֳנִי עַמִּי אֲשֶׁר בְּמִצְרָיִם; וְאֶת
צַעֲקָתָם שָׁמַעְתִּי מִפְּנֵי נֹגְשָׂיו, כִּי יָדַעְתִּי אֶת מַכְאֹבָיו.

וָאֵרֵד לְהַצִּילוֹ מִיַּד מִצְרַיִם וּלְהַעֲלֹתוֹ מִן הָאָרֶץ הַהִוא,
אֶל אֶרֶץ טוֹבָה וּרְחָבָה, אֶל אֶרֶץ זָבַת חָלָב וּדְבָשׁ; אֶל
מְקוֹם הַכְּנַעֲנִי וְהַחִתִּי וְהָאֱמֹרִי וְהַפְּרִזִּי וְהַחִוִּי וְהַיְבוּסִי.

וְעַתָּה, הִנֵּה צַעֲקַת בְּנֵי יִשְׂרָאֵל בָּאָה אֵלָי; וְגַם
רָאִיתִי אֶת הַלַּחַץ אֲשֶׁר מִצְרַיִם לֹחֲצִים אֹתָם.

וְעַתָּה לְכָה וְאֶשְׁלָחֲךָ אֶל פַּרְעֹה; וְהוֹצֵא
אֶת עַמִּי בְנֵי יִשְׂרָאֵל מִמִּצְרָיִם."

וַיֹּאמֶר מֹשֶׁה אֶל הָאֱלֹקִים, "מִי אָנֹכִי כִּי אֵלֵךְ אֶל
פַּרְעֹה, וְכִי אוֹצִיא אֶת בְּנֵי יִשְׂרָאֵל מִמִּצְרָיִם?"

וַיֹּאמֶר, "כִּי אֶהְיֶה עִמָּךְ, וְזֶה לְּךָ הָאוֹת כִּי
אָנֹכִי שְׁלַחְתִּיךָ: בְּהוֹצִיאֲךָ אֶת הָעָם מִמִּצְרַיִם,
תַּעַבְדוּן אֶת הָאֱלֹקִים עַל הָהָר הַזֶּה."

וַיֹּאמֶר מֹשֶׁה אֶל הָאֱלֹקִים, "הִנֵּה אָנֹכִי בָא אֶל בְּנֵי
יִשְׂרָאֵל וְאָמַרְתִּי לָהֶם, 'אֱלֹקֵי אֲבוֹתֵיכֶם שְׁלָחַנִי
אֲלֵיכֶם'; וְאָמְרוּ לִי, 'מַה שְּׁמוֹ?', מָה אֹמַר אֲלֵהֶם?"

וַיֹּאמֶר אֱלֹקִים אֶל מֹשֶׁה, "אֶהְיֶ־ה אֲשֶׁר אֶהְיֶ־ה"; וַיֹּאמֶר:
"כֹּה תֹאמַר לִבְנֵי יִשְׂרָאֵל, 'אֶהְיֶ־ה שְׁלָחַנִי אֲלֵיכֶם'."

Moses was shepherding the flock of his father-in-law, Jethro, the priest of Midian. He led the flock after the desert, and he came to the mountain of G-d, to Horeb.

And an angel of G-d appeared to him in a heart of fire, from within the thornbush; and he saw that, behold, the thornbush is burning with fire, and the thornbush is not consumed.

And Moses said, "Let me turn away and see this great sight; why is the thornbush not burned?"

G-d saw that he had turned away to see. And G-d called to him from within the thornbush, and He said: "Moses! Moses!" And he said, "Here I am."

And He said: "Do not come near to here; shed your shoes from your feet, as the place upon which you are standing, it is holy ground."

And He said: "I am the G-d of your father, the G-d of Abraham, the G-d of Isaac, and the G-d of Jacob"; and Moses hid his face, as he was afraid to look toward G-d.

And G-d said: "I have seen, seen the affliction of My people who are in Egypt; I have heard their cries before their taskmasters; I know their hurt.

"And I have descended to save them from the hand of Egypt and to bring them up from that land to a good and broad land, to a land that flows with milk and honey; to the place of the Canaanite and the Hittite and the Emorite and the Perizzite and the Hivite and the Jebusite.

"And now, behold the cry of the Children of Israel has come to Me; I have also seen the oppression that the Egyptians are oppressing them.

"Now go, and I will send you to Pharaoh; and take out My people, the Children of Israel, from Egypt."

And Moses said to G-d: "Who am I that I should go to Pharaoh, and that I should take out the Children of Israel from Egypt?"

And He said: "For I will be with you. And this is your sign that I Myself have sent you: when you take the people out of Egypt, you will serve G-d on this mountain."

And Moses said to G-d: "Here I am coming to the Children of Israel, and I will say to them, 'The G-d of your fathers has sent me to you,' and they will say to me, 'What is His name?' What should I say to them?"

And G-d said to Moses, "I will be that which I will be." And He said: "So you shall say to the Children of Israel: *Eh-yeh* ('I will be') has sent me to you."

The Thornbush

Midrash Tanchuma, Shemot 14

Why did G-d appear to Moses in a thornbush? For G-d said: I wrote in My Torah, "I am with them in their affliction" (Psalms 91:15). They are enslaved, so I, too, am in in a place of constriction, in a bush that is full of thorns.

Rabbi Yisrael Baal Shem Tov, cited in *Sefer Hasichot* 5702

"The heart of fire" that Moses beheld in his vision at Mount Horeb is the heart of the simple Jew.

The Torah (Deuteronomy 20:19) likens the human being to a "tree of the field." But the field has many types of trees. The Talmud (Taanit 7a) compares the righteous Torah scholars to fruit trees—stately, beautiful trees that bestow fragrance and nourishment upon the world. These trees burn: They burn with the ecstasy of their Torah learning, with the fervor of their prayer, with the warmth of their good deeds. But theirs is a fire that is satiated by the sense of achievement and fulfillment they experience in their G-dly endeavors.

The thornbush, however, burns with a fire that is never satiated. The simple Jew who has a limited understanding of the Torah, of the words of the prayers they utter, and of the significance of the *mitzvot* they perform—theirs is a thirst never quenched. Their heart burns with a yearning for G-d they can never hope to still, with a love they can never hope to consummate.

When Moses beheld the sight of "the thornbush that burns with fire but is not consumed," he said: "Let me turn away and see this great sight." Moses recognized that he must turn away from his own lofty station in order to awaken in himself the insatiable fire of the simple Jew.

G-d's Names

Midrash Rabah, Shemot 3:6

G-d said to Moses: You wish to know My name? I am called by My deeds. When I judge the creations, I am called *Elokim*. When I battle the wicked, I am called *Tzevakot*. When I abide with the sins of humanity, I am called *Kel Shakai*. When I have compassion upon my world, I am called YHVH.

The Holy Life

LEVITICUS 19:1–18

וַיְדַבֵּר ה' אֶל מֹשֶׁה לֵּאמֹר.

דַּבֵּר אֶל כָּל עֲדַת בְּנֵי יִשְׂרָאֵל וְאָמַרְתָּ אֲלֵהֶם:
קְדֹשִׁים תִּהְיוּ, כִּי קָדוֹשׁ אֲנִי ה' אֱלֹקֵיכֶם.

אִישׁ אִמּוֹ וְאָבִיו תִּירָאוּ וְאֶת שַׁבְּתֹתַי תִּשְׁמֹרוּ; אֲנִי ה' אֱלֹקֵיכֶם.

אַל תִּפְנוּ אֶל הָאֱלִילִם וֵאלֹהֵי מַסֵּכָה לֹא תַעֲשׂוּ לָכֶם; אֲנִי ה' אֱלֹקֵיכֶם...

וּבְקֻצְרְכֶם אֶת קְצִיר אַרְצְכֶם, לֹא תְכַלֶּה פְּאַת שָׂדְךָ לִקְצֹר,
וְלֶקֶט קְצִירְךָ לֹא תְלַקֵּט. וְכַרְמְךָ לֹא תְעוֹלֵל, וּפֶרֶט כַּרְמְךָ
לֹא תְלַקֵּט; לֶעָנִי וְלַגֵּר תַּעֲזֹב אֹתָם, אֲנִי ה' אֱלֹקֵיכֶם.

לֹא תִּגְנֹבוּ, וְלֹא תְכַחֲשׁוּ, וְלֹא תְשַׁקְּרוּ אִישׁ בַּעֲמִיתוֹ.

וְלֹא תִשָּׁבְעוּ בִשְׁמִי לַשָּׁקֶר; וְחִלַּלְתָּ אֶת שֵׁם אֱלֹקֶיךָ, אֲנִי ה'.

לֹא תַעֲשֹׁק אֶת רֵעֲךָ, וְלֹא תִגְזֹל; לֹא תָלִין פְּעֻלַּת שָׂכִיר אִתְּךָ עַד בֹּקֶר.

לֹא תְקַלֵּל חֵרֵשׁ, וְלִפְנֵי עִוֵּר לֹא תִתֵּן מִכְשֹׁל; וְיָרֵאתָ מֵּאֱלֹקֶיךָ, אֲנִי ה'.

לֹא תַעֲשׂוּ עָוֶל בַּמִּשְׁפָּט, לֹא תִשָּׂא פְנֵי דָל,
וְלֹא תֶהְדַּר פְּנֵי גָדוֹל; בְּצֶדֶק תִּשְׁפֹּט עֲמִיתֶךָ.

לֹא תֵלֵךְ רָכִיל בְּעַמֶּיךָ, לֹא תַעֲמֹד עַל דַּם רֵעֶךָ; אֲנִי ה'.

לֹא תִשְׂנָא אֶת אָחִיךָ בִּלְבָבֶךָ; הוֹכֵחַ תּוֹכִיחַ
אֶת עֲמִיתֶךָ, וְלֹא תִשָּׂא עָלָיו חֵטְא.

לֹא תִקֹּם וְלֹא תִטֹּר אֶת בְּנֵי עַמֶּךָ, וְאָהַבְתָּ לְרֵעֲךָ כָּמוֹךָ; אֲנִי ה'.

G-d spoke to Moses, saying:

Speak to the entire congregation of the Children of Israel, and say to them: You shall be holy, for I, G-d your G-d, am holy.

Every person should fear their mother and their father, and you shall observe My Sabbaths; I am G-d your G-d.

Do not turn to the idols, and do not make molten gods for yourselves; I am G-d your G-d. . . .

And when you reap the harvest of your land, do not finish the edge of your field with your harvesting, and do not collect the gleanings of your harvest. Do not pick the underdeveloped clusters of your vineyard, and do not collect the gleanings of your vineyard; leave them for the pauper and the stranger. I am G-d your G-d.

Do not steal, and do not falsely deny a claim, and do not lie, one person to their fellow.

Harvest Gleanings for the Poor

Maimonides, *Mishneh Torah*, Laws of Gifts to the Poor 1:1–5

When harvesting one's field, one should not harvest the entire field. Rather, one should leave a small portion of the standing grain at the end of the field for the poor, as the Torah states, "Do not finish the edge of your field in your harvesting." . . . The grain left standing is referred to as *pe'ah* ("edge"). . . .

Similarly, with regard to *leket* ("gleanings"): When harvesting the grain and binding it into sheaves, one should not collect the stalks that fall away during the harvest, . . . as it is stated, "Do not collect the gleanings of your harvest." . . . The same applies to *peret*, individual grapes that fall off during the harvest, and to underdeveloped grape clusters (*olelot*), as it is stated, "Do not pick the underdeveloped clusters of your vineyard, and do not collect the gleanings of your vineyard."

The Torah on One Foot

Talmud, Shabbat 31a

A gentile came before Shamai and said to him, "I wish to convert to Judaism, on condition that you teach me the entire Torah while I stand on one foot." Shamai drove him away with the builder's measuring stick that was in his hand.

He then came to Hillel. Hillel converted him, and said to him: "What is hateful to you, do not do to your fellow. This is the entire Torah. The rest is commentary—go and learn it."

Do not swear falsely by My name, profaning the name of your G-d; I am G-d.

Do not oppress your fellow, and do not rob; do not keep a hired worker's wage with you overnight until morning.

Do not curse a deaf person, and do not place a stumbling block before a blind person; and you shall fear your G-d, I am G-d.

Do not commit an injustice in judgment, do not favor a pauper, and do not respect a great person; judge your fellow with righteousness.

Do not go around as a gossipmonger amidst your people; do not stand by the shedding of your fellow's blood; I am G-d.

Do not hate your brother in your heart; rebuke, rebuke your fellow, and do not bear a sin on his account.

Do not take revenge and do not bear a grudge against the members of your people, and you shall love your fellow as yourself; I am G-d.

Journeys in the Desert

NUMBERS 9:15–23

וּבְיוֹם הָקִים אֶת הַמִּשְׁכָּן, כִּסָּה הֶעָנָן אֶת הַמִּשְׁכָּן לְאֹהֶל
הָעֵדֻת; וּבָעֶרֶב יִהְיֶה עַל הַמִּשְׁכָּן כְּמַרְאֵה אֵשׁ עַד בֹּקֶר.

כֵּן יִהְיֶה תָמִיד, הֶעָנָן יְכַסֶּנּוּ; וּמַרְאֵה אֵשׁ לָיְלָה.

וּלְפִי הֵעָלֹת הֶעָנָן מֵעַל הָאֹהֶל, וְאַחֲרֵי כֵן יִסְעוּ בְּנֵי יִשְׂרָאֵל;
וּבִמְקוֹם אֲשֶׁר יִשְׁכָּן שָׁם הֶעָנָן, שָׁם יַחֲנוּ בְּנֵי יִשְׂרָאֵל.

עַל פִּי ה' יִסְעוּ בְּנֵי יִשְׂרָאֵל, וְעַל פִּי ה' יַחֲנוּ;
כָּל יְמֵי אֲשֶׁר יִשְׁכֹּן הֶעָנָן עַל הַמִּשְׁכָּן יַחֲנוּ.

וּבְהַאֲרִיךְ הֶעָנָן עַל הַמִּשְׁכָּן יָמִים רַבִּים;
וְשָׁמְרוּ בְנֵי יִשְׂרָאֵל אֶת מִשְׁמֶרֶת ה' וְלֹא יִסָּעוּ.

וְיֵשׁ אֲשֶׁר יִהְיֶה הֶעָנָן יָמִים מִסְפָּר עַל הַמִּשְׁכָּן;
עַל פִּי ה' יַחֲנוּ, וְעַל פִּי ה' יִסָּעוּ.

וְיֵשׁ אֲשֶׁר יִהְיֶה הֶעָנָן מֵעֶרֶב עַד בֹּקֶר, וְנַעֲלָה הֶעָנָן
בַּבֹּקֶר וְנָסָעוּ; אוֹ יוֹמָם וָלַיְלָה, וְנַעֲלָה הֶעָנָן וְנָסָעוּ.

אוֹ יֹמַיִם, אוֹ חֹדֶשׁ, אוֹ יָמִים, בְּהַאֲרִיךְ הֶעָנָן עַל הַמִּשְׁכָּן
לִשְׁכֹּן עָלָיו, יַחֲנוּ בְנֵי יִשְׂרָאֵל וְלֹא יִסָּעוּ; וּבְהֵעָלֹתוֹ יִסָּעוּ.

עַל פִּי ה' יַחֲנוּ, וְעַל פִּי ה' יִסָּעוּ; אֶת מִשְׁמֶרֶת
ה' שָׁמָרוּ, עַל פִּי ה' בְּיַד מֹשֶׁה.

On the day the Tabernacle was erected, the cloud covered the Tabernacle that was a tent for the Testimony; and at evening there was over the Tabernacle like an appearance of fire, until morning.

So it was always, the cloud covered it; and an appearance of fire at night.

According to the cloud's ascent from over the Tent, after that, the Children of Israel would journey; and in the place where the cloud settled, there the Children of Israel would encamp.

At G-d's bidding the Children of Israel journeyed, and at G-d's bidding they encamped; all the days that the cloud would rest above the Tabernacle, they encamped.

When the cloud lingered over the Tabernacle for many days, the Children of Israel kept the charge of G-d and did not journey.

There were times when the cloud would be for several days above the Tabernacle; at G-d's bidding they encamped, and at G-d's bidding they journeyed.

And there were times when the cloud would be from evening until morning, and the cloud would ascend in the morning, and they would journey; or, for a day and a night, and the cloud would ascend and they would journey.

Or for two days, or for a month, or for a year, when the cloud lengthened its time over the Tabernacle to rest upon it, the Children of Israel would encamp and not journey; and when it ascended they would journey.

At G-d's bidding they would encamp, and at G-d's bidding they would journey; they kept the charge of G-d, by the word of G-d through Moses.

The Birth of a People

DEUTERONOMY 4:32-35

כִּי שְׁאַל נָא לְיָמִים רִאשֹׁנִים אֲשֶׁר הָיוּ לְפָנֶיךָ, לְמִן הַיּוֹם
אֲשֶׁר בָּרָא אֱלֹקִים אָדָם עַל הָאָרֶץ, וּלְמִקְצֵה הַשָּׁמַיִם וְעַד
קְצֵה הַשָּׁמָיִם; הֲנִהְיָה כַּדָּבָר הַגָּדוֹל הַזֶּה, אוֹ הֲנִשְׁמַע כָּמֹהוּ.

הֲשָׁמַע עָם קוֹל אֱלֹקִים מְדַבֵּר מִתּוֹךְ
הָאֵשׁ כַּאֲשֶׁר שָׁמַעְתָּ אַתָּה וַיֶּחִי.

אוֹ הֲנִסָּה אֱלֹקִים לָבוֹא לָקַחַת לוֹ גוֹי מִקֶּרֶב גּוֹי, בְּמַסֹּת בְּאֹתֹת
וּבְמוֹפְתִים וּבְמִלְחָמָה וּבְיָד חֲזָקָה וּבִזְרוֹעַ נְטוּיָה וּבְמוֹרָאִים
גְּדֹלִים; כְּכֹל אֲשֶׁר עָשָׂה לָכֶם ה' אֱלֹקֵיכֶם בְּמִצְרַיִם לְעֵינֶיךָ.

אַתָּה הָרְאֵתָ לָדַעַת, כִּי ה' הוּא הָאֱלֹקִים; אֵין עוֹד מִלְבַדּוֹ.

Ask now after the early days that came before you, from the day that G-d created man upon the earth, and from one end of the heavens to the other; has there ever been the likes of this great thing, or has anything like it been heard?

Have a people heard the voice of G-d speaking from within the fire, as you have heard, and lived?

Or has G-d endeavored to take for Himself a nation from the bowels of a nation, with trials, with signs, with miracles, with battle, with a mighty hand and with an outstretched arm, and with great awesome deeds; as all that G-d your G-d has done for you in Egypt before your eyes?

You were shown to know that G-d is the L-rd; there is none else besides Him.

A Unique Event

Kuzari, 4:11

Moses, our first leader, was not like [the founders of other religions]. He brought the entire people to stand at Mount Sinai, for them to see with their own eyes, each in accordance with their ability, the revelation that he saw. . . . As the verse states (Exodus 24:10), "They saw the G-d of Israel." . . . They all could affirm to each other what they saw and heard. This removed from the heart of the nation the terrible suspicion: Perhaps all of this is just the claim of a few individuals that prophecy came to them? For it is not possible to create a conspiracy in full sight of the masses.

The Shema

DEUTERONOMY 6:4-9

שְׁמַע יִשְׂרָאֵל ה' אֱלֹקֵינוּ ה' אֶחָד.

וְאָהַבְתָּ אֵת ה' אֱלֹקֶיךָ בְּכָל לְבָבְךָ
וּבְכָל נַפְשְׁךָ וּבְכָל מְאֹדֶךָ.

וְהָיוּ הַדְּבָרִים הָאֵלֶּה אֲשֶׁר אָנֹכִי מְצַוְּךָ הַיּוֹם עַל לְבָבֶךָ.
וְשִׁנַּנְתָּם לְבָנֶיךָ וְדִבַּרְתָּ בָּם בְּשִׁבְתְּךָ בְּבֵיתֶךָ
וּבְלֶכְתְּךָ בַדֶּרֶךְ וּבְשָׁכְבְּךָ וּבְקוּמֶךָ.

וּקְשַׁרְתָּם לְאוֹת עַל יָדֶךָ וְהָיוּ לְטֹטָפֹת בֵּין עֵינֶיךָ.

וּכְתַבְתָּם עַל מְזֻזוֹת בֵּיתֶךָ וּבִשְׁעָרֶיךָ.

Hear O Israel, G-d is our G-d, G-d is one.

You shall love G-d your G-d with all your heart, with all your soul, and with all your might.

And these words that I command you today shall be upon your heart. Teach them to your children, and speak of them when you sit in your home and when you travel on the way, when you lie down and when you rise up.

Bind them as a sign on your arm, and they shall be *tefilin* between your eyes.

Write them on the doorposts of your home and on your gates.

Heart, Soul, and Might

Mishnah, Berachot 9:5

"With all your heart"—with both your inclinations: with your good inclination, and your evil inclination.

"With all your soul"—even if He takes your life.

"With all your might (*me'od*)"—with all your money. Another meaning of the phrase "with all your *me'od*": With each and every measure (*midah*) that G-d metes out (*moded*) to you, be exceedingly-exceedingly (*me'od me'od*) grateful (*modeh*) to Him.

Also see Text 11 in Lesson 2

PROPHETS

SAMUEL

Nathan's Rebuke of King David

II SAMUEL 11:27–12:13

וַיֵּרַע הַדָּבָר אֲשֶׁר עָשָׂה דָוִד בְּעֵינֵי ה'.
וַיִּשְׁלַח ה' אֶת נָתָן אֶל דָּוִד, וַיָּבֹא אֵלָיו וַיֹּאמֶר לוֹ:

שְׁנֵי אֲנָשִׁים הָיוּ בְּעִיר אֶחָת, אֶחָד עָשִׁיר וְאֶחָד רָאשׁ. לְעָשִׁיר הָיָה צֹאן וּבָקָר הַרְבֵּה מְאֹד. וְלָרָשׁ אֵין כֹּל, כִּי אִם כִּבְשָׂה אַחַת קְטַנָּה אֲשֶׁר קָנָה וַיְחַיֶּהָ, וַתִּגְדַּל עִמּוֹ וְעִם בָּנָיו יַחְדָּו; מִפִּתּוֹ תֹאכַל וּמִכֹּסוֹ תִשְׁתֶּה וּבְחֵיקוֹ תִשְׁכָּב, וַתְּהִי לוֹ כְּבַת.

וַיָּבֹא הֵלֶךְ לְאִישׁ הֶעָשִׁיר; וַיַּחְמֹל לָקַחַת מִצֹּאנוֹ וּמִבְּקָרוֹ לַעֲשׂוֹת לָאֹרֵחַ הַבָּא לוֹ, וַיִּקַּח אֶת כִּבְשַׂת הָאִישׁ הָרָאשׁ וַיַּעֲשֶׂהָ לָאִישׁ הַבָּא אֵלָיו.

וַיִּחַר אַף דָּוִד בָּאִישׁ מְאֹד; וַיֹּאמֶר אֶל נָתָן: "חַי ה', כִּי בֶן מָוֶת הָאִישׁ הָעֹשֶׂה זֹאת! וְאֶת הַכִּבְשָׂה יְשַׁלֵּם אַרְבַּעְתָּיִם, עֵקֶב אֲשֶׁר עָשָׂה אֶת הַדָּבָר הַזֶּה, וְעַל אֲשֶׁר לֹא חָמָל."

וַיֹּאמֶר נָתָן אֶל דָּוִד: "אַתָּה הָאִישׁ!"...

וַיֹּאמֶר דָּוִד אֶל נָתָן, "חָטָאתִי לַה'."

The thing that David had done was bad in the eyes of G-d. And G-d sent Nathan to David, and he came to him and said to him:

There were two men in one city, one rich and one poor. The rich man had very many flocks and herds. The poor man had nothing, save one little ewe lamb that he had bought and reared, and it grew up together with him and his sons; of his bread it would eat and from his cup it would drink, and in his bosom it would lie, and it was to him like a daughter.

There came a wayfarer to the rich man; and he spared to take of his own flock and of his own herd to prepare for the guest that had come to him, so he took the poor man's lamb and prepared it for the man that had come to him.

David's rage was exceedingly enflamed at the man, and he said to Nathan: "As G-d lives, the man who has done this deserves to die! And the ewe lamb he shall repay fourfold, because he did this thing, and because he had no pity."

And Nathan said to David: "You are the man!" . . .

Said David to Nathan, "I have sinned against G-d."

ISAIAH

The Future Redemption

ISAIAH 2:1–4

הַדָּבָר אֲשֶׁר חָזָה יְשַׁעְיָהוּ בֶּן אָמוֹץ עַל יְהוּדָה וִירוּשָׁלָם:

וְהָיָה בְּאַחֲרִית הַיָּמִים, נָכוֹן יִהְיֶה הַר בֵּית ה' בְּרֹאשׁ הֶהָרִים וְנִשָּׂא מִגְּבָעוֹת; וְנָהֲרוּ אֵלָיו כָּל הַגּוֹיִם.

וְהָלְכוּ עַמִּים רַבִּים וְאָמְרוּ: לְכוּ וְנַעֲלֶה אֶל הַר ה', אֶל בֵּית אֱלֹקֵי יַעֲקֹב; וְיֹרֵנוּ מִדְּרָכָיו וְנֵלְכָה בְּאֹרְחֹתָיו. כִּי מִצִּיּוֹן תֵּצֵא תוֹרָה וּדְבַר ה' מִירוּשָׁלָם.

וְשָׁפַט בֵּין הַגּוֹיִם, וְהוֹכִיחַ לְעַמִּים רַבִּים. וְכִתְּתוּ חַרְבוֹתָם לְאִתִּים וַחֲנִיתוֹתֵיהֶם לְמַזְמֵרוֹת. לֹא יִשָּׂא גוֹי אֶל גּוֹי חֶרֶב, וְלֹא יִלְמְדוּ עוֹד מִלְחָמָה.

The word that Isaiah, son of Amoz, prophesied concerning Judah and Jerusalem:

It shall come to pass in the last days, that the mount of the house of G-d will be established atop the mountains and be exalted above the hills; and all nations will stream to it.

Many nations will go, and say: "Come, let us go up to the mountain of G-d, to the house of the G-d of Jacob; and He will teach us of His ways and we will walk in His paths." For from Zion shall go forth Torah, and the word of G-d from Jerusalem.

[Mashiach] will judge between nations, and reprove many peoples. They will beat their swords into plowshares, and their spears into pruning hooks. Nation will not lift up sword upon nation, neither will they learn war anymore.

The Messiah

ISAIAH 11:1-9

וְיָצָא חֹטֶר מִגֵּזַע יִשָׁי; וְנֵצֶר מִשָּׁרָשָׁיו יִפְרֶה.

וְנָחָה עָלָיו רוּחַ ה'; רוּחַ חָכְמָה וּבִינָה, רוּחַ עֵצָה וּגְבוּרָה, רוּחַ דַּעַת וְיִרְאַת ה'.

וַהֲרִיחוֹ בְּיִרְאַת ה'; וְלֹא לְמַרְאֵה עֵינָיו יִשְׁפּוֹט, וְלֹא לְמִשְׁמַע אָזְנָיו יוֹכִיחַ.

וְשָׁפַט בְּצֶדֶק דַּלִּים, וְהוֹכִיחַ בְּמִישׁוֹר לְעַנְוֵי אָרֶץ; וְהִכָּה אֶרֶץ בְּשֵׁבֶט פִּיו, וּבְרוּחַ שְׂפָתָיו יָמִית רָשָׁע.

וְהָיָה צֶדֶק אֵזוֹר מָתְנָיו; וְהָאֱמוּנָה אֵזוֹר חֲלָצָיו.

וְגָר זְאֵב עִם כֶּבֶשׂ, וְנָמֵר עִם גְּדִי יִרְבָּץ; וְעֵגֶל וּכְפִיר וּמְרִיא יַחְדָּו, וְנַעַר קָטֹן נֹהֵג בָּם.

וּפָרָה וָדֹב תִּרְעֶינָה, יַחְדָּו יִרְבְּצוּ יַלְדֵיהֶן; וְאַרְיֵה כַּבָּקָר יֹאכַל תֶּבֶן.

וְשִׁעֲשַׁע יוֹנֵק עַל חֻר פָּתֶן; וְעַל מְאוּרַת צִפְעוֹנִי גָּמוּל יָדוֹ הָדָה.

לֹא יָרֵעוּ וְלֹא יַשְׁחִיתוּ בְּכָל הַר קָדְשִׁי; כִּי מָלְאָה הָאָרֶץ דֵּעָה אֶת ה' כַּמַּיִם לַיָּם מְכַסִּים.

A shoot shall come forth from the stem of Jesse; and a twig shall sprout from his roots.

The spirit of G-d will rest upon him; a spirit of wisdom and understanding, a spirit of counsel and might, a spirit of knowledge and fear of G-d.

He will be animated by the fear of G-d; and neither with the sight of his eyes shall he judge, nor with the hearing of his ears shall he chastise.

He will judge the poor with equity, and decide with justice for the lowly of the land; he will smite the earth with the rod of his mouth, and with the breath of his lips he shall put the wicked to death.

Righteousness will be the girdle of his loins, and faith the girdle of his waist.

The wolf will dwell with the lamb, and the leopard will lie with the kid; a calf and a lion cub and a fatling together, and a small child shall lead them.

The cow and the bear will graze, together will their children lie; the lion, like cattle, will eat straw.

A suckling child will play on the cobra's hole, and on the lair of an adder a weaned child shall stretch forth its hand.

They shall neither harm nor destroy on all My holy mountain; for the world will be filled with knowledge of G-d as waters cover the sea.

The Wolf and the Lamb

Rabbi David Kimchi ("Radak"), commentary to Isaiah 11:6

There are those who explain the meaning of this verse as follows: In the days of Mashiach, the nature of the animals will change, reverting back to what it was in the beginning of Creation and in Noah's ark, before they became predators.

Others explain that this is all an analogy—that the wolf, the leopard, the bear, and the lion represent the wicked people who persecute and rob, and behave toward the weak as predators toward their prey; while the lamb, the cow, the calf, and the kid represent the humble of the world. The prophet is saying that in the days of Mashiach, there will be peace in the world, and no person will harm their fellow.

The Prophecy of the Dry Bones

EZEKIEL 37:1–14

הָיְתָה עָלַי יַד ה', וַיּוֹצִאֵנִי בְרוּחַ ה' וַיְנִיחֵנִי בְּתוֹךְ הַבִּקְעָה; וְהִיא מְלֵאָה עֲצָמוֹת.

וְהֶעֱבִירַנִי עֲלֵיהֶם סָבִיב סָבִיב; וְהִנֵּה רַבּוֹת מְאֹד עַל פְּנֵי הַבִּקְעָה, וְהִנֵּה יְבֵשׁוֹת מְאֹד.

וַיֹּאמֶר אֵלַי: "בֶּן אָדָם, הֲתִחְיֶינָה הָעֲצָמוֹת הָאֵלֶּה?"; וָאֹמַר, "אֲדֹנָ־י ה' אַתָּה יָדָעְתָּ".

וַיֹּאמֶר אֵלַי: "הִנָּבֵא עַל הָעֲצָמוֹת הָאֵלֶּה; וְאָמַרְתָּ אֲלֵיהֶם: הָעֲצָמוֹת הַיְבֵשׁוֹת, שִׁמְעוּ דְּבַר ה'.

כֹּה אָמַר אֲדֹנָ־י ה' לָעֲצָמוֹת הָאֵלֶּה:
הִנֵּה אֲנִי מֵבִיא בָכֶם רוּחַ וִחְיִיתֶם.

וְנָתַתִּי עֲלֵיכֶם גִּדִים, וְהַעֲלֵתִי עֲלֵיכֶם בָּשָׂר, וְקָרַמְתִּי עֲלֵיכֶם עוֹר, וְנָתַתִּי בָכֶם רוּחַ וִחְיִיתֶם; וִידַעְתֶּם כִּי אֲנִי ה'."

וְנִבֵּאתִי כַּאֲשֶׁר צֻוֵּיתִי; וַיְהִי קוֹל כְּהִנָּבְאִי, וְהִנֵּה רַעַשׁ, וַתִּקְרְבוּ עֲצָמוֹת, עֶצֶם אֶל עַצְמוֹ.

וְרָאִיתִי, וְהִנֵּה עֲלֵיהֶם גִּדִים, וּבָשָׂר עָלָה, וַיִּקְרַם עֲלֵיהֶם עוֹר מִלְמָעְלָה; וְרוּחַ אֵין בָּהֶם.

וַיֹּאמֶר אֵלַי: "הִנָּבֵא אֶל הָרוּחַ; הִנָּבֵא בֶן אָדָם וְאָמַרְתָּ אֶל הָרוּחַ, כֹּה אָמַר אֲדֹנָ־י ה': מֵאַרְבַּע רוּחוֹת בֹּאִי הָרוּחַ, וּפְחִי בַּהֲרוּגִים הָאֵלֶּה וְיִחְיוּ".

וְהִנַּבֵּאתִי כַּאֲשֶׁר צִוָּנִי; וַתָּבוֹא בָהֶם הָרוּחַ וַיִּחְיוּ, וַיַּעַמְדוּ עַל רַגְלֵיהֶם, חַיִל גָּדוֹל מְאֹד מְאֹד.

וַיֹּאמֶר אֵלַי: "בֶּן אָדָם! הָעֲצָמוֹת הָאֵלֶּה כָּל בֵּית יִשְׂרָאֵל הֵמָּה; הִנֵּה אֹמְרִים: יָבְשׁוּ עַצְמוֹתֵינוּ וְאָבְדָה תִקְוָתֵנוּ, נִגְזַרְנוּ לָנוּ.

לָכֵן הִנָּבֵא וְאָמַרְתָּ אֲלֵיהֶם: כֹּה אָמַר אֲדֹנָ־י ה': הִנֵּה אֲנִי פֹתֵחַ אֶת קִבְרוֹתֵיכֶם, וְהַעֲלֵיתִי אֶתְכֶם מִקִּבְרוֹתֵיכֶם, עַמִּי; וְהֵבֵאתִי אֶתְכֶם אֶל אַדְמַת יִשְׂרָאֵל.

וִידַעְתֶּם כִּי אֲנִי ה'; בְּפִתְחִי אֶת קִבְרוֹתֵיכֶם, וּבְהַעֲלוֹתִי אֶתְכֶם מִקִּבְרוֹתֵיכֶם עַמִּי.

וְנָתַתִּי רוּחִי בָכֶם וִחְיִיתֶם, וְהִנַּחְתִּי אֶתְכֶם עַל אַדְמַתְכֶם; וִידַעְתֶּם כִּי אֲנִי ה' דִּבַּרְתִּי וְעָשִׂיתִי." נְאֻם ה'.

The hand of G-d was upon me, and He carried me out in the spirit of G-d, and He set me down in the midst of the valley; and it was full of bones.

He made me pass by them round and round; and behold, there were very many in the open valley, and behold, they were exceedingly dry.

And He said to me: "Son of man, can these bones live?" And I said, "O L-rd G-d, You know."

And He said to me: "Prophesy unto these bones. Say to them: Dry bones! Hear the word of G-d.

"So said the L-rd G-d to these bones: Behold, I will bring spirit into you and you will live.

"I will lay sinews upon you, and I will bring up flesh upon you, and I will cover you with skin, and I will put breath in you, and you will live; and you will know that I am G-d."

I prophesied as I was commanded; as I prophesied there was a sound, and behold a commotion, and the bones came together, a bone to its bone.

I looked, and behold, there were sinews on them, and flesh came up upon them, and the skin covered them above; but there was no spirit in them.

And He said to me: "Prophesy to the spirit; prophesy, O son of man, and say to the spirit: So says the L-rd G-d: From the four winds come, O spirit, and breathe into these slain ones that they should live."

I prophesied as He commanded me; and spirit entered into them, and they lived, and stood up upon their feet, a very great army, exceedingly so.

And He said to me: "Son of man! These bones, they are the whole house of Israel; behold, they say, 'Our bones are dried, our hope is lost, we are cut off from ourselves.'

"Therefore, prophesy and say unto them: So says the L-rd G-d: My people, behold, I will open your graves, and I will raise you up from your graves; and I will bring you to the soil of Israel.

"And you will know that I am G-d; when I open your graves, and when I raise you from your graves, My people.

"I will put My spirit into you and you will live, and I will set you down on your own soil; and you will know that I, G-d, have spoken it and done it. So says G-d."

What Does G-d Want?

MICAH 6:6–8

בַּמָּה אֲקַדֵּם ה', אִכַּף לֵאלֹקֵי מָרוֹם?
הַאֲקַדְּמֶנּוּ בְעוֹלוֹת בַּעֲגָלִים בְּנֵי שָׁנָה?

הֲיִרְצֶה ה' בְּאַלְפֵי אֵילִים, בְּרִבְבוֹת נַחֲלֵי שָׁמֶן?
הַאֶתֵּן בְּכוֹרִי פִּשְׁעִי, פְּרִי בִטְנִי חַטַּאת נַפְשִׁי?

הִגִּיד לְךָ אָדָם מַה טּוֹב, וּמָה ה' דּוֹרֵשׁ מִמְּךָ:
כִּי אִם עֲשׂוֹת מִשְׁפָּט, וְאַהֲבַת חֶסֶד,
וְהַצְנֵעַ לֶכֶת עִם אֱלֹקֶיךָ.

With what shall I come before G-d, bow before the most-high G-d? Shall I come before Him with burnt offerings, with yearling calves?

Will G-d be pleased with thousands of rams, with myriad streams of oil? Shall I give my firstborn for my transgression, the fruit of my body for the sin of my soul?

He has told you, O man, what is good, and what G-d seeks of you: But to do justice, to love kindness, and to walk modestly with your G-d.

WRITINGS

PSALMS

The Path of Torah

PSALMS 1

אַשְׁרֵי הָאִישׁ אֲשֶׁר לֹא הָלַךְ בַּעֲצַת רְשָׁעִים,
וּבְדֶרֶךְ חַטָּאִים לֹא עָמָד, וּבְמוֹשַׁב לֵצִים לֹא יָשָׁב.

כִּי אִם בְּתוֹרַת ה' חֶפְצוֹ, וּבְתוֹרָתוֹ יֶהְגֶּה יוֹמָם וָלָיְלָה.

וְהָיָה כְּעֵץ שָׁתוּל עַל פַּלְגֵי מָיִם; אֲשֶׁר פִּרְיוֹ יִתֵּן
בְּעִתּוֹ, וְעָלֵהוּ לֹא יִבּוֹל, וְכֹל אֲשֶׁר יַעֲשֶׂה יַצְלִיחַ.

לֹא כֵן הָרְשָׁעִים; כִּי אִם כַּמֹּץ אֲשֶׁר תִּדְּפֶנּוּ רוּחַ.

עַל כֵּן לֹא יָקֻמוּ רְשָׁעִים בַּמִּשְׁפָּט, וְחַטָּאִים בַּעֲדַת צַדִּיקִים.

כִּי יוֹדֵעַ ה' דֶּרֶךְ צַדִּיקִים; וְדֶרֶךְ רְשָׁעִים תֹּאבֵד.

Fortunate is the person who did not walk in the counsel of the wicked, who stood not in the path of sinners, who did not sit in the company of scorners.

But only in G-d's Torah is his desire; and in his Torah he deliberates day and night.

He shall be as a tree replanted upon rivulets of water; which gives its fruit in its season, and its leaves do not wilt, and all that it does prospers.

Not so the wicked; they are like chaff driven off by the wind.

Therefore, the wicked shall not stand up in judgment, and the sinners in the community of the righteous.

For G-d knows the way of the righteous; and the way of the wicked shall be lost.

Six Truths about the Torah

Talmud, Avodah Zarah 19a–b

Rabbi [Yehudah Hanasi] said: A person can only learn Torah in the area that their heart desires. As it is written, "But only in G-d's Torah is his desire."

Rava said: At first, the Torah is called by G-d's name, but afterward, it is called by the name of the person [who studies it]. As it is written, ". . . in G-d's Torah is his desire, and in his Torah he deliberates day and night."

Rava also said: A person should first learn [the basic meaning of] Torah, and after that, they should study [the underlying reasoning]. As it is written, "in G-d's Torah," and after that, "and in his Torah he deliberates."

"He shall be as a tree replanted upon rivulets of water." In the study house of Rabbi Yana'i, they said: As a replanted tree, rather than a planted tree. A person who learns only from one teacher does not see success. . . .

"Upon rivulets of water." Rabbi Tanchum ben Chanila'i said: A person should divide their years [of learning] into three parts: one-third in Scripture, one-third in Mishnah, and one-third in Talmud.

"Which brings forth its fruit in its season, [and its leaves do not wilt]." Said Rava: If [the student of Torah] produces fruit [i.e., their learning results in action], their leaves will not wither; but if not, then for both student and teacher, it is as the verse continues, "Not so the wicked, [who are as chaff driven by the wind]."

Also see: Lesson 1, Texts 9 and 15.

G-d Is My Shepherd

PSALMS 23

מִזְמוֹר לְדָוִד: ה' רֹעִי לֹא אֶחְסָר.

בִּנְאוֹת דֶּשֶׁא יַרְבִּיצֵנִי; עַל מֵי מְנֻחוֹת יְנַהֲלֵנִי.

נַפְשִׁי יְשׁוֹבֵב; יַנְחֵנִי בְמַעְגְּלֵי צֶדֶק לְמַעַן שְׁמוֹ.

גַּם כִּי אֵלֵךְ בְּגֵיא צַלְמָוֶת לֹא אִירָא רָע, כִּי אַתָּה
עִמָּדִי; שִׁבְטְךָ וּמִשְׁעַנְתֶּךָ הֵמָּה יְנַחֲמֻנִי.

תַּעֲרֹךְ לְפָנַי שֻׁלְחָן נֶגֶד צֹרְרָי;
דִּשַּׁנְתָּ בַשֶּׁמֶן רֹאשִׁי, כּוֹסִי רְוָיָה.

אַךְ טוֹב וָחֶסֶד יִרְדְּפוּנִי כָּל יְמֵי חַיָּי,
וְשַׁבְתִּי בְּבֵית ה' לְאֹרֶךְ יָמִים.

A song of David: G-d is my shepherd, I shall not want.

He makes me lie down in green pastures; He leads me beside still waters.

He restores my soul; He leads me on paths of righteousness for the sake of His name.

Though I walk in the valley of the shadow of death, I fear no evil, for You are with me; Your rod and Your staff, they comfort me.

You set a table before me in the presence of my adversaries; You anointed my head with oil, my cup runs over.

May only goodness and kindness pursue me all the days of my life, and I shall dwell in the house of G-d for length of days.

The Song of Nature

PSALMS 104

בָּרְכִי נַפְשִׁי אֶת ה'.

ה' אֱלֹקַי גָּדַלְתָּ מְּאֹד; הוֹד וְהָדָר לָבָשְׁתָּ.

עֹטֶה אוֹר כַּשַּׂלְמָה; נוֹטֶה שָׁמַיִם כַּיְרִיעָה.

הַמְקָרֶה בַמַּיִם עֲלִיּוֹתָיו, הַשָּׂם עָבִים
רְכוּבוֹ; הַמְהַלֵּךְ עַל כַּנְפֵי רוּחַ.

עֹשֶׂה מַלְאָכָיו רוּחוֹת; מְשָׁרְתָיו אֵשׁ לֹהֵט.

יָסַד אֶרֶץ עַל מְכוֹנֶיהָ; בַּל תִּמּוֹט עוֹלָם וָעֶד.

תְּהוֹם כַּלְּבוּשׁ כִּסִּיתוֹ; עַל הָרִים יַעַמְדוּ מָיִם.

מִן גַּעֲרָתְךָ יְנוּסוּן; מִן קוֹל רַעַמְךָ יֵחָפֵזוּן.

יַעֲלוּ הָרִים יֵרְדוּ בְקָעוֹת; אֶל מְקוֹם זֶה יָסַדְתָּ לָהֶם.

גְּבוּל שַׂמְתָּ בַּל יַעֲבֹרוּן; בַּל יְשׁוּבוּן לְכַסּוֹת הָאָרֶץ.

הַמְשַׁלֵּחַ מַעְיָנִים בַּנְּחָלִים; בֵּין הָרִים יְהַלֵּכוּן.

יַשְׁקוּ כָּל חַיְתוֹ שָׂדָי; יִשְׁבְּרוּ פְרָאִים צְמָאָם.

עֲלֵיהֶם עוֹף הַשָּׁמַיִם יִשְׁכּוֹן; מִבֵּין עֳפָאיִם יִתְּנוּ קוֹל.

מַשְׁקֶה הָרִים מֵעֲלִיּוֹתָיו; מִפְּרִי מַעֲשֶׂיךָ תִּשְׂבַּע הָאָרֶץ.

מַצְמִיחַ חָצִיר לַבְּהֵמָה, וְעֵשֶׂב לַעֲבֹדַת
הָאָדָם; לְהוֹצִיא לֶחֶם מִן הָאָרֶץ.

וְיַיִן יְשַׂמַּח לְבַב אֱנוֹשׁ, לְהַצְהִיל פָּנִים
מִשָּׁמֶן; וְלֶחֶם לְבַב אֱנוֹשׁ יִסְעָד.

יִשְׂבְּעוּ עֲצֵי ה'; אַרְזֵי לְבָנוֹן אֲשֶׁר נָטָע.

אֲשֶׁר שָׁם צִפֳּרִים יְקַנֵּנוּ; חֲסִידָה בְּרוֹשִׁים בֵּיתָהּ.

הָרִים הַגְּבֹהִים לַיְּעֵלִים; סְלָעִים מַחְסֶה לַשְׁפַנִּים.

עָשָׂה יָרֵחַ לְמוֹעֲדִים; שֶׁמֶשׁ יָדַע מְבוֹאוֹ.

תָּשֶׁת חֹשֶׁךְ וִיהִי לָיְלָה; בּוֹ תִרְמֹשׂ כָּל חַיְתוֹ יָעַר.

הַכְּפִירִים שֹׁאֲגִים לַטָּרֶף; וּלְבַקֵּשׁ מֵאֵל אָכְלָם.

תִּזְרַח הַשֶּׁמֶשׁ יֵאָסֵפוּן; וְאֶל מְעוֹנֹתָם יִרְבָּצוּן.

יֵצֵא אָדָם לְפָעֳלוֹ; וְלַעֲבֹדָתוֹ עֲדֵי עָרֶב.

מָה רַבּוּ מַעֲשֶׂיךָ ה', כֻּלָּם בְּחָכְמָה עָשִׂיתָ; מָלְאָה הָאָרֶץ קִנְיָנֶךָ.

זֶה הַיָּם גָּדוֹל וּרְחַב יָדָיִם, שָׁם רֶמֶשׂ וְאֵין מִסְפָּר;
חַיּוֹת קְטַנּוֹת עִם גְּדֹלוֹת.

שָׁם אֳנִיּוֹת יְהַלֵּכוּן; לִוְיָתָן זֶה יָצַרְתָּ לְשַׂחֶק בּוֹ.

כֻּלָּם אֵלֶיךָ יְשַׂבֵּרוּן; לָתֵת אָכְלָם בְּעִתּוֹ.

תִּתֵּן לָהֶם יִלְקֹטוּן; תִּפְתַּח יָדְךָ יִשְׂבְּעוּן טוֹב.

תַּסְתִּיר פָּנֶיךָ יִבָּהֵלוּן, תֹּסֵף רוּחָם יִגְוָעוּן; וְאֶל עֲפָרָם יְשׁוּבוּן.

תְּשַׁלַּח רוּחֲךָ יִבָּרֵאוּן; וּתְחַדֵּשׁ פְּנֵי אֲדָמָה.

יְהִי כְבוֹד ה' לְעוֹלָם; יִשְׂמַח ה' בְּמַעֲשָׂיו.

הַמַּבִּיט לָאָרֶץ וַתִּרְעָד; יִגַּע בֶּהָרִים וְיֶעֱשָׁנוּ.

אָשִׁירָה לַה' בְּחַיָּי; אֲזַמְּרָה לֵאלֹקַי בְּעוֹדִי.

יֶעֱרַב עָלָיו שִׂיחִי; אָנֹכִי אֶשְׂמַח בַּה'.

יִתַּמּוּ חַטָּאִים מִן הָאָרֶץ, וּרְשָׁעִים עוֹד
אֵינָם, בָּרְכִי נַפְשִׁי אֶת ה'; הַלְלוּ יָ־הּ.

My soul, bless G-d!

My L-rd G-d, You are verily great; with splendor and beauty You have clothed Yourself.

Who dons light like a robe; who spreads the heavens like a tapestry.

Who roofs His lofts with water, who makes clouds His chariot; who traverses upon wings of wind.

He makes the winds His messengers; flaming fire His ministers.

He set the earth upon its foundations; lest it ever falter.

You covered the watery depths like a garment; above the mountains are stood the waters.

From Your shout they flee; from the sound of Your thunder they rush off.

They climb the mountains, they descend the valleys; to this place You established for them.

You set a boundary for them that they may not cross; lest they return to cover the earth.

Who sends forth wellsprings along the riverbeds; between the mountains they traverse.

They water every beast of the field; the wild ones quench their thirst.

Upon them the birds of heaven dwell; from between the branches they give voice.

He waters the mountains from His lofts; from the fruit of Your works is the earth satiated.

He grows fodder for cattle, and herbage to be worked by man; to bring forth bread from the earth.

And wine that will gladden the heart of the human, oil to brighten the face; and bread that sustains the human heart.

The trees of G-d are satiated; the cedars of Lebanon which He planted.

There birds do nest; the stork makes her home in the cypresses.

The high mountains are for the gazelles; the rocks shelter the badgers.

He made the moon to mark times; the sun knows its setting.

You set darkness and night becomes; in it do crawl all beasts of the forest.

The lions roar for prey; to request their food from G-d.

The sun shines and they gather in; and lie down unto their dens.

Man goes forth to their doings; to their labors until evening.

How manifold are Your works, O G-d! You made them all with wisdom; the world is filled with Your possessions.

This sea is great and wide, there are creeping things without number; beasts small and large.

There the ships go; You formed this leviathan with which to sport.

They all look to You with hope; to give their food in its time.

You give them and they gather it; You open Your hand and they are sated with goodness.

You hide Your countenance and they are frightened, You gather in their spirit and they perish; and return to their dust.

You send forth Your spirit and they are created; and You renew the face of the earth.

The glory of G-d shall be forever; G-d shall rejoice in His works.

Who looks upon the earth and it quakes; He touches the mountains and they smoke.

I shall sing to G-d while I am alive; I shall make songs to my G-d as long as I exist.

May my speech be pleasing to Him; I shall rejoice in G-d.

May sins cease from the earth and the wicked be no more; my soul shall bless G-d. Praise G-d!

Guardian of Israel

PSALMS 121

שִׁיר לַמַּעֲלוֹת: אֶשָּׂא עֵינַי אֶל הֶהָרִים, מֵאַיִן יָבֹא עֶזְרִי.
עֶזְרִי מֵעִם ה', עֹשֵׂה שָׁמַיִם וָאָרֶץ.
אַל יִתֵּן לַמּוֹט רַגְלֶךָ; אַל יָנוּם שֹׁמְרֶךָ.
הִנֵּה לֹא יָנוּם וְלֹא יִישָׁן שׁוֹמֵר יִשְׂרָאֵל.
ה' שֹׁמְרֶךָ; ה' צִלְּךָ עַל יַד יְמִינֶךָ.
יוֹמָם הַשֶּׁמֶשׁ לֹא יַכֶּכָּה וְיָרֵחַ בַּלָּיְלָה.
ה' יִשְׁמָרְךָ מִכָּל רָע; יִשְׁמֹר אֶת נַפְשֶׁךָ.
ה' יִשְׁמָר צֵאתְךָ וּבוֹאֶךָ, מֵעַתָּה וְעַד עוֹלָם.

A song of ascents: I raise my eyes to the mountains; from where will come my help?

My help is from G-d, maker of heaven and earth.

He will not allow your foot to falter; your guardian will not slumber.

Behold, the guardian of Israel neither slumbers nor sleeps.

G-d is your guardian; G-d is your shadow, at your right hand.

The sun shall not smite you by day; nor the moon at night.

G-d will guard you from all evil; He will guard your soul.

G-d will guard your goings and your comings, from now and to eternity.

Selected Sayings from the Book of Proverbs

בְּכָל דְּרָכֶיךָ דָעֵהוּ

Know Him in all your ways. (3:6)

לֵךְ אֶל נְמָלָה עָצֵל רְאֵה דְרָכֶיהָ וַחֲכָם

Go to the ant, you sluggard;
see her ways and become wise. (6:6)

אַל תּוֹכַח לֵץ פֶּן יִשְׂנָאֶךָּ הוֹכַח לְחָכָם וְיֶאֱהָבֶךָּ

Reprove not a scorner lest they hate you;
reprove a wise person and they will love you. (9:8)

וְעַל כָּל פְּשָׁעִים תְּכַסֶּה אַהֲבָה

Love covers all sins. (10:12)

בִּרְכַּת ה' הִיא תַעֲשִׁיר וְלֹא יוֹסִף עֶצֶב עִמָּהּ

The blessing of G-d will bring riches,
and toil will add nothing to it. (10:22)

כַּעֲבוֹר סוּפָה וְאֵין רָשָׁע וְצַדִּיק יְסוֹד עוֹלָם

When the whirlwind passes, the wicked
person is no more; but the righteous person
is the foundation of the world. (10:25)

תֻּמַּת יְשָׁרִים תַּנְחֵם וְסֶלֶף בּוֹגְדִים יְשָׁדֵּם

The innocence of the honest guides them;
the treacherous are robbed by their
own contortions. (11:3)

לֹא יוֹעִיל הוֹן בְּיוֹם עֶבְרָה; וּצְדָקָה תַּצִּיל מִמָּוֶת

Riches will not avail on the day of wrath;
but charity will save from death. (11:4)

בְּכָל עֶצֶב יִהְיֶה מוֹתָר

In every distress will be a gain. (14:23)

וּרְקַב עֲצָמוֹת קִנְאָה

Jealousy rots the bones. (14:30)

מַעֲנֶה רַּךְ יָשִׁיב חֵמָה

A gentle reply turns away wrath. (15:1)

כֹּל פָּעַל ה' לַמַּעֲנֵהוּ, וְגַם רָשָׁע לְיוֹם רָעָה

G-d made everything for His sake,
also the wicked for the day of evil. (16:4)

בִּרְצוֹת ה' דַּרְכֵי אִישׁ גַּם אוֹיְבָיו יַשְׁלִם אִתּוֹ

When a person's ways please G-d, also
their enemies will make peace with them. (16:7)

לֵב אָדָם יְחַשֵּׁב דַּרְכּוֹ וַה' יָכִין צַעֲדוֹ

A person's heart plans their way,
but G-d prepares their steps. (16:9)

לִפְנֵי שֶׁבֶר גָּאוֹן, וְלִפְנֵי כִשָּׁלוֹן גֹּבַהּ רוּחַ

Before ruin comes pride,
and before stumbling a haughty spirit. (16:18)

טוֹב פַּת חֲרֵבָה וְשַׁלְוָה בָהּ, מִבַּיִת מָלֵא זִבְחֵי רִיב

Better a piece of dry bread and tranquility
with it, than a house full of meat of strife. (17:1)

גַּם אֱוִיל מַחֲרִישׁ חָכָם יֵחָשֵׁב

Even a fool, when they keep silent,
is considered wise. (17:28)

נֵר ה' נִשְׁמַת אָדָם

The soul of man is a lamp of G-d. (20:27)

חֲנֹךְ לַנַּעַר עַל פִּי דַרְכּוֹ גַּם כִּי יַזְקִין לֹא יָסוּר מִמֶּנָּה

Educate the child according to their way,
so that also when they grow old they
will not turn away from it. (22:6)

אַל תַּסֵּג גְּבוּל עוֹלָם אֲשֶׁר עָשׂוּ אֲבוֹתֶיךָ

Do not remove an ancient boundary
that your forefathers set. (22:28)

בִּנְפֹל אוֹיִבְךָ אַל תִּשְׂמָח וּבִכָּשְׁלוֹ אַל יָגֵל לִבֶּךָ.
פֶּן יִרְאֶה ה' וְרַע בְּעֵינָיו וְהֵשִׁיב מֵעָלָיו אַפּוֹ.

When your enemy falls, do not rejoice,
and when they stumble, let your heart not exult;
lest G-d see and be displeased, and turn
His wrath from them [onto you]. (24:17–18)

כְּבֹד אֱלֹקִים הַסְתֵּר דָּבָר

The glory of G-d is to conceal a matter. (25:2)

רִיבְךָ רִיב אֶת רֵעֶךָ וְסוֹד אַחֵר אַל תְּגָל

Have your quarrel with your friend,
but do not divulge another's secret. (25:9)

אַל תַּעַן כְּסִיל כְּאִוַּלְתּוֹ פֶּן תִּשְׁוֶה לּוֹ גַם אָתָּה

Do not answer a fool according to their folly,
lest you too become like them. (26:4)

בְּאֶפֶס עֵצִים תִּכְבֶּה אֵשׁ וּבְאֵין נִרְגָּן יִשְׁתֹּק מָדוֹן

Without wood the fire goes out;
so without a grumbler the quarrel quiets down. (26:20)

כֹּרֶה שַּׁחַת בָּהּ יִפֹּל וְגֹלֵל אֶבֶן אֵלָיו תָּשׁוּב

One who digs a pit will fall into it;
one who rolls a stone, it will come back to them. (26:27)

אַל תִּתְהַלֵּל בְּיוֹם מָחָר כִּי לֹא תֵדַע מַה יֵּלֶד יוֹם

Do not boast for tomorrow,
for you do not know what the day will bear. (27:1)

יְהַלֶּלְךָ זָר וְלֹא פִיךָ

Let a stranger praise you, not your own mouth. (27:2)

טוֹבָה תּוֹכַחַת מְגֻלָּה מֵאַהֲבָה מְסֻתָּרֶת

Better open rebuke than concealed love. (27:5)

בְּאֵין חָזוֹן יִפָּרַע עָם

Where there is no vision, a people perish. (29:18)

The Knock

SONG OF SONGS 5:2-6

אֲנִי יְשֵׁנָה וְלִבִּי עֵר. קוֹל דּוֹדִי דוֹפֵק: פִּתְחִי לִי אֲחֹתִי רַעְיָתִי
יוֹנָתִי תַמָּתִי, שֶׁרֹּאשִׁי נִמְלָא טָל קְוֻצּוֹתַי רְסִיסֵי לָיְלָה.

פָּשַׁטְתִּי אֶת כֻּתָּנְתִּי אֵיכָכָה אֶלְבָּשֶׁנָּה?
רָחַצְתִּי אֶת רַגְלַי אֵיכָכָה אֲטַנְּפֵם?

דּוֹדִי שָׁלַח יָדוֹ מִן הַחֹר וּמֵעַי הָמוּ עָלָיו.

קַמְתִּי אֲנִי לִפְתֹּחַ לְדוֹדִי; וְיָדַי נָטְפוּ מוֹר
וְאֶצְבְּעֹתַי מוֹר עֹבֵר עַל כַּפּוֹת הַמַּנְעוּל.

פָּתַחְתִּי אֲנִי לְדוֹדִי וְדוֹדִי חָמַק עָבָר; נַפְשִׁי יָצְאָה בְדַבְּרוֹ;
בִּקַּשְׁתִּיהוּ וְלֹא מְצָאתִיהוּ, קְרָאתִיו וְלֹא עָנָנִי.

I am asleep, but my heart is awake. The sound of my lover knocking: Open for me, my sister, my friend, my dove, my perfect one; for my head is full of dew, my locks with the drops of the night.

I have taken off my shirt, how can I put it on? I have washed my feet, how can I soil them?

My beloved withdrew his hand from the latch, and my insides stirred over him.

I arose to open for my beloved, and my hands dripped with myrrh, and my fingers with flowing myrrh, upon the handles of the lock.

I opened for my beloved, but my beloved had eluded and was gone. My soul went out when he spoke; I sought him, but I did not find him; I called him, but he did not answer me.

Our Wakeful Heart

Shir Hashirim Rabah, 5:2

"I am asleep but my heart is awake"—The community of Israel says to G-d: Although I am asleep regarding the *mitzvot*, my heart is awake to acts of kindness. Although I am asleep regarding the Holy Temple, my heart is awake to our synagogues and study halls. Although I am asleep regarding the end of the exile, my heart is awake to the redemption.

The Moabite Convert

RUTH 1:1-18

וַיְהִי בִּימֵי שְׁפֹט הַשֹּׁפְטִים, וַיְהִי רָעָב בָּאָרֶץ; וַיֵּלֶךְ אִישׁ מִבֵּית
לֶחֶם יְהוּדָה לָגוּר בִּשְׂדֵי מוֹאָב, הוּא וְאִשְׁתּוֹ וּשְׁנֵי בָנָיו.

וְשֵׁם הָאִישׁ אֱלִימֶלֶךְ, וְשֵׁם אִשְׁתּוֹ נָעֳמִי, וְשֵׁם שְׁנֵי בָנָיו מַחְלוֹן
וְכִלְיוֹן, אֶפְרָתִים מִבֵּית לֶחֶם יְהוּדָה; וַיָּבֹאוּ שְׂדֵי מוֹאָב וַיִּהְיוּ שָׁם.

וַיָּמָת אֱלִימֶלֶךְ אִישׁ נָעֳמִי; וַתִּשָּׁאֵר הִיא וּשְׁנֵי בָנֶיהָ.

וַיִּשְׂאוּ לָהֶם נָשִׁים מֹאֲבִיּוֹת, שֵׁם הָאַחַת עָרְפָּה,
וְשֵׁם הַשֵּׁנִית רוּת; וַיֵּשְׁבוּ שָׁם כְּעֶשֶׂר שָׁנִים.

וַיָּמוּתוּ גַם שְׁנֵיהֶם, מַחְלוֹן וְכִלְיוֹן; וַתִּשָּׁאֵר
הָאִשָּׁה מִשְּׁנֵי יְלָדֶיהָ וּמֵאִישָׁהּ.

וַתָּקָם הִיא וְכַלֹּתֶיהָ, וַתָּשָׁב מִשְּׂדֵי מוֹאָב; כִּי שָׁמְעָה
בִּשְׂדֵה מוֹאָב כִּי פָקַד ה' אֶת עַמּוֹ לָתֵת לָהֶם לָחֶם.

וַתֵּצֵא מִן הַמָּקוֹם אֲשֶׁר הָיְתָה שָׁמָּה, וּשְׁתֵּי כַלֹּתֶיהָ
עִמָּהּ; וַתֵּלַכְנָה בַדֶּרֶךְ לָשׁוּב אֶל אֶרֶץ יְהוּדָה.

וַתֹּאמֶר נָעֳמִי לִשְׁתֵּי כַלֹּתֶיהָ, "לֵכְנָה שֹּׁבְנָה אִשָּׁה לְבֵית
אִמָּהּ; יַעַשׂ ה' עִמָּכֶם חֶסֶד, כַּאֲשֶׁר עֲשִׂיתֶם עִם הַמֵּתִים וְעִמָּדִי.

יִתֵּן ה' לָכֶם וּמְצֶאןָ מְנוּחָה, אִשָּׁה בֵּית אִישָׁהּ";
וַתִּשַּׁק לָהֶן, וַתִּשֶּׂאנָה קוֹלָן וַתִּבְכֶּינָה.

וַתֹּאמַרְנָה לָּהּ, "כִּי אִתָּךְ נָשׁוּב לְעַמֵּךְ".

וַתֹּאמֶר נָעֳמִי, "שֹׁבְנָה בְנֹתַי, לָמָּה תֵלַכְנָה עִמִּי?
הַעוֹד לִי בָנִים בְּמֵעַי, וְהָיוּ לָכֶם לַאֲנָשִׁים?

שֹׁבְנָה בְנֹתַי לֵכְןָ, כִּי זָקַנְתִּי מִהְיוֹת לְאִישׁ; כִּי אָמַרְתִּי יֶשׁ
לִי תִקְוָה? גַּם הָיִיתִי הַלַּיְלָה לְאִישׁ וְגַם יָלַדְתִּי בָנִים. הֲלָהֵן
תְּשַׂבֵּרְנָה עַד אֲשֶׁר יִגְדָּלוּ? הֲלָהֵן תֵּעָגֵנָה לְבִלְתִּי הֱיוֹת
לְאִישׁ? אַל בְּנֹתַי כִּי מַר לִי מְאֹד מִכֶּם, כִּי יָצְאָה בִי יַד ה'.

וַתִּשֶּׂנָה קוֹלָן וַתִּבְכֶּינָה עוֹד; וַתִּשַּׁק עָרְפָּה
לַחֲמוֹתָהּ, וְרוּת דָּבְקָה בָּהּ.

וַתֹּאמֶר, "הִנֵּה שָׁבָה יְבִמְתֵּךְ אֶל עַמָּהּ וְאֶל
אֱלֹהֶיהָ; שׁוּבִי אַחֲרֵי יְבִמְתֵּךְ".

וַתֹּאמֶר רוּת, "אַל תִּפְגְּעִי בִי לְעָזְבֵךְ לָשׁוּב מֵאַחֲרָיִךְ; כִּי אֶל אֲשֶׁר
תֵּלְכִי אֵלֵךְ, וּבַאֲשֶׁר תָּלִינִי אָלִין, עַמֵּךְ עַמִּי, וֵאלֹקַיִךְ אֱלֹקָי.

בַּאֲשֶׁר תָּמוּתִי אָמוּת, וְשָׁם אֶקָּבֵר; כֹּה יַעֲשֶׂה ה'
לִי וְכֹה יֹסִיף, כִּי הַמָּוֶת יַפְרִיד בֵּינִי וּבֵינֵךְ".

וַתֵּרֶא כִּי מִתְאַמֶּצֶת הִיא לָלֶכֶת אִתָּהּ; וַתֶּחְדַּל לְדַבֵּר אֵלֶיהָ.

It was in the days when the judges judged, that there was a famine in the land; and a man went from Bethlehem of Judah to sojourn in the fields of Moab, he and his wife and his two sons.

The man's name was Elimelech, and his wife's name was Naomi, and his two sons' names were Mahlon and Chilion, Ephrathites from Bethlehem of Judah; and they came to the fields of Moab and remained there.

And Naomi's husband Elimelech died; and she was left with her two sons.

And they married Moabite women, one named Orpah, and the other named Ruth; and they dwelt there for about ten years.

And both Mahlon and Chilion also died, and the woman was left bereft of her two children and of her husband.

She arose with her daughters-in-law, and returned from the fields of Moab; for she had heard in the field of Moab that G-d had remembered His people to give them bread.

She went forth from the place where she had been, and her two daughters-in-law with her; and they went on the road to return to the land of Judah.

And Naomi said to her two daughters-in-law, "Go and return, each woman to her mother's house; may G-d do kindness with you, as you have done with the dead and with me.

"May G-d grant you that you find rest, each woman in her husband's house"; and she kissed them, and they raised their voices and wept.

They said to her: "But we will return with you to your people."

And Naomi said, "Return, my daughters, why should you go with me? Have I yet sons in my womb that they should be your husbands?

"Return, my daughters, go, for I have become too old to marry. Could I say that I have hope? Even if I had a husband tonight, and even if I bore sons. Would you wait for them until they grew up? Would you tie yourselves down for them and not marry? No, my daughters, for it is much more bitter for me than for you, as the hand of G-d has gone forth against me."

And they raised their voices and wept again; and Orpah kissed her mother-in-law, but Ruth cleaved to her.

And she said: "Here your sister-in-law has returned to her people and to her god; return after your sister-in-law."

And Ruth said, "Do not entreat me to leave you, to return from following you; for wherever you go I will go, and wherever you lodge I will lodge, your people are my people, and your G-d is my G-d.

"Where you die I shall die, and there I will be buried; so may G-d do to me and so may He continue, if anything but death shall separate between me and you."

And she saw that she was determined to go with her; and she stopped speaking to her.

Accepting a Convert

Ruth Rabah, 2:16

Three times Naomi says to Ruth, "Return," for three times we dissuade a convert from converting. But if they persist, we accept them. . . . We reject with the left hand, and draw near with the right.

Talmud, Yevamot 47a

We were taught: When a person comes to us to convert to Judaism, we say to them: "Why do you wish to convert? Don't you know that these days the Jewish people are anguished, persecuted, suppressed, and despised, and many troubles befall them?" If they say, "I know, I am unworthy, and nevertheless I desire it," we accept them immediately. . . . As the verse states, "She saw that she was determined to go with her; and she stopped speaking to her."

Times and Seasons

ECCLESIASTES 3:1-8

לַכֹּל זְמָן; וְעֵת לְכָל חֵפֶץ תַּחַת הַשָּׁמָיִם.

עֵת לָלֶדֶת וְעֵת לָמוּת; עֵת לָטַעַת וְעֵת לַעֲקוֹר נָטוּעַ.

עֵת לַהֲרוֹג וְעֵת לִרְפּוֹא, עֵת לִפְרוֹץ וְעֵת לִבְנוֹת.

עֵת לִבְכּוֹת וְעֵת לִשְׂחוֹק, עֵת סְפוֹד וְעֵת רְקוֹד.

עֵת לְהַשְׁלִיךְ אֲבָנִים וְעֵת כְּנוֹס אֲבָנִים;
עֵת לַחֲבוֹק וְעֵת לִרְחֹק מֵחַבֵּק.

עֵת לְבַקֵּשׁ וְעֵת לְאַבֵּד, עֵת לִשְׁמוֹר וְעֵת לְהַשְׁלִיךְ.

עֵת לִקְרוֹעַ וְעֵת לִתְפּוֹר, עֵת לַחֲשׁוֹת וְעֵת לְדַבֵּר.

עֵת לֶאֱהֹב וְעֵת לִשְׂנֹא, עֵת מִלְחָמָה וְעֵת שָׁלוֹם.

To every thing there is a season; a time to every purpose under the heavens:

A time to give birth and a time to die; a time to plant and a time to uproot what is planted.

A time to kill and a time to heal, a time to break and a time to build.

A time to weep and a time to laugh, a time to mourn and a time to dance.

A time to cast stones and a time to gather stones; a time to embrace and a time to refrain from embracing.

A time to search and a time to lose, a time to keep and a time to cast away.

A time to rend and a time to mend, a time to be silent and a time to speak.

A time to love and a time to hate, a time for war and a time for peace.

The Ten Commandments

DERIVED MITZVOT	TABLET 1 BETWEEN US AND G-D	TABLET 2 A PERSON AND THEIR FELLOW	DERIVED MITZVOT
▪ Love and awe of G-d ▪ Prayer ▪ The service in the Holy Temple ▪ The signs and reminders of our relationship with G-d: *tefilin*, *mezuzah*, *tztzit*, etc.	**1** I AM G-D YOUR G-D	**6** DO NOT MURDER	▪ Mitzvot governing preservation of life ▪ The judging of capital cases ▪ Laws of warfare
▪ All prohibitions of idolatry and idolatrous practices ▪ The laws of ritual purity	**2** DO NOT HAVE ANY OTHER GODS BEFORE ME	**7** DO NOT COMMIT ADULTERY	▪ Laws of marriage and divorce ▪ Forbidden relations
▪ Laws of prophecy ▪ The sanctification of G-d's name ▪ Blasphemy, false oaths, and the fulfillment of vows ▪ Not to curse or insult a fellow	**3** DO NOT TAKE THE NAME OF G-D IN VAIN	**8** DO NOT STEAL	▪ All financial and property laws
▪ The festivals ▪ The Sabbatical and Jubilee years	**4** REMEMBER THE DAY OF SHABBAT TO SANCTIFY IT	**9** DO NOT BEAR FALSE WITNESS UNTO YOUR FELLOW	▪ Laws pertaining to the hearing of evidence and the proper execution of justice ▪ Prohibitions against slander, defamation, and gossip
▪ Procreation ▪ Circumcision ▪ Mourning relatives ▪ Laws of inheritance ▪ Charity and aiding a fellow in need ▪ Gifts to *kohanim* and Levites	**5** HONOR YOUR FATHER AND YOUR MOTHER	**10** DO NOT COVET . . . ANYTHING THAT IS YOUR FELLOW'S	▪ Love your fellow as yourself ▪ Laws pertaining to diet and dress

PARALLEL COMMANDMENTS

1/6

The human soul is "literally a part of G-d above." Without belief in G-d, there is ultimately no respect for the sanctity of human life; without respect for the sanctity of human life, there is no true belief in G-d.

2/7

Our relationship with G-d is a marriage, and human marriage reflects its Divine analog. The loyalty that G-d expects from us is no less than that which we expect from our spouse. Conversely, love between a man and a woman will attain its fullest potential when it is true to its Divine essence.

3/8

G-d allocates to every individual his or her "portion in the world"—the resources they require to fulfill their mission in life. Violating the property rights of one's fellow is an act that debases G-d's own ownership of His creation.

4/9

By observing the Shabbat, we testify to G-d's creation of the world. To violate the Shabbat is to make a lie of this testimony.

5/10

Both these commandments indicate an inherent synonymy of the two tablets. On the face of it, the 5th commandment would seem to belong with the "between a person and their fellow" precepts, while the 10th Commandment, an act performed in the heart, appears to be wholly a matter "between us and G-d." Yet honoring those who brought us into the world with the distinctly Divine power of creation acknowledges the G-dly in the human being; and the precept "Do not covet" acknowledges that our spiritual transgressions also impact a fellow's life.

Major Biblical Commentaries

1070
RASHI

Commentary by Rabbi Shlomo Yitzchaki (1040–1105) of Troyes, France. Foremost of the biblical elucidators, Rashi's commentary on Torah is a first point of reference for schoolchild and scholar alike. Drawn almost entirely from Talmudic and Midrashic sources, under Rashi's pen these are blended, rephrased, and edited into a lucid, internally consistent commentary, addressing virtually every question and ambiguity arising from the text. By Rashi's own attestation, "I come only to explain the plain meaning of the text, and to present those Midrashim that aid its understanding."

1200
RADAK

Rabbi David Kimchi (1160–1235) was a primary authority on biblical Hebrew. In addition to his philological works, Kimchi wrote commentaries on many of the biblical books, including all the books of the Prophets and the book of Psalms.

1291
BECHAYEI

Commentary on the Torah by Rabbi Bechayei (or Bachya) ben Asher (1255–1340, Spain) that is a synthesis of elucidation, allegory, homilies, and mysticism.

1494
AKEIDAT YITZCHAK

("Binding of Isaac") Philosophical and mystical essays in order of the weekly Torah portions by Rabbi Yitzchak Arama (1420–1494) of Spain.

100 500 1000 1100 1200 13

100
ONKELOS

Aramaic translation of the Bible authored by Onkelos (c. 35–120 CE), a prominent Roman nobleman (and nephew of the Roman emperor Titus) who converted to Judaism. The Talmud attests that Onkelos's translation incorporates the authentic interpretation of the Torah as received in the Sinaitic tradition.

1156
IBN EZRA

Classic commentary on the Torah by Rabbi Abraham ibn Ezra (1092–1167). Born in Tudela in northern Spain, the wanderings of his turbulent life brought him to France, Italy, England, and the Middle East. Ibn Ezra employs grammatical and lexical analysis to support a rigorous *peshat* (plain meaning of the verse) approach to biblical elucidation, and draws on explanations given by earlier philologists and commentators, many of whom are known only from his work. Ibn Ezra also wrote works of poetry, philosophy, medicine, astronomy, and other topics.

1264
NACHMANIDES

Classic commentary on the Torah, intermingled with agadic and mystical interpretations, by Rabbi Moshe ben Nachman (1194–1270). Toward the end of his life, Nachmanides left his native Spain and settled in the Holy Land, where he revived the Jewish community in Jerusalem. Nachmanides also authored a commentary on the Talmud and works of Halachah and Musar.

1321
RALBAG

Rabbi Levi ben Gershon (1288–1344) of France, also known by the acronym "Ralbag" and by the patronymic "Gersonides," was a philosopher, mathematician, astronomer, and inventor. His commentary on Tanach defines word meanings, explains the narrative, and lists dozens of philosophical, ethical, and Halachic conclusions derived from each chapter.

1550
SEFORNO

Popular commentary by Rabbi Ovadiah Seforno (1475–1550), who lived in Rome and Bologna, Italy. While in Rome, Seforno taught Hebrew to the German humanist Johann Reuchlin, who later put this knowledge to use in defending German Jewry against religious attacks.

1500
ABARBANEL
Rabbi Don Yitzchak Abarbanel (1437–1508) was a scholar, philosopher, statesman, and financier who served as treasurer to several monarchs in Portugal and Spain. Following the infamous Edict of Expulsion in 1492, he settled in Italy. Abarbanel authored a series of commentaries on the Tanach, and numerous other important Torah works.

1732
ME'AM LO'EZ
Encyclopedic biblical commentary covering all areas of Jewish life, originally written in Ladino. Begun by Rabbi Yaakov Culi (1689–1732), chief rabbinical magistrate of Constantinople, with other prominent rabbis of Turkey completing the remaining volumes after his passing.

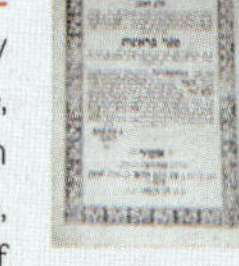

1593
ALSHICH
Homiletical commentary on the Torah by Rabbi Moshe Alshich (c. 1508–1593) of Safed, Israel.

1742
OHR HACHAYIM
Commentary on the Torah combining *peshat*, homiletics, and mysticism by Rabbi Chaim ibn Atar (1696–1743) of Morocco and Israel.

1860
NETZIV
Commentary on the Torah entitled *Haamek Davar* ("Delve into the Matter") by Rabbi Naftali Tzvi Yehudah Berlin (1817–1893), head of the yeshiva in Volozhin, Russia. Netziv also authored commentaries on the Halachic Midrashim, Talmud, and *She'iltot*.

1601
KELI YAKAR
A popular commentary containing many philosophical and psychological insights by Rabbi Shlomo Ephraim Luntshitz (1550–1619), who lived in Lublin, Lvov, and Prague.

1780
METZUDOT
A pair of commentaries on the "Prophets" section of Tanach and most of the "Writings" section by Rabbi David Altschuler (18th century, Prague). *Metzudat David* explains the plain sense of the text, and *Metzudat Tzion* explains the meaning of difficult words. The commentary was assembled and completed by Altschuler's son, Rabbi Yechiel Hillel.

1774
CHIDA
Commentaries by Rabbi Chaim Yosef David Azulai (1724–1806) of Jerusalem. Chida traveled extensively throughout Europe and North Africa, and was a noted bibliophile and a prolific writer in many areas of Torah.

1868
MALBIM
Commentary on the entire Tanach by Rabbi Meir Leibush Wisser (1809–1879), who served as rabbi in a number of prestigious communities across Europe. Malbim's commentary endeavors to explain the precise meaning of every word and synonym of the biblical text, while also introducing philosophical and mystical perspectives on the narrative.

1875
BEN ISH CHAI
Series of lectures on the weekly Torah portion with mystical discussions and practical Halachah by Rabbi Yosef Chaim of Baghdad (1834–1909).

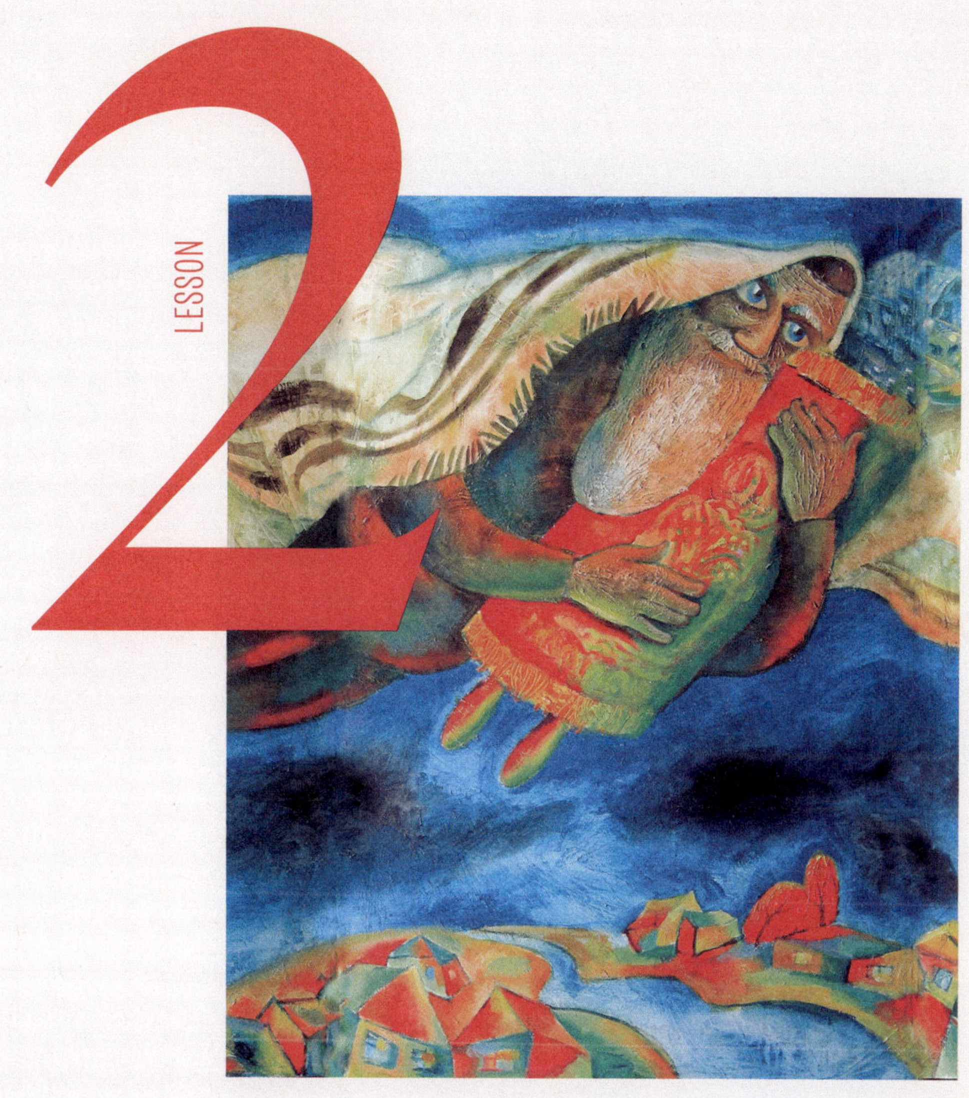

THE MIDRASH

What is Midrash? Is it a set of books, a methodology, or both? In this lesson, we learn about the methods by which the sages excavate the multiple layers of meaning contained within the words—and between the lines—of the biblical text, and we explore the mysterious pathways of the Midrashic parable.

FLYING WITH TORAH
Leon Zernitsky, acrylic on canvas.

I. WHAT IS MIDRASH?

Midrash means "to seek out" and "to expound." The principle behind Midrash is that every verse in the Written Torah incorporates multiple layers of meaning. Midrash is the process by which the additional layers of meaning contained within the words—or between the lines—of the Written Torah are expounded.

TEXT 1

Exploding Particles

Talmud, Sanhedrin 34a

"וּכְפַטִּישׁ יְפוֹצֵץ סָלַע" (יִרְמְיָה כג, כט).
מָה פַּטִּישׁ זֶה מִתְחַלֵּק לְכַמָּה נִיצוֹצוֹת,
אַף מִקְרָא אֶחָד יוֹצֵא לְכַמָּה טְעָמִים.

"[My words are like fire, says G-d,] and like a hammer that shatters a rock" (JEREMIAH 23:29). As the hammer explodes many particles, so does one verse of Scripture diverge into many meanings.

Jeremiah 23 in the Leningrad Codex, the oldest complete manuscript of the Tanach, produced in Cairo, c. 1008. (National Library of Russia, St. Petersburg)

BABYLONIAN TALMUD

A literary work of monumental proportions that draws upon the legal, spiritual, intellectual, ethical, and historical traditions of Judaism. The 37 tractates of the Babylonian Talmud contain the teachings of the Jewish sages from the period after the destruction of the 2nd Temple through the 5th century CE. It has served as the primary vehicle for the transmission of the Oral Law and the education of Jews over the centuries; it is the entry point for all subsequent legal, ethical, and theological Jewish scholarship.

II. HALACHAH AND AGADAH

The Midrashic teachings fall under two general categories: Halachic Midrashim and Agadic Midrashim. The Halachic Midrashim document how the laws governing the observance of the *mitzvot* are derived from the words of the Written Torah. The Agadic Midrashim include moral, philosophical, and mystical teachings, as well as stories, parables, and narratives.

TORAH STUDY UNDER A TREE
Rosa Katznelson

FIGURE 2.1

Types of Midrashic Texts

	TYPE OF MIDRASH	EXAMPLES
HALACHIC MIDRASHIM	**Legal Exposition:** Midrashim that derive the particulars of the Torah's laws from the biblical text, using one of the traditional methods of Torah exposition.	The details of the placement of the *tefilin* are derived from the Torah's description in Deuteronomy 11:18–20, by using the "association" and "juxtaposition" methods—see text from *Mechilta DeRabbi Yishma'el* on pp. 74–75.
AGADIC MIDRASHIM	**Historical Narratives:** Narratives of biblical events not explicitly recounted in the Written Torah and only hinted to in the text, which are part of the oral tradition and are recorded in the Midrash.	The account of Abraham's early years and his discovery of the truth of the One G-d—see texts on p. 88.
	Moral and Ethical Teachings: Non-legal teachings that impart guidance on proper behavior and attitudes, which are derived from the biblical text and narratives.	The power of speech—see texts on p. 90.
	Philosophical and Mystical Midrashim: Insights into the "big questions" of life and the secrets of Creation, derived from the biblical text.	The paradox of truth and peace—see text from *Bereshit Rabah* on pp. 66–67. The relationship between the spiritual and material dimensions of Creation—see text on p. 90.
	Parables: Teachings conveyed by means of a parable, often associated with a verse of the Written Torah.	See text from *Bereshit Rabah* on p. 64, and texts on p. 89.
	Torah Commentary: Explanations of the biblical text and narrative. Many of these Midrashim serve as sources for the later works of biblical commentary by Rashi and others.	The meaning of the phrase, "the souls they made in Charan" (Genesis 12:5)—see text from *Shir Hashirim Rabah* on p. 32. The allegorical meanings of the imagery in "Song of Songs"—see p. 48.
	Biographical accounts: Stories from the lives of the sages.	The story of the thirteen years Rabbi Shimon bar Yocha'i and his son spent hiding from the Romans in a cave—see text on p. 91.

Also see "Compendium of Agadic Midrashim" in Additional Features for this lesson (pp. 88–92)

III. THE MIDRASHIC WORKS

While the term "Midrash" is sometimes more loosely applied to a wide range of teachings that expound the Torah, the term is more properly applied to those quoted by the sages of the Mishnaic and Talmudic periods (approximately 100 BCE to 500 CE), which are considered to be more authoritative than teachings expounded in later generations.

A THEOLOGICAL DEBATE
Eduard Frankfort (1864–1920), oil on canvas, Amsterdam, 1888.

FIGURE 2.2

Major Midrashic Works

2ND CENTURY CE

135 CE
MECHILTA DE'RABBI YISHMA'EL
Exegeses on the book of Exodus from the school of Rabbi Yishma'el ben Elisha.

MECHILTA DE'RASHBI
Exegeses on the book of Exodus from the school of Rabbi Akiva, attributed to his disciple, Rabbi Shimon bar Yocha'i.

SIFRA
also called
TORAT KOHANIM
Exegeses on the book of Leviticus from the school of the Mishnaic sage Rabbi Yehudah (a disciple of Rabbi Akiva). According to Maimonides, it was compiled by the Talmudic sage Rav.

SIFREI
Exegeses on the books of Numbers and Deuteronomy.

HALACHIC MIDRASHIM

1 CE — 200 — 400 — 600

AGADIC MIDRASHIM

50 CE
PIRKEI RABBI ELIEZER
Expositions on biblical events from Creation until the Israelites' journeys in the wilderness. Attributed to 1st-century Mishnaic sage R. Eliezer ben Hyrcanus.

150 CE
SEDER OLAM
Chronicles biblical and post-biblical history from Creation to the Bar Kochba revolt. Attributed to the 2nd-century Mishnaic sage R. Yosei ben Chalafta of Sepphoris.

200–400 CE
MIDRASH RABAH
A series of ten separate works, containing textual exegeses, historical narratives, and moral teachings structured as commentaries on the Five Books of Moses and the five scriptural "scrolls." These Midrashic anthologies were compiled between the 3rd and 12th centuries, and cite the teachings of Talmudic sages from the Land of Israel from the 3rd and 4th centuries CE.

350 CE
MIDRASH TANCHUMA
A foundational Midrashic work containing exposition on the Five Books of Moses, bearing the name of the 4th-century Talmudic sage Rabbi Tanchuma, who is quoted often in it.

3760 YEAR ON JEWISH CALENDAR — 3960 — 4160 — 4360

219–505 CE
THE TALMUD
While the Talmud is not an exclusively Midrashic work, it includes a wealth of Midrashic expositions of biblical verses, of both the Halachic and Agadic genres.

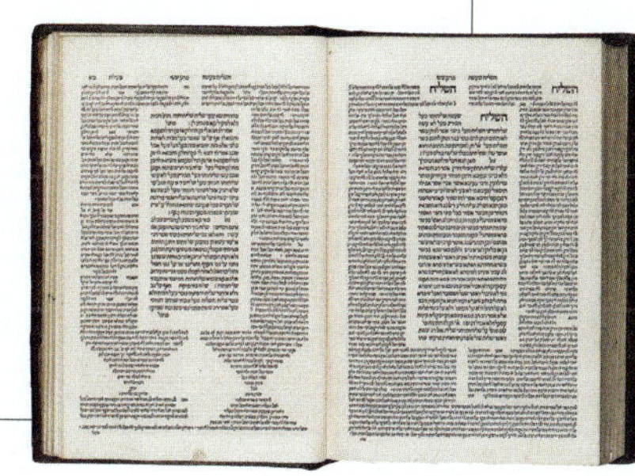

800 1000 1200 1400

1000
MIDRASH TEHILIM
A Midrashic commentary on the book of Psalms. While the date of its compilation has not been conclusively determined, it is cited as early as the 11th century.

1250
YALKUT SHIMONI
A voluminous Midrashic anthology covering all 24 books of the Tanach. Compiled by Rabbi Shimon Hadarshan of Frankfort, Germany.

1300
MIDRASH HAGADOL
Midrashic anthology attributed to Rabbi David bar Amram al-Adani of Aden, Yemen.

1500
EIN YAAKOV
Extraction of the agadic sections of the Talmud. Compiled by Rabbi Yaakov ibn Habib, who lived in Spain and Greece.

BERESHIT RABAH
Expositions on the book of Genesis

SHEMOT RABAH
Expositions on the book of Exodus

VAYIKRA RABAH
Expositions on the book of Leviticus

BAMIDBAR RABAH
Expositions on the book of Numbers

DEVARIM RABAH
Expositions on the book of Deuteronomy

RUTH RABAH
Expositions on the book of Ruth

SHIR HASHIRIM RABAH
Expositions on Song of Songs

KOHELET RABAH
Expositions on Ecclesiastes

ESTHER RABAH
Expositions on the book of Esther

EICHAH RABATI
Expositions on Lamentations

4560 4760 4960 5160

IV. STORIES, PARABLES, AND SECRETS

A most fascinating area of Midrashic literature are the stories, narratives, and parables in its Agadic component, which convey many of the mystical secrets of the Torah.

TEXT 2

Iron and the Trees

Midrash, *Bereshit Rabah* 5:10

כֵּיוָן שֶׁנִּבְרָא הַבַּרְזֶל, הִתְחִילוּ הָאִילָנוֹת מְרַתְּתִים.
אָמַר לָהֶן: "מַה לָכֶם מְרַתְּתִים?
עֵץ מִכֶּם אַל יִכָּנֵס בִּי, וְאֵין אֶחָד מִכֶּם נִזּוֹק!"

When iron was created, the trees started trembling. Said iron to them: "Why are you trembling? If no tree among you enters into me [to provide a handle for my blade], not a single one of you will be hurt!"

BERESHIT RABAH

An early rabbinic commentary on the Book of Genesis. This Midrash bears the name of Rabbi Oshiya Rabah (Rabbi Oshiya "the Great"), whose teaching opens this work. This Midrash provides textual exegeses and stories, expounds upon the biblical narrative, and develops and illustrates moral principles. Produced by the sages of the Talmud in the Land of Israel, its use of Aramaic closely resembles that of the Jerusalem Talmud. It was first printed in Constantinople in 1512 together with 4 other Midrashic works on the other 4 books of the Pentateuch.

Cover page to volume two of the book *Ein Yaakov*, a compilation—by Rabbi Yaakov ibn Habib and his son Rabbi Levi ibn Habib—of Agadic content in the Talmud. (Vilna: Romm Printing House—Yosef Reuven ben Menachem Mann Romm, 1863). (Russian State Library. Moscow)

QUESTION

What is the purpose of a parable? What are the advantages of using a parable, instead of just communicating the idea that lies behind it?

TEXT 3

Agadah and the Mystical

Rabbi Shneur Zalman of Liadi, *Tanya*, Igeret Hakodesh 23

אַגָּדָה שֶׁבְּסֵפֶר עֵין יַעֲקֹב,
שֶׁרֹב סוֹדוֹת הַתּוֹרָה גְנוּזִין בָּהּ.

Most of the esoteric wisdom of the Torah is hidden in the *Agadot* in the book *Ein Yaakov*.

RABBI SHNEUR ZALMAN OF LIADI (ALTER REBBE) 1745–1812

Chasidic rebbe, Halachic authority, and founder of the Chabad movement. The Alter Rebbe was born in Liozna, Belarus, and was among the principal students of the Magid of Mezeritch. His numerous works include the *Tanya*, an early classic containing the fundamentals of Chabad Chasidism; and *Shulchan Aruch HaRav*, an expanded and reworked code of Jewish law.

TEXT 4

The Battle of the Angels

Midrash, *Bereshit Rabah* 8:3–5

"וַיֹּאמֶר אֱלֹקִים נַעֲשֶׂה אָדָם" (בְּרֵאשִׁית א, כו). בְּמִי נִמְלַךְ? . . .

אָמַר רַבִּי סִימוֹן: בְּשָׁעָה שֶׁבָּא הַקָּדוֹשׁ בָּרוּךְ הוּא לִבְרֹאת אֶת אָדָם הָרִאשׁוֹן, נַעֲשׂוּ מַלְאֲכֵי הַשָּׁרֵת כִּתִּים כִּתִּים וַחֲבוּרוֹת חֲבוּרוֹת. מֵהֶם אוֹמְרִים: "אַל יִבָּרֵא", וּמֵהֶם אוֹמְרִים: "יִבָּרֵא". הֲדָא הוּא דִכְתִיב: "חֶסֶד וֶאֱמֶת נִפְגָּשׁוּ, צֶדֶק וְשָׁלוֹם נָשָׁקוּ" (תְּהִלִּים פה, יא). חֶסֶד אוֹמֵר: "יִבָּרֵא, שֶׁהוּא גוֹמֵל חֲסָדִים", וֶאֱמֶת אוֹמֵר: "אַל יִבָּרֵא, שֶׁכֻּלּוֹ שְׁקָרִים". צֶדֶק אוֹמֵר: "יִבָּרֵא, שֶׁהוּא עוֹשֶׂה צְדָקוֹת", שָׁלוֹם אוֹמֵר: "אַל יִבָּרֵא, דְכוּלֵּיהּ קְטָטָה".

מָה עָשָׂה הַקָּדוֹשׁ בָּרוּךְ הוּא? נָטַל אֱמֶת וְהִשְׁלִיכוֹ לָאָרֶץ. הֲדָא הוּא דִכְתִיב: "וְתַשְׁלֵךְ אֱמֶת אַרְצָה" (דָּנִיֵּאל ח, יב). אָמְרוּ מַלְאֲכֵי הַשָּׁרֵת לִפְנֵי הַקָּדוֹשׁ בָּרוּךְ הוּא: "רִבּוֹן הָעוֹלָמִים, מָה אַתָּה מְבַזֶּה תַּכְסִיס אַלְטִיכְסִיָה שֶׁלְּךָ?", "תַּעֲלֶה אֱמֶת מִן הָאָרֶץ". הֲדָא הוּא דִכְתִיב: "אֱמֶת מֵאֶרֶץ תִּצְמָח" (תְּהִלִּים פה, יב).

[It is written,] "And G-d said, 'Let us make a human'" (GENESIS 1:26). With whom did G-d consult . . . ?

Said Rabbi Simon: When G-d came to create the first human being, the ministering angels formed different factions, different parties. Some of them said, "The human being should not be created," while others said, "The human being should be created." Thus it is written, "Kindness and Truth encountered each other; Righteousness and Peace abutted" (PSALMS 85:11). Kindness said, "Create them, for they do acts of kindness"; and Truth said, "Do not create them, as they are full of lies." Righteousness said, "Create them, for they do acts of righteousness"; Peace said, "Do not create them, as they are full of quarrels."

What did G-d do? He took Truth and hurled it to the earth. Thus it is written, "You cast truth to the ground" (DANIEL 8:12). Said the ministering angels to G-d: "Master of the world! Why do You insult Your signet?" [Said G-d:] "May Truth rise from the earth." Thus it is written, "Truth sprouts forth from the earth" (PSALMS 85:12).

THE SIXTH DAY OF CREATION
Ofra Friedland, oil on canvas, Israel.

V. THE MIDRASHIC METHODOLOGIES

A central component of the Oral Torah and the Sinaitic tradition is a set of rules describing the methods by which the Torah is expounded. These are the methodologies that the Midrash employs to derive laws and teachings from the verses and words of the Written Torah. In today's class, we will be studying examples of four of these methodologies.

TEXT 5

Thirteen Methodologies

Midrash Hagadol, Exodus 21:1

"וְאֵלֶּה הַמִּשְׁפָּטִים אֲשֶׁר תָּשִׂים לִפְנֵיהֶם" (שְׁמוֹת כא, א). רַבִּי יִשְׁמָעֵאל אוֹמֵר: אֵלּוּ שְׁלֹשׁ עֶשְׂרֵה מִדּוֹת שֶׁהַתּוֹרָה נִדְרֶשֶׁת בָּהֶן שֶׁנִּמְסְרוּ לוֹ לְמֹשֶׁה בְּסִינַי.

"These are the laws that you shall place before them" (EXODUS 21:1). Rabbi Yishma'el says: These are the thirteen methods by which the Torah is expounded, which were given to Moses at Sinai.

MIDRASH HAGADOL

A midrashic work on the 5 books of the Pentateuch. Midrash is the designation of a particular genre of rabbinic literature usually forming a running commentary on specific books of the Bible. *Midrash Hagadol* quotes widely from Talmud and other earlier Midrashic works, serving as a valuable resource to reconstruct lost sections of Midrash. A traveler, Yaakov Sapir, first discovered the anonymous Midrash in Yemen in the middle of the 19th century. Some ascribe it to Rabbi Avraham, son of Maimonides.

Why Is the Oral Torah so Concise: Couldn't G-d Just Say Everything in a Straightforward Way?
myjli.com/booksmart

FIGURE 2.3

Four Methods of Torah Exposition

TALMUDIC NAME	METHOD OF EXPOSITION	EXAMPLES
קַל וָחֹמֶר *kal vachomer*	logical deduction	Texts 6, 7, 8
רִבּוּי וּמִיעוּט *ribui umi'ut*	textual exposition	Text 9
הֶקֵּשׁ; גְּזֵרָה שָׁוָה; סְמִיכוּת *hekeish; gezerah shavah; semichut*	association	Texts 10, 11
קְרִי וּכְתִיב; אַל תִּקְרֵי ___ אֶלָּא ___ *keri uketiv; al tikrei ___, ela ___*	alternate readings	Texts 12, 13, 14, 15

TALMUDIC DISCUSSION
Mark Gertler (1891–1939), oil on canvas, London, 1911. (Ben Uri Gallery and Museum, London, England)

VI. LOGICAL DEDUCTION

One of the rules of Torah exposition is that the Torah will state one law, from which a second law can be logically derived. For example, when the Torah instructs that one is obligated to help unload an overburdened animal belonging to one's enemy, then certainly one is obligated to assist in the case of a friend's animal. The fact that the Torah chooses to tell us the law in this manner (rather than by stating it explicitly) is also significant, as it establishes the limits of the derived law, which can never be stronger than the source law from which it derives.

TEXT 6

The *Kal Vachomer* Argument

Genesis 44:8

הֵן כֶּסֶף אֲשֶׁר מָצָאנוּ בְּפִי אַמְתְּחֹתֵינוּ
הֱשִׁיבֹנוּ אֵלֶיךָ מֵאֶרֶץ כְּנָעַן,
וְאֵיךְ נִגְנֹב מִבֵּית אֲדֹנֶיךָ כֶּסֶף אוֹ זָהָב?

Behold, the money that we found in the opening of our bags, we returned to you from the land of Canaan; how, then, would we steal gold or silver from the house of your master?

Judah pleads for his brother Benjamin before Joseph, from *Old Testament History*, Willam Hole. (London, England: Eyre and Spottiswoode, 1925)

TEXT 7

The Roadside Assistance Law

Exodus 23:5

כִּי תִרְאֶה חֲמוֹר שֹׂנַאֲךָ רֹבֵץ תַּחַת מַשָּׂאוֹ
וְחָדַלְתָּ מֵעֲזֹב לוֹ, עָזֹב תַּעֲזֹב עִמּוֹ.

When you see the donkey of your enemy collapsing under its burden, and you are inclined to desist from assisting him, assist you must assist with him.

TEXT 8

The "*Dayo*" Rule

Talmud, Bava Kama 25a

דַיוֹ לַבָּא מִן הַדִּין לִהְיוֹת כַּנִדוֹן.

It is enough that a matter derived from a law should be as strong as [but not stronger than] the source law.

VII. TEXTUAL EXPOSITION

Another rule of Torah exposition emphasizes the significance of the precise wording and spelling of the Written Torah. When a verse contains a seemingly superfluous word, or even a seemingly unneeded letter, these are interpreted as conveying an additional clause to the law stated in the verse, or an additional insight to its teaching.

TEXT 9

Conditions of Assistance

Mishnah, Bava Metzi'a 2:10

פָּרַק וְטָעַן, פָּרַק וְטָעַן, אֲפִלּוּ אַרְבָּעָה וַחֲמִשָּׁה פְּעָמִים, חַיָּב. שֶׁנֶּאֱמַר: "עָזֹב תַּעֲזֹב".

הָלַךְ וְיָשַׁב לוֹ וְאָמַר: "הוֹאִיל וְעָלֶיךָ מִצְוָה, אִם רְצוֹנְךָ לִפְרֹק, פְּרֹק!" פָּטוּר, שֶׁנֶּאֱמַר: "עִמּוֹ".

If one unloaded and reloaded, unloaded and reloaded, even four or five times, one is still obligated [to unload again]. As it is written, "assist you must assist."

If [the animal's owner] walked away and sat down and said, "Since it is a mitzvah that is incumbent on you, if you wish to unload, then unload!"—in such a case one is not obligated. As it is written, "with him."

MISHNAH

The first authoritative work of Jewish law that was codified in writing. The Mishnah contains the oral traditions that were passed down from teacher to student; it supplements, clarifies, and systematizes the commandments of the Torah. Due to the continual persecution of the Jewish people, it became increasingly difficult to guarantee that these traditions would not be forgotten. Rabbi Yehudah Hanasi therefore redacted the Mishnah at the end of the 2nd century. It serves as the foundation for the Talmud.

VIII. THE ASSOCIATION METHOD

When the Torah chooses to associate Law A with Law B—for example, by placing two laws next to each other, or by using identical phraseology in both laws—this tells us that we should apply what we know about Law A to Law B.

TEXT 10

Learn, Bind, Write

Deuteronomy 11:18–20

וְשַׂמְתֶּם אֶת דְּבָרַי אֵלֶּה עַל לְבַבְכֶם וְעַל נַפְשְׁכֶם,
וּקְשַׁרְתֶּם אֹתָם לְאוֹת עַל יֶדְכֶם, וְהָיוּ לְטוֹטָפֹת בֵּין עֵינֵיכֶם.

וְלִמַּדְתֶּם אֹתָם אֶת בְּנֵיכֶם לְדַבֵּר בָּם,
בְּשִׁבְתְּךָ בְּבֵיתֶךָ וּבְלֶכְתְּךָ בַדֶּרֶךְ וּבְשָׁכְבְּךָ וּבְקוּמֶךָ.

וּכְתַבְתָּם עַל מְזוּזוֹת בֵּיתֶךָ וּבִשְׁעָרֶיךָ.

Set these words of Mine upon your hearts and upon your souls; bind them as a sign on your hands, and they shall be phylacteries between your eyes.

Teach them to your children, to speak of them when you sit in your home and when you travel on the way, when you lie down and when you rise up.

Write them on the doorposts of your home, and on your gates.

FIGURE 2.4

Placement of the *Tefilin*

INCORRECT

CORRECT

TEXT 11

Midrashic Sources for *Tefilin* Placement

Mechilta DeRabbi Yishma'el, Exodus 13

"עַל יָדְךָ" . . . עַל גֹּבַהּ שֶׁל יָד. אוֹ אֵינוֹ אֶלָּא עַל יָדְךָ כְּמַשְׁמָעוֹ? תַּלְמוּד לוֹמַר: "וְשַׂמְתֶּם אֶת דְּבָרַי אֵלֶּה עַל לְבַבְכֶם". לֹא אָמַרְתִּי אֶלָּא דָּבָר שֶׁהוּא מְכֻוָּן כְּנֶגֶד הַלֵּב, וְאֵיזֶהוּ מְכֻוָּן כְּנֶגֶד הַלֵּב? זֶה גֹּבַהּ שֶׁל יָד.

"עַל יָדְכָה", זֶה שְׂמֹאל. אַתָּה אוֹמֵר זֶה שְׂמֹאל, אוֹ אֵינוֹ אֶלָּא יָמִין? . . . "וּקְשַׁרְתֶּם . . . וּכְתַבְתֶּם", מָה כְּתִיבָה בְּיָמִין, אַף קְשִׁירָה בְּיָמִין.

"בֵּין עֵינֶיךָ" עַל גֹּבַהּ שֶׁל רֹאשׁ. אַתָּה אוֹמֵר גֹּבַהּ שֶׁל רֹאשׁ, אוֹ אֵינוֹ אֶלָּא בֵּין עֵינֶיךָ כְּמַשְׁמָעוֹ? תַּלְמוּד לוֹמַר: "בָּנִים אַתֶּם לַה' אֱלֹקֵיכֶם וְגוֹ'". מָה "בֵּין עֵינֵיכֶם" הָאָמוּר לְהַלָּן עַל גֹּבַהּ שֶׁל רֹאשׁ, אַף "בֵּין עֵינֶיךָ" [הָאָמוּר כָּאן] עַל גֹּבַהּ שֶׁל רֹאשׁ.

MECHILTA

A Halachic Midrash to Exodus. Midrash is the designation of a particular genre of rabbinic literature usually forming a running commentary on specific books of the Bible. The name *Mechilta* means "rule" and was given to this Midrash because its comments and explanations are based on fixed rules of exegesis. This work is often attributed to Rabbi Yishmael ben Elisha, a contemporary of Rabbi Akiva, though there are some references to later sages in this work.

"On your hand" . . . meaning, on the upper arm. But perhaps it means literally on the hand? The Torah therefore teaches us [by stating in the first part of this verse], "Set these words of Mine upon your hearts." We are speaking of a place that is aligned with the heart. What is aligned with the heart? The upper arm.

"On your hand." This is the left hand. You say that it is the left, but perhaps it is the right? . . . [But we know this from the juxtaposition of the two verses], "Bind them" and "Write them." Just as the writing [of the *mezuzah*] is done with the right hand, so is the tying [of the *tefilin*] done with the right.

"Between your eyes." Meaning, on the top of the head. You say that it means on top of the head, but perhaps it means literally between the eyes? The Torah therefore teaches us by writing, "You are children of the L-rd your G-d. [Do not gash yourselves, and do not make a baldness between your eyes, for the dead]" (DEUTERONOMY 14:1). Just as there, [in the case of the prohibition to tear out one's hair in mourning the dead,] the phrase "between your eyes" means [the corresponding spot] on the top of the head, so, too, the phrase "between your eyes" in our verse [regarding the placement of the *tefilin*] refers to the top of the head.

How to Put On *Tefilin:*
myjli.com/booksmart

IX. ALTERNATIVE READINGS: WHY NO VOWELS?

The Sinaitic tradition includes, as part of the Oral Torah, the pronunciation and syntax for the text of the Written Torah. But the Written Torah itself consists of consonants only, without vowels or punctuation marks. This means that in addition to the basic meaning of the text, every word and sentence in the Written Torah can be read in a number of different ways, each expressing a different meaning.

FIGURE 2.5

Eats Shoots and Leaves

EATS SHOOTS AND LEAVES

EATS, SHOOTS AND LEAVES

FIGURE 2.6

Consonants, Vowels, and Punctuation

1.	Consonants, vowels, and punctuation	**Eats, shoots and leaves.**
2.	Consonants and vowels only	**eats shoots and leaves**
3.	Consonants only	**_ts sts _nd lvs**

TEXT 12

Versatile Text

Responsa of Radbaz, vol. 1, Responsum 1068 (643)

שָׁאַלְתָּ . . . לָמָה אֵין כּוֹתְבִין הַנְקוּדָה בְּסֵפֶר תּוֹרָה, כֵּיוָן שֶׁהַכֹּל נִתָּן לְמֹשֶׁה רַבֵּנוּ עָלָיו הַשָּׁלוֹם בְּסִינַי? וְגַם הַטְעָמִים רָאוּי שֶׁיִכְתְּבוּ אוֹתָם, כְּדֵי שֶׁיִקְרָא הַקוֹרֵא קְרִיאָה יְשָׁרָה לְלֹא שִׁבּוּשׁ, שֶׁהֲרֵי גַם הַטְעָמִים מְבָאֲרִים טַעַם הַכְּתוּבִים לִפְעָמִים.

תְּשׁוּבָה . . . כִּי הָאוֹתִיּוֹת בְּלֹא נְקוּדוֹת וּטְעָמִים יֵשׁ בָּהֶם מַשְׁמָעֻיּוֹת הַרְבֵּה וְצֵרוּפִים שׁוֹנִים וּקְרִיאוֹת הָפְכִיּוֹת . . . פָּנִים לִפְנִים מִפָּנִים וְתַעֲלוּמוֹת לִפְנִים מִתַּעֲלוּמוֹת . . . וְאִם נְנַקֵּד הַסֵפֶר תּוֹרָה, הָיָה לוֹ גְבוּל וְשִׁעוּר, כְּדִמְיוֹן הַחֹמֶר שֶׁהִגִּיעָה לוֹ צוּרָה יְדוּעָה, וְלֹא הָיָה אֶפְשָׁר לוֹ לִהְיוֹת נִדְרָשׁ . . . וּלְפִיכָךְ אָמְרוּ חֲכָמֵינוּ זַ"ל "שִׁבְעִים פָּנִים לַתּוֹרָה" . . .

וְלָכֵן לֹא נִתְּנוּ הַנְקוּדוֹת וְהַטְעָמִים לִכָּתֵב בְּסֵפֶר תּוֹרָה. וְיִכָּתְבוּ בַּחֻמָּשִׁים מִשּׁוּם "עֵת לַעֲשׂוֹת לַה'" כְּדֵי שֶׁלֹּא תִּשְׁתַּכַּח תּוֹרַת הַקְרִיאָה, כִּשְׁאַר תּוֹרָה שֶׁבְּעַל פֶּה . . .

RABBI DAVID IBN ZIMRA (RADBAZ) 1479–1573

Noted halachist. Radbaz was born in Spain and immigrated to Safed, Israel, upon the expulsion of the Jews from Spain in 1492. In 1513, he moved to Egypt and served as rabbi, judge, and head of the yeshiva in Cairo. He also ran many successful business ventures and was independently wealthy. In 1553, he returned to Safed where he would later be buried. He authored what would later become a classic commentary to Maimonides's code of law and wrote many Halachic responsa, of which more than 10,000 are extant.

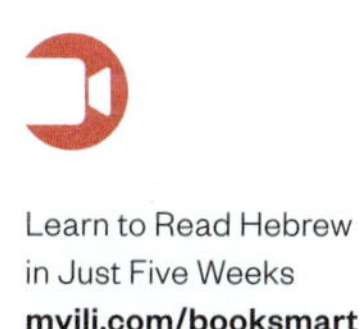

Learn to Read Hebrew in Just Five Weeks
myjli.com/booksmart

You asked: . . . Why are the vowel marks not written in the Torah scroll, seeing that it was all given to Moses at Sinai? Likewise, it would have been fitting that the cantillation marks should have been written [in the Torah scroll], so that the reader could read smoothly without error; indeed, the cantillation marks will sometimes explicate the meaning of the text.

Answer: . . . The letters without the vowel and cantillation marks have numerous meanings, various possible compositions, and [even] contrary readings. . . . Each and every letter contains facets within facets and mysteries within mysteries. . . . But if the Torah scroll were vowelized, it would be finite and limited, like matter that has been given a definitive form, and it could not be expounded. . . . This is why the sages say, "There are seventy faces to the Torah." . . .

For this reason, we were not permitted to write the vowels and cantillation marks in the Torah scroll. But they are recorded in *Chumashim,* in keeping with the principle that "it is a time to act for G-d," so that the rules of reading the Torah should not be forgotten—as was done regarding the rest of the Oral Torah. . . .

A kabbalist reveals: *Secrets of the Hebrew Letters and Vowels*
myjli.com/booksmart

X. KINDNESS AND TRUTH REVISITED

In this section, we apply the "Alternative Readings" method of Torah exposition to a verse in the book of Psalms. The basic meaning of this verse is that it is a prayer by King David expressing his yearning for closeness to G-d; but by a different reading of four of its words, this verse represents a dialogue between King David and G-d on a profound philosophical and sociological dilemma. We then apply the insight gleaned from this Midrash to revisit the mysterious narrative of "The Battle of the Angels" (Text 4 above), and discover how our materialistic world may contain the ultimate resolution to the cosmic paradox of goodness and truth.

TEXT 13

A King's Prayer

Psalms 61:8

יֵשֵׁב עוֹלָם לִפְנֵי אֱלֹקִים,
חֶסֶד וֶאֱמֶת מַן יִנְצְרֻהוּ.

May he dwell forever before G-d; kindness and truth shall be summoned to guard him.

King David plays the harp in an introductory illustration to the book of Psalms. This volume was copied and decorated in 1723 by Moshe Yehudah Leib ben Wolf Broda of Trebitsch, an accomplished painter who was responsible for some of the most famous Hebrew manuscripts of the seventeenth century. (Braginsky Collection 222)

PSALMS

Biblical book. The book of Psalms contains 150 psalms expressing praise for G-d, faith in G-d, and laments over tragedies. The primary author of the psalms was King David, who lived in the 9th century BCE. Psalms also contains material from earlier figures. The feelings and circumstances expressed in the psalms resonate throughout the generations and they have become an important part of communal and personal prayer.

FIGURE 2.7

Alternate Word Meanings in Psalms 61:8

WORD	BASIC MEANING	ALTERNATE MEANING
יֵשֵׁב **YESHEV**	"may he dwell"	"may it be settled" (in the sense of stability and equanimity)
עוֹלָם **OLAM**	"forever"	"the world"
מַן **MAN**	"summoned"	the question, "who will?"
יִנְצְרֻהוּ **YINTZERUHU**	"to guard him"	"keep it" (in the sense of "to practice")

TEXT 14

A King's Dilemma

Psalms 61:8 (alternate translation)

יֵשֵׁב עוֹלָם לִפְנֵי אֱלֹקִים,
חֶסֶד וֶאֱמֶת מַן יִנְצְרֻהוּ.

May the world be settled before G-d.
Who will keep kindness and truth?

TEXT 15

A Dialogue on Wealth Inequality and the Purpose of Life

Midrash, *Tanchuma*, Mishpatim 9

אָמַר דָוִד לִפְנֵי הַקָדוֹשׁ בָּרוּךְ הוּא: רִבּוֹן הָעוֹלָם, "יֵשֵׁב עוֹלָם לִפְנֵי אֱלֹקִים" – תְּיַשֵּׁב עוֹלָמְךָ בְּשָׁוֶה, הָעֲשִׁירִים וְהָעֲנִיִּים.

אָמַר לוֹ: אִם כֵּן, "חֶסֶד וֶאֱמֶת מַן יִנְצְרֻהוּ"? אִם יִהְיוּ כֻּלָּם עֲשִׁירִים אוֹ עֲנִיִּים, מִי יוּכַל לַעֲשׂוֹת חֶסֶד?

Said King David to the Almighty: "Master of the world! *May the world be settled before G-d*. Why don't You balance Your world, and make equal the rich and the poor?"

Replied G-d: "If such were the case, *who will practice kindness and truth?* If all were rich or all were poor, how would there be an opportunity for human kindness?"

TANCHUMA

A Midrashic work bearing the name of Rabbi Tanchuma, a 4th-century Talmudic sage quoted often in this work. "Midrash" is the designation of a particular genre of rabbinic literature usually forming a running commentary on specific books of the Bible. *Tanchuma* provides textual exegeses, expounds upon the biblical narrative, and develops and illustrates moral principles. *Tanchuma* is unique in that many of its sections commence with a Halachic discussion, which subsequently leads into non-Halachic teachings.

TSDAKA
Natan Cooper.

TEXT 16

Truth from the Earth

The Rebbe, Rabbi Menachem Mendel Schneerson, *Likutei Sichot* (Hebrew Edition), vol. 16, pp. 45–46

מִדַּת הָאֱמֶת, הָאֱמֶת שֶׁל אֱלוֹקוּת שֶׁבְּסֵדֶר הַהִשְׁתַּלְשְׁלוּת, שֶׁיֵּשׁ לָהּ מְדִידָה וְהַגְבָּלָה . . . מַגִּיעָה רַק עַד הַדַּרְגָּה שֶׁבָּהּ נִכָּר שֶׁה' אֱמֶת. וְכֵיוָן שֶׁהָעוֹלָם הַזֶּה הוּא עָלְמָא דְשִׁקְרָא, שֶׁבּוֹ אֵין נִכֶּרֶת "אֱמֶת ה'", לָכֵן "אֱמֶת אָמַר אַל יִבָּרֵא".

אֲבָל הָאֱמֶת שֶׁל עַצְמוּתוֹ יִתְבָּרֵךְ אֵינָהּ מְגֻבֶּלֶת כְּלָל. אֵין הִיא מְגֻבֶּלֶת לַדַּרְגָּה שֶׁבָּהּ מַכִּירִים בַּאֲמִתּוּת ה' . . . לָכֵן אֲפִלּוּ "עִנְיְנֵי בְּנֵי בֵיתוֹ" שֶׁל יְהוּדִי, שֶׁהוּא מִתְכַּוֵּן לַעֲשׂוֹתָם לְצֹרֶךְ "גַשְׁמִיּוּת", אֲשֶׁר עַל כֵּן הֵם נִרְאִים כְּ"דִבְרֵי שֶׁקֶר" שֶׁאֵין לָהֶם כְּלַל קֶשֶׁר לְ"אֱמֶת ה'"–גַּם גַשְׁמִיּוּת זוֹ קְשׁוּרָה לְ"אֲמִתַּת הִמָּצְאוֹ". וְזֶה מִתְבַּטֵּא בְּכָךְ שֶׁלַּמְרוֹת שֶׁיְּהוּדִי חָשׁ רַק בַּגַּשְׁמִיּוּת שֶׁל עִנְיְנֵי הָעוֹלָם הַזֶּה שֶׁלּוֹ, הוּא מְנַצְּלָם בְּפֹעַל לְצֹרֶךְ טוֹב וּקְדוּשָּׁה.

The attribute of truth, which is the truth of G-d as it relates to the spiritual processes of creation, is limited in that it only manifests itself where the Divine truth is recognized. So, because the material world is a place of falsehood, a place where the Divine truth is not recognized, the attribute of Truth said, "Do not create."

But the quintessential truth of G-d is not constrained in any way. It is not limited to those places where the Divine truth is recognized. . . .

RABBI MENACHEM MENDEL SCHNEERSON 1902–1994

The towering Jewish leader of the 20th century, known as "the Lubavitcher Rebbe," or simply as "the Rebbe." Born in southern Ukraine, the Rebbe escaped Nazi-occupied Europe, arriving in the U.S. in June 1941. The Rebbe inspired and guided the revival of traditional Judaism after the European devastation, impacting virtually every Jewish community the world over. The Rebbe often emphasized that the performance of just one additional good deed could usher in the era of Mashiach. The Rebbe's scholarly talks and writings have been printed in more than 200 volumes.

Therefore, even a person's mundane household affairs, in which the person engages solely for materialistic purposes—and which therefore seem to be a pack of lies that have no connection with the truth of G-d—these are also bound to the Divine reality. This expresses itself when the person, despite the fact that they experience only the materialistic nature of these pursuits, utilizes them for goodness and holiness.

FEEST HOUDINGE DER IODEN (FESTIVE ATTITUDE OF THE JEWS)
Etching on paper: illustration in *School of the Jews, Understanding the Entire Jewish Faith*, by Johannes Buxtorf (Leiden, South Holland: Daniel van den Dalen and Hendrik van Damme, 1702). (Rijksmuseum, Amsterdam)

Why Doesn't G-d Feed the Poor? **Rabbi Shalom Paltiel** explains: **myjli.com/booksmart**

KEY POINTS

1 *The Meaning of "Midrash": Midrash* means "to seek out" and "to expound." Midrash is the process by which the additional layers of meaning contained within the words—or between the lines—of the Written Torah are expounded. "Midrash" is also the general name given to a number of works that cite the Midrashic teachings by the sages of the Talmudic era (approximately 100 BCE to 500 CE).

2 *Halachah and Agadah:* Midrashic literature falls under two general categories: Halachah and Agadah. The Halachic Midrashim document how the laws governing the observance of the *mitzvot* are derived from the biblical text. "Agadah" is a term that describes all non-Halachic Midrashic material: moral, philosophical, and mystical teachings, as well as parables, historical narratives not explicitly recorded in the Written Torah, stories from the lives of the sages, and so on.

3 *The Mystical Element in Midrash:* The Midrash contains many of the deepest secrets of the Torah. This is particularly the case with the stories and parables of the Agadah, which encapsulate ideas that are too abstract and too complex to communicate by direct teaching.

4 *The Methodology of Torah Exposition:* A central component of the Oral Torah and the Sinaitic tradition is a set of Midrashic rules outlining the methods by which the Torah is expounded. These methodologies include: (1) logical deduction, (2) textual exposition, (3) association, and (4) alternate readings.

5 *Logical Deduction:* One example of "logical deduction" is the a fortiori argument; namely, "If A is the case, then B is certainly the case." A corollary to this argument is the rule that if Case B is derived from Case A, the derived law cannot be stronger than the source law. Thus, when the Torah instructs in Exodus 23:5 that we are obligated to help unload the overburdened donkey of an enemy, we know that we are certainly obligated to help unload a friend's donkey. On the other hand, the obligation to unload a friend's donkey cannot be greater than the obligation to unload the enemy's donkey, from which it is derived.

6 *Textual Exposition:* The particularities of the wording and spelling of the Torah's text also serve as sources for the derivation of additional laws. For example, the repetitive wording in Exodus 23:5, "assist you must assist with him," teaches us to assist even multiple times with the same animal. On the other hand, the qualifying clause "with him" in that verse teaches us that the obligation is limited to assisting along with the owner's own efforts.

7 *The "Association" Methods:* When two laws are placed next to each other in the text, or when identical wording is used in two different laws, this tells us to apply what we know about one law to the other. A number of details regarding the placement of the *tefilin* (i.e., that the head-*tefilin* are placed on the top of the head rather than literally "between your eyes," and that the hand-*tefilin* are tied to the upper arm of the weaker hand) are derived by "association" methods.

8 *Alternative Readings:* While the Sinaitic tradition includes, as part of the "Oral Torah," the pronunciation and syntax for the text of the Tanach, the Written Torah itself consists of consonants only, without vowels or punctuation marks. This means that in addition to the basic meaning of the text, every word and sentence in the Written Torah can be read in a number of different ways, each expressing a different meaning.

9 *The Paradox of Goodness and Truth:* One example of an "alternative reading" is the way that a verse in the book of Psalms (61:8), containing a prayer by King David for closeness to G-d, also reads as a philosophical dialogue on the seeming unfairness of life. The insights gleaned from this dialogue also shed light on the deeper meaning of a mysterious Midrash describing a

"battle of the angels" over the creation of the human being, and the way that our materialistic existence holds the key to resolving the cosmic paradox of goodness and truth.

Abraham's Early Years

TANCHUMA, LECH LECHA 4

Said Rabbi Acha in the name of Rabbi Chanina: At the age of three, Abraham recognized his Creator. As it is written (Genesis 26:5), "In consequence of that which Abraham listened to My voice." The word עקב ("in consequence") has a numerical value of 172, and Abraham lived 175 years; this teaches us that at the age of three, Abraham recognized his Creator.

ZOHAR, VOL. 1, P. 86A

When Abraham saw the sun rising in the east in the morning, he said, "This is the sovereign who created me!" All that day, he worshipped the sun.

In the evening, he saw that the sun had set and the moon was giving light to the world. Said he, "Surely this one rules over the one I worshipped all day, for that one has gone dark and no longer gives light." He worshipped the moon all that night.

In the morning, he saw the moon fading and the east lighting up, and he said, "Surely, all these have a sovereign over them, a ruler who controls them all."

BERESHIT RABAH, 38:13

Terah [the father of Abraham] was a maker of idols. One day, he installed Abraham as a seller in his shop.

When a person would come to purchase an idol, Abraham would ask him, "How old are you?" The man would say, "I am fifty years old," or, "I am sixty years old." Abraham would then cry out: "Woe is to this man! He is sixty years old, and he wishes to worship an object that was made yesterday?" The man would be ashamed and leave.

One day, a woman came carrying a dish of fine flour as an offering to the idols. Abraham took an axe and smashed them all. He then placed the axe in the hand of the largest idol.

When Terah came, he said to Abraham: "Who did this?"

Said Abraham to his father: "Why should I hide it from you? A woman came bearing a dish of fine flour. That one said, 'I shall eat first,' and the other one said, 'I shall eat first.' So the biggest one took the axe and smashed them all."

Said Terah to Abraham: "Why are you mocking me? Do I not know that they cannot eat, speak, or move?"

Said Abraham to his father: "Don't your ears hear what your mouth is saying?"

Terah took his son and handed him over to [the Babylonian king] Nimrod.

Nimrod said to Abraham: "Let us worship fire."

Said Abraham: "Better we should worship water, which puts out fire."

Said Nimrod: "Let us then worship water."

Said Abraham: "We should rather worship the clouds, which bear water."

Said Nimrod: "Let us then worship the clouds."

Said Abraham: "We should worship the wind, which scatters the clouds."

Said Nimrod: "Let us then worship the wind."

Said Abraham: "In that case, we should worship the human being, who contains the wind of life in himself."

Said Nimrod: "It is but words that you speak. I worship fire; I shall throw you into the fire, and let the god whom you serve come and save you from it."

[Abraham's brother] Haran was there. He said to himself, "If Abraham is victorious, I will say that I am with Abraham; if Nimrod wins, I shall declare myself with Nimrod."

When Abraham descended into the fiery furnace and was saved, they asked Haran: "Whom are you for?" Said he to them, "I am with Abraham." So they took him and threw him into the fire, and his innards melted; he emerged and died in front of his father. Thus it is written (Genesis 11:28), "Haran died in the face of his father Terah, in the land of his birth, Ur Casdim."

Men in a Boat

***VAYIKRA RABAH*, 4:6**

"Shall one man sin, and unto the entire community is Your fury?" (Numbers 16:22).

Rabbi Shimon bar Yocha'i taught: This is analogous to a group of people who were traveling in a boat. One of them took an awl and began to drill a hole beneath himself.

His companions said to him: "Why are you doing this?"

Replied the man: "What concern is it of yours? Am I not drilling under my own place?"

Said they to him: "But the water that will come up will drown us all!"

So, too, Job said: "And if indeed I erred, my error shall reside with me" (Job 19:4). To which his friends responded, "When one adds to one's failings, the crime strikes among us" (Ibid., 34:37).

The Fox and the Vineyard

***KOHELET RABAH*, 5:14**

"As he left his mother's womb, naked shall he return to go as he came; he will carry nothing from his toil that he will take in his hand" (Ecclesiastes 5:14).

A fox found a vineyard that was fenced in all around from all sides. There was one hole in the fence through which the fox tried to enter, but was not able. What did the fox do? He fasted for three days, until he was skinny and thin, and entered through the hole. He ate his fill and got fat. He tried leaving, but was unable to fit through at all. So again he fasted for three days, until he grew weak and skinny as before, and got out.

When he got outside, he turned his face back to gaze at the vineyard, and said: "Vineyard, O vineyard! How goodly are you, and how goodly are the fruits within you, and all that is in you is beautiful and praiseworthy! But what pleasure can one derive from you? As one enters into you, so does one leave. . . ."

So it is with our world.

The Two Watchmen

***VAYIKRA RABAH*, 4:5**

There was a king who had an orchard in which there were beautiful fruits. The king placed two guardians in it; one was lame and the other was blind. The king said to them: "Take care of these beautiful fruits."

A while later, the king came to the orchard and said to them, "Where are the beautiful fruits?"

Said the blind one, "Your majesty, am I then able to see?" Said the lame one, "Your majesty, am I then able to walk?"

Now, this king was a wise man. What did he do with them? He placed the lame one on the shoulders of the blind one, and said to them: "This is what you did to eat the fruits."

So, too, in the World to Come, G-d says to the soul, "Why did you sin?"

Says the soul, "Master of the world! I did not sin. The body sinned. From the moment that I left the body, I am like a pure bird flying through the air. How would I sin before You?"

G-d says to the body, "Why did you sin?"

Says the body, "Master of the world! I did not sin. The soul sinned. From the moment that it left me, I am like a stone that has been cast to the ground. How would I sin before You?"

What does G-d do with them? He brings the soul and inserts it into the body, and judges them as one, as it is written (Psalms 50:4), "He summons the heavens above and the earth to judge His people."

The Power of Speech

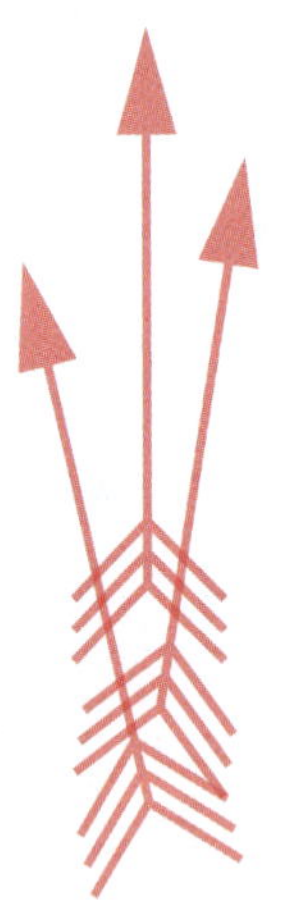

***BERESHIT RABAH*, 38:13**

It is written (Psalms 120:4), "G-d, save my soul from false lips, from a deceitful tongue . . . sharp arrows of the warrior, coals of broom."

Why, of all other weapons, is slanderous speech compared to arrows? All other weapons strike at close quarters, while the arrow strikes from a distance. So is it with slander: What is spoken in Rome kills in Syria.

And of all other coals, slanderous speech is compared to coals of broom. All other coals, when extinguished, are extinguished without and within; but coals of broom are still burning within when they are extinguished without. So is it with words of slander: Even after it seems that their effects have been put out, they continue to smolder within those who heard them. It once happened that a broom tree was set on fire and it burned eighteen months—winter, summer, and winter.

***MIDRASH TEHILIM*, PSALM 120**

Evil talk is like an arrow. A person may unsheathe a sword to kill their fellow, but the latter begs for mercy, and the killer regrets their intention and returns the sword to its sheath. But the arrow—once the killer shoots it, even if they desire to retrieve it, they no longer can.

***YALKUT SHIMONI, DEVARIM* 933**

To what may the tongue be compared? To a dog tied with an iron chain and locked in a room within a room within a room, yet when it barks, the entire populace is terrified of it. Imagine if it were loose outside! So the tongue: It is secured behind the teeth and behind the lips, yet it does no end of damage. Imagine if it were on the outside!

***TALMUD, PESACHIM* 3A**

A person should never allow a derogatory expression to pass their lips. For we find that the Torah deviated by adding eight extra letters in order not to use a derogatory word, when it said (Genesis 7:8), "From the animals that are pure and from the animals that are not pure."

MORAL TEACHINGS

The *Bet* of Bereshit

***BERESHIT RABAH*, 1:10**

Rabbi Yonah said in the name of Rabbi Levi: Why was the world created with the letter ב (*bet*)? Just as a ב is closed on all sides and open in the front, so are we not able to inquire what is beneath [the created reality], what is above it, what came before it, or what will come after it. Rather we can only inquire from the day the world was created and after. . . .

Rabbi Yehudah ben Pazi expounded on the Creation story according to Bar Kapara: Why was the world created with a *bet*? To teach us there are two worlds: this world and the world-to-come. Another explanation: Why with a *bet*? Because it is [the initial letter of] *berachah* ("blessing") . . .

Another interpretation: Why with a ב? The ב has two points—one on its top, and one behind it. They say to the *bet*, "Who created you?" and it points with its point on top, and says: "The One Above created me." "And what is His name?" and it points behind [to the preceding letter, *alef*] and says, "G-d is His name."

Said Rabbi Elazar bar Chanina in the name of Rabbi Acha: For twenty-six generations the letter *alef* protested before the throne of G-d, saying to Him, "Master of the universe! I am the first of the letters, and You did not create the world with me!" G-d said to her: The world and all that it contains were only created due to the merit of Torah, as it is written (Proverbs 3:19): "G-d founded the world with wisdom". . . . Tomorrow I come to give Torah at Sinai, and I am going to open at first instance only with you, as it says: "*Anochi* (I am) G-d your G-d" (Exodus 20:2).

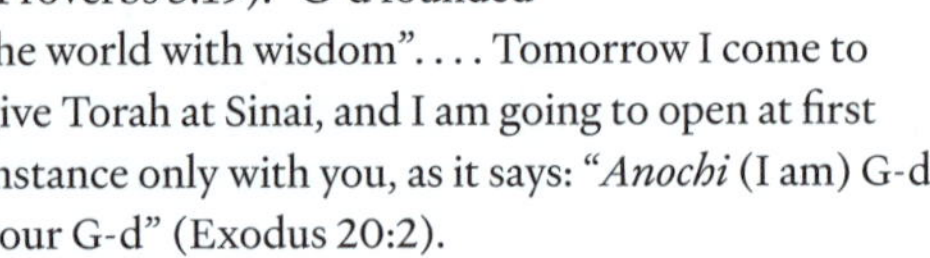

***BERESHIT RABAH*, 1:15**

The School of Shamai and the School of Hillel debated. The School of Shamai said: The heavens were created first, and after that the earth was created. The School of Hillel said: The earth was created first and after that the heavens. . . .

MYSTICAL TEACHINGS

Rabbi Tanchuma said: I will tell the reasoning for this. Regarding their creation, the heavens were first, as it is written (Genesis 1:1), "In the beginning G-d created the heavens and the earth." And regarding their completion, the earth was first, as it is written (Genesis 2:4), "On the day that Almighty G-d made earth and heaven."

Rabbi Shimon bar Yocha'i said: I am amazed at how the fathers of the world, the School of Shamai and School of Hillel, were divided on the creation of the heavens and the earth. I would say that both were created together, like a pot and its lid, as it is written (Isaiah 48:13): "Even My hand founded the earth, and My right hand spanned the heavens; I call unto them, they stand together."

Said Rabbi Eliezer ben Rabbi Shimon: If it is according to the opinion of my father, why in some places does the Torah put the earth before the heavens, and in some places it puts the heavens before the earth? But this is to teach that both are equal to each other.

Rabbi Shimon's Cave

***TALMUD, SHABBAT* 33B**

Rabbi Yehudah [bar Ila'i], Rabbi Yosei, and Rabbi Shimon [bar Yocha'i] were sitting, and Judah, a son of converts, was sitting near them. Rabbi Yehudah said, "How fine are the works of [the Romans]! They have set up marketplaces, they have built bridges, they have erected bathhouses." Rabbi Yosei was silent. Rabbi Shimon said, "Everything that they did, they did only for themselves. They built marketplaces in order to place harlots in them. They built bathhouses to pamper themselves. They built bridges to collect tolls."

Judah the son of converts repeated their talk, which reached the government, which decreed: Yehudah, who exalted us, shall be promoted. Yosei, who was silent, shall be exiled. Shimon, who denounced us, shall be executed.

Rabbi Shimon and his son [Rabbi Elazar] hid in a cave. A carob tree and a wellspring were miraculously created for them. The whole day they studied Torah. . . . After twelve years, Elijah the Prophet stood at the entrance to the cave and exclaimed: "Who will inform the son of Yocha'i that the emperor is dead and his decree annulled?" So they emerged.

They saw people plowing and sowing. Said Rabbi Shimon, "They forsake the eternal life [of Torah] and engage in temporal life?" Whatever met their gaze was immediately burnt. A heavenly voice proclaimed: "Have you come out to destroy My world? Return to your cave!"

So they lived there another year. [When they emerged,] wherever Rabbi Elazar wounded, Rabbi Shimon healed. . . . As the sun was setting on Shabbat eve, they saw an elderly man holding two bundles of myrtle branches and running at twilight. Said Rabbi Shimon to his son: "See how precious the *mitzvot* are to Israel." And their minds were put at ease.

Beruria

TALMUD, BERACHOT 10A

In the neighborhood of Rabbi Me'ir, there were thugs who caused him a great deal of distress. Rabbi Me'ir prayed that they should die.

His wife Beruria said to him: "What is your thinking? Is it because it is written (Psalms 104:35), 'Sins shall cease from the earth, and the wicked are no more'? But it doesn't say, 'sinners shall cease,' only that 'sins shall cease.'... Pray for them that they should repent, and then, as the verse concludes, 'the wicked are no more.'"

Rabbi Me'ir prayed for them and they repented.

MIDRASH MISHLEI, 31

It happened that one Shabbat afternoon, while Rabbi Me'ir was lecturing at the study hall, his two sons died. What did their mother do? She laid them on the bed and covered them with a sheet.

After Shabbat, Rabbi Me'ir arrived from the study hall, and said to her, "Where are my two sons?"

Said she to him, "They went to the study hall."

Said he to her, "But I looked in the study hall and I did not see them."

She handed him a cup of wine for Havdalah. [After reciting Havdalah,] he again asked, "Where are my two sons?"

Said she to him, "They went somewhere and will soon return."

She served him dinner. After he recited the Grace after Meals, she said, "My teacher, I have a question to ask."

Said he to her, "Ask."

Said she to him, "A while ago, someone left an item with me for safekeeping, and now he has come to collect it. Shall we return the item or not?"

Said he to her, "My daughter, is not a custodian required to return the deposit to its master?"

Said she to him, "My teacher, if not for your words, I could not have brought myself to return it."

What did she do next? She grasped his hand, led him up to that room, brought him near the bed, and removed the sheet from over them, and he saw the two of them lying dead upon the bed. He began to weep, saying, "My children, my children! My teachers, my teachers!" (Meaning, my children in the natural sense, and my teachers who enlightened my eyes with words of Torah.)

At that moment, she said to him, "Rabbi Me'ir, my teacher, did you not tell me that we are required to return the deposit to its master? 'G-d has given, and G-d has taken' (Job 1:21)." With these words, she consoled him, and his mind was eased and settled.

3

LESSON

THE TALMUD

*The Talmud is much more than a book, or even a library of books; in many ways, it defines the experience of Jewish learning. In this lesson, we dive deep into the "sea of Talmud." We learn about the unique historical circumstance that led to the Talmud's composition, acquaint ourselves with the Talmudic "*daf*," sample some of the distinctive features of Talmudic logic, and participate in mind-sharpening adventures of Talmudic exposition and Talmudic debate.*

A YESHIVAH BOY READING
Alois Heinrich Priechenfried (1867–1953), oil on panel, Vienna.

I. WHAT IS THE TALMUD?

The Talmud is the most important and the most authoritative record of the "Oral Torah." More than any other work, it has defined the experience of Jewish learning through the centuries.

FIGURE 3.1

A *Daf* of Talmud

יציאות השבת פרק ראשון שבת כ:

THE ORIGINAL HYPERTEXT

The complexity of the Talmudic text and the variety of approaches among the commentaries makes the study of Talmud a challenging and immersive intellectual journey.

The distinctive format of the Talmudic *daf* (folio page) was created to enable a simultaneous consultation of numerous Talmudic commentaries. On an oversize page (typically 11 x 16 inches), the text of the Talmud is laid out in the center of the page, with surrounding blocks of text containing the major commentaries. Additional commentaries are reproduced, in similar format, as addenda following the text. A single volume of Talmud will often contain close to 100 works authored over the course of 1,800 years.

Depicted here is the first page of the 2nd chapter of the Talmudic tractate *Shabbat*.

A) MISHNAH

The first official transcription of the Oral Torah, compiled by Rabbi Yehudah Hanasi at the end of the 2nd century CE. Consists primarily of rulings and debates concerning lesser-known decisions and special circumstances of Torah law. The Mishnah cites the teachings of the *tana'im* (Mishnaic sages) who lived and taught in the Holy Land in the years 100 BCE to 200 CE.

(B) GEMARA

Analysis and interpretation of the Mishnah, as well as other Halachic and agadic discussions by the *amora'im* (sages of the Gemara), who lived and taught in the great *yeshivot* of Babylonia and the Holy Land in the 3rd, 4th, and 5th centuries. Also includes citations from Mishnaic sages not included in the Mishnah.

(C) RASHI

The most important commentary on the Talmud, explaining the basic meaning of its often obscure wording. Composed by Rabbi Shlomo Yitzchaki (1040–1105).

(D) TOSAFOT

Anthology of commentaries by dozens of sages who lived in western Europe in the 12th and 13th centuries, including a number of Rashi's disciples and descendants. The analytical and dialectical style of the Tosafot commentaries—which labor to reconcile seemingly inconsistent Talmudic passages—strongly influenced the manner in which Talmud has been studied over the centuries throughout Europe and beyond.

(E) RABBEINU CHANANEL

Commentary by Rabbi Chananel of Kairouan, Tunisia (c. 965–1055), the first to write a running commentary on the Talmud.

(F) BACH

Glosses on the Talmud, Rashi, and Tosafot by Rabbi Yoel Sirkis (c. 1560–1640).

(G) GRA

Glosses and brief notes by Rabbi Eliyahu, the "Gaon of Vilna" (1720–1797).

(H) GILYON HASHAS

Notes by Rabbi Akiva Eiger of Posen, Poland (1761–1837).

(I) MASORET HASHAS

Cross-references showing where specific passages are cited and discussed elsewhere in the Talmud.

(J) EIN MISHPAT

References indicating where key Talmudic statements are cited in the various Halachic codes—Maimonides's Mishneh Torah, Semag, Tur, and Shuchan Aruch.

(K) TORAH OHR

References for biblical citations.

Additional Talmudic Commentaries

RIF

Halachic digest of the Talmud by Rabbi Yitzchak Alfasi (1013–1103) of Fez, Morocco.

RAN

Commentary by Rabbi Nisim Gerondi (1320–1376) of Gerona, Spain.

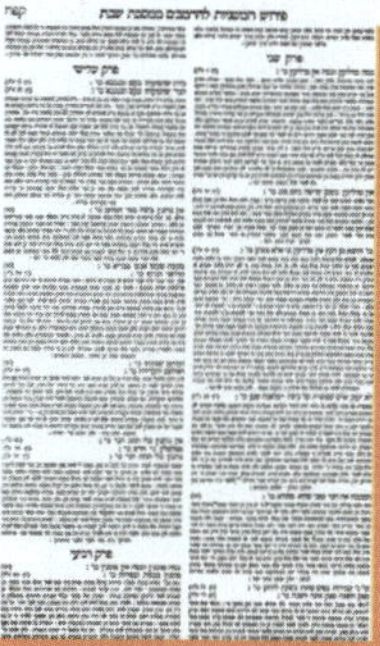

RAMBAM

Commentary on the Mishnah by Rabbi Moshe ben Maimon ("Maimonides," 1135–1204), Egypt.

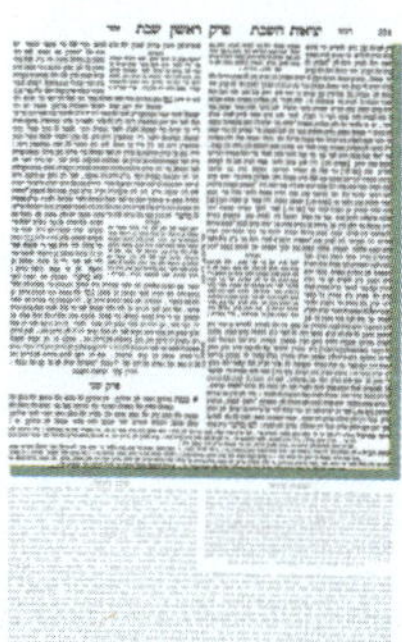

ROSH

Halachic digest of the Talmud by Rabbi Asher ben Yechiel (1250–1328) of Germany and later Spain.

MAHARSHA

Commentary on Talmud, Rashi, and Tosafot by Rabbi Shmuel Eidels (1565–1631) of Poland.

MAHARSHAL

Commentaries by Rabbi Shlomo Luria (1510–1574) of Lublin, Poland.

MAHARAM

Commentaries by Rabbi Meir of Lublin (1558–1616).

II. THE MISHNAH

The Talmud consists of two primary components: the "Mishnah," composed at the end of the second century CE; and the "Gemara," structured as commentaries and discussions on the Mishnah, compiled 300 years later. The Mishnah summarizes 35 generations of the Sinaitic tradition from Moses to Rabbi Yehudah Hanasi, who took the unprecedented step of officially transcribing the core teachings of the Oral Torah.

TEXT 1

The Early History of the Oral Torah

Maimonides, Introduction to *Mishneh Torah*

כָּל הַמִּצְווֹת שֶׁנִּתְּנוּ לוֹ לְמֹשֶׁה בְּסִינַי, בְּפֵרוּשָׁן נִתְּנוּ . . . הִיא הַנִּקְרֵאת "תּוֹרָה שֶׁבְּעַל פֶּה".

כָּל הַתּוֹרָה כְּתָבָהּ מֹשֶׁה רַבֵּנוּ קֹדֶם שֶׁיָּמוּת בִּכְתַב יָדוֹ . . . וְהַמִּצְוָה שְׁהִיא פֵּרוּשׁ הַתּוֹרָה, לֹא כְּתָבָהּ, אֶלָּא צִוָּה בָּהּ לַזְּקֵנִים וְלִיהוֹשֻׁעַ וְלִשְׁאָר כָּל יִשְׂרָאֵל . . . וּמִפְּנֵי זֶה נִקְרֵאת תּוֹרָה שֶׁבְּעַל פֶּה . . .

וּמִימוֹת מֹשֶׁה וְעַד רַבֵּנוּ הַקָּדוֹשׁ, לֹא חִבְּרוּ חִבּוּר שֶׁמְּלַמְּדִין אוֹתוֹ בָּרַבִּים בַּתּוֹרָה שֶׁבְּעַל פֶּה. אֶלָּא בְּכָל דּוֹר וָדוֹר, רֹאשׁ בֵּית דִּין אוֹ נָבִיא שֶׁיִּהְיֶה בְּאוֹתוֹ הַדּוֹר כּוֹתֵב לְעַצְמוֹ זִכָּרוֹן בַּשְּׁמוּעוֹת שֶׁשָּׁמַע מֵרַבּוֹתָיו, וְהוּא מְלַמֵּד עַל פֶּה בָּרַבִּים. וְכֵן כָּל אֶחָד וְאֶחָד כּוֹתֵב לְעַצְמוֹ כְּפִי כּוֹחוֹ מִבֵּאוּר הַתּוֹרָה וּמֵהִלְכוֹתֶיהָ כְּמוֹ שֶׁשָּׁמַע, וּמִדְּבָרִים שֶׁנִּתְחַדְּשׁוּ בְּכָל דּוֹר וָדוֹר, בְּדִינִים שֶׁלֹּא לְמָדוּם מִפִּי הַשְּׁמוּעָה

RABBI MOSHE BEN MAIMON (MAIMONIDES, RAMBAM) 1135-1204

Halachist, philosopher, author, and physician. Maimonides was born in Córdoba, Spain. After the conquest of Córdoba by the Almohads, he fled Spain and eventually settled in Cairo, Egypt. There, he became the leader of the Jewish community and served as court physician to the vizier of Egypt. He is most noted for authoring the *Mishneh Torah*, an encyclopedic arrangement of Jewish law; and for his philosophical work, *Guide for the Perplexed*. His rulings on Jewish law are integral to the formation of Halachic consensus.

אֶלָּא בְּמִדָּה מִשְּׁלוֹשׁ עֶשְׂרֵה מִדּוֹת וְהִסְכִּימוּ עֲלֵיהֶן בֵּית דִּין הַגָּדוֹל. וְכֵן הָיָה הַדָּבָר תָּמִיד עַד רַבֵּנוּ הַקָּדוֹשׁ.

All the commandments that were given to Moses at Mount Sinai were given together with their explanation. . . . [The explanation] is what we call "the Oral Torah."

Moses transcribed the entire Torah by his own hand before his passing. . . . But he did not transcribe its explanations. Rather, he instructed them to the elders and to Joshua and to the rest of Israel. . . . This is why it is called the "Oral Torah." . . .

From the days of Moses until Rabbi Yehudah Hanasi, no one composed a text for the purpose of disseminating the Oral Torah in public. Rather, in each generation, the head of the court or the prophet of that generation would write their own notes of the teachings they received from their teachers, and teach them orally to the public. Similarly, each person would write down for themselves, according to their ability, the teachings they heard regarding the explanation of the Torah and its laws, as well as the new concepts that were deduced in each generation using one of the thirteen rules of Biblical exegesis and accepted by the high court. So it continued until the time of Rabbi Yehudah Hanasi.

The Written and Oral Bible, Explained:
myjli.com/booksmart

TEXT 2

The Sanhedrin System

Talmud, Pesachim 88b

מִתְּחִלָּה לֹא הָיוּ מַרְבִּין מַחְלֹקֶת בְּיִשְׂרָאֵל. אֶלָּא, בֵּית דִּין שֶׁל שִׁבְעִים וְאֶחָד יוֹשְׁבִין בְּלִשְׁכַּת הַגָּזִית, וּשְׁנֵי בָּתֵּי דִּינִין שֶׁל עֶשְׂרִים וּשְׁלֹשָׁה – אֶחָד יוֹשֵׁב עַל פֶּתַח הַר הַבַּיִת וְאֶחָד יוֹשֵׁב עַל פֶּתַח הָעֲזָרָה, וּשְׁאָר בָּתֵּי דִּינִין שֶׁל עֶשְׂרִים וּשְׁלֹשָׁה יוֹשְׁבִין בְּכָל עֲיָרוֹת יִשְׂרָאֵל.

הֻצְרַךְ הַדָּבָר לִשְׁאֹל, שׁוֹאֲלִין מִבֵּית דִּין שֶׁבְּעִירָן. אִם שָׁמְעוּ, אָמְרוּ לָהֶן; וְאִם לַאו, בָּאִין לְזֶה שֶׁסָּמוּךְ לְעִירָן. אִם שָׁמְעוּ, אָמְרוּ לָהֶם; וְאִם לַאו, בָּאִין לְזֶה שֶׁעַל פֶּתַח הַר הַבַּיִת. אִם שָׁמְעוּ, אָמְרוּ לָהֶם; וְאִם לַאו, בָּאִין לְזֶה שֶׁעַל פֶּתַח הָעֲזָרָה, וְאוֹמֵר: "כָּךְ דָּרַשְׁתִּי, וְכָךְ דָּרְשׁוּ חֲבֵרַי; כָּךְ לָמַדְתִּי, וְכָךְ לָמְדוּ חֲבֵרַי". אִם שָׁמְעוּ, אָמְרוּ לָהֶם; וְאִם לַאו, אֵלּוּ וָאֵלּוּ בָּאִין לְלִשְׁכַּת הַגָּזִית שֶׁשָּׁם יוֹשְׁבִין מִתָּמִיד שֶׁל שַׁחַר עַד תָּמִיד שֶׁל בֵּין הָעַרְבַּיִם, וּבְשַׁבָּתוֹת וּבְיָמִים טוֹבִים יוֹשְׁבִין בַּחֵיל. נִשְׁאֲלָה שְׁאֵלָה בִּפְנֵיהֶם; אִם שָׁמְעוּ, אָמְרוּ לָהֶם, וְאִם לַאו, עוֹמְדִין לְמִנְיָן. רַבּוּ הַמְטַמְּאִים, טִמְּאוּ; רַבּוּ הַמְטַהֲרִין, טִהֲרוּ.

At first, there were few disputes [on matters of Torah law] in Israel. Rather, a court of seventy-one magistrates sat in the Chamber of Chiseled Stone [in the Holy Temple in Jerusalem]; two additional courts of twenty-three magistrates sat at the entrance of the Temple Mount, and at the entrance of the Temple courtyard; and additional courts of twenty-three sat in all the cities of Israel.

BABYLONIAN TALMUD

A literary work of monumental proportions that draws upon the legal, spiritual, intellectual, ethical, and historical traditions of Judaism. The 37 tractates of the Babylonian Talmud contain the teachings of the Jewish sages from the period after the destruction of the 2nd Temple through the 5th century CE. It has served as the primary vehicle for the transmission of the Oral Law and the education of Jews over the centuries; it is the entry point for all subsequent legal, ethical, and theological Jewish scholarship.

When a matter [under dispute] needed to be addressed, they would inquire of the court in their city. If the [sages of the court] had received a tradition [regarding this matter], they told it to them; if not, they would go to a court in a nearby city. If they had received a tradition, they told them; if not, they went to the court at the entrance of the Temple Mount. If they had received a tradition, they told them; if not, they went to the court at the entrance of the Temple courtyard, and said: "So I expounded, and so have my colleagues expounded; so I learned, and so my colleagues learned." If they had received a tradition, they told them; if not, they both went to the Chamber of Chiseled Stone, where the court sat from the time of the daily morning offering to the time of the daily afternoon offering; on Shabbat and festival days, they sat in the *cheil*. The question was presented to them. If they had received a tradition, they told them; if not, they took a vote. If a majority said "impure," they deemed it impure; if a majority said "pure," they deemed it pure.

What Is the Mishnah?
myjli.com/booksmart

TEXT 3

The Mishnah Is Transcribed

Maimonides, Introduction to *Mishneh Torah*

וְהוּא קִבֵּץ כָּל הַשְּׁמוּעוֹת וְכָל הַדִּינִין וְכָל הַבֵּאוּרִין וְהַפֵּרוּשִׁין שֶׁשָּׁמְעוּ מִמֹּשֶׁה רַבֵּנוּ, וְשֶׁלָּמְדוּ בֵּית דִּין שֶׁל כָּל דּוֹר וָדוֹר בְּכָל הַתּוֹרָה כֻּלָּהּ. וְחִבֵּר מֵהַכֹּל סֵפֶר הַמִּשְׁנָה וְשִׁנְּנוֹ בָּרַבִּים, וְנִגְלָה לְכָל יִשְׂרָאֵל; וּכְתָבוּהוּ כֻּלָּם, וְרִבְּצוּ בְּכָל מָקוֹם . . .

וְלָמָּה עָשָׂה רַבֵּנוּ הַקָּדוֹשׁ כָּךְ, וְלֹא הִנִּיחַ הַדָּבָר כְּמוֹת שֶׁהָיָה? לְפִי שֶׁרָאָה שֶׁהַתַּלְמִידִים מִתְמַעֲטִים וְהוֹלְכִים, וְהַצָּרוֹת מִתְחַדְּשׁוֹת וּבָאוֹת, וּמַמְלֶכֶת הָרִשְׁעָה פּוֹשֶׁטֶת בָּעוֹלָם וּמִתְגַּבֶּרֶת, וְיִשְׂרָאֵל מִתְגַּלְגְּלִים וְהוֹלְכִים לַקְּצָווֹת - חִבֵּר חִבּוּר אֶחָד לִהְיוֹת בְּיַד כֻּלָּם, כְּדֵי שֶׁיִּלְמְדוּהוּ בִּמְהֵרָה, וְלֹא יִשָּׁכַח.

[Rabbi Yehudah Hanasi] collected all the teachings, all the laws, and all the explanations and commentaries that were handed down from Moses, and those that were taught by the courts in each generation, concerning the entire Torah. From all of these, he composed the text of the Mishnah. He taught it publicly and revealed it to the Jewish people, who all wrote it down, and disseminated it everywhere. . . .

Why did Rabbi Yehudah do this, and not leave matters as they were? Because he saw that the students of Torah were becoming fewer, new troubles were constantly arising, the Roman Empire [which was suppressing the study and practice of Judaism] was spreading throughout the world and becoming more powerful, and the Jewish people were being dispersed to the far ends of the earth. He therefore composed a single text that would be available to everyone, so that it could be learned quickly and would not be forgotten.

THE COMPILATION OF THE TALMUD
George Derville Rowlandson, from *Hutchinson's History of the Nations*, edited by Walter Hutchinson (London, U.K: Hutchinson and Son, c. 1915).

FIGURE 3.2

The Six "Orders" of the Mishnah

		SUBJECT	NUMBER OF TRACTATES
	ZERA'IM **("SEEDS")**	The daily prayers; agricultural laws	11
	MO'ED **("APPOINTED TIMES")**	Shabbat and the festivals; the Jewish calendar	12
	NASHIM **("WOMEN")**	Marriage and divorce	7
	NEZIKIN **("DAMAGES")**	Civil and criminal law	10
	KODOSHIM **("SACRAMENTS")**	The Temple service; the kosher dietary laws	11
	TAHAROT **("PURITIES")**	Laws of ritual purity	12

See "Map of the Talmud" on page 134 134–140 for a more detailed map of the Talmud.

III. THE GEMARA

The Gemara documents the teachings and deliberations of hundreds of sages who studied and taught in the great centers of Torah learning in the Land of Israel and in Babylonia during the three centuries following the compilation of the Mishnah. While the Gemara is structured as commentary on the Mishnah, it also includes many other topics and areas of the Oral Torah.

A fragment from a twelfth-century manuscript of the Babylonian Talmud. (British Library, London).

Watch **Rabbi Adin Even-Israel Steinsaltz** demonstrate *what the Talmud is, and how it should be studied:* **myjli.com/booksmart**

FIGURE 3.3

The Making of the Talmud

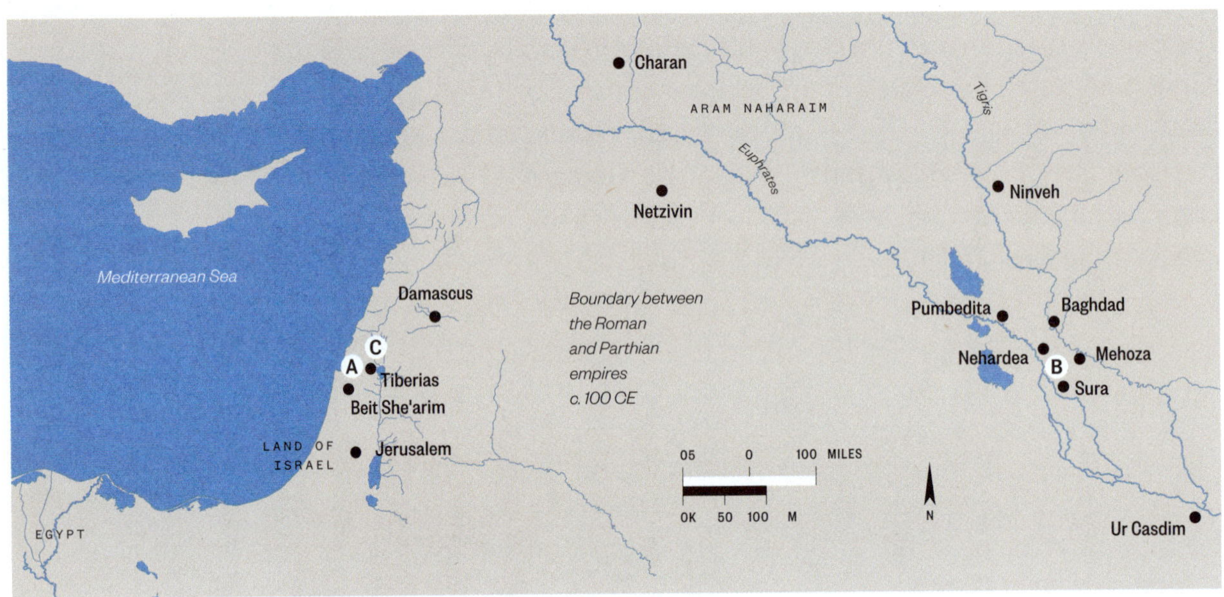

(A) 189 CE

THE MISHNAH

After the destruction of the Second Temple in 69 CE, the Land of Israel continued to serve as the seat of the Sanhedrin and the center of Jewish learning. Toward the end of the 2nd century, Rabbi Yehudah Hanasi completed his redaction of the Mishnah, which encapsulates 35 generations of legal Torah rulings from Moses to his time. But the Roman persecution of the Jewish people and their suppression of the Jewish faith were taking their toll, and in the years following Rabbi Yehudah's passing, the flourishing Babylonian Jewish community replaced the Holy Land as the center of Torah learning and Jewish life.

(B) 219–505 CE

THE BABYLONIAN TALMUD

Two of Rabbi Yehudah Hanasi's disciples, Rav (Abba Arichta) and Shmuel, established Torah academies in Babylonia—the former in Sura and the latter in Nehardea. The academy in Sura would serve as a major center of Torah learning for nearly 1000 years. Other Babylonian academies included those in the town of Pumbedita (near modern-day Fallujah), headed in the 3rd and 4th centuries by Rav Yehudah, Rabah bar Nachmani, and Abayei; and in Mehoza, the seat of Abayei's colleague, Rava.

It was in Sura that Rav Ashi and Ravina embarked, in the beginning of the 5th century, on the monumental task of compiling the Babylonian Talmud, a task that was completed by their disciples 80 years later. The Talmud records three centuries of teachings by the greatest Torah sages of Babylon and the Holy Land, formulated as deliberations on the Mishnah. This vast compendium of legal and moral teachings is second in importance only to the Bible as a foundational text of Judaism.

(C) 200–350 CE

THE JERUSALEM TALMUD

During the Talmudic period, Torah learning continued in the Land of Israel, with scholars and students traveling to and from Babylon, although the difficult conditions in the Holy Land prevented its centers from achieving the prominence of the Babylonian academies. The Holy Land produced a sister Talmud of its own—the "Jerusalem Talmud"—whose foundations were laid by the sages Rabbi Yochanan, Reish Lakish, and Rabbi Elazar at the Tiberias academy in the 3rd and 4th centuries.

FIGURE 3.4

Talmudic Exposition of the Mishnah

BACKWARD
Tracing the Mishnah's sources and underlying principles

What is the source of this law?
מנא הני מילי

What is the basis for and/or reasoning behind the different opinions cited in the Mishnah?
במאי קמפלגי

LATERAL
Analyzing the Mishnah and comparing it with parallel Mishnaic teachings

Introducing other Mishnaic-era teachings that explain or expand on the Mishnah
תניא, תנו רבנן

What are the circumstances of the case cited in this Mishnah?
הכא במאי עסקינן

Resolving contradictions between the two Mishnaic-era teachings
רמינהו

What is the Mishnah teaching us by adding this particular detail?
מאי קמשמע לן

Which of the opinions cited in the Mishnah should be followed in practice?
כמאן הילכתא

Why did the Mishnah need to tell us this law, which is similar to another law that was already stated?
צריכותא

THE

Mishnah

FORWARD
Extending the Mishnah to additional cases and circumstances

The Mishnah tells us the law in case A. But how should we rule in cases B, C, or D?
אבעיא להו

Rabbi A says X, and Rabbi B disagrees and says Y. What proofs can we bring from the Mishnah for A or B's opinion?
תא שמע

IV. THE UNIQUE STATUS OF THE TALMUD

Although many thousands of Torah works have been produced in the centuries after the closing of the Talmud, no subsequent work has achieved the degree of authority that the Talmud commands as a documentation of the Oral Torah.

TEXT 4

The Last Consensus

Maimonides, Introduction to *Mishneh Torah*

וְאַחַר בֵּית דִּינוֹ שֶׁל רַב אָשִׁי, שֶׁחִבֵּר הַתַּלְמוּד . . . נִתְפַּזְּרוּ יִשְׂרָאֵל בְּכָל הָאֲרָצוֹת פִּזּוּר יָתֵר . . . וְרָבְתָה קְטָטָה בָּעוֹלָם, וְנִשְׁתַּבְּשׁוּ הַדְּרָכִים בִּגְיָסוֹת, וְנִתְמַעֵט תַּלְמוּד תּוֹרָה. וְלֹא נִתְכַּנְסוּ יִשְׂרָאֵל לִלְמֹד בִּישִׁיבוֹתֵיהֶם אֲלָפִים וּרְבָבוֹת כְּמוֹ שֶׁהָיוּ מִקֹּדֶם, אֶלָּא מִתְקַבְּצִים יְחִידִים הַשְּׂרִידִים אֲשֶׁר ה' קוֹרֵא בְּכָל עִיר וָעִיר וּבְכָל מְדִינָה וּמְדִינָה וְעוֹסְקִים בַּתּוֹרָה, וּמְבִינִים בְּחִבּוּרֵי הַחֲכָמִים . . .

וְכָל בֵּית דִּין שֶׁעָמַד אַחַר הַתַּלְמוּד . . . לֹא פָּשְׁטוּ מַעֲשָׂיו בְּכָל יִשְׂרָאֵל . . . וֶהֱיוֹת בֵּית דִּין שֶׁל אוֹתָהּ הַמְּדִינָה יְחִידִים, וּבֵית דִּין הַגָּדוֹל שֶׁל שִׁבְעִים בָּטֵל מִכַּמָּה שָׁנִים קֹדֶם חִבּוּר הַתַּלְמוּד.

לְפִיכָךְ, אֵין כּוֹפִין אַנְשֵׁי מְדִינָה זוֹ לִנְהֹג בְּמִנְהַג מְדִינָה אַחֶרֶת, וְאֵין אוֹמְרִין לְבֵית דִּין זֶה לִגְזֹר גְּזֵרָה שֶׁגְּזָרָהּ בֵּית דִּין אַחֵר בִּמְדִינָתוֹ. וְכֵן אִם לִמֵּד אֶחָד מִן הַגְּאוֹנִים שֶׁדֶּרֶךְ הַמִּשְׁפָּט כָּךְ הוּא, וְנִתְבָּאֵר לְבֵית דִּין אַחֵר שֶׁעָמַד

אַחֲרָיו שְׁאֵין זֶה דֶרֶךְ הַמִּשְׁפָּט הַכָּתוּב בַּתַּלְמוּד - אֵין שׁוֹמְעִין לָרִאשׁוֹן, אֶלָּא לְמִי שֶׁהַדַּעַת נוֹטָה לִדְבָרָיו . . .

וּדְבָרִים הַלָּלוּ - בְּדִינִים וּגְזֵרוֹת וְתַקָּנוֹת וּמִנְהָגוֹת שֶׁנִּתְחַדְּשׁוּ אַחַר חִבּוּר הַתַּלְמוּד. אֲבָל כָּל הַדְּבָרִים שֶׁבַּתַּלְמוּד הַבַּבְלִי, חַיָּבִין כָּל בֵּית יִשְׂרָאֵל לָלֶכֶת בָּהֶם . . . הוֹאִיל וְכָל אוֹתָן הַדְּבָרִים שֶׁבַּתַּלְמוּד הִסְכִּימוּ עֲלֵיהֶם כָּל יִשְׂרָאֵל, וְאוֹתָן הַחֲכָמִים שֶׁהִתְקִינוּ אוֹ שֶׁגָּזְרוּ אוֹ שֶׁהִנְהִיגוּ אוֹ שֶׁדָּנוּ דִין וְלִמְדוּ שֶׁהַמִּשְׁפָּט כָּךְ הוּא, הֵם כָּל חַכְמֵי יִשְׂרָאֵל אוֹ רֻבָּן, וְהֵם שֶׁשָּׁמְעוּ הַקַּבָּלָה בְּעִיקְּרֵי הַתּוֹרָה כֻּלָּהּ, אִישׁ מִפִּי אִישׁ עַד מֹשֶׁה רַבֵּנוּ.

[In the years] after the *beit din* (court of Torah law) headed by Rav Ashei, compiler of the Talmud, . . . the dispersion of the people of Israel spread even farther, . . . conflicts abounded in the world, travel became unsafe, and the study of Torah diminished. Jews no longer gathered in the thousands and tens of thousands to study in their academies, as before. Only the remnant few called by G-d would gather in each city and country to study the Torah and understand the works of the sages. . . .

[As a result,] the courts of Torah law that were established in each country after the Talmudic era . . . did not have their decisions accepted by the entire Jewish people. . . . These were only individual [authorities] for

From Where Does the Talmud Get Its Authority?
myjli.com/booksmart

their country, as the great seventy-member court had been disbanded a number of years before the compilation of the Talmud.

Therefore, we do not compel the people of one country to follow the customs followed in a different country, nor do we tell one *beit din* to enact the ordinances enacted by another *beit din*. . . . By the same token, if one of the post-Talmudic sages taught that the meaning of a law is a certain way, and a later *beit din* understands the meaning of this Talmudic law differently, we don't give precedence to the former or the latter, only to the one whose view is more supported by reasoning.

All this applies to the laws, edicts, ordinances, and customs that were innovated after the compilation of the Talmud. But as regards everything that is in the Babylonian Talmud, the whole of Israel is obligated to follow it . . . because all that is in the Talmud was accepted by the entire Jewish people. The sages who instituted these ordinances and customs, and who deliberated these laws and taught these rulings, constituted all or the majority of the sages of Israel who were the recipients of the tradition of the principles of the entire Torah, as was given over to each generation from the mouth of the previous generation, up to our teacher Moses.

V. THE TWO TALMUDS

As noted earlier, there are actually two versions of the Talmud: the "Jerusalem Talmud" and the "Babylonian Talmud." In this section, we look at the different learning models that the two Talmuds represent.

TEXT 5

The Dark Room of the Questing Mind

Talmud, Sanhedrin 24a

"בְּמַחְשַׁכִּים הוֹשִׁיבַנִי . . ." (אֵיכָה ג, ו).
אָמַר רַבִּי יִרְמְיָה: זֶה תַּלְמוּדָהּ שֶׁל בָּבֶל.

"He has set me in dark places . . ." (LAMENTATIONS 3:6). Said Rabbi Yirmiyah: This is the learning of Babylonia.

Decorated initial word panel to the book of Lamentations in a thirteenth-century Italian manuscript. (British Library, London)

TEXT 6

Violent Debate

Talmud, Sanhedrin 24a

מַאי דִכְתִיב (זְכַרְיָה יא, ז), "וָאֶקַּח לִי שְׁנֵי מַקְלוֹת, לְאַחַד קָרָאתִי נֹעַם וּלְאַחַד קָרָאתִי חֹבְלִים"?

"נֹעַם" אֵלוּ תַּלְמִידֵי חֲכָמִים שֶׁבְּאֶרֶץ יִשְׂרָאֵל, שֶׁמַּנְעִימִין זֶה לָזֶה בַּהֲלָכָה. "חוֹבְלִים" אֵלוּ תַּלְמִידֵי חֲכָמִים שֶׁבְּבָבֶל, שֶׁמְּחַבְּלִים זֶה לָזֶה בַּהֲלָכָה.

What is the meaning of the verse (ZECHARIAH 11:7), "I took for myself two staffs; the one I called *No'am* ('pleasantness'), and the other I called *Chovlim* ('saboteurs')"?

"*No'am*" are the sages of the Land of Israel, who are gracious to each other in their deliberations of Torah law. "*Chovlim*" are Babylonian sages, who assault each other in their deliberations of Torah law.

VIEW OF JERUSALEM FROM OVER THE POOL OF HEZEKIAH
From *All Round the World: An Illustrated Record of Voyages, Travels, and Adventures in All Parts of the Globe, First Series*, edited by W. F. Ainsworth (Glasgow and London, U.K.: William Collins, Sons, and Company, 1873).

Why Is Judaism Full of Debates? **Rabbi Lord Jonathan Sacks** explains: **myjli.com/booksmart**

VI. *SUGYA* SAMPLE I: EXPOUNDING A MISHNAH

In this section, we study one example of how the Gemara analyzes a Mishnah, defining the circumstances of the case that the Mishnah presents, identifying the biblical source of this law, contrasting it with other Mishnaic rulings, and discussing how the resulting legal principles should be applied in a variety of cases.

TEXT 7

The Contested Garment

Mishnah, Bava Metzi'a 1:1

שְׁנַיִם אוֹחֲזִין בְּטַלִּית. זֶה אוֹמֵר: "אֲנִי מְצָאתִיהָ", וְזֶה אוֹמֵר: "אֲנִי מְצָאתִיהָ". זֶה אוֹמֵר: "כֻּלָּהּ שֶׁלִּי", וְזֶה אוֹמֵר: "כֻּלָּהּ שֶׁלִּי" - זֶה יִשָּׁבַע שֶׁאֵין לוֹ בָּהּ פָּחוֹת מֵחֶצְיָהּ, וְזֶה יִשָּׁבַע שֶׁאֵין לוֹ בָּהּ פָּחוֹת מֵחֶצְיָהּ, וְיַחֲלֹקוּ.

Two people are grasping a garment. This one says, "I found it," and this one says, "I found it." This one says, "All of it is mine," and this one says, "All of it is mine." This one should swear that his share in it is no less than half, and this one should swear that his share in it is no less than half. And they divide it.

MISHNAH

The first authoritative work of Jewish law that was codified in writing. The Mishnah contains the oral traditions that were passed down from teacher to student; it supplements, clarifies, and systematizes the commandments of the Torah. Due to the continual persecution of the Jewish people, it became increasingly difficult to guarantee that these traditions would not be forgotten. Rabbi Yehudah Hanasi therefore redacted the Mishnah at the end of the 2nd century. It serves as the foundation for the Talmud.

TEXT 8

The *Chazakah* Principle

Talmud, Bava Kama 46b

אָמַר רַבִּי שְׁמוּאֵל בַּר נַחְמָנִי: מִנַּיִן לְהַמּוֹצִיא מֵחֲבֵרוֹ עָלָיו הָרְאָיָה? שֶׁנֶּאֱמַר (שְׁמוֹת כד, יד): "מִי בַעַל דְּבָרִים יִגַּשׁ אֲלֵיהֶם". יַגִּישׁ רְאָיָה אֲלֵיהֶם.

Said Rabbi Shmuel bar Nachmani: From where do we know the rule that the one who is seeking to take property out of his fellow's possession, it is incumbent upon him to provide the evidence? From the verse (EXODUS 24:14), "Whoever has a matter for adjudication should approach them"—he must present the evidence.

Reproduction of *Talmud*, by Lazar Krestin, on a postcard (Wiener Art Postcards, after 1907). (Library of the JTS, New York)

TEXT 9

Two Possessors

Rashi's Commentary to Talmud, Bava Metzi'a 2a

דַוְקָא "אוֹחֲזִין", דִשְׁנֵיהֶם מֻחְזָקִים בָּהּ, וְאֵין לָזֶה כֹּחַ בָּהּ יוֹתֵר מִזֶּה. שֶׁאִלּוּ הָיְתָה בְּיַד אֶחָד לְבַדוֹ, הֱוֵי אִידָךְ "הַמּוֹצִיא מֵחֲבֵרוֹ" וְעָלָיו לְהָבִיא רְאָיָה בְּעֵדִים שֶׁהִיא שֶׁלּוֹ, וְאֵינוֹ נֶאֱמָן זֶה לִטֹּל בִּשְׁבוּעָה.

It is specifically in the case that they are both *grasping* the garment, meaning that both are in possession of it, and neither one has a stronger hold on it than the other. But if only one of them were holding the garment, then the other one has the status of "one who is seeking to take property out of his fellow's possession," and it would be incumbent upon him to provide proof by bringing witnesses that it is his. He would not be believed [to get any part of the garment] with just an oath.

RABBI SHLOMO YITZCHAKI (RASHI) 1040–1105

Most noted biblical and Talmudic commentator. Born in Troyes, France, Rashi studied in the famed *yeshivot* of Mainz and Worms. His commentaries on the Pentateuch and the Talmud, which focus on the straightforward meaning of the text, appear in virtually every edition of the Talmud and Bible.

TEXT 10

The Free-Floating Boat

Talmud, Bava Batra 34b

הַהוּא אַרְבָּא דַהֲווּ מִינְצוּ עֲלָהּ בֵּי תְּרֵי. הַאי אָמַר: "דִּידִי הִיא", וְהַאי אָמַר: "דִּידִי הִיא".

אָתָא חַד מִינַּיְיהוּ לְבֵי דִּינָא וְאָמַר: "תִּיפְסוּהָ, אַדְמַיְיתִינָא סַהֲדֵי דְּדִידִי הִיא". תָּפְסִינַן אוֹ לֹא תָּפְסִינַן?

רַב הוּנָא אָמַר: "תָּפְסִינַן", רַב יְהוּדָה אָמַר: "לָא תָּפְסִינַן".

אֲזַל וְלֹא אַשְׁכַּח סַהֲדֵי. אָמַר לְהוּ: "אַפְּקוּהָ, וְכֹל דְּאַלִּים גָּבַר". מַפְּקִינַן אוֹ לֹא מַפְּקִינַן?

רַב יְהוּדָה אָמַר: "לֹא מַפְּקִינַן", רַב פָּפָּא אָמַר: "מַפְּקִינַן".

וְהִלְכְתָא: לֹא תָּפְסִינַן, וְהֵיכָא דְּתָפַס לֹא מַפְּקִינַן.

There was a certain boat that two people were quarreling about. This one said, "It is mine," and the other one said, "It is mine."

One of them came to the court and said, "Seize it until I am able to bring witnesses that it is mine." Do we seize it or do we not seize it?

Rav Huna said, "We seize it." Rav Yehudah said, "We do not seize it."

[The court seized the boat, but] the man went and did not find witnesses. He then said to the court,

"Release the boat, and whoever is stronger will prevail." Do we release it or do we not release it?

Rav Yehudah said, "We do not release it." Rav Papa said, "We release it."

The law is: We do not seize the property [in such a case]. But if the court did seize it, we do not release it.

THE SANHEDRIN IN SESSION
From *The People's Cyclopedia of Universal Knowledge, Volume III* (New York and San Francisco: Phillips and Hunt; Cincinnati, Chicago, and St. Louis: Jones Bros. and Co., 1883).

TEXT 11

When Should the Court Impose an Imperfect Solution?

Rulings of the Rosh, Bava Metzi'a 1:1

דְּכֵיוָן דִּשְׁנֵיהֶם בָּאִים לְפָנֵינוּ מְחֻזָּקִים בְּגוּף הַטַּלִּית, אָנוּ צְרִיכִין לִפְסֹק לְהוּ דִּין חֲלֻקָּה. דְּכָל דָּבָר שֶׁאָנוּ רוֹאִין בְּיַד אָדָם חַשְׁבִינַן לֵיהּ שֶׁהוּא שֶׁלּוֹ, אַף עַל פִּי שֶׁאַחֵר מְעַרְעֵר וְאוֹמֵר שֶׁלִּי הוּא . . . הִלְכָּךְ, אִי אֶפְשָׁר לִפְסֹק כָּאן דִּין "כָּל דְּאַלִּים גְּבַר", כִּדְאַמְרִינָן פֶּרֶק חֶזְקַת הַבָּתִּים (בָּבָא בַּתְרָא לד, ב) גַּבֵּי אַרְבָּא . . .

דְּהָתָם שַׁאנִי, שֶׁאֵין אֶחָד מֵהֶן מְחֻזָּק בַּדָּבָר שֶׁמְּעַרְעֲרִין עָלָיו, וְאֵין בֵּית דִּין מְחֻיָּבִין לִמְחוֹת לְמִי שֶׁבָּא לִקַּח דָּבָר שֶׁאֵין אָנוּ יוֹדְעִין שֶׁל מִי הוּא וְהוּא אוֹמֵר: שֶׁלּוֹ הוּא. הִלְכָּךְ, אֵין רָאוּי לִפְסֹק לָהֶן דִּין חֲלֻקָּה, שֶׁמָּא נַפְסִיד לְאֶחָד מֵהֶן שֶׁלֹּא כַּדִּין . . .

אֲבָל הָכָא, דִּשְׁנֵיהֶם מְחֻזָּקִין בְּגוּף הַטַּלִּית, אָנוּ מְחֻיָּבִין לִמְחוֹת, שֶׁלֹּא יִגְזֹל הָאֶחָד אֶת חֲבֵרוֹ . . . הִלְכָּךְ אָנוּ צְרִיכִין לִפְסֹק לָהֶן דִּין חֲלֻקָּה.

When the two claimants stand before us holding the garment, we are compelled to rule that the garment should be divided. Because any time that we see something in a person's possession, we need to regard it as their property, even though another person is contesting this and claiming that "It is mine." . . . Consequently, we cannot rule that

RABBI ASHER BEN YECHIEL (ROSH) 1250–1328

Rabbi, author, and Talmudist, he is widely known by the acronym "Rosh." Rabbi Asher was a native of Germany, where he was a prominent disciple and successor of Rabbi Meir (Maharam) of Rothenburg. Due to the persecution and massacres of German Jewry under Emperor Rudolph I, Rabbi Asher was forced to flee, and in 1305, he arrived in Toledo, Spain. He is best known for his Halachic commentary on the Talmud. Rabbi Asher was the father of Rabbi Yaakov, the author of the *Arbaah Turim.*

"whoever is stronger will prevail," as we do in the case cited in Bava Kama 34b regarding the boat. . . .

That case, however, is different. Because neither of them is in possession of the property they are claiming, the court has no cause to stop any person from taking something that they claim is theirs, when we don't know who it belongs to. It would therefore be wrong to rule that it should be divided, as we might be depriving a person of their property without just cause. . . .

But in our case, where both claimants are "possessors" of the garment, we are obligated to prevent one of them from robbing the other. . . . So we have no choice but to rule that the garment should be divided.

WARTEZIMMER BEI GERICHT (WAITING ROOM AT THE COURT)
Isidor Kaufmann (1853–1921), Vienna.

TEXT 12

The Contested Deposit

Mishnah, Bava Metzi'a 3:4

שְׁנַיִם שֶׁהִפְקִידוּ אֵצֶל אֶחָד, זֶה מָנֶה וְזֶה מָאתַיִם. זֶה אוֹמֵר: "שֶׁלִּי מָאתַיִם", וְזֶה אוֹמֵר: "שֶׁלִּי מָאתַיִם". נוֹתֵן לָזֶה מָנֶה וְלָזֶה מָנֶה, וְהַשְּׁאָר יְהֵא מֻנָּח עַד שֶׁיָּבֹא אֵלִיָּהוּ.

אָמַר רַבִּי יוֹסֵי: אִם כֵּן, מַה הִפְסִיד הָרַמַּאי? אֶלָּא הַכֹּל יְהֵא מֻנָּח עַד שֶׁיָּבֹא אֵלִיָּהוּ.

Two people entrusted money with a [third] person. One deposited 100 dinars, and one deposited 200 dinars. This one says, "The 200 are mine," and this one says, "The 200 are mine." We give 100 to one, and 100 to the other, and the remainder is put away until [the prophet] Elijah comes.

Said Rabbi Yosei: If we do that, the swindler loses nothing! Rather, all of the money should be put away until Elijah comes.

QUESTION

In the case of "The Contested Deposit" (Text 12), who are the "possessors" of the contested property—one of the claimants, both claimants, or neither claimant?

THE THREE JUDGES
Honoré-Victorin Daumier, watercolor and brush and black gouache, with charcoal, heightened with gray gouache over touches of graphite, on ivory laid paper, France, c. 1860. (Art Institute of Chicago)

TEXT 13

The “Extended Hand” of the Depositors

Rulings of the Rosh, Bava Metzi’a 1:1

דְהַוֵי כְּאִלוּ שְׁנֵיהֶם מַחְזִיקִין בּוֹ, מִשּׁוּם דְהַנִפְקָד מַחְזִיק מִכֹּחַ שְׁנֵיהֶם, וְהַסָפֵק נוֹלַד בִּרְשׁוּתוֹ, וְיַד הַנִפְקָד כְּיָדָם.

It is as if both of them are holding the money, since the bailee, in whose possession the question of ownership was born, is holding the money on the strength of their authorization, and his hand is legally regarded as the extension of their hands.

TEXT 14

An Honest vs. a Dishonest Dispute

Talmud, Bava Metzi’a 3a

הָתָם וַדַאי אִיכָּא רַמַאי. הָכָא, מִי יֵימַר דְאִיכָּא רַמַאי? אֵימָא תַּרְוַיְהוּ בַּהֲדֵי הֲדָדֵי אַגְבְּהוּהָ.

In that case [of the disputed deposit], there is certainly a swindler. In our case, who is to say that there is a swindler? Perhaps both of them picked up [the garment] together.

FIGURE 3.5

Disputed Property—Four Resolutions

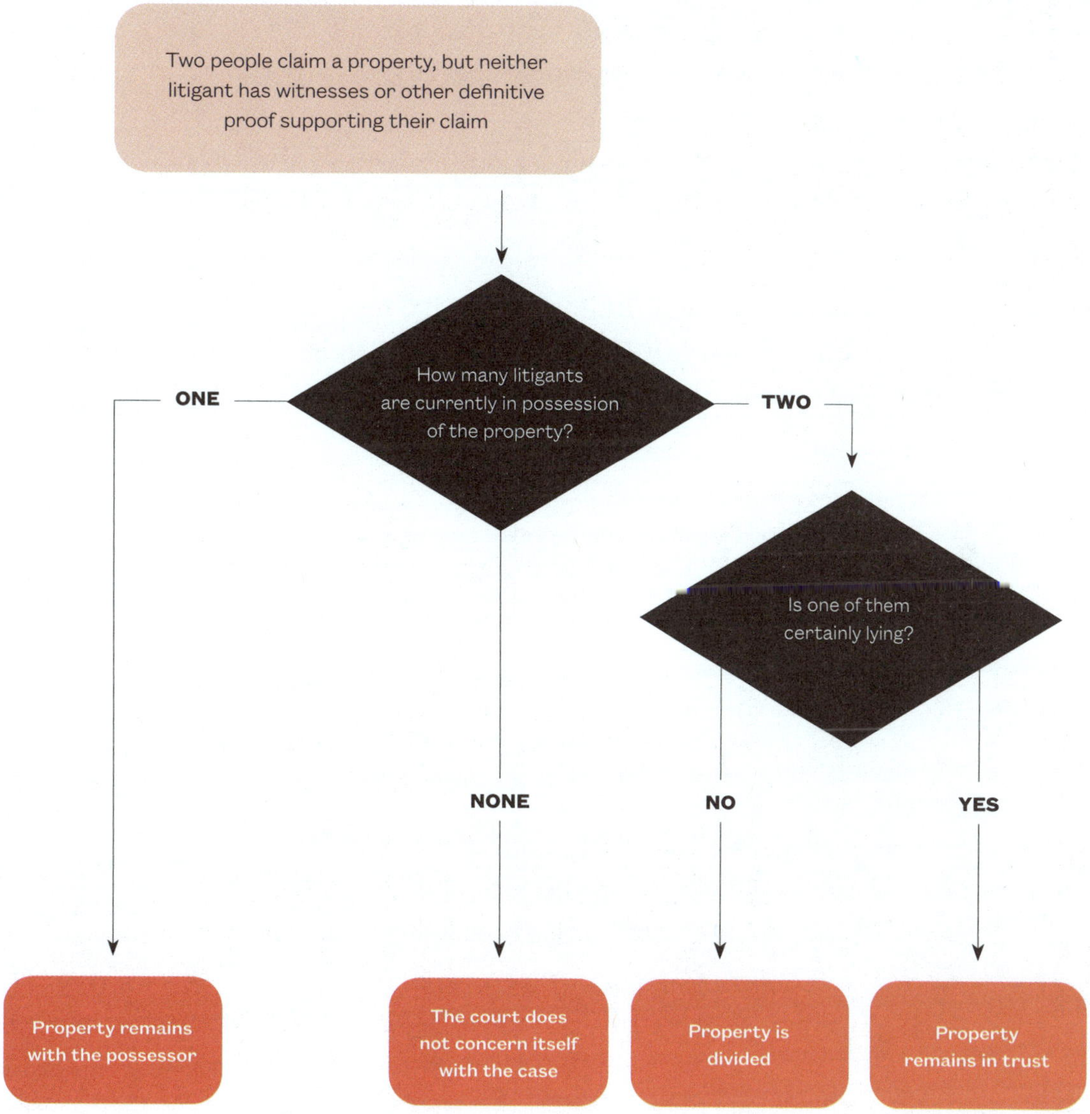

VII. *SUGYA* SAMPLE II: THE TALMUDIC DISPUTATION

In this section, we examine the phenomenon of *machloket*—the arguments and debates between the sages that populate virtually every page of the Talmud. We analyze one of these disputations and explore its wider applications. In the process, we discover how, rather than a "necessary evil" of the human participation in the Oral Torah process, the *machloket* brings to light the multifaceted nature of the Divine truth of Torah and its illumination of the complexities of human life.

TEXT 15

The Words of the Living G-d

Talmud, Eruvin 13b

שָׁלֹשׁ שָׁנִים נֶחְלְקוּ בֵּית שַׁמַאי וּבֵית הִלֵּל. הַלָּלוּ אוֹמְרִים: "הֲלָכָה כְּמוֹתֵנוּ", וְהַלָּלוּ אוֹמְרִים: "הֲלָכָה כְּמוֹתֵנוּ". יָצְאָה בַּת קוֹל וְאָמְרָה: "אֵלוּ וָאֵלוּ דִבְרֵי אֱלֹקִים חַיִּים הֵן".

For three years, the sages of the school of Shamai and the sages of the school of Hillel were disputing. These said, "The law is as we say," and these said, "The law is as we say." Then a heavenly voice issued forth and proclaimed: "These and these are both the words of the living G-d."

If the Bible Is the Word of G-d, How Are There Differing Opinions? **Rabbi Yitzchak Breitowitz** answers: **myjli.com/booksmart**

TEXT 16

Ascending Lights or Descending Lights?

Talmud, Shabbat 21b

בֵּית שַׁמַּאי אוֹמְרִים: "יוֹם רִאשׁוֹן מַדְלִיק שְׁמֹנָה, מִכָּאן וְאֵילָךְ פּוֹחֵת וְהוֹלֵךְ". וּבֵית הִלֵּל אוֹמְרִים: "יוֹם רִאשׁוֹן מַדְלִיק אַחַת, מִכָּאן וְאֵילָךְ מוֹסִיף וְהוֹלֵךְ" . . .

טַעְמָא דְבֵית שַׁמַּאי כְּנֶגֶד יָמִים הַנִּכְנָסִין, וְטַעְמָא דְבֵית הִלֵּל כְּנֶגֶד יָמִים הַיּוֹצְאִין.

The sages of the school of Shamai say: "On the first day [of Chanukah], one kindles eight lights, and on each subsequent day, one light less." The sages of the School of Hillel say: "On the first day, one kindles one light, and on each subsequent day, one additional light."

The reasoning of the school of Shamai is to represent the coming days. The reasoning of the school of Hillel is to represent the days that have passed.

TEXT 17

Potential vs. Actual

Rabbi Shlomo Yosef Zevin, *Le'or Hahalachah*, pp. 396–397

הַקַו הַזֶה שֶׁל "בְּכֹחַ" וְ"בְּפֹעַל" חוֹדֵר וְחוֹרֵז בְּתוֹךְ הַרְבֵּה הֲלָכוֹת פְּרָטִיוֹת שֶׁנֶחְלְקוּ בָּהֶן בֵּית שַׁמַאי וּבֵית הִלֵל. בֵּית שַׁמַאי מַבִּיטִים עַל הַדָבָר כְּפִי מָה שֶׁהוּא עֲדַיִן בְּכֹחַ, וּבֵית הִלֵל מַשְׁקִיפִים עָלָיו מִבְּחִינַת יְצִיאָתוֹ לַפֹּעַל . . .

בְּעֶצֶם, כְּבָר הָיָה בַּלַיְלָה הָרִאשׁוֹן . . . שֶׁמֶן שֶׁל נֵס עַל כָּל שְׁמוֹנֶה הַלֵילוֹת, שֶׁהֲרֵי כְּבָר נִתְעַצֵם כֹּחוֹ שֶׁל הַשֶׁמֶן פִּי שְׁמוֹנָה . . . לְמָחֳרָתוֹ, לֹא הָיָה לָהֶם שֶׁמֶן שֶׁל נֵס אֶלָא כְּדֵי שִׁבְעָה יָמִים. וְכֵן בְּכָל לַיְלָה הָיָה הַשֶׁמֶן הוֹלֵךְ וְחָסוֹר, פּוֹחֵת וְהוֹלֵךְ.

אֶלָא שֶׁכָּל זֶה הָיָה בְּכֹחַ . . . בְּפֹעַל הָיָה לְהֵפֶךְ: בַּיוֹם הָרִאשׁוֹן רָאוּ הַנֵס בְּלַיְלָה אֶחָד בִּלְבַד, וּלְמָחֳרָתוֹ רָאוּ עוֹד בְּלַיְלָה אֶחָד, וְכֵן בְּכָל לַיְלָה הוֹסִיפוּ לִרְאוֹת הַנֵס.

וּבְכָךְ נֶחְלְקוּ בֵּית שַׁמַאי וּבֵית הִלֵל. בֵּית שַׁמַאי לְשִׁיטָתָם מַחֲשִׁיבִים אֶת הַדֶרֶךְ כְּפִי מָה שֶׁהוּא בְּכֹחַ, וּבֵית הִלֵל לְשִׁיטָתָם מַעֲרִיכִים אוֹתוֹ מִנְקֻדַת הוֹצָאָתוֹ לְפֹעַל.

The theme of "potential" versus "actuality" runs as a thread through many of the disputations between the school of Shamai and the school of Hillel. The school of Shamai views things as they are in their potential state, whereas the school of Hillel views things as they are in actuality. . . .

RABBI SHLOMO YOSEF ZEVIN
1886–1978

Editor in chief of the *Talmudic Encyclopedia*. Rabbi Zevin was born in Kazimirov, Belarus, and was ordained by numerous prominent rabbis, including Rabbi Yosef Rosen of Rogatchov and Rabbi Michel Epstein. In 1934, he immigrated to Israel.

In essence, on the very first night [of the Chanukah miracle], we already had eight-days' worth of miraculous oil, as the potential of the oil had already been intensified eightfold. . . . On the next day, however, we only had miracle oil with the power to burn for seven days. And so on with each successive night as the oil diminished.

All this, however, is when we view the miracle in terms of how much potential there is. . . . But when we view it in terms of actuality, the opposite is the case: On the first day, we only saw one night of the miracle, on the following day we experienced two days of miraculous light, and so on. With each additional night, we experienced more of the miracle in actuality.

This is the *machloket* between the school of Shamai and the school of Hillel. The school of Shamai follows their approach of regarding things in terms of their potential, while the school of Hillel follows their approach of viewing things from the perspective of what has emerged into actuality.

TEXT 18

Looking Beyond the Surface Reality

Mishnah, Avot 4:20

אַל תִּסְתַּכֵּל בַּקַּנְקַן, אֶלָּא בְמַה שֶּׁיֵּשׁ בּוֹ.

Don't look at the container, but at what it contains.

AVOT (ETHICS OF THE FATHERS; PIRKEI AVOT)

A 6-chapter work on Jewish ethics that is studied widely by Jewish communities, especially during the summer. The first 5 chapters are from the Mishnah, tractate Avot. Avot differs from the rest of the Mishnah in that it does not focus on legal subjects; it is a collection of the sages' wisdom on topics related to character development, ethics, healthy living, piety, and the study of Torah.

TEXT 19

Reality Check

Mishnah, Avot 1:17

וְלֹא הַמִּדְרָשׁ הוּא הָעִקָּר, אֶלָּא הַמַּעֲשֶׂה.

The main thing is not learning, but action.

TEXT 20

All Was Received from a Single Pastor

Talmud, Chagigah 3b

תַּלְמִידֵי חֲכָמִים שֶׁיּוֹשְׁבִין אֲסוּפּוֹת אֲסוּפּוֹת וְעוֹסְקִין בַּתּוֹרָה, הַלָּלוּ מְטַמְּאִין וְהַלָּלוּ מְטַהֲרִין, הַלָּלוּ אוֹסְרִין וְהַלָּלוּ מַתִּירִין, הַלָּלוּ פּוֹסְלִין וְהַלָּלוּ מַכְשִׁירִין.

שֶׁמָּא יֹאמַר אָדָם: הֵיאַךְ אֲנִי לָמֵד תּוֹרָה מֵעַתָּה? תַּלְמוּד לוֹמַר: "כּוּלָּם נִתְּנוּ מֵרוֹעֶה אֶחָד". קֵל אֶחָד נְתָנָן, פַּרְנָס אֶחָד אֲמָרָן מִפִּי אֲדוֹן כָּל הַמַּעֲשִׂים בָּרוּךְ הוּא, דִּכְתִיב:

"וַיְדַבֵּר אֱלֹקִים אֵת כָּל הַדְּבָרִים הָאֵלֶּה". אַף אַתָּה עֲשֵׂה אָזְנֶיךָ כַּאֲפַרְכֶּסֶת, וּקְנֵה לְךָ לֵב מֵבִין לִשְׁמוֹעַ אֶת דִּבְרֵי מְטַמְּאִים וְאֶת דִּבְרֵי מְטַהֲרִים, אֶת דִּבְרֵי אוֹסְרִין וְאֶת דִּבְרֵי מַתִּירִין, אֶת דִּבְרֵי פּוֹסְלִין וְאֶת דִּבְרֵי מַכְשִׁירִין.

Torah scholars sit in numerous groups and study the Torah. One group deems a thing impure, and another deems it pure; one group forbids a deed and another permits it; one group disqualifies something and another renders it fit.

Should a person then ask: How, then, might I study Torah? We are therefore taught, "All was received from a single pastor" (ECCLESIASTES 12:11). One G-d gave it, one provider said it all from the mouth of the Master of all works; as it is written, "And G-d spoke all these words" (EXODUS 20:1). So make your ears as a hopper and acquire a perceptive heart to understand the words of those who deem impure and the words of those who deem pure, the words of those who forbid and the words of those who permit, the words of those who disqualify and the words of those who render fit.

Why Are So Many of Our Religious Practices Rooted in Arguments? A lecture by **Rabbi Shais Taub: myjli.com/booksmart**

KEY POINTS

1 *The Hallmark of Jewish Learning:* More than any other work, the Talmud defines "Jewish learning." This is because the Talmud is the most comprehensive and authoritative record of the "Oral Torah"—the process by which we engage with the Divine truths revealed in the Torah.

2 *The Making of the Mishnah:* For 35 generations, from the Giving of the Torah at Mount Sinai in 1313 BCE until the end of the 2nd century CE, the Oral Torah was an exclusively oral tradition handed down from teacher to disciple. But when the increasing dispersion of the Jewish people created the danger that this tradition would be lost, Rabbi Yehudah Hanasi took the unprecedented step of compiling the Mishnah, which documents the core teachings of the Oral Torah in 63 "tractates" covering every area of Jewish life.

3 *The Structure and Contents of the Talmud:* The Talmud incorporates the Mishnah and adds to it the "Gemara," which records the teachings and deliberations of hundreds of sages who studied and taught in the great centers of Torah learning in the Land of Israel and in Babylonia in the three centuries following the

Mishnah's compilation. A primary function of the Gemara is to "expound" the Mishnah: to explain the Mishnah's meaning, compare and contrast it with other Mishnaic teachings, trace the source of the laws and principles presented in the Mishnah, and apply these laws and principles to new questions and circumstances. The Gemara also includes numerous other teachings and discussions, in both the Halachic (legal) and Agadic (non-legal) areas of the Oral Torah.

4 *The Unique Status of the Talmud:* The Talmud was compiled at a time when, as a result of the growing dispersion of the Jewish people, the global Torah leadership in Babylonia was being replaced by numerous localized Torah centers. The Talmud is therefore the last work that was accepted by the whole of the Jewish people as a definitive record of the Oral Torah. As a result, no subsequent Torah work has achieved the degree of authority that the Talmud commands.

5 *The Two Talmuds:* There are actually two versions of the Talmud: the "Jerusalem Talmud," which records the learning of the Torah academies of the Holy Land in the years 200 to 350 CE; and the "Babylonian Talmud," created in the learning centers of Mesopotamia in the 3rd, 4th, and 5th centuries. The Jerusalem Talmud is characterized by a "direct approach" that zeroes in on

the solution, whereas the Babylonian Talmud reaches its conclusions with a greater degree of roundabout reasoning, rejected hypotheses, and contentious debate. Yet it is the Babylonian version that became the hallmark of Jewish wisdom and learning.

6 *The Case of the Contested Garment:* A classic example of the Talmudic exposition of a Mishnah is the Gemara's analysis of the case of *Shnayim ochazin be'talis* ("Two people are grasping a garment"), in which two people claim ownership of an object, yet neither can provide evidence for their claim. The Gemara examines the particulars of the Mishnah's case, identifies its biblical source, and contrasts it with parallel cases in other Mishnaic sources. In the process, we discover four different possible outcomes for this type of scenario. Depending on who is currently in possession of the object, as well as on the question of whether this is an honest dispute or an attempt by one of the parties to defraud the other, the court will either: (1) award the property to one of the two parties, (2) divide it between them, (3) refuse to get involved, or (4) hold on to the property until the truth comes to light.

7 *The Talmudic Disputation:* A prevalent feature of the Talmud is *machloket*—arguments and debates among the sages. These can be viewed as a "necessary

evil" of the human participation in the Oral Torah process. Yet the Talmud insists that "these and these are both the words of the living G-d"—that *machloket* serves to reveal the multidimensional nature of the Divine truths contained in the Torah.

8 *Potential vs. Actual:* A *machloket* that illustrates this paradigm is the classic debate between the sages of Shamai and the sages of Hillel regarding the kindling of the Chanukah lights, which also has multiple applications in many areas of Torah law. The dispute hinges on the question of which should be given precedence over the other: the potential that a thing possesses or its actual state. The legal ruling in these cases follows the opinion of the school of Hillel; but in the inner life of the mind, both sides of the *machloket* are sustained. Regarding our spiritual self-perception and our relationships with others, the potential takes precedence over the actual, while at the same time, the supremacy of the actual over the potential is also affirmed.

9 *The Talmudic Mind:* Talmudic learning leverages the "flaws" of the human mind—its circuitous reasoning, its contentiousness, and its inconsistencies—to reveal the multifaceted nature of the Divine wisdom and apply it to the complexities of human life.

Map of the Talmud

ORDER 1: ZERA'IM / "SEEDS"

The daily prayers; agricultural laws

BERACHOT — *"Blessings"*

Reading of the Shema; daily prayers; blessings on food

 9  64  68

+ Mealtime etiquette; the life of King David; the meaning of dreams

PE'AH — *"Sides"*

Agricultural leavings for the poor; charity

8  37

+ Laws and practices of Torah study; prohibitions against gossip and slander

DEMAI — *"Mixtures"*

Produce whose tithed status is in doubt

7  34

KILAYIM — *"Hybrids"*

Forbidden hybrids in planting, breeding animals, and garment making

9  44

SHEVIIT — *"Seventh Year"*

Laws of the Sabbatical and Jubilee years

10 31

TERUMOT — *"Upliftings"*

Portion of produce that is consecrated and given to the *Kohanim*

11 59

MAASROT — *"Tithes"*

Tithes of the produce given to the Levites and the poor

5 26

MAASER SHENI — *"Second Tithe"*

Portions of the land's produce that were eaten in Jerusalem

5 28

CHALAH — *"Loaf"*

Portion of the dough that is consecrated and given to the *Kohanim*

4  28

ORLAH — *"Stoppage"*

Laws governing the first three years' produce of fruit trees

3  20

BIKURIM — *"First Fruits"*

First fruits of the year's harvest, which were brought to the Holy Temple in Jerusalem

3 13

ICON KEYS

 **Mishnah** (chapters)

 **Babylonian Talmud** (folios)

 **Jerusalem Talmud** (folios)

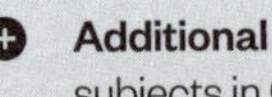 **Additional** subjects in Gemara

ZERA'IM · MO'ED · NASHIM · NEZIKIN · KODOSHIM · TAHAROT

ORDER 2: MO'ED / "APPOINTED TIMES"

Shabbat and the festivals; the Jewish calendar

SHABBAT

Laws of Shabbat observance

24 · 157 · 92

The festival of Chanukah; account of the Giving of the Torah at Mount Sinai; laws of circumcision

EIRUVIN

Continuation of the laws of Shabbat, focusing primarily on the *eiruv* mechanisms that permit carrying objects and traveling in specially designated spaces

10 · 105 · 92

Tips and pointers on the study and acquisition of knowledge

PESACHIM *"Passovers"*

Observances of the festival of Passover

10 · 121 · 71

Proper speech; guidelines in following the local custom; Kiddush and Havadalah

SHEKALIM

The annual half-shekel coin contributed by each Jew toward the service in the Holy Temple; rules pertaining to the daily management of the Holy Temple

8 · 33

YOMA *"The Day"*

Observances of Yom Kippur; repentance

8 · 88 · 42

SUKKAH

Observances of the festival of Sukkot

5 · 56 · 26

BEITZAH *"Egg"*

Laws pertaining to the prohibition of work on the festivals; laws of *muktzeh* (objects that should not be handled on Shabbat and the festivals)

5 · 40 · 22

ROSH HASHANAH *"Head of the Year"*

Setting of the Jewish calendar; observances of Rosh Hashanah

4 · 35 · 22

TAANIT *"Fasting"*

Observances of the fast days; prayers for rain; notable dates and events in Jewish history

4 · 31 · 26

Narratives on the lives of the sages

MEGILAH *"Scroll"*

Observances of Purim; laws pertaining to the synagogue, the synagogue service, and the public Torah readings

4 · 32 · 34

The story of Purim; expositions on the Book of Esther

MO'ED KATAN *"Minor Festival"*

Laws of the "intermediate days" of the festivals; laws of mourning for the dead

3 · 29 · 14

CHAGIGAH *"Festival Offering"*

The three annual pilgrimages to the Holy Temple in Jerusalem

3 · 27 · 22

Mystical secrets of the Creation cosmology

ORDER 3: NASHIM / "WOMEN"

Marriage and divorce

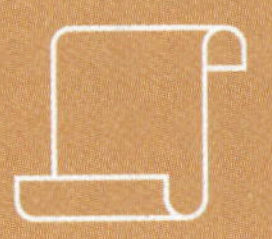

YEVAMOT — *"Levirates"*

Laws of *yibum* (levirate marriage) and *chalitzah*; the *arayot* (forbidden incestuous relations)

Mishnah: 16 · Babylonian Talmud: 122 · Jerusalem Talmud: 85

+ Conversion to Judaism

KETUVOT — *"Marriage Contracts"*

The financial and marital obligations of a husband to his wife

Mishnah: 13 · Babylonian Talmud: 112 · Jerusalem Talmud: 72

+ Legal contracts, veracity of testimony in court, and numerous other topics; this tractate is often called "the minor Talmud" due to the multitude of legal subjects it touches on

NEDARIM — *"Vows"*

Laws governing personal vows and pledges

Mishnah: 11 · Babylonian Talmud: 91 · Jerusalem Talmud: 40

+ Circumcision; the mitzvah of visiting the sick

NAZIR — *"The Nazirite"*

Laws of the "Nazirite" who takes a vow not to drink wine, cut their hair, or become ritually impure through contact with the dead

Mishnah: 9 · Babylonian Talmud: 66 · Jerusalem Talmud: 47

+ The different levels of ritual impurity

SOTAH — *"Wayward Wife"*

Laws of the *sotah* (a woman suspected of adultery); the priestly blessing and other prayers; laws of warfare; the procedure for an unsolved murder (*eglah arufah*)

Mishnah: 9 · Babylonian Talmud: 49 · Jerusalem Talmud: 47

+ Divine reward and retribution; accounts of the Egyptian exile, the Exodus, and the Israelites' entry into the Promised Land; the story of Samson; expositions on Job; descriptions of the eve of the messianic era

GITIN — *"Writs of Divorce"*

Laws of divorce; *shelichut* (legal agency) ; various rabbinic ordinances instituted for the common good

Mishnah: 9 · Babylonian Talmud: 90 · Jerusalem Talmud: 54

+ Events surrounding the destruction of Jerusalem and the Holy Temple

KIDUSHIN — *"Consecration"*

Laws of marriage; laws pertaining to purchases and acquisitions; the differing obligations of men and women regarding various *mitzvot*

Mishnah: 4 · Babylonian Talmud: 82 · Jerusalem Talmud: 48

+ The mitzvah to honor one's parents; paternal obligations toward their children

ICON KEYS

- **Mishnah** (chapters)
- **Babylonian Talmud** (folios)
- **Jerusalem Talmud** (folios)
- **Additional** subjects in Gemara

ZERA'IM · MO'ED · NASHIM · NEZIKIN · KODOSHIM · TAHAROT

ORDER 4: NEZIKIN / "DAMAGES"

Civil and criminal law

BAVA KAMA *"First Gate"**

A person's responsibility for damages caused by their person or property; theft and robbery

10 · 110 · 44

BAVA METZI'A *"Middle Gate"**

Determining the ownership of disputed property; the obligation to return a lost object; responsibilities of a bailee; loans; usury, exchange rates, and fraud; employment and leasing

10 · 119 · 37

BAVA BATRA *"Last Gate"**

Partnerships; neighbor law; proof of ownership; purchases and acquisitions; financial contracts and appraisals; inheritance

10 · 176 · 34

+ Intangible damages; municipal levies and taxes; the collection and distribution of charity; composition of the Tanach; the Rabbah bar bar Chanah legends

SANHEDRIN *"High Court"*

Structure of the criminal justice system; judicial procedures; capital punishment; kidnapping and murder; self-defense; treason; government

11 · 113 · 57

+ Fundamental beliefs of Judaism; prophecy; principles of morality; the preservation of life; the seven Noahide laws; warfare; burial; the messianic era and the World to Come

MAKOT *"Lashings"*

Corporal punishment; the penalties for unintentional killing and false testimony

3 · 24 · 9

SHEVU'OT *"Oaths"*

Oaths and vows

8 · 49 · 44

+ Honesty and truth-telling

EDUYOT *"Testimonies"*

Record of a variety of legal traditions and disputations

8

AVODAH ZARAH *"Alien Worship"*

Idolatry; relations with non-Jews

5 · 76 · 37

+ Agadot on various events in Jewish history; the methodologies of Torah study; the responsibility not to be the cause of another person's transgression

AVOT *"Fathers"*

Ethics and character

5

HORAYOT *"Rulings"*

Mistaken rulings issued by the court

3 · 14 · 19

* These three tractates were originally part of one tractate called *Nezikin* ("Damages"), which was divided into three parts due to its size

ORDER 5: **KODOSHIM** / **"SACRAMENTS"**

The Temple service; the kosher dietary laws

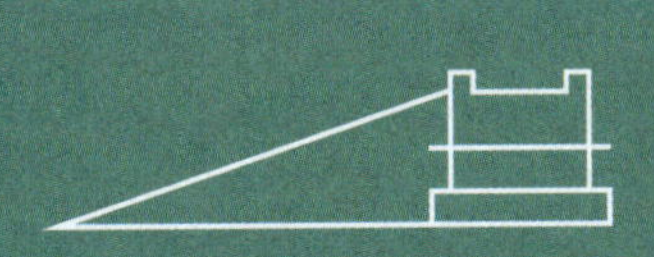

ZEVACHIM *"Sacrifices"*

Laws pertaining to the animal sacrifices brought in the Holy Temple in Jerusalem

Mishnah 14 · Babylonian Talmud 120

+ The principles of Halachic exposition

MENACHOT *"Offerings"*

The grain, wine, and oil offerings brought in the Holy Temple

Mishnah 13 · Babylonian Talmud 11

+ *Tzitzit* and *tefilin*

CHULIN *"Non-Sacred Foods"*

The kosher dietary laws

Mishnah 12 · Babylonian Talmud 148

BECHOROT *"Firstborns"*

Redemption of the firstborn; the firstborn animals and the animal tithe that were offered in the Holy Temple

Mishnah 9 · Babylonian Talmud 61

ARACHIN *"Estimations"*

Property pledged to the Holy Temple

Mishnah 9 · Babylonian Talmud 34

+ The Levite musicians in the Holy Temple; the prohibition of various types of negative speech (*lashon hara*)

TEMURAH *"Exchange"*

Temple offerings that got mixed with other animals, or were disqualified for other reasons

Mishnah 7 · Babylonian Talmud 34

KERITOT *"Cutting Off"*

The *chatat* and *asham* offerings brought in atonement for various transgressions

Mishnah 6 · Babylonian Talmud 29

+ The formula for the *ketoret* (incense) offered daily in the Holy Temple

ME'ILAH *"Betrayal"*

Penalties for the unauthorized use of Temple property

Mishnah 6 · Babylonian Talmud 22

TAMID *"Constant"*

The daily service in the Holy Temple

Mishnah 7 · Babylonian Talmud 8

MIDOT *"Measurements"*

Detailed description of the physical structure of the Holy Temple in Jerusalem

Mishnah 5

KINIM *"Nests"*

Laws dealing with various types of bird offerings that got mixed up with each other

Mishnah 3

ICON KEYS

 **Mishnah** (chapters)

 **Babylonian Talmud** (folios)

 **Jerusalem Talmud** (folios)

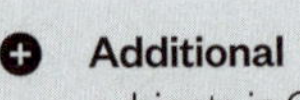 **Additional** subjects in Gemara

ZERA'IM · MO'ED · NASHIM · NEZIKIN · KODOSHIM · TAHAROT

ORDER 6: TAHAROT / "PURITIES"

Laws of ritual purity

KELIM *"Vessels"*

The different types of ritual purity and impurity, and the status of various vessels regarding their susceptibility to contamination

30

OHALOT *"Canopies"*

Ritual impurity acquired through contact with a dead body

18

NEGA'IM *"Afflictions"*

Laws of *tzaraat* ("leprosy") that afflicts a person, clothes, or home

14

PARAH *"Heifer"*

Laws of the "red heifer"

12

TAHAROT *"Purities"*

Laws of ritual purity and impurity

10

MIKVA'OT *"Pools"*

Laws of the *mikveh* (ritually cleansing pool of water)

10

NIDAH *"Menstruant"*

Laws pertaining to the prohibition of marital relations during menstruation, and the state of ritual impurity it engenders

10  72 13

Conception, pregnancy, and birth; the soul's descent into the physical world

MACHSHIRIN *"Preparation"*

The manner in which the "seven liquids" make foods susceptible to ritual contamination

6

ZAVIM *"Emissions"*

Ritual impurity engendered by bodily emissions

5

TEVUL YOM *"Day Immersion"*

Ritual status of one who has immersed in a *mikveh* but must wait until sunset to be fully purified

4

YADAYIM *"Hands"*

Ritual washing of the hands; disputations between the Pharisees and the Sadducees

4

UKTZIN *"Stems"*

The status of various components and containers of foods in regard ritual impurity; the rewards of the righteous in the World to Come

3

THE "MINOR TRACTATES"

The Minor Tractates are Baraitot ("external teachings"), i.e., Mishnaic-era teachings not included in the Mishnah

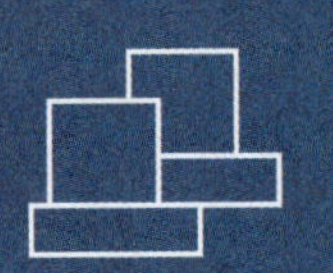

AVOT D'RABBI NATAN
"Rabbi Nathan's 'Fathers'"

An expansion of the Mishnaic tractate *Avot* ("Ethics of the Fathers")

CHAPTERS: 41

SOFRIM *"Scribes"*

The writing of a Torah scroll; the annual Torah reading cycle

CHAPTERS: 21

SEMACHOT *"Happy Occasions"*

Burial and mourning

CHAPTERS: 14

KALAH *"Bride"*

Marriage and marital relations

CHAPTERS: 1

KALAH RABATI *"Greater Bride"*

Modesty and etiquette in various areas of everyday life

CHAPTERS: 10

DERECH ERETZ RABAH
"Greater Everyday Behavior"

Proper behavior in various areas of everyday life

CHAPTERS: 11

DERECH ERETZ ZUTA
"Minor Everyday Behavior"

Proper behavior for a Torah scholar; the value of peace

CHAPTERS: 11

GERIM *"Converts"*

Conversion to Judaism; the status of a non-Jewish "resident-sojourner"

CHAPTERS: 4

KUTIM *"Cuthites"*

Laws governing relations between Jews and Cuthites (Samaritans)

CHAPTERS: 2

AVADIM "SERVANTS"

Laws of the indentured servant

CHAPTERS: 3

SEFER TORAH *"Torah Scroll"*

The writing and format of a Torah scroll

CHAPTERS: 5

TEFILIN *"Phylacteries"*

Laws of *tefilin*

CHAPTERS: 1

TZITZIT *"Fringes"*

Laws of *tzitzit*

CHAPTERS: 1

MEZUZAH *"Doorpost"*

Laws of *mezuzah*

CHAPTERS: 2

The Chain of Tradition

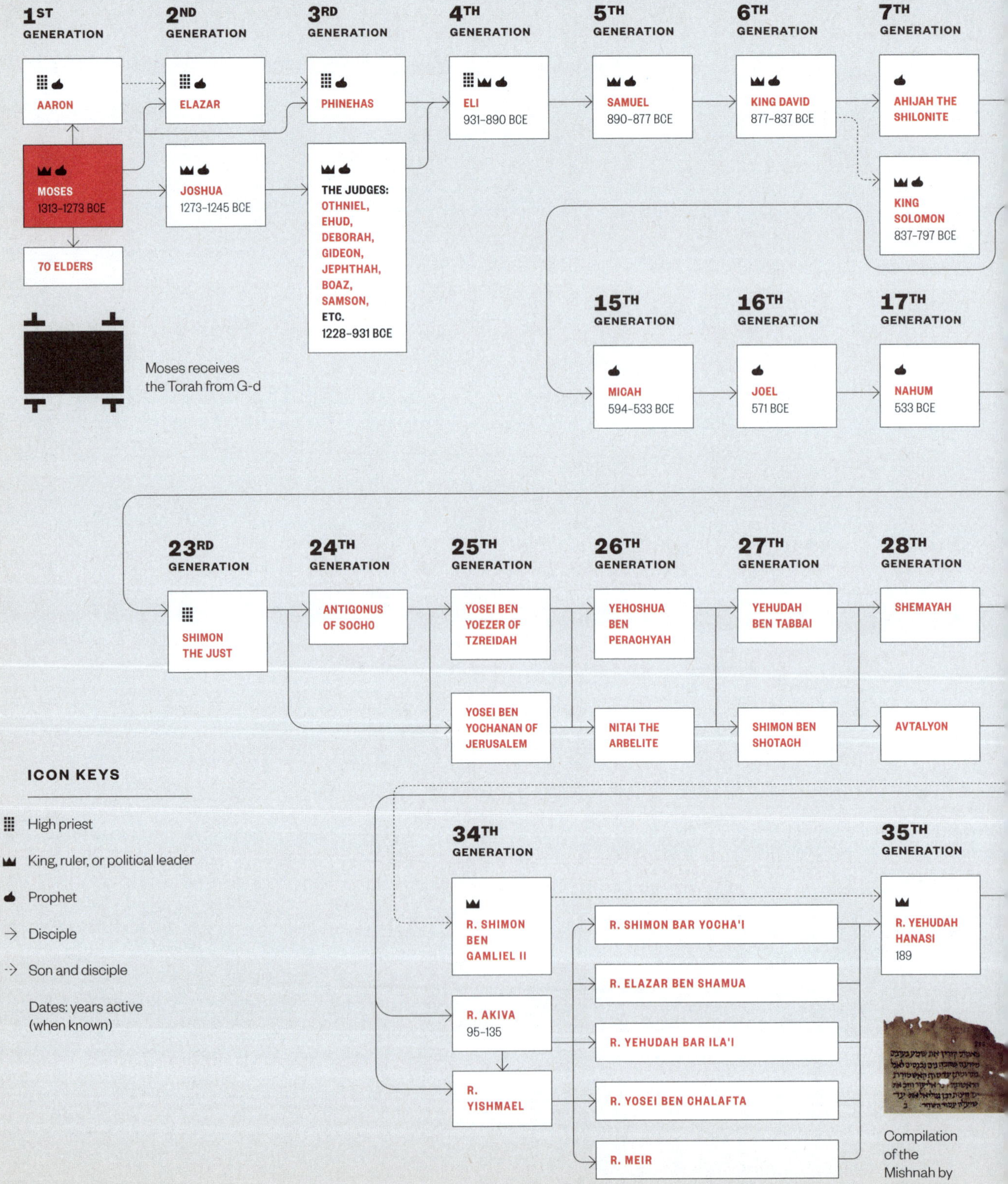

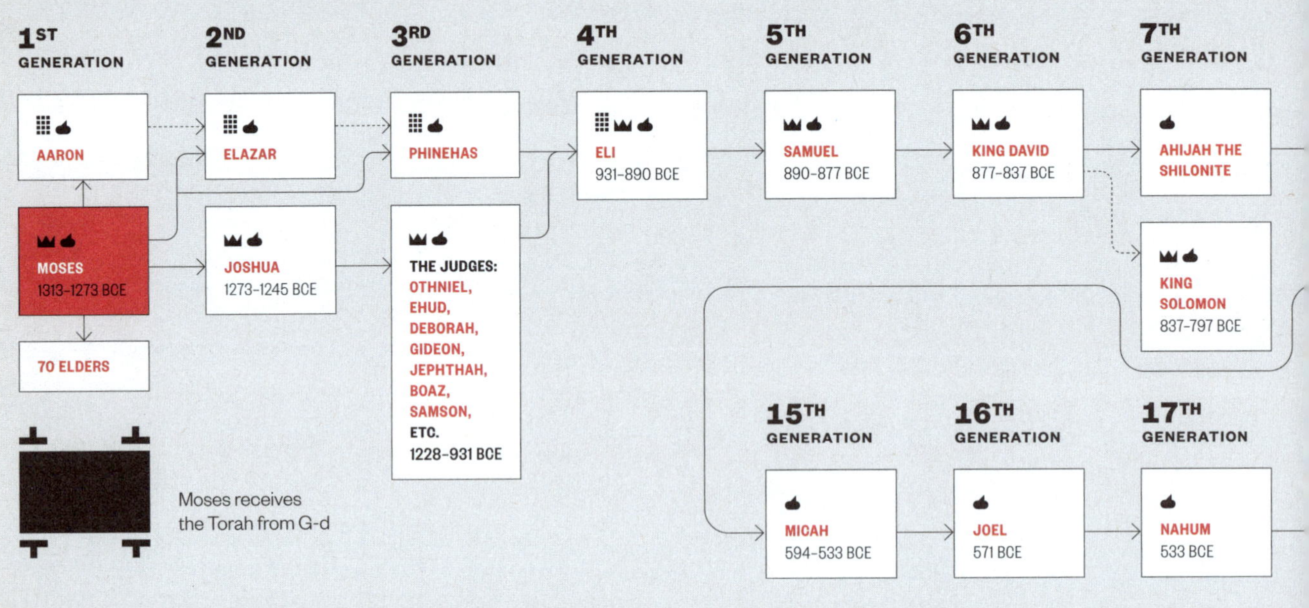

23RD GENERATION
SHIMON THE JUST

24TH GENERATION
ANTIGONUS OF SOCHO

25TH GENERATION
YOSEI BEN YOEZER OF TZREIDAH
YOSEI BEN YOCHANAN OF JERUSALEM

26TH GENERATION
YEHOSHUA BEN PERACHYAH
NITAI THE ARBELITE

27TH GENERATION
YEHUDAH BEN TABBAI
SHIMON BEN SHOTACH

28TH GENERATION
SHEMAYAH
AVTALYON

34TH GENERATION
R. SHIMON BEN GAMLIEL II
R. AKIVA
95–135
R. YISHMAEL

R. SHIMON BAR YOCHA'I
R. ELAZAR BEN SHAMUA
R. YEHUDAH BAR ILA'I
R. YOSEI BEN CHALAFTA
R. MEIR

35TH GENERATION
R. YEHUDAH HANASI
189

Compilation of the Mishnah by R. Yehudah ha-Nasi

ICON KEYS

- High priest
- King, ruler, or political leader
- Prophet
- Disciple
- Son and disciple

Dates: years active (when known)

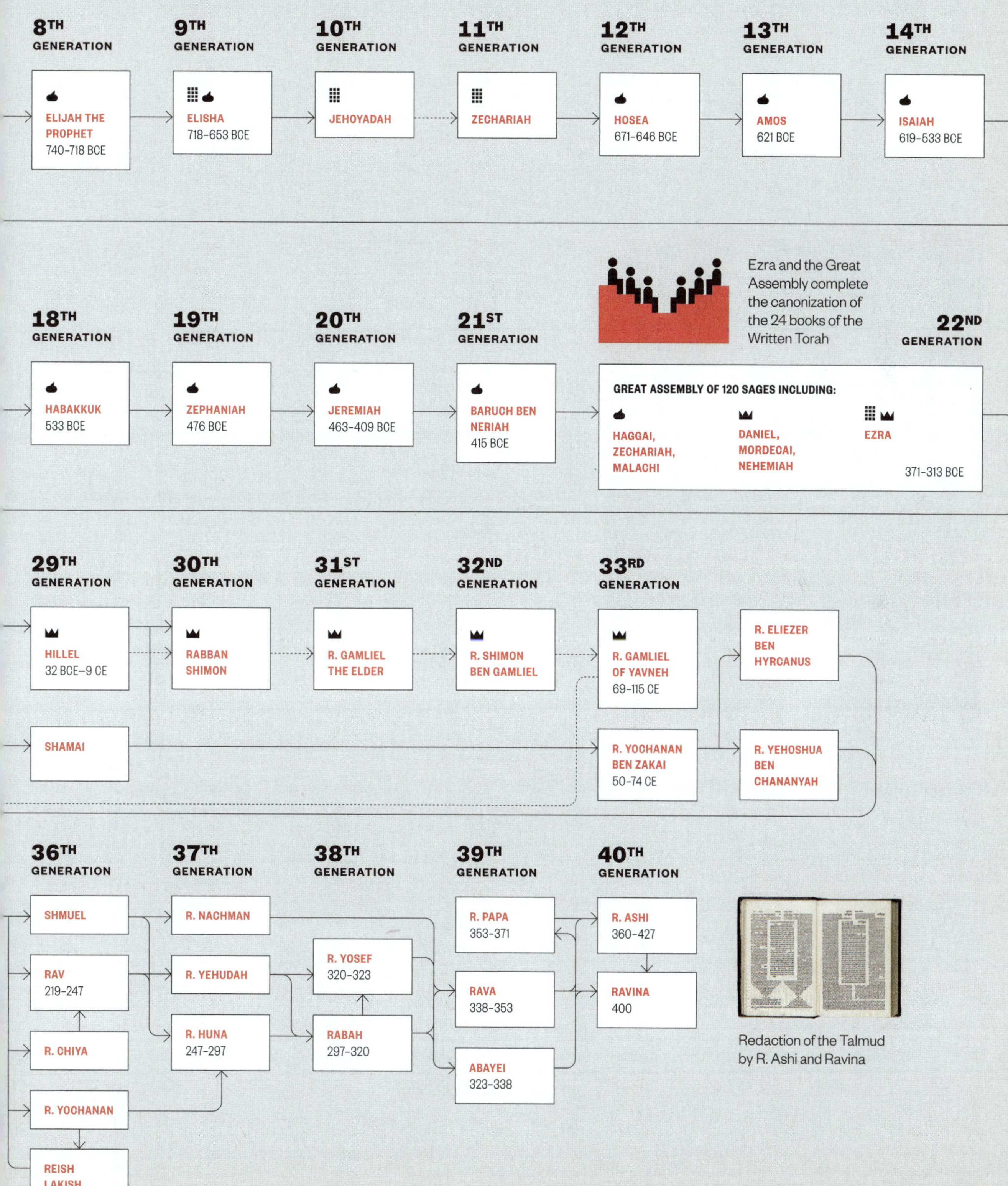

Redaction of the Talmud by R. Ashi and Ravina

A Symposium of Generations

From a talk delivered in 1971

RABBI JOSEPH B. SOLOVEITCHIK
1903–1993

Talmudist and philosopher. A scion of a renowned Lithuanian rabbinical family, Rabbi Soloveitchik was one of the most influential Jewish personalities, leaders, and thinkers of the 20th century. In 1941, he became professor of Talmud at RIETS—Yeshiva University; in this capacity, he ordained close to 2000 rabbis. Among his published works are *Halakhic Man* and *The Lonely Man of Faith.*

I enter the classroom, which is crowded with boys who could be, as far as age is concerned, my grandchildren. I enter the classroom as an old man, with a wrinkled face and eyes reflecting fatigue and the sadness of old age. It's a very strange sadness: the melancholy of remembering things which disappear, which no longer exist. I sit down, and opposite me are rows of young boys with beaming eyes, beaming faces, clear eyes, radiating the joy of being young.

I always enter the class in a very pessimistic mood; I always enter in despair. I ask myself: Can there be a dialogue between an old teacher and young students? Between a *rebbe* in his Indian summer and boys enjoying the spring of their lives?

I start the *shiur*; the door opens, and another old man walks in and sits down. He is older than I am. All the students call me the Rav, but he is older than the Rav. He is the grandfather of the Rav; his name is Reb Chaim Brisker, without whom no *shiur* can be delivered nowadays. Then, the door opens quietly again and another old man comes in; he is older than Reb Chaim, he lived in the 17th century. What's his name? Shabsai Kohen—the famous Shach—who must be present when *dinei mamonos* (property law) is being discussed; when we study [the

Talmudic tractates] *Bava Metzia* and *Bava Kama*. And then, more visitors show up. Some of the visitors lived in the 11th century, some in the 12th century, some in the 13th century, some lived in antiquity. Rabbi Akiva, Rashi, Rabbeinu Tam, the Raavad, the Rashba; more and more come in.

I introduce them to my pupils and the dialogue commences. The Rambam (Maimonides) says something, the Raavad disagrees; and sometimes he's very nasty. Very sharp, harsh language he uses against the Rambam. A boy jumps up to defend the Rambam against the Raavad, and the boy is fresh—you know how young boys are fresh—so the language he uses is improper. So, I correct him. And another jumps up with a new idea; the Rashba smiles gently. I try to analyze what the young boy meant, another boy intervenes, we call upon the Rabbeinu Tam to express his opinion, and suddenly a symposium of generations comes into existence.

Generations! Young boys, 22, 23, 24 years of age, there are boys who are just 18 years old in my class: one generation. Then my generation, then the generation of Reb Chaim Brisker, then the generation of the Shach, then the generation of the Rashba, the Ramban, the generation of the Rambam, the generation of Rabbeinu Tam, the generation of Rashi, and then, I mean there is no end! What about Rav Hai Gaon? What about Rabbi Akiva, Rabbi Elazar, Rabban Yochanan ben Zakai?

We all speak one language; "The entire earth was one language and singular words" (Genesis 11:1). We all chat, we all laugh, we all enjoy the company, and we all pursue one goal; we all are committed to a common vision, and we all operate in the same categories. There is *mesorah* collegiality, friendship, comradeship between old and young, between antiquity, middle-ages, and modern times.

This unity of generations, this march of centuries, this conversation of generations, this dialogue between antiquity and present will finally bring the redemption of the Jew.

Let me tell you that at the conclusion of three and sometimes four hours, I emerge young and elated, younger than my pupils. They are tired, exhausted, some of them yawn. I feel happy. I have defeated age. I have defeated oldness; I emerge young, less fatigued, less exhausted than my young pupils.

We belong to the same *mesorah* community, where generations meet. Where hands, no matter how wrinkled and parchment-dry one hand is and how soft and wan the other hand is, grasp each other and unite in a community where the great dialogue continues.

HALACHAH

Halachah is the "bottom line" of Torah, where the Torah's source texts, commentaries, and deliberations translate into the dos and don'ts of daily life. In this lesson, we explore the history of Halachah, and survey the great variety of issues and dilemmas that Halachah addresses. We then bring it all to life via a case study that traces a Halachic issue from its biblical origins through more than a dozen citations across the entire spectrum of Halachic literature.

BETH HAMEDRASH AND BETH DIN (HOUSE OF LEARNING AND JUDGMENT)—A JEWISH COURT
Detail from illustration from London newspaper *The Graphic*, August 11, 1906. The detailed drawing depicts the members of the London Beth Din at the time, which functioned as a Jewish court and oversaw kosher certification.

I. WHAT IS HALACHAH?

Halachah is the "bottom line" of Torah, where the biblical commandments, rabbinical ordinances, and Talmudic learning translate into the dos and don'ts of daily life. Halachah addresses every part of a Jew's life, from waking to bedtime, from birth to burial, and from everyday activities to the most extraordinary situations and dilemmas.

TEXT 1

The Path of Action

Exodus 18:20

וְהִזְהַרְתָּה אֶתְהֶם אֶת הַחֻקִּים וְאֶת הַתּוֹרֹת, וְהוֹדַעְתָּ
לָהֶם אֶת הַדֶּרֶךְ יֵלְכוּ בָהּ, וְאֶת הַמַּעֲשֶׂה אֲשֶׁר יַעֲשׂוּן.

Instruct them on the statutes and the teachings; make known to them the way on which they should go, and the actions that they should do.

Initial word panel to the book of Exodus in the *Duke of Sussex's German Pentateuch*, a decorated Hebrew parchment codex of the fourteenth century. (British Library, London)

TEXT 2

The Meaning of "Torah"

Rabbi Yehudah Loew ("Maharal") of Prague, *Gur Aryeh*, Genesis 1:1

שֶׁהֲרֵי לָשׁוֹן 'תּוֹרָה' הוּא לָשׁוֹן הוֹרָאָה, לְהוֹרוֹת לָנוּ הַמַּעֲשֶׂה אֲשֶׁר נַעֲשֶׂה. וּלְפִיכָךְ דַּוְקָא תּוֹרַת מֹשֶׁה נִקְרָא "תּוֹרָה", מִפְּנֵי שֶׁבָּהּ כְּתוּבִים הַמִּצְוֹת.

The word *torah* means "instruction" (as in the word *horaah*). [For the function of Torah is] to instruct us in the actions that we should do. That is why it is specifically the Five Books of Moses that are called "Torah," as they contain the *mitzvot*.

RABBI YEHUDAH LOEW (MAHARAL OF PRAGUE) 1525–1609

Talmudist and philosopher. Maharal rose to prominence as leader of the famed Jewish community of Prague. He is the author of more than a dozen works of original philosophic thought, including *Tiferet Yisrael* and *Netsach Yisrael*. He also authored *Gur Aryeh*, a supercommentary to Rashi's biblical commentary; and a commentary on the nonlegal passages of the Talmud. He is buried in the Old Jewish Cemetery of Prague.

ALEPH BEIT
Loren Hodes, charcoal on paper

FIGURE 4.1

Queries in Torah Law through the Ages

Adapted from the *Book of Jewish Knowledge* (Brooklyn, NY: The Rohr Jewish Learning Institute, 2022)

Jews are a scattered people, and from the earliest days of the Diaspora, queries in Torah law were dispatched to Halachic authorities who responded with written answers called *teshuvot*, or "responsa." This correspondence—which continues to this day —has produced a vast trove of Halachic literature, with some rabbinic responders authoring thousands of *teshuvot*. A typical responsum may run for many pages, citing and analyzing dozens of sources from the Talmud, the Talmudic commentaries, the Halachic codes and their commentaries, and previous responsa, and weighing the merits of several proposed solutions before rendering its decision. Presented here is a sampling of queries posed to different Halachists addressing issues of their time and place.

ATLANTA
R. Tobias Geffen
1935 Is Coca-Cola kosher?

NEW YORK
R. Moshe Feinstein
1977 Conjoined twins share a single six-chambered heart, and separating them would save the life of one of them but kill the other. Should the procedure be performed?
1978 When volunteers respond to a medical emergency on Shabbat, are they permitted to drive home after the emergency has been taken care of?

WORMS
R. Ya'ir Bacharach
1699 A woman committed adultery and fears that she is pregnant. Is she permitted to drink a potion that would terminate her pregnancy?
1699 When calculating one's earning for tithing (giving 10% to charity), may a person deduct their business expenses?

ZURICH
R. Mordechai Yaakov Breisch
1963 May a person undergo cosmetic surgery for the purpose of improving their appearance?

BARCELONA
R. Shelomo ben Aderet (Rashba)
c. 1275 Is it appropriate to inscribe the donor's name on a synagogue annex that he donated?

ENTRE RIOS
R. Yosef Aharon Taran
1894 Is the Muscovy duck, a New World species, kosher?

MANCHESTER
R. Yitzchak Yaakov Weiss
c. 1970 Are organ transplants permitted according to Torah law?

KOVNO GHETTO
R. Ephraim Oshry
c. 1941 Should Jews who daily experience starvation, abuse, and forced labor at the hands of the Nazis recite the blessing (instituted by the sages as part of the daily morning prayers) thanking G-d for "not making me a slave"?
c. 1941 Is it permitted to steal a worker's "white card" from the offices of the Ghetto Council to save oneself from being sent to the death camps, knowing that, as a result, someone else will not be saved?

LOMZA
R. Malkiel Tenenbaum
1891 May a couple who are unable to conceive resort to artificial insemination?
1891 Does taking a photograph violate the biblical prohibition against making a graven image?

LVOV
R. Yosef Shaul Nathansohn
1859 Can machine-made matzah be used for the Passover *seder*?
R. Yitzchak Shmelkes
c. 1875 Is it permissible to turn on an electric light on Shabbat?

TIBERIAS
The Sanhedrin under Hillel II
c. 361 Now that a preset calendar has been established for the Jewish year, should Diaspora communities nevertheless continue to observe the additional days of the festivals, which they have been keeping because they were uninformed of the date of the new month set by the Sanhedrin in Israel?

CAIRO
R. David ben Zimra (Radbaz)
c. 1550 May one use medicinal potions made from unearthed mummies?

PUMBEDITA
R. Sherira Gaon
992 Is it permissible to pray in Aramaic?
c. 998 Is one permitted to travel on Shabbat in order to keep up with a caravan that is crossing the desert?

VIENNA
R. Yisrael Isserlin
c. 1450 May one dress as a non-Jew when traveling to a city where Jews are forbidden to enter?

PRESSBURG
R. Moshe Schreiber (Chatam Sofer)
1818 Can the synagogue service be conducted in German instead of Hebrew?

JERUSALEM
R. Ovadia Yosef
1976 Should terrorists be released in order to free the hostages being held in Entebbe?
c. 1995 Is it permissible to walk past a video camera that's recording on Shabbat?
R. Eliezer Waldenberg
1982 Should a Halachic prohibition be issued against smoking, in light of the evidence of the health risks it entails?
1992 In cases of surrogate motherhood, who is the Halachic mother?

PRAGUE
R. Yechezkel Landau (Noda BiYehudah)
c. 1760 A patient died during surgery to remove bladder stones. May an autopsy be performed in order to further medical knowledge for this procedure?
c. 1760 Is it permitted to hunt animals for sport?

KRAKOW
R. Yoel Sirkis (Bach)
c. 1630 Is it permitted to sing in the synagogue a tune that is used in church liturgy?
c. 1630 A thief asked me if he is allowed to recite the Hamotzi blessing and Grace After Meals on stolen bread.

ELEPHANTINE
Hananiah (a Jewish military officer of the Persian Empire)
c. 400 BCE Instructions to the Jewish garrison regarding the observance of the festival of Passover

MANTUA
R. Yosef Colon (Maharik)
c. 1470 May a Jew wear the "doctors' cape" that attests to their academic accreditation, or does this fall under the Halachic prohibition against "gentile custom"?

ALGIERS
R. Yitzchak bar Sheshet (Rivash)
c. 1400 Two Jews who were forced to convert to Christianity during the 1391 riots in Spain are signed on a *get* (Jewish religious bill of divorce) as witnesses. Is the document valid?

JOHANNESBURG
R. Moshe Sternbuch
c. 1990 What is the blessing for chocolate?
c. 1990 Can one own stock in a company that sells non-kosher food?

II. A HISTORY OF HALACHAH

The Tanach, the Talmud, and the Midrashim are "generic" books of Torah, in which different types of teachings—historical, legal, philosophical, moral, mystical, etc.—are included in the same books and woven into the same narratives. Following the completion of the Talmud, Torah learning underwent a transition from being exclusively teacher-based to an increasing reliance on books as sources of Torah knowledge. This resulted in the creation of more specialized Torah works, including books of Halachah.

TEXT 3

Laws of the Reading of the Shema—Version 1

Mishnah, Berachot 1:1–3

מֵאֵימָתַי קוֹרִין אֶת שְׁמַע בְּעַרְבִית? מִשָּׁעָה שֶׁהַכֹּהֲנִים נִכְנָסִים לֶאֱכֹל בִּתְרוּמָתָן, עַד סוֹף הָאַשְׁמוּרָה הָרִאשׁוֹנָה, דִּבְרֵי רַבִּי אֱלִיעֶזֶר. וַחֲכָמִים אוֹמְרִים: עַד חֲצוֹת. רַבָּן גַּמְלִיאֵל אוֹמֵר: עַד שֶׁיַּעֲלֶה עַמּוּד הַשָּׁחַר. מַעֲשֶׂה שֶׁבָּאוּ בָנָיו מִבֵּית הַמִּשְׁתֶּה, אָמְרוּ לוֹ: לֹא קָרִינוּ אֶת שְׁמַע. אָמַר לָהֶם: אִם לֹא עָלָה עַמּוּד הַשַּׁחַר, חַיָּבִין אַתֶּם לִקְרוֹת. וְלֹא זוֹ בִּלְבַד, אֶלָּא כָּל מַה שֶּׁאָמְרוּ חֲכָמִים עַד חֲצוֹת, מִצְוָתָן עַד שֶׁיַּעֲלֶה עַמּוּד הַשָּׁחַר. הֶקְטֵר חֲלָבִים וְאֵבָרִים, מִצְוָתָן עַד שֶׁיַּעֲלֶה עַמּוּד הַשָּׁחַר. וְכָל הַנֶּאֱכָלִים לְיוֹם אֶחָד, מִצְוָתָן עַד שֶׁיַּעֲלֶה עַמּוּד הַשָּׁחַר. אִם כֵּן, לָמָּה אָמְרוּ חֲכָמִים עַד חֲצוֹת? כְּדֵי לְהַרְחִיק אֶת הָאָדָם מִן הָעֲבֵרָה.

MISHNAH

The first authoritative work of Jewish law that was codified in writing. The Mishnah contains the oral traditions that were passed down from teacher to student; it supplements, clarifies, and systematizes the commandments of the Torah. Due to the continual persecution of the Jewish people, it became increasingly difficult to guarantee that these traditions would not be forgotten. Rabbi Yehudah Hanasi therefore redacted the Mishnah at the end of the 2nd century. It serves as the foundation for the Talmud.

מֵאֵימָתַי קוֹרִין אֶת שְׁמַע בְּשַׁחֲרִית? מִשֶּׁיַּכִּיר בֵּין תְּכֵלֶת לְלָבָן. רַבִּי אֱלִיעֶזֶר אוֹמֵר: בֵּין תְּכֵלֶת לְכַרְתִּי. וְגוֹמְרָהּ עַד הָנֵץ הַחַמָּה. רַבִּי יְהוֹשֻׁעַ אוֹמֵר: עַד שָׁלֹשׁ שָׁעוֹת, שֶׁכֵּן דֶּרֶךְ בְּנֵי מְלָכִים לַעֲמֹד בְּשָׁלֹשׁ שָׁעוֹת . . .

בֵּית שַׁמַּאי אוֹמְרִים: בָּעֶרֶב כָּל אָדָם יַטּוּ וְיִקְרְאוּ, וּבַבֹּקֶר יַעַמְדוּ, שֶׁנֶּאֱמַר: "וּבְשָׁכְבְּךָ וּבְקוּמֶךָ" (דְּבָרִים ו, ז). וּבֵית הִלֵּל אוֹמְרִים: כָּל אָדָם קוֹרֵא כְדַרְכּוֹ, שֶׁנֶּאֱמַר: "וּבְלֶכְתְּךָ בַדֶּרֶךְ" (שָׁם). אִם כֵּן, לָמָּה נֶאֱמַר "וּבְשָׁכְבְּךָ וּבְקוּמֶךָ"? בְּשָׁעָה שֶׁבְּנֵי אָדָם שׁוֹכְבִים, וּבְשָׁעָה שֶׁבְּנֵי אָדָם עוֹמְדִים.

From when do we read Shema in the evening? From the time when the *Kohanim* enter to partake of their *terumah*, until the end of the first watch. This is the opinion of Rabbi Eliezer. The sages say: Until midnight. Rabban Gamliel says: Until dawn. It once happened that [Rabban Gamliel's] sons returned from a party, and they said to him, "We did not read the Shema." Said he to them: "If dawn has not risen, you are obligated to read." And not only in this case, but in every case that the sages said "until midnight," the mitzvah can be fulfilled until dawn. The mitzvah of burning of fats and limbs [of the offerings in the Holy Temple] is until dawn. For all the [Temple] offerings that can be eaten for one day, the mitzvah is until dawn. If so, why did the sages say, "Until midnight"? In order to distance a person from transgressing.

From when do we read Shema in the morning? From when a person can distinguish between sky-blue and white. Rabbi Eliezer says: From when a person can distinguish between sky-blue and leek-green. And one should finish it until sunrise. Rabbi Yehoshua says: Until three hours [into the day], as that is the habit of royalty—to rise at three hours. . . .

The sages of the school of Shamai say: In the evening, every person should recline [while reading the Shema], and in the morning they should stand, as it is written, "When you lie down and when you rise" (DEUTERONOMY 6:7). The sages of the school of Hillel say: Every person should read after their manner, as it is written, "And when you go on your way" (IBID.). If so, why does it say, "When you lie down and when you rise"? At the time when people lie down, and the time when people rise.

TEXT 4

Laws of the Reading of the Shema—Version 2

Maimonides, *Mishneh Torah*, Laws of the Reading of Shema, 1:1–11

פַּעֲמַיִם בְּכָל יוֹם קוֹרְאִין קְרִיאַת שְׁמַע, בָּעֶרֶב וּבַבֹּקֶר.
שֶׁנֶּאֱמַר: "וּבְשָׁכְבְּךָ וּבְקוּמֶךָ" (דְּבָרִים ו, ז),
בְּשָׁעָה שֶׁדֶּרֶךְ בְּנֵי אָדָם שׁוֹכְבִין, וְזֶה הוּא לַיְלָה;
וּבְשָׁעָה שֶׁדֶּרֶךְ בְּנֵי אָדָם עוֹמְדִין, וְזֶה הוּא יוֹם.

וּמַה הוּא קוֹרֵא? שְׁלֹשָׁה פָּרָשִׁיּוֹת. אֵלּוּ הֵן: "שְׁמַע" (דְּבָרִים ו, ד-ט), "וְהָיָה אִם שָׁמֹעַ" (שָׁם יא, יג-כא), "וַיֹּאמֶר" (בַּמִּדְבָּר טו, לז-מא) . . . וּקְרִיאַת שָׁלֹשׁ פָּרָשִׁיּוֹת אֵלּוּ עַל סֵדֶר זֶה הִיא הַנִּקְרֵאת "קְרִיאַת שְׁמַע" . . .

אֵיזֶה הוּא זְמַן קְרִיאַת שְׁמַע בַּלַּיְלָה? מִצְוָתָהּ מִשְּׁעַת יְצִיאַת הַכּוֹכָבִים עַד חֲצִי הַלַּיְלָה. וְאִם עָבַר וְאִחֵר וְקָרָא עַד שֶׁלֹּא עָלָה עַמּוּד הַשַּׁחַר, יָצָא יְדֵי חוֹבָתוֹ. שֶׁלֹּא אָמְרוּ עַד חֲצוֹת אֶלָּא כְּדֵי לְהַרְחִיק אָדָם מִן הַפְּשִׁיעָה . . .

וְאֵי זֶה הוּא זְמַנָּהּ בַּיּוֹם? מִצְוָתָהּ שֶׁיַּתְחִיל לִקְרוֹת קֹדֶם הָנֵץ הַחַמָּה, כְּדֵי שֶׁיִּגְמֹר לִקְרוֹת וּלְבָרֵךְ בְּרָכָה אַחֲרוֹנָה עִם הָנֵץ הַחַמָּה. וְשִׁעוּר זֶה כְּמוֹ [עִשּׂוּר] שָׁעָה קֹדֶם שֶׁתַּעֲלֶה הַשֶּׁמֶשׁ. וְאִם אִחֵר וְקָרָא קְרִיאַת שְׁמַע אַחַר שֶׁתַּעֲלֶה הַשֶּׁמֶשׁ, יָצָא יְדֵי חוֹבָתוֹ, שֶׁעוֹנָתָהּ עַד סוֹף שָׁלֹשׁ שָׁעוֹת בַּיּוֹם לְמִי שֶׁעָבַר וְאִחֵר.

The Shema is read twice every day, in the evening and in the morning. As it is written, "When you lie down and when you rise" (DEUTERONOMY 6:7)—meaning, during the time when people lie down [to sleep], which is at night, and during the time when people get up, which is the day.

What does one read? Three Torah portions. These are: "Hear, O Israel . . ." (DEUTERONOMY 6:4–9), "And it will be . . . " (DEUTERONOMY 11:13–21), "And [G-d] said . . ." (NUMBERS 15:37–41). . . .

RABBI MOSHE BEN MAIMON (MAIMONIDES, RAMBAM) 1135–1204

Halachist, philosopher, author, and physician. Maimonides was born in Córdoba, Spain. After the conquest of Córdoba by the Almohads, he fled Spain and eventually settled in Cairo, Egypt. There, he became the leader of the Jewish community and served as court physician to the vizier of Egypt. He is most noted for authoring the *Mishneh Torah*, an encyclopedic arrangement of Jewish law; and for his philosophical work, *Guide for the Perplexed*. His rulings on Jewish law are integral to the formation of halachic consensus.

Reading these three portions in this order is what is called "reading the Shema." . . .

When is the time for reading the Shema? In the evening, the mitzvah can be fulfilled from when the stars come out, until midnight. However, if a person transgressed and delayed, as long as they read the Shema before dawn, they have fulfilled their obligation, as the rule "until midnight" was only said in order to distance a person from negligence. . . .

When is its time by day? The mitzvah is to begin reading before sunrise, so as to conclude the reading of the Shema and make the last blessing [which follows the Shema] with the rising of the sun. This interval is about a tenth of an hour before sunrise. One who delayed and read the Shema after sunrise has fulfilled their obligation, as the time for reading the Shema, for one who delayed, is until the end of the first three hours of the day.

QUESTION

What are the main differences between Text 3 and Text 4?

III. THE HALACHIC WORKS

Halachic works fall under four general categories: (1) Halachic digests of the Talmud, which isolate the final Halachic rulings from the plethora of debates and deliberations in the Talmudic text; (2) Halachic codes, which arrange the Torah's laws by topic and are designed to serve as a Halachic guide for the "end user"; (3) Halachic commentaries, which explain, debate, supplement, and compare between other Halachic works; (4) Halachic responsa, which address specific queries in Torah law.

FIGURE 4.2

The Tree of Halachah

See next page.

TEACHER AND STUDENT
Inbal Levin, New York.

FIGURE 4.2

The Tree of Halachah

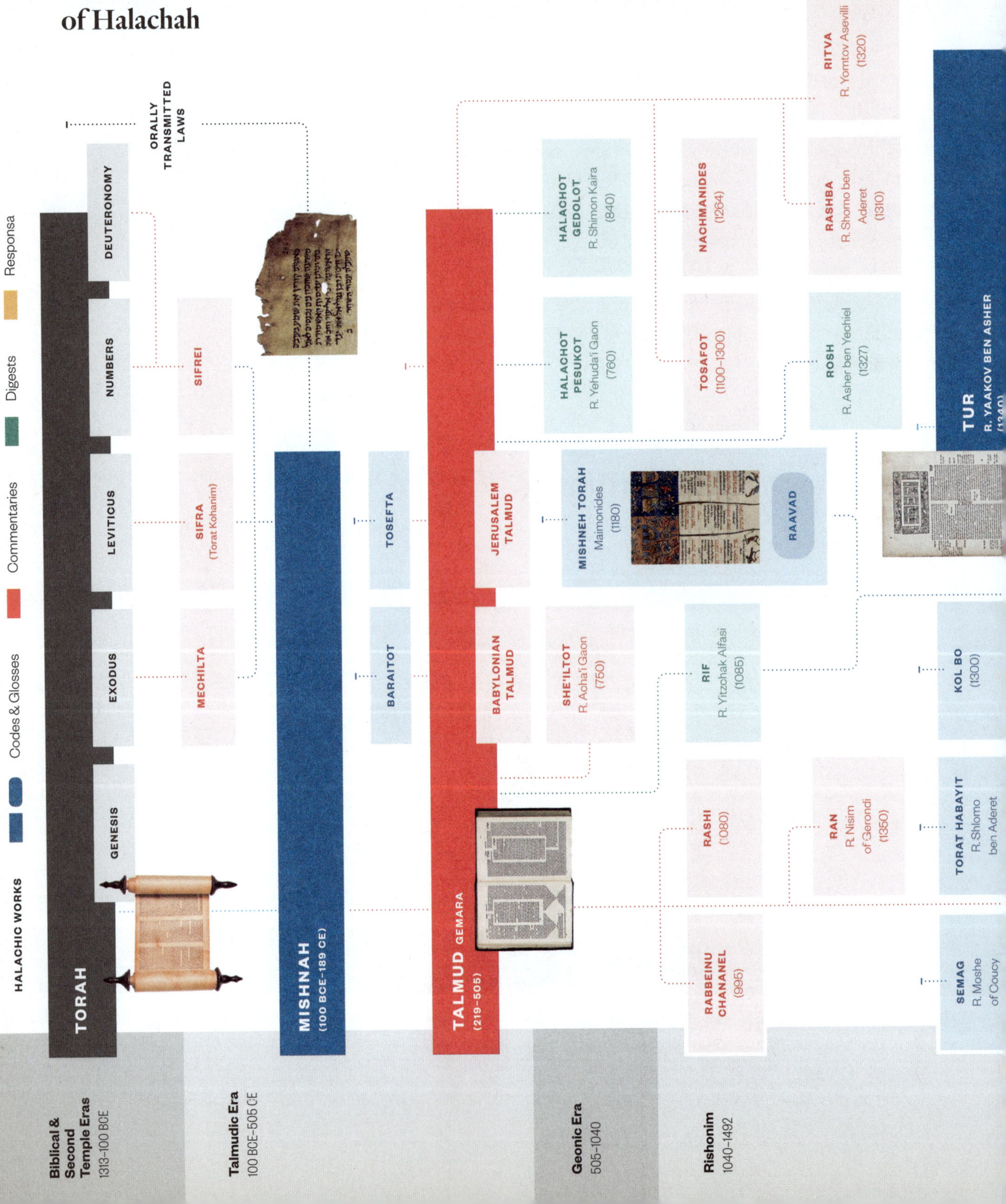

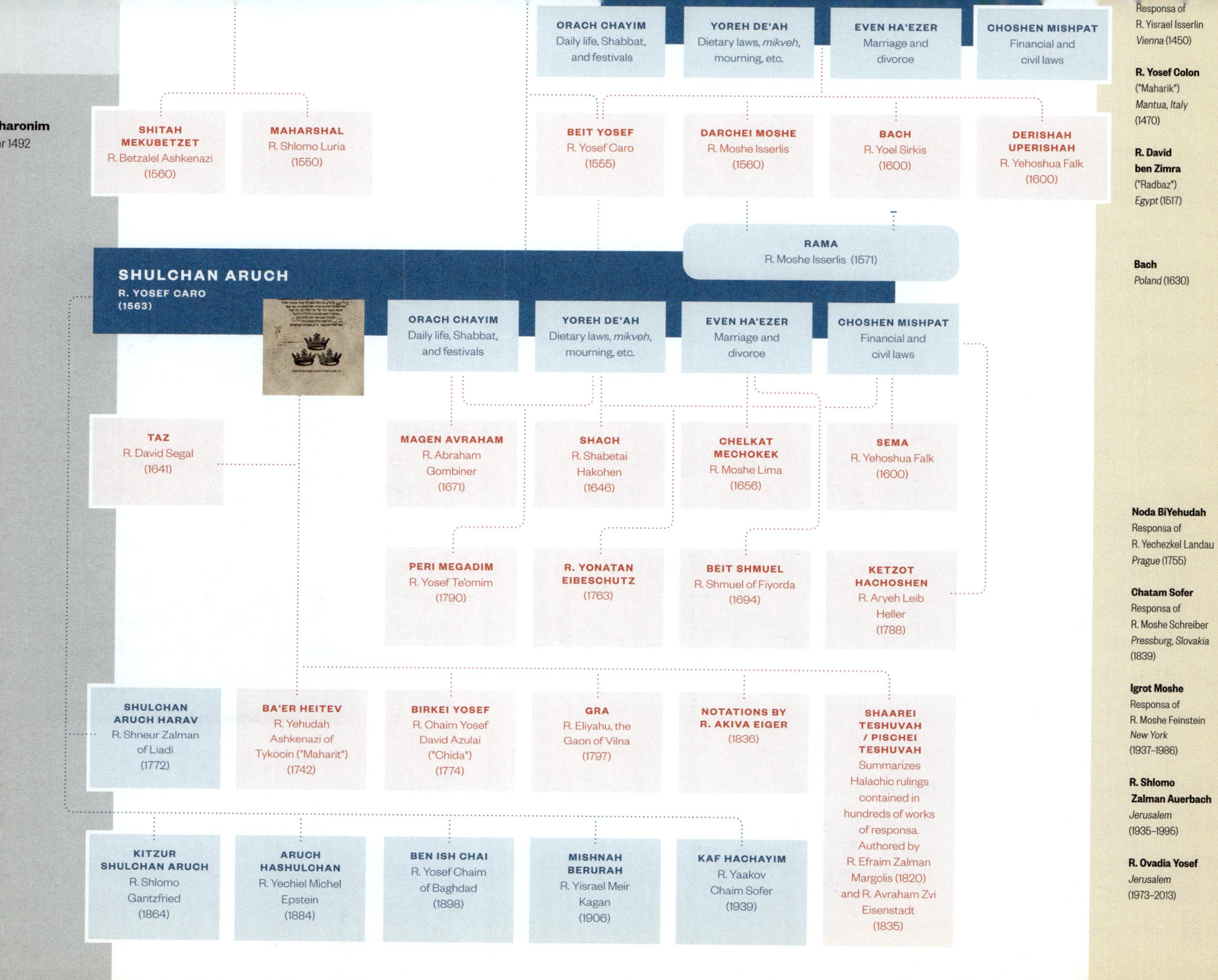

ORACH CHAYIM
Daily life, Shabbat, and festivals
YOREH DE'AH
Dietary laws, mikveh, mourning, etc.
EVEN HA'EZER
Marriage and divorce
CHOSHEN MISHPAT
Financial and civil laws
Responsa of R. Yisrael Isserlin Vienna (1450)
R. Yosef Colon ("Maharik") Mantua, Italy (1470)
R. David ben Zimra ("Radbaz") Egypt (1517)
Acharonim
After 1492
SHITAH MEKUBETZET
R. Betzalel Ashkenazi (1560)
MAHARSHAL
R. Shlomo Luria (1550)
BEIT YOSEF
R. Yosef Caro (1555)
DARCHEI MOSHE
R. Moshe Isserlis (1560)
BACH
R. Yoel Sirkis (1600)
DERISHAH UPERISHAH
R. Yehoshua Falk (1600)
RAMA
R. Moshe Isserlis (1571)
Bach
Poland (1630)
SHULCHAN ARUCH
R. YOSEF CARO (1563)
ORACH CHAYIM
Daily life, Shabbat, and festivals
YOREH DE'AH
Dietary laws, mikveh, mourning, etc.
EVEN HA'EZER
Marriage and divorce
CHOSHEN MISHPAT
Financial and civil laws
TAZ
R. David Segal (1641)
MAGEN AVRAHAM
R. Abraham Gombiner (1671)
SHACH
R. Shabetai Hakohen (1646)
CHELKAT MECHOKEK
R. Moshe Lima (1656)
SEMA
R. Yehoshua Falk (1600)
Noda BiYehudah
Responsa of R. Yechezkel Landau Prague (1755)
PERI MEGADIM
R. Yosef Te'omim (1790)
R. YONATAN EIBESCHUTZ
(1763)
BEIT SHMUEL
R. Shmuel of Fiyorda (1694)
KETZOT HACHOSHEN
R. Aryeh Leib Heller (1788)
Chatam Sofer
Responsa of R. Moshe Schreiber Pressburg, Slovakia (1839)
SHULCHAN ARUCH HARAV
R. Shneur Zalman of Liadi (1772)
BA'ER HEITEV
R. Yehudah Ashkenazi of Tykocin ("Maharit") (1742)
BIRKEI YOSEF
R. Chaim Yosef David Azulai ("Chida") (1774)
GRA
R. Eliyahu, the Gaon of Vilna (1797)
NOTATIONS BY R. AKIVA EIGER
(1836)
SHAAREI TESHUVAH / PISCHEI TESHUVAH
Summarizes Halachic rulings contained in hundreds of works of responsa. Authored by R. Efraim Zalman Margolis (1820) and R. Avraham Zvi Eisenstadt (1835)
Igrot Moshe
Responsa of R. Moshe Feinstein New York (1937–1986)
R. Shlomo Zalman Auerbach
Jerusalem (1935–1995)
KITZUR SHULCHAN ARUCH
R. Shlomo Gantzfried (1864)
ARUCH HASHULCHAN
R. Yechiel Michel Epstein (1884)
BEN ISH CHAI
R. Yosef Chaim of Baghdad (1898)
MISHNAH BERURAH
R. Yisrael Meir Kagan (1906)
KAF HACHAYIM
R. Yaakov Chaim Sofer (1939)
R. Ovadia Yosef
Jerusalem (1973–2013)

IV. A HALACHIC CASE STUDY: CAN WE SAVE ONE LIFE AT THE EXPENSE OF ANOTHER?

In this section, we explore a Halachic case study, tracing a set of Halachic principles from their biblical and Talmudic origins, through the writings of the early Halachists, to their codification in the Shulchan Aruch and its commentaries, all the way to their application in a 20th-century responsum.

TEXT 5

The Divine Image

Genesis 1:27

וַיִּבְרָא אֱלֹקִים אֶת הָאָדָם בְּצַלְמוֹ,
בְּצֶלֶם אֱלֹקִים בָּרָא אֹתוֹ;
זָכָר וּנְקֵבָה בָּרָא אֹתָם.

G-d created the human in His image;
in the image of G-d He created him;
male and female He created them.

NOTE: Shaded area shows the placement of this text on "The Tree of Halachah" map on pages 158–159.

DAY 6 (detail)
From the series *The Seven Days of Creation*, Yoram Raanan, pastel crayon over acrylic, Israel.

TEXT 6

The First Commandment

Mechilta DeRabbi Yishma'el, Exodus 20:14

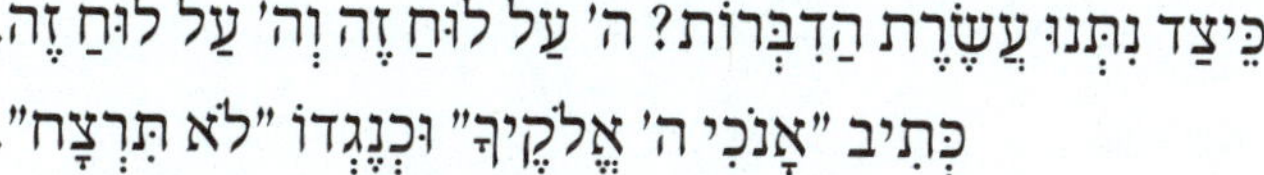

כֵּיצַד נִתְּנוּ עֲשֶׂרֶת הַדִּבְּרוֹת? ה' עַל לוּחַ זֶה וְה' עַל לוּחַ זֶה.
כְּתִיב "אָנֹכִי ה' אֱלֹקֶיךָ" וּכְנֶגְדוֹ "לֹא תִרְצָח".
מַגִּיד הַכָּתוּב שֶׁכָּל מִי שֶׁשּׁוֹפֵךְ דָּם -
מַעֲלֶה עָלָיו הַכָּתוּב כְּאִלּוּ מְמַעֵט בִּדְמוּת הַמֶּלֶךְ.

How were the Ten Commandments given? Five on one tablet, and five on the other tablet. [On one tablet] it says, "I am the L-rd your G-d," and opposite it [on the other tablet] it says, "Do not murder." This teaches us that anyone who spills blood, the Torah considers it as if they have diminished the stature of the Almighty.

MECHILTA

A halachic Midrash to Exodus. Midrash is the designation of a particular genre of rabbinic literature usually forming a running commentary on specific books of the Bible. The name *Mechilta* means "rule" and was given to this Midrash because its comments and explanations are based on fixed rules of exegesis. This work is often attributed to Rabbi Yishmael ben Elisha, a contemporary of Rabbi Akiva, though there are some references to later sages in this work.

TEXT 7

Mitzvot to Live By

Leviticus 18:5

וּשְׁמַרְתֶּם אֶת חֻקֹּתַי וְאֶת מִשְׁפָּטַי,
אֲשֶׁר יַעֲשֶׂה אֹתָם הָאָדָם וָחַי בָּהֶם;
אֲנִי ה'.

You shall keep My statutes and My laws,
which a person shall do and live by them;
I am G-d.

TEXT 8

Transgression or Death?

Talmud, Sanhedrin 74a

כָּל עֲבֵרוֹת שֶׁבַּתּוֹרָה, אִם אוֹמְרִין לְאָדָם עֲבוֹר וְאַל תֵּהָרֵג,
יַעֲבוֹר וְאַל יֵהָרֵג . . .
"וָחַי בָּהֶם", וְלֹא שֶׁיָּמוּת בָּהֶם.

With all the transgressions of the Torah, if a person is told, "transgress, so that you should not be killed," they should transgress rather than be killed. . . . [For the Torah states,] "Live by them"—not die by them.

BABYLONIAN TALMUD

A literary work of monumental proportions that draws upon the legal, spiritual, intellectual, ethical, and historical traditions of Judaism. The 37 tractates of the Babylonian Talmud contain the teachings of the Jewish sages from the period after the destruction of the 2nd Temple through the 5th century CE. It has served as the primary vehicle for the transmission of the Oral Law and the education of Jews over the centuries; it is the entry point for all subsequent legal, ethical, and theological Jewish scholarship.

TEXT 9

Saving a Life on Shabbat

Mishnah, Yoma 8:7

מִי שֶׁנָּפְלָה עָלָיו מַפּוֹלֶת,
סָפֵק הוּא שָׁם סָפֵק אֵינוֹ שָׁם, סָפֵק חַי סָפֵק מֵת . . .
מְפַקְּחִין עָלָיו אֶת הַגַּל.
מְצָאוּהוּ חַי, מְפַקְּחִין.

If a collapsed building falls on someone [on Shabbat], even if it is doubtful whether they are there or they aren't there, [and furthermore it is doubtful] whether they are alive or dead, . . . we must clear the rubble heap from them. If the person is found alive, we continue clearing the rubble.

TEXT 10

The Life of the Mortally Wounded

Talmud, Yoma 85a

"מְצָאוּהוּ חַי", פְּשִׁיטָא!
לֹא צְרִיכָא דַאֲפִילוּ לְחַיֵּי שָׁעָה.

[The Mishnah states:] "If the person is found alive, [we continue clearing the rubble]."
Isn't this obvious?
This needs to be stated in order to tell us [that we continue our efforts] even in the case [that the person is mortally wounded and] can only live a short while.

TEXT 11

The Value of a Moment

Rabbi Yitzchak Alfasi, Mo'ed Katan, Chapter 3

הַגּוֹסֵס, הֲרֵי הוּא כְּחַי לְכָל דָּבָר . . . שֶׁנֶּאֱמַר:
(קֹהֶלֶת יב, ו) "עַד אֲשֶׁר לֹא יֵרָתֵק חֶבֶל הַכֶּסֶף" . . .
וְהַנּוֹגֵעַ בּוֹ, הֲרֵי זֶה שׁוֹפֵךְ דָּמִים.

A dying person has the [legal] status of a living person in every respect, . . . as it is written (ECCLESIASTES 12:6), "Not until the silver cord snaps . . ." One who touches a dying person [in any way that hastens their death] is a murderer.

RABBI YITZCHAK ALFASI (RIF) 1013–1103

Halachist. A native of the North African Maghreb, Rabbi Yitzchak Alfasi (Rif) studied with Rabbi Chananel of Kairouan, Tunisia. He lived and taught in the Maghreb for most of his life and lived his final years in Spain. Rabbi Alfasi authored a digest of the Talmud, known as Rif, containing only the practical conclusions of the Talmud, excluding the lengthy debates and nonlegal material. As the first comprehensive work of practical Jewish law, Rif had a decisive influence in shaping the consensus of Jewish law.

TEXT 12

Whose Blood Is Redder?

Talmud, Pesachim 25b

הַהוּא דְאָתָא לְקַמֵּיה דְרָבָא. אָמַר לֵיה: "אָמַר לִי מָרֵי דוּרָאִי:
קַטְלֵיה לִפְלָנְיָא, וְאִי לָא קָטִילְנָא לָךְ".
אָמַר לֵיה: "נִקְטְלָךְ וְלָא תִּקְטוֹל. מַאי חָזֵית דְדָמָא דִידָךְ
סוּמָק טְפֵי? דִילְמָא דָמָא דְהַהוּא גַבְרָא סוּמָק טְפֵי?"

A person came before Rava, and said to him: "The chieftain of my village said to me, 'Kill so-and-so, and if you do not do so, I will kill you.'"
Rava said to him: "Let yourself be killed, rather than that you should kill. Why do you think that your blood is redder than theirs? Perhaps the blood of that person is redder?"

QUESTION

How does the argument that "your blood is not redder than theirs" imply that you cannot kill someone in order to save your own life?

TEXT 13

The Logic behind the "Redder Blood" Rule

Rashi's Commentary to Talmud, Pesachim 25b

כְּלוֹמַר: כְּלוּם בָּאתָה לִשָּׁאֵל עַל כָּךְ, אֶלָּא מִפְּנֵי שֶׁאַתָּה יוֹדֵעַ
שֶׁאֵין מִצְוָה עוֹמֶדֶת בִּפְנֵי פִּקּוּחַ נֶפֶשׁ, וְסָבוּר אַתָּה שֶׁאַף זוֹ
תִּדָּחֶה מִפְּנֵי פִּקּוּחַ נַפְשְׁךָ. אֵין זוֹ דוֹמָה לִשְׁאָר עֲבֵרוֹת, דְּמִכָּל
מָקוֹם יֵשׁ כָּאן אִבּוּד נֶפֶשׁ. וְהַתּוֹרָה לֹא הִתִּירָה לִדְחוֹת אֶת
הַמִּצְוָה אֶלָּא מִפְּנֵי חִבַּת נַפְשׁוֹ שֶׁל יִשְׂרָאֵל . . . מִי יֹאמַר
שֶׁנַּפְשְׁךָ חֲבִיבָה לִפְנֵי הַמָּקוֹם יוֹתֵר מִשֶּׁל זֶה? דִּלְמָא שֶׁל
זֶה חֲבִיבָה טְפֵי עָלָיו, וְנִמְצָא עֲבֵרָה נַעֲשֵׂית וְנֶפֶשׁ אֲבוּדָה!

[Rava] is saying: Your premise is that every mitzvah is set aside in order to preserve a life, so you think that also this mitzvah [i.e., the prohibition against murder] should be set aside in order to preserve your life. But this transgression is different from other transgressions in that, in any case, there will be a loss of life. The Torah only allowed the *mitzvot* to be set aside because of the preciousness of a Jewish life. . . . But who says that your life is more precious in G-d's eyes than the other person's life? Perhaps that person's life is more precious, with the result that a transgression will be committed and a life will also be lost!

RABBI SHLOMO YITZCHAKI (RASHI) 1040–1105

Most noted biblical and Talmudic commentator. Born in Troyes, France, Rashi studied in the famed yeshivot of Mainz and Worms. His commentaries on the Pentateuch and the Talmud, which focus on the straightforward meaning of the text, appear in virtually every edition of the Talmud and Bible.

TEXT 14

The Dilemma of the Water Jug

Talmud, Bava Metzi'a 62a

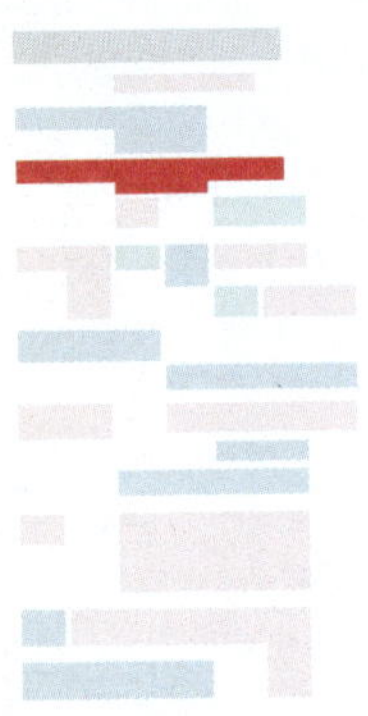

שְׁנַיִם שֶׁהָיוּ מְהַלְּכִין בַּדֶּרֶךְ, וּבְיַד אֶחָד מֵהֶן
קִיתוֹן שֶׁל מַיִם. אִם שׁוֹתִין שְׁנֵיהֶם, מֵתִים;
וְאִם שׁוֹתֶה אֶחָד מֵהֶן, מַגִּיעַ לַיִּשׁוּב.

דָּרַשׁ בֶּן פְּטוּרָא: מוּטָב שֶׁיִּשְׁתּוּ שְׁנֵיהֶם וְיָמוּתוּ,
וְאַל יִרְאֶה אֶחָד מֵהֶם בְּמִיתָתוֹ שֶׁל חֲבֵרוֹ.

עַד שֶׁבָּא רַבִּי עֲקִיבָא וְלִמֵּד: "וְחֵי אָחִיךָ עִמָּךְ"
(וַיִּקְרָא כה, לו), חַיֶּיךָ קוֹדְמִים לְחַיֵּי חֲבֵרְךָ.

Two people are traveling, and one of them has a jug of water. If they both drink, both will die [of thirst]; if only one drinks, he will make it to a settled place.

Ben Petora expounded: Better that both should drink and die, than one should witness the death of the other.

But then Rabbi Akiva came and taught: The Torah states, "Your brother shall live *with you*" (LEVITICUS 25:36). Your life comes before the life of your fellow.

QUESTION

What is the difference between Rava's case (Text 12) and Rabbi Akiva's case (Text 14)?

TEXT 15

Whose Water?

Rabbi Betzalel Ashkenazi, *Shitah Mekubetzet*, Bava Metzi'a 62a

שְׁנַיִם שֶׁהָיוּ מְהַלְּכִין בַּדֶּרֶךְ וְכוּ' . . . וְאוֹתוֹ אָדָם שֶׁהַמַּיִם בְּיָדוֹ שׁוֹתֶה וּמַצִּיל נַפְשׁוֹ, דְחַיָיו קוֹדְמִים לְהַצִיל אֶת עַצְמוֹ. חֲטָפָן אֶחָד מֵהֶם וְשָׁתָה וּמֵת חֲבֵרוֹ עַל יָדוֹ, חַיָב בְּדִינֵי שָׁמַיִם. כֵּן נִרְאֶה, דְ"מַאי חָזִית דְדָמֵיה סוּמָק טְפֵי".

Regarding the case of the two travelers . . . where the law is that the one who has the water may drink it to save their own life, based on the principle that "your life comes before the life of your fellow": . . . It would seem, however, that if one of them grabbed the water away from the other and drank it, causing the other to die, that person would be guilty in the eyes of Heaven, as the principle, "Why do you think that your blood is redder?" would apply in this case.

RABBI BETZALEL ASHKENAZI, C. 1520–1592

Rabbi and scholar; lived in Egypt and Israel. While in Egypt he studied under the Radbaz and, upon the latter's immigration to Israel, assumed leadership of the community. Later, he himself immigrated to Israel, where he became the leader of the Jerusalem community. He is best known for his *Shitah Mekubetset*, an anthology of classical commentaries to the Talmud. His most important disciple was the famous kabbalist, Rabbi Yitzchak Luria.

TEXT 16

The Besieged Caravan

Jerusalem Talmud, Terumot 8:4

סִיעוֹת בְּנֵי אָדָם שֶׁהָיוּ מְהַלְּכִין בַּדֶּרֶךְ, וּפָגְעוּ לָהֶן גּוֹיִם וְאָמְרוּ:
"תְּנוּ לָנוּ אֶחָד מִכֶּם וְנַהֲרוֹג אוֹתוֹ,
וְאִם לָאו הֲרֵי אָנוּ הוֹרְגִין אֶת כּוּלְּכֶם".
אֲפִילוּ כּוּלָּן נֶהֱרָגִים, אַל יִמְסְרוּ נֶפֶשׁ אַחַת מִיִּשְׂרָאֵל.

If a group of people are traveling on the road, and
they encounter heathens who say to them,
"Give us one of you that we may kill him,
otherwise we shall kill you all,"
even if all of them will be killed, they should
not hand over a single Jewish soul.

JERUSALEM TALMUD

A commentary to the Mishnah, compiled during the 4th and 5th centuries. The Jerusalem Talmud predates its Babylonian counterpart by 100 years and is written in both Hebrew and Aramaic. While the Babylonian Talmud is the most authoritative source for Jewish law, the Jerusalem Talmud remains an invaluable source for the spiritual, intellectual, ethical, historical, and legal traditions of Judaism.

LA CARAVANE (THE CARAVAN), Jacques Gabriel Huquier (1730–1805), France, mid- to late eighteenth century. (The Metropolitan Museum of Art, New York)

TEXT 17

The "White Cards" in the Kovno Ghetto

Rabbi Ephraim Oshry, *Responsa from the Depths*, Vol. 5, Responsum 1

בְּיוֹם ט"ז אֱלוּל תש"א, 8 סֶפְּטֶמְבֶּר שְׁנַת 1941 לְמִסְפָּרָם, בָּא לְלִיטָא . . . "אוֹבֶּערְפִירֶער" שֶׁל הָס.ס. גֶעקֶע, שֶׁחִסֵּל בְּסוֹפוֹ שֶׁל דָּבָר גַּם אֶת גֵּטוֹ קוֹבְנָה. שְׁמוֹ הַמְנֹאָץ שֶׁל רָשָׁע מְרֻשָּׁע גֶּרְמָנִי זֶה הָלַךְ לְפָנָיו כְּרוֹצֵחַ שׁוֹאֵף דָּם מִמַּדְרֵגָה רִאשׁוֹנָה, וּדְבַר בּוֹאוֹ לְלִיטָא עוֹרֵר בֶּהָלָה גְדוֹלָה בֵּין כְּלוּאֵי הַגֵּטוֹ, כִּי מִיָּד לְבוֹאוֹ הוֹצִיא לַהוֹרֵג מִסְפַּר יְהוּדִים. וְאָז נִתְעוֹרְרָה שְׁאֵלַת הַכַּרְטִיסִים הַלְּבָנִים שֶׁהָיוּ יְדוּעִים לְשִׁמְצָה . . .

וְזֶה הַדָּבָר: הַמְפַקֵּד הַגֶּרְמָנִי, יִמַּח שְׁמוֹ, עַל עִנְיְנֵי גֵּטוֹ קוֹבְנָה, יַארְדָאן, נָתַן צַו לְמוֹעֶצֶת הַזְּקֵנִים שֶׁל הַגֵּטוֹ . . . שֶׁעֲלֵיהֶם לְחַלֵּק בֵּין בַּעֲלֵי הַמְּלָאכָה הַנִּמְצָאִים בַּגֵּטוֹ 5000 כַּרְטִיסִים לְבָנִים שֶׁמָּסַר לָהֶם, וְרַק לְאֵלֶּה תִּנָּתֵן הָרְשׁוּת לְהִשָּׁאֵר בַּגֵּטוֹ עִם מִשְׁפְּחוֹתֵיהֶם, וְהַיֶּתֶר יְחֻסְלוּ. וּבָעֵת הַהִיא נִמְצְאוּ בַּגֵּטוֹ כִּשְׁלוֹשִׁים אֶלֶף יְהוּדִים וּבֵינֵיהֶם כַּעֲשֶׂרֶת אֲלָפִים בַּעֲלֵי מְלָאכָה.

נִשְׁאַלְתִּי, הַאִם יָאוּת עַבְדֵי אֵלֶּה שֶׁחוֹטְפִים כַּרְטִיסִים לְבָנִים כְּדֵי לְהַצִּיל אֶת נַפְשָׁם, כִּי הֲלֹא בָּזֶה . . . דּוֹחִים נֶפֶשׁ יְהוּדִי אַחֵר וּמוֹנְעִים אֶת הַצָּלָתוֹ וְהַצָּלַת מִשְׁפַּחְתּוֹ?

On Elul 16, 5701 (September 8, 1941), the Nazi SS Commander Gocke arrived in Lithuania (it was he who in the end liquidated the Kovno Ghetto). The reputation of this evil and bloodthirsty murderer had preceded him, evoking panic among those

RABBI EPHRAIM OSHRY
1914–2003

Halachist. Rabbi Oshry was a young rabbinical scholar in Kovno, the second-largest city in Lithuania, when the Nazis invaded in June 1941. He carefully recorded the halachic questions that Lithuanian Jews asked him during the war, as well as his responses—writing them on bits of paper torn from cement sacks he carried on forced labor—and buried them in tin cans. He dug up the cans after the war and used these notes as the basis for his collection of Holocaust responsa, the five-volume *She'elot Uteshuvot Mimaamakim*.

imprisoned in the ghetto, as immediately upon his arrival, he executed a number of Jews. At that time, there arose the issue of the notorious "white cards." . . .

The matter was as follows: Yardan, the German commander of the Kovno Ghetto, instructed the Jewish Council to distribute among the workers in the ghetto 5,000 white cards, which he gave to them. These individuals would be the only ones allowed to remain in the ghetto with their families, while the rest would be liquidated. At the time, there were about 30,000 Jews in the ghetto, including 10,000 workers. . . .

I was asked: Are those who were grabbing white cards for themselves to save themselves acting properly, knowing that they are preventing another Jewish family from being saved?

KOVNO GHETTO, MAIN GATE 1943
Esther Lurie, lithograph of ink and pencil on paper. (The United States Holocaust Memorial Museum Collection, Washington, D.C.)

QUESTION

Based on the Halachic precedents we reviewed so far (Texts 12, 13, 14, 15, and 16), how would you rule on the question posed to Rabbi Oshry? Is a person permitted to steal a "white card" from the ghetto council offices in order to save their own life and their family's?

TEXT 18

Deflecting Damage (Part I)

Rabbi Moshe Isserlis, Glosses to Shulchan Aruch, *Choshen Mishpat*, 388:2

הָיָה רוֹאֶה נֶזֶק בָּא עָלָיו,
מֻתָּר לְהַצִּיל עַצְמוֹ,
אַף עַל פִּי שֶׁעַל יְדֵי זֶה בָּא הַנֶּזֶק לְאַחֵר
(נִמּוּקֵי יוֹסֵף, פֶּרֶק הַשֻּׁתָּפִין).

A person who anticipates damage that will occur to them is permitted to save themselves, even though this will cause the damage to come to another person, [as cited in the] *Nimukei Yosef* commentary to [Talmud, Bava Batra], chapter of *Hashutafin*.

RABBI MOSHE ISSERLIS (RAMA) 1525–1572

Halachist. Rama served as rabbi in Krakow, Poland, and is considered the definitive authority on Jewish law among Ashkenazic Jewry. Rama authored glosses (known as the *Mapah*) on the Shulchan Aruch; and *Darchei Moshe*, a commentary on the halachic compendium *Arbaah Turim*.

TEXT 19

Deflecting Damage (Part II)

Rabbi Yehoshua Falk, *Sema*, ad loc.

שָׁם בְּנִמּוּקֵי יוֹסֵף סִיֵּם וְכָתַב,
דְּאִם כְּבָר בָּא עָלָיו, אָסוּר לְסַלְּקוֹ מִמֶּנּוּ
כְּשֶׁגּוֹרֵם בָּזֶה הֶזֵּק לַחֲבֵרוֹ.

However, as the *Nimukei Yosef* concludes there, if the damage already arrived in their domain, a person is not permitted to remove it from themselves if that will cause damage to their fellow.

RABBI YEHOSHUA FALK HAKOHEN KATZ
1555–1614

Polish rabbi, Talmudist, and authority on Jewish law. Rabbi Falk is best known for his *Perishah* and *Derishah* commentaries on the *Arbaah Turim*, as well as *Sefer Me'irat Einayim* on the Shulchan Aruch. Rabbi Falk was a pupil of Rabbi Moshe Isserlis and served as head of the yeshiva in Lemberg as well as on the Council of Four Lands, a central body of Jewish authority in Poland.

Initial word panel to the section on damages in Maimonides's *Mishneh Torah*. Produced in Northern Italy, c. 1457, the illumination of this elaborate manuscript is attributed to "Master of the Barbo Missal," and gives a glimpse into the aesthetic of Italy's Jewish community at the time. (The Israel Museum, Jerusalem, and the Metropolitan Museum of Art, New York)

TEXT 20

Deflecting Damage (Part III)

Rabbi Eliyahu of Vilna, Gra's commentary on Shulchan Aruch, ad loc.

יְרוּשַׁלְמִי, בָּבָא קַמָּא, פֶּרֶק ג, הֲלָכָה א:

רָאָה אַמַּת הַמַּיִם שׁוֹטֶפֶת וּבָאָה לְתוֹךְ שָׂדֵהוּ - עַד שֶׁלֹּא נִכְנְסוּ הַמַּיִם לְתוֹךְ שָׂדֵהוּ, רַשַּׁאי לְפַנּוֹתָן לְמָקוֹם אַחֵר; מִשֶּׁנִּכְנְסוּ, אֵין רַשַּׁאי לְפַנּוֹתָן לְמָקוֹם אַחֵר . . .

הָדֵין אַכְסְנַיי פִּרְכָא: עַד דְּלֹא יֵיתוּן רוֹמָאֵי, שָׁרֵי מֵיחַשְׁדוּנֵיה; וּמִן דְּיֵיתוּן רוֹמָאֵי, אָסִיר.

[The source of these laws is from the cases presented in] the Jerusalem Talmud, Bava Kama 3:5:

A person who sees that a water channel is about to flood their field, as long as the water has not yet entered their field, is permitted to divert the water [even though this will cause another's field to be flooded]. But once the water has entered the person's field, they are not permitted to divert it [to another's field]. . . .

Regarding a quartermaster: As long as the legions have not yet arrived, a person is permitted to bribe [the quartermaster not to lodge soldiers in their home, even though this will result in the soldiers being lodged in someone else's home]. But once the legions have arrived, it is forbidden to do so.

RABBI ELIYAHU OF VILNA (VILNA GA'ON, GRA) 1720–1797

Talmudist, halachist, and kabbalist. The Vilna Ga'on was one of the greatest scholars of his day. In addition to Talmud, he excelled in all aspects of Torah study, including kabbalah, and was proficient in secular subjects as well. He left a tremendous legacy, both from his vast writings on the Tanach, Talmud, and Shulchan Aruch, and from the many students that he inspired to Torah and scholarship.

KEY POINTS

1. *The Field of Halachah.* Halachah—meaning "going" and "the way"—is the bottom line of Torah. The field of Halachah is where the biblical commandments, rabbinical ordinances, and Talmudic learning translate into the dos and don'ts of daily life. Halachah addresses every part of a Jew's life, from waking to bedtime, from birth to burial,and from everyday activities to the most extraordinary situations and dilemmas.

2. *The Emergence of Specialized Branches of Torah.* The Tanach, the Talmud, and the Midrashim are "generic" works of Torah, in which various types of teachings—historical, legal, philosophical, moral, mystical, etc.—are incorporated in the same book and woven into the same narratives. Following the completion of the Talmud at the end of the 5th century CE, Torah learning underwent a transition from being exclusively teacher-based to an increased reliance on books as sources of Torah knowledge. This resulted in the creation of more specialized Torah works, including books of Halachah.

3 *Types of Halachic Works.* Halachic works fall under four general categories: (1) Halachic digests of the Talmud, which isolate the final Halachic rulings from the plethora of opinions and deliberations in the Talmudic text; (2) Halachic codes, which arrange the Torah's laws by topic and are designed to serve as a Halachic guide for the "end user"; (3) Halachic commentaries, which explain, debate, supplement, and compare between other Halachic works; (4) Halachic responsa, which address specific queries in Torah law.

4 *Major Halachic Codes.* Two central Halachic codes are: (1) The 14-volume *Mishneh Torah,* authored by Maimonides in the 12th century, which was the first work that systematically codified all the laws of the Torah. (2) The *Shulchan Aruch,* which combines two monumental Halachic works representing, respectively, the Sefardic and Ashkenazic Halachic traditions: the code of law compiled in 1563 by Rabbi Yosef Caro, and the "glosses" appended to it by Rabbi Moshe Isserlis in 1571. The Shulchan Aruch was accepted by all Jewish communities as the fundamental "code of Jewish law," and it became the baseline work on which many subsequent Halachic commentaries and codifications were written.

5 *A Case Study of the Halachic Process.* The Halachic process applies the macro-principles of the Torah to the particulars of everyday life. A case in point is the absolute value that the Torah places on human life, which results in a number of Halachic rules that may, at times, conflict with each other. The Halachic process navigates these conflicts, addressing a number of scenarios in which saving one life results in the loss of another, to determine how a person should act in each case.

6 *Focus on Action.* This case study emphasizes the Torah's conception of moral choice as action-based rather than consequence-based, with the focus being on what a person should or should not do in a given situation.

APPENDIX: THE CASE OF THE CONJOINED TWINS

TEXT 21

The Self-Defense Doctrine

Bamidbar Rabah 21:4

"צָרוֹר אֶת הַמִּדְיָנִים" (בַּמִּדְבָּר כה, יז),
לָמָּה? "כִּי צֹרְרִים הֵם לָכֶם" (שָׁם, יח).
מִכָּאן אָמְרוּ חֲכָמִים: בָּא לְהָרָגְךָ הַשְׁכֵּם לְהָרְגוֹ.

"Attack the Midianites" (NUMBERS 25:17). Why? Because "they are belligerent to you" (IBID., VERSE 18). From here the sages derived: If someone is coming to kill you, preempt them and kill them first.

BAMIDBAR RABAH

An exegetical commentary on the first seven chapters of the book of Numbers and a homiletic commentary on the rest of the book. The first part of *Bamidbar Rabah* is notable for its inclusion of esoteric material; the second half is essentially identical to *Midrash Tanchuma* on the book of Numbers. It was first printed in Constantinople in 1512, together with four other midrashic works on the other four books of the Pentateuch.

FIGHT AGAINST THE MIDIANITES
Print of an illustration by Gerard Hoet, engraving on paper, Gilliam van der Gouwen printmaker (Amsterdam and The Hague: Pieter de Hondt, 1728). (Rijksmuseum, Amsterdam)

TEXT 22

The Parachute

Rabbi Dr. Moshe David Tendler, as cited in "Siamese Twins: An Agonizing Choice," *Assia: A Journal of Jewish Ethics and Halacha*, Vol. IV, No. 1, February 1, 2001

Two men jump out of a burning airplane. The parachute of the first man opens and he falls slowly and safely to earth. The parachute of the second man does not open. As he plunges past his friend, he manages to grab onto his foot and hold on. But the parachute is too small to support both of them. Now they are both plunging to their death. It is morally justified for the first man to kick his friend away, because they would both die if he didn't.

RABBI DR. MOSHE D. TENDLER, PHD
1926–2021

Rabbi and professor. Rabbi Tendler, a son-in-law of Rabbi Moshe Feinstein, was the Rabbi Isaac and Bella Tendler Professor of Jewish Medical Ethics and a Professor of Biology at Yeshiva University. He also served as a Rosh Yeshiva in Yeshivat Rav Yitzchak Elchanan (RIETS) at Yeshiva University. Rabbi Tendler was a renowned expert on medical Halachah, and he wrote a book on the subject.

TEXT 23

The Life-Endangering Birth

Mishnah, Ohalot 7:6

הָאִשָּׁה שֶׁהִיא מַקְשָׁה לֵילֵד,
מְחַתְּכִין אֶת הַוָּלָד בְּמֵעֶיהָ וּמוֹצִיאִין אוֹתוֹ אֵבָרִים אֵבָרִים,
מִפְּנֵי שֶׁחַיֶּיהָ קוֹדְמִין לְחַיָּיו.

יָצָא רֹאשׁוֹ, אֵין נוֹגְעִין בּוֹ, שֶׁאֵין דוֹחִין נֶפֶשׁ מִפְּנֵי נֶפֶשׁ.

If a woman is in difficulty during childbirth,
we cut up the fetus inside her womb
and remove it limb by limb,
for her life takes precedence over the fetus's life.

But if the fetus's head has emerged, we may not touch it, for we may not set aside one life for the sake of another.

TEXT 24

Is the Fetus a *Rodef*?

Talmud, Sanhedrin 72b

אֵיתִיבֵיהּ רַב חִסְדָּא לְרַב הוּנָא:
"יָצָא רֹאשׁוֹ אֵין נוֹגְעִין בּוֹ,
לְפִי שֶׁאֵין דּוֹחִין נֶפֶשׁ מִפְּנֵי נֶפֶשׁ".
וְאַמַּאי? רוֹדֵף הוּא!

שַׁאֲנִי הָתָם, דְּמִשְּׁמַיָּא קָא רָדְפֵי לָהּ.

Rav Chisda raised an objection to Rav Huna:
[The Mishnah states that] "if the fetus's head has emerged, we may not touch it, for we may not set aside one life for the sake of another."
But why? The fetus is a *rodef*!

[The Talmud responds:]
That case is different, as she is being pursued from Heaven.

TEXT 25

Two Babies, One Heart

Rabbi Dr. Moshe Dovid Tendler, "So One May Live," *Assia: A Journal of Ethics and Halacha*, Vol. IV, No. 1, February 1, 2001

Early in September 1977, . . . in Lakewood, New Jersey, Siamese twins were born to a prestigious family of Torah educators. The twins were taken by helicopter, on September 15, to the Children's Hospital in Philadelphia, where Dr. C. Everett Koop, who subsequently became the surgeon general of the United States, was then the hospital's chief of surgery. Immediately after the initial evaluation, it was obvious to all the physicians called in to evaluate the twins that both would die unless they were separated. However, the only way one child would be viable was if the other child was killed during surgery. The question was referred to Rav Moshe Feinstein for his evaluation and decision.

The children, designated Baby A and Baby B, . . . shared one six-chambered heart. The wall separating the essentially normal four chambers from the other two, most likely the stunted heart of Baby A, was too thin to be divided. It was not possible to give the two-chambered heart to Baby A. . . . The entire six-chambered heart had to be given to Baby B, and the life of Baby A would have to be sacrificed.

It was clear to all concerned that this was a major ethical issue. . . . Nurses and doctors at Children's Hospital consulted with their religious guides, and many reported back that they would not be able to participate in the surgery. . . . When the team of twenty or so professionals were awaiting Rav Feinstein's decision, and, indeed, were expressing impatience at the lapse of time, . . . Dr. Koop quieted the group with the following statement: "The ethics and morals involved in this decision are too complex for me. I believe they are too complex for you as well. Therefore, I referred it to an old rabbi on the Lower East Side of New York. He is a great scholar, a saintly individual. He knows how to answer such questions. When he tells me, I too will know."

Doctoral diploma of Israel Baruch Olmo, son of a rabbi from Ferrara, Italy, from the University of Padua, Italy. Handwritten in Latin using ink and gouache on parchment, 1755. (Braginsky Collection 332)

The Four Captives

RABBI ABRAHAM IBN DA'UD (RAAVAD I)
C. 1110–1180

Philosopher and historian. A resident of Spain, Rabbi Abraham ibn Da'ud wrote *Ha'emunah Haramah*, an early work of Jewish philosophy, and is best known as the author of *Sefer Hakabbalah*, which chronicles the transmission of the Oral Torah through the generations, and Jewish history in Spain.

RABBI ABRAHAM IBN DAUD
***SEFER HAKABBALAH*, PP. 13–14, (MANTUA: 1514)**

Some time before [the decline of the Babylonian gaonate], it was ordained by Divine providence that [centers of Torah learning should be established in the west]. This is how it came about.

The commander of a pirate fleet, whose name was Ibn Rumahis, sailed from Cordoba. The fleet sailed as far as the coast of the Land of Israel and swung about to the Greek sea, where it encountered a ship carrying four great scholars, who were traveling from Bari to a city called Sefastin on a fundraising mission.

Ibn Rumahis captured the ship and took the sages prisoneRabbi One of them was Rabbi Chushiel, the father of Rabbi Chananel. Another was Rabbi Moshe, who was taken prisoner with his wife and his young son, Rabbi Hanoch. The third sage was Rabbi Shemariah the son of Rabbi Elchanan. As for the fourth, I do not know his name.

The commander wanted to forcibly violate Rabbi Moshe's wife, as she was exceedingly beautiful. She cried out in Hebrew to her husband, Rabbi Moshe, asking him if those who drown in the sea will be brought back to life at the time of the resurrection of the dead. He replied to her by citing the verse (Psalms 68:23), "Says the L-rd: I will bring them back from Bashan; I will bring them back from the depths of the sea." Upon hearing his words, she threw herself into the sea and drowned.

These sages did not tell a soul about themselves or their wisdom. The

commander sold Rabbi Shemariah for ransom [to the Jewish community] in Alexandria of Egypt, from which Rabbi Shemariah proceeded to the Egyptian capital where he became head [of the academy]. Rabbi Chushiel was ransomed on the African coast, from which he proceeded to the city of Kairouan, which at that time was the greatest of all Muslim cities in the land of the Maghreb. There, Rabbi Chushiel became the head of the academy, and there his son Rabbi Chananel was born. The commander then arrived at Cordoba, where the local Jews ransomed Rabbi Moshe and his son Rabbi Chanoch. They were under the impression that he was an ignoramus.

Now, in Cordoba there was a Torah academy that was presided over by a magistrate by the name of Rabbi Natan, who was a very pious person. The Jews of Spain were not thoroughly versed in the words of the sages; nevertheless, with the little knowledge they did possess, they held study sessions and deliberated their meanings. [One day,] Rabbi Natan was explaining the law in the Talmudic tractate Yoma that "each sprinkling requires immersion," but he was unable to explain it correctly. Thereupon, Rabbi Moshe, who was seated in the corner like an attendant, arose before Rabbi Natan and said to him, "Rabbi, this would result in an excess of immersions!" When Rabbi Natan and the students heard his words, they marveled to each other and asked him to explain the law to them. This he did quite properly. Then each of them asked him all the difficulties that they had, and he replied to them out of the abundance of his wisdom.

When Rabbi Natan walked out of the study hall and the waiting litigants approached him, he said to them: "I shall no longer be your magistrate. This stranger who is garbed in rags is my master, and I will be his disciple. You ought to appoint him magistrate of the community of Cordoba."

This they did. The community assigned Rabbi Moshe a large stipend and honored him with costly garments and a carriage. As a result, the pirate commander wished to retract his sale. However, the king would not permit him to do so, for he was delighted by the fact that the Jews of his domain no longer had need of the people of Babylonia.

Word spread through all of Spain and the Maghreb, and students came to study under him. Moreover, all questions that had formerly been addressed to the Babylonian academies were now directed to him. This affair occurred in the days of R. Sherira Gaon, in about the year 4750 [990 CE].

LESSON 5

MUSAR AND JEWISH PHILOSOPHY

In this lesson, we explore the parallel yet overlapping fields of Torah psychology and Torah philosophy. Musar is the body of Torah teachings that deals with ethics, character development, and spiritual self-improvement; while Jewish philosophy, also known as "Chakirah," discusses the theology and ideology of Judaism. After surveying some of the primary authors and works in both fields, we will also study their treatment of a number of topics such as the origins of Creation, trust, and anger.

LIEDER DES VOLKES (SONG OF THE PEOPLE)
Ephraim Moses Lillian. Illustration from *Lieder des Ghetto (Songs of the Ghetto)*, by Morris Rosenfeld (Berlin, Germany: S. Cavalry & Co., 1903).

I. THE PHILOSOPHY AND PSYCHOLOGY OF JUDAISM

In this section, we introduce the two genres of Torah learning covered in this lesson: Musar, a body of teaching that deals with ethics and character development; and Chakirah, which is the rational exploration of the philosophy and theology of Judaism.

TEXT 1

Inner *Teshuvah*

Maimonides, *Mishneh Torah*, Laws of *Teshuvah* 7:3

אַל תֹּאמַר שֶׁאֵין תְּשׁוּבָה אֶלָּא מֵעֲבֵירוֹת שֶׁיֵּשׁ בָּהֶן מַעֲשֶׂה . . . כָּךְ הוּא צָרִיךְ לְחַפֵּשׂ בְּדֵעוֹת רָעוֹת שֶׁיֵּשׁ לוֹ, וְלָשׁוּב מִן הַכַּעַס וּמִן הָאֵיבָה וּמִן הַקִּנְאָה וּמִן הַהִתּוּל וּמֵרְדִיפַת הַמָּמוֹן וְהַכָּבוֹד וּמֵרְדִיפַת הַמַּאֲכָלוֹת וְכַיּוֹצֵא בָּהֶן; מִן הַכֹּל צָרִיךְ לַחֲזֹר בִּתְשׁוּבָה.

Do not think that *teshuvah* (repentance) is only for sinful actions. . . . A person should also examine their negative character traits—anger, hatred, envy, frivolity, the pursuit of money and honor, gluttony, etc.—and do *teshuvah* for them as well.

RABBI MOSHE BEN MAIMON (MAIMONIDES, RAMBAM) 1135–1204

Halachist, philosopher, author, and physician. Maimonides was born in Córdoba, Spain. After the conquest of Córdoba by the Almohads, he fled Spain and eventually settled in Cairo, Egypt. There, he became the leader of the Jewish community and served as court physician to the vizier of Egypt. He is most noted for authoring the *Mishneh Torah*, an encyclopedic arrangement of Jewish law; and for his philosophical work, *Guide for the Perplexed*. His rulings on Jewish law are integral to the formation of Halachic consensus.

TEXT 2

Faith vs. Understanding

Rabbi Yeshayahu Halevi Horowitz,
Shenei Luchot Haberit 1:40a

"וְיָדַעְתָּ הַיּוֹם וַהֲשֵׁבֹתָ אֶל לְבָבֶךָ כִּי ה' הוּא הָאֱלֹקִים" (דְּבָרִים ד, לט). רָצָה לוֹמַר, יְדִיעָה בַּלֵּב בְּהַשָּׂגָה מוֹפְתִית, נוֹסָף עַל הַקַּבָּלָה מִצַּד אֲבוֹתָיו . . . וְזֶהוּ מְרֻמָּז בְּמַה שֶּׁכָּתוּב: "דַּע אֶת אֱלֹקֵי אָבִיךָ" (דִּבְרֵי הַיָּמִים א כח, ט). רָצָה לוֹמַר, נוֹסָף עַל מַה שֶּׁהֻקְבַּע אֱמוּנָה הָאֱלֹקוּת בִּלְבָבְךָ מִצַּד אָבִיךָ, דְּהַיְנוּ הַקַּבָּלָה אִישׁ מִפִּי אִישׁ, דַּע אַתָּה בְּעַצְמְךָ מִצַּד הַהַשָּׂגָה.

וְזֶהוּ רֶמֶז הַפָּסוּק "זֶה קֵלִי וְאַנְוֵהוּ אֱלֹקֵי אָבִי וַאֲרֹמְמֶנְהוּ" (שְׁמוֹת טו, ב). רָצָה לוֹמַר, כְּשֶׁ"זֶה קֵלִי", שֶׁהוּא קֵלִי מִצַּד הַשָּׂגָתִי וִידִיעָתִי, אָז "וְאַנְוֵהוּ", מִלָּשׁוֹן "אֲנִי וָהוּ" (רַשִׁ"י, שַׁבָּת קלג, ב). רָצָה לוֹמַר, אֲנִי וְהוּא דְּבוּקִים בְּיַחַד כִּבְיָכוֹל, כִּי הַיְדִיעָה נִתְפֶּסֶת בַּלֵּב. אָמְנָם כְּשֶׁאֵין לִי הַיְדִיעָה מִצַּד הַהַשָּׂגָה, רַק מִצַּד הַקַּבָּלָה שֶׁהוּא "אֱלֹקֵי אָבִי", אָז "וַאֲרֹמְמֶנְהוּ", כִּי הוּא רָם וְנִשְׂגָּב מִמֶּנִּי, וַאֲנִי מְרֻחָק מֵאִתּוֹ בְּמַצְפּוּן הַלֵּב.

עַל כֵּן חָל הַחִיּוּב לִהְיוֹת בָּקִי בַּמּוֹפְתִים שֶׁל חוֹבַת הַלְּבָבוֹת, וְיִהְיוּ מוּבָנִים בַּלֵּב הֵיטֵב הֵיטֵב . . . לֵדַע וּלְהָבִין כִּי "ה' אֶחָד וּשְׁמוֹ אֶחָד".

RABBI YESHAYAHU HALEVI HOROWITZ (*SHALAH*)
1565–1630

Kabbalist and author. Rabbi Horowitz was born in Prague and served as rabbi in several prominent Jewish communities, including Frankfurt am Main and his native Prague. After the passing of his wife in 1620, he moved to Israel. In Tiberias, he completed his *Shenei Luchot Haberit*, an encyclopedic compilation of kabbalistic ideas. He is buried in Tiberias, next to Maimonides.

Rabbi Dr. J. Immanuel Schochet illuminates the fundamental connection between faith and knowledge
myjli.com/booksmart

[The Torah states,] "Know today, and bring unto your heart, that G-d is the G-d" (DEUTERONOMY 4:39). That is to say, know G-d with an in-depth knowledge and with logical proofs, in addition to the tradition received from our ancestors. . . . This is alluded to in the verse (I CHRONICLES 28:9), "Know the G-d of your fathers." Meaning to say, in addition to the faith established in your heart by "your fathers"—by the tradition handed down through the generations—you should also know on your own, by means of your own understanding.

This is also alluded to in the verse (EXODUS 15:2), "This is my G-d, and I shall beautify Him; the G-d of my fathers, and I shall exalt Him." That is to say: When He is *my* G-d, due to my own knowledge and understanding, then *ve'anvehu* ["I shall beautify Him," which also can be read as a combination of the words] *ani vahu*, "I and He" (as Rashi explains in his commentary on the Talmud, Shabbat 133b); meaning, I and He are bonded together, so to speak, because my knowledge of Him is internalized in my heart. However, when I do not possess a knowledge of G-d that is the product of my understanding, only the tradition that He is "the G-d of my fathers," then "I shall exalt Him"—G-d remains aloof and elevated from me, and I am distant from Him in the inner recesses of my heart.

A person is therefore obligated to be well-versed in the logical proofs cited in *Chovot Halevavot*, that these be well-understood in their heart, . . . to know and understand that "G-d is One, and His name is one" (ZECHARIAH 14:9).

Initial word panel to the book of Zechariah, in the *Duke of Sussex's German Pentateuch*. (British Library, London)

What Is the Difference between Knowing and Believing in G-d? **Rabbi Manis Friedman** gives a fascinating explanation: **myjli.com/booksmart**

TEXT 3

Learning to Love

Rabbi Dov Ber of Mezeritch, *Magid Devarav LeYaakov*, Addendum 26

מָה שֶׁכָּתוּב "וְאָהַבְתָּ אֵת ה' אֱלֹקֶיךָ וְגוֹ'" – הֲלֹא אַהֲבָה הִיא מִדָּה שֶׁבַּלֵּב, וְאֵיךְ שַׁיָּךְ עִנְיַן הַצִּוּוּי? דְּמִי שֶׁיֵּשׁ לוֹ אַהֲבָה הוּא אוֹהֵב; וּמָה יַעֲשֶׂה מִי אֲשֶׁר, חַס וְשָׁלוֹם, אֵין הָאַהֲבָה תְּקוּעַ בְּלִבּוֹ? וְאֵיךְ אוֹמֵר "וְאָהַבְתָּ" לְשׁוֹן צִוּוּי, כְּאִלּוּ הוּא בַּעַל בְּחִירָה בָּזֶה?

אֶלָּא שֶׁהַצִּוּוּי הוּא עַל הַהִתְבּוֹנְנוּת הַקָּדוּם לָהּ בַּפָּסוּק "שְׁמַע יִשְׂרָאֵל". דְ"שְׁמַע" עִנְיָנוֹ הֲבָנָה . . . וְזֶהוּ "וְאָהַבְתָּ" לְשׁוֹן צִוּוּי, דְּהַצִּוּוּי הוּא עַל הִתְבּוֹנְנוּת.

It is written, "You shall love G-d your G-d" (DEUTERONOMY 6:5). But love is a feeling in the heart; how can it be commanded? One who loves G-d, loves; but what should a person do if this love is not embedded in their heart, G-d forbid? How can the Torah say, in the manner of a command, "You shall love," as if a person has a choice in the matter?

But the commandment is regarding the contemplation described in the preceding verse (DEUTERONOMY 6:4), "Hear O Israel, [G-d is our G-d, G-d is one]." The Hebrew word *shema* ("hear") also means "understand". . . . This is why it says "You shall love" as an imperative, as the commandment is to contemplate and understand.

RABBI DOV BER "THE MAGID" OF MEZERITCH
D. 1772

Primary disciple and eventual successor of the Baal Shem Tov. Among his disciples were the founders of various Chasidic dynasties, including Rabbi Nachum of Chernobyl, Rabbi Levi Yitzchak of Berditchev, and Rabbi Shne'ur Zalman of Liadi. His teachings, recorded by his students, appear in various volumes, including *Magid Devarav LeYaakov.*

II. OVERVIEW OF MAJOR WORKS OF MUSAR AND CHAKIRAH

In this section, we review the history of Musar and Chakirah, noting the major authors and works in each field and their contributions.

SABBATH AFTERNOON
Moritz Daniel Oppenheim (1800-1882), oil on canvas, 1860.

FIGURE 5.1

Major Works of Musar and Jewish Philosophy

1080
DUTIES OF THE HEARTS
The first systematic work of Jewish ethical philosophy, authored by Rabbi Bachya ibn Pakudah (c. 1050–1120) of Saragossa, Spain. The work consists of ten "gates" exploring ten principles of inner spiritual life: unity of G-d, Divine providence, worship, trust, sincerity, humility, repentance, self-examination, asceticism, and love. Originally written in Judeo-Arabic, the work is also known by its Hebrew title, *Chovot Halevavot*.

1200
SEFER CHASIDIM
"Book of the Pious." An ethical work by Rabbi Yehudah heChasid (1140–1217) of Germany, one of the initiators of the *Chasidei Ashkenaz* movement, which stressed piety and asceticism.

1400
ORCHOT TZADDIKIM
"Ways of the Righteous." A 15th-century collection of ethical teachings by an unknown author that became a classic of Musar teachings.

1250
SHAAREI TESHUVAH
"Gates of Repentance." One of several moralistic works by Rabbi Yonah Gerondi (d. 1263) of Spain.

1575
RESHIT CHOCHMAH
"Genesis of Wisdom." A moral-mystical work by Rabbi Eliyahu de Vidas, 1518–1587, of Safed, a disciple of the master kabbalist Rabbi Isaac Luria ("Ari").

MUSAR

900 CE | 1000 | 1100 | 1200 | 1300 | 1400

JEWISH PHILOSOPHY (CHAKIRAH)

933
SAADIA GAON
The earliest extant work that systematically organized the philosophy and theology of Juadism was "Beliefs and Opinions," composed in Judeo-Arabic by Rabbi Saadia Gaon (882–942), who lived in Egypt, Israel, and Babylonia. Translated into Hebrew under the title *Emunot Vede'ot*.

1139
KUZARI
Considered one of Judaism's most important theological works, *The Kuzari* presents the beliefs and ideology of Judaism in the form of a dialogue between a Jewish scholar and the 8th-century Khazar king who converted to Judaism. Authored by Rabbi Yehudah Halevi (c. 1075–1141, Spain), who was also one of the greatest Hebrew poets and liturgists in Jewish history.

1250
CHINUCH
"Book of Education." An overview of the reasons behind each of the 613 biblical commandments, and the ethical lessons they convey. Composed in the 13th century by an anonymous author who identifies himself only as "a Levite from Barcelona."

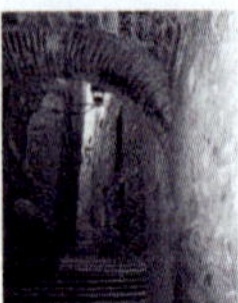

1352
DERASHOT HA-RAN
A series of discourses exploring fundamental ideas in Jewish philosophy such as creation, free choice, prophesy, the chosenness of the people of Israel, nature and miracles, the *mitzvot*, and Torah learning. Authored by 14th-century Torah sage Rabbi Nisim Gerondi ("Ran").

1040
IBN GABIROL
In his short life, Rabbi Shlomo ibn Gabirol created works in numerous fields, including philosophy, ethics, Kabbalah, and Hebrew literature. His *Font of Life* is a classic in both Jewish and Islamic ethical philosophy.

1190
GUIDE FOR THE PERPLEXED
Philosophical work by Maimonides employing Aristotelian and classical Arabic philosophy to present the fundamental principles of Judaism.

1321
RALBAG
Rabbi Levi ben Gershon, 1288–1344, of France; also known as "Gersonides." A philosopher, mathematician, astronomer, scientist, and inventor, his works include the philosophical treatise *Milchamot Hashem* ("Battles of G-d"), and a commentary on the Bible that presents his philosophical, ethical, and Halachic conclusions from the narrative.

4560 YEAR ON JEWISH CALENDAR | 4760 | 4960 | 5160

1740
RAMCHAL
Rabbi Moshe Chaim Luzzatto, 1707–1746, who lived in Italy and Holland, was a prodigious author in numerous areas of Torah learning, including Kabbalah, philosophy, ethics, and poetry. His most famous ethical work is *Mesilat Yesharim* ("Path of the Upright").

1845
THE MUSAR MOVEMENT
Rabbi Yisrael Lipkind (1809–1883, Lithuania) was the founder of the modern Musar movement, which brought a new emphasis to ethical behavior, character refinement, and spiritual self-improvement in the *yeshivot* of Europe, alongside the study of Talmud and Torah law. Over the next two generations, various schools within this movement were established by Rabbi Salanter's disciples, including the Kelm school, founded by Rabbi Simchah Zisel Ziv (1824–1898), which emphasized orderliness, thoughtfulness, and dedication; the Slabodka school (R. Nathan Zvi Finkel, 1849–1927), which focused on the human being's striving for perfection; and the Novardok school (Rabbi Yosef Yozel Horowitz, 1847–1919), which emphasized trust in G-d, and humility and self-effacement.

1873
CHAFETZ CHAYIM
Rabbi Yisrael Meir Kagan (1839–1933), of Radun, Belarus, was a foremost Halachist, ethicist, leader, and mentor of Eastern European Jewry in the late 19th and early 20th centuries. Known as *Chafetz Chayim* ("Desires Life") after his first published work, a digest of laws pertaining to proper ethical speech.

1953
MICHTAV ME'ELIYAHU
"Letter from Eliyahu." The teachings of Rabbi Eliyahu Dessler, 1892–1953, of the UK and Israel.

1500 1600 1700 1800 1900

1410
RABBI CHASDAI CRESCAS

Author of *Ohr Hashem* ("Light of G-d"), a defense of classical Jewish theology in face of the popularity of Aristotelian philosophy among medieval Jewish scholars.

1440
IKARIM
"Book of Fundamentals." A classic of Torah philosophy authored by Rabbi Yosef Albo (c. 1380–1444, Spain). The work stresses three fundamental aspects of Jewish belief: the existence of G-d, the Divine origin of the Torah, and reward and punishment.

1578
MAHARAL
Rabbi Yehudah Loew, 1520–1609, known as "the Maharal of Prague." Considered one of the great sages of his time, many subsequent schools of Torah philosophy are based on or derive from his numerous works.

1820
NEFESH HACHAYIM
"Soul of Life." A philosophical and kabbalistic work authored by Rabbi Chaim of Volozhin (1749–1821), a protégé of the Gaon of Vilna. In 1803, Rabbi Chaim founded the famed yeshiva of Volozhin, which would produce many of the leading Torah scholars of the next century and a half.

1836
RABBI SAMSON REPHAEL HIRSCH
1808–1888; Germany. Founder of the *Torah im derech eretz* approach to Judaism, advocating a symbiosis of Torah learning with secular sciences and engagement with the modern world. His commentaries on the Bible contain his philosophical and psychological insights into the biblical narratives. He also authored *Horeb*, a philosophical exploration of the *mitzvot*; and *Nineteen Letters on Judaism*.

1900
RABBI ABRAHAM ISAAC KOOK
1864–1935. First Ashkenazic chief rabbi of Israel in the modern era. Rabbi Kook's many works on Jewish thought and law are composed in a distinctive philosophical, mystical, and poetic style, and form the ideological underpinning for Religious Zionism.

1965
RABBI JOSEPH B. SOLOVEITCHIK
1903–1993, Boston. Talmudist, philosopher, and a seminal figure of Modern Orthodox Judaism. Served at the helm of the rabbinical seminary at Yeshiva University in New York. His philosophy of Judaism is expressed in two landmark essays, *The Lonely Man of Faith* and *Halakhic Man*, and in numerous articles and talks.

5360 5560

III. FIRST TOPIC: CREATION

In the next three sections, we will study three topics in Chakirah and Musar: (a) Creation, (b) *bitachon* (trust in G-d), and (c) anger. We will also see how the philosophical and psychological aspects of these topics are intertwined.

The Torah famously begins with the statement, "In the beginning G-d created the heavens and the earth." But is this the most important thing we need to know about G-d and about our own existence? If a person believed that the world always existed—as was the prevailing scientific view until less than a century ago—could they not still believe in a Higher Power, moral responsibility, and Divine purpose?

TEXT 4

The Beginning

Genesis 1:1

בְּרֵאשִׁית בָּרָא אֱלֹקִים
אֵת הַשָּׁמַיִם וְאֵת הָאָרֶץ.

In the beginning G-d created
the heavens and the earth.

TEXT 5

Rashi's Question

Rashi, Genesis 1:1

לֹא הָיָה צָרִיךְ לְהַתְחִיל אֶת הַתּוֹרָה אֶלָּא מֵ"הַחֹדֶשׁ הַזֶּה לָכֶם" (שְׁמוֹת יב, ב), שֶׁהִיא מִצְוָה רִאשׁוֹנָה שֶׁנִּצְטַוּוּ בָּהּ יִשְׂרָאֵל. וּמָה טַעַם פָּתַח בְּ"בְּרֵאשִׁית"?

The Torah ought to have begun [with the verse], "This month shall be to you . . ." (EXODUS 12:2), which is the first mitzvah commanded to the people of Israel. Why, then, does it begin with "In the beginning [G-d created the heavens and the earth]"?

RABBI SHLOMO YITZCHAKI (RASHI) 1040–1105

Most noted biblical and Talmudic commentator. Born in Troyes, France, Rashi studied in the famed *yeshivot* of Mainz and Worms. His commentaries on the Pentateuch and the Talmud, which focus on the straightforward meaning of the text, appear in virtually every edition of the Talmud and Bible.

THE FIRST DAY OF CREATION
Ofra Friedland, oil on canvas, Israel.

TEXT 6

Creation as a Foundation of Torah

Nachmanides's Commentary on Torah, Genesis 1:1

זוֹ אַגָּדָה שֶׁכְּתָבָהּ רַבֵּנוּ שְׁלֹמֹה בְּפֵרוּשָׁיו.
וְיֵשׁ לִשְׁאֹל בָּהּ, כִּי צֹרֶךְ גָּדוֹל הוּא לְהַתְחִיל הַתּוֹרָה
בְּ"בְּרֵאשִׁית בָּרָא אֱלֹקִים", כִּי הוּא שֹׁרֶשׁ הָאֱמוּנָה.
וְשֶׁאֵינוֹ מַאֲמִין בָּזֶה וְחוֹשֵׁב שֶׁהָעוֹלָם קַדְמוֹן,
הוּא כּוֹפֵר בָּעִקָּר וְאֵין לוֹ תּוֹרָה כְּלָל.

This is a Midrashic teaching that Rashi cites in his commentary. But we can question this: Indeed, there is a great need to begin the Torah with "In the beginning G-d created," as this is the very root of our faith. One who does not believe this, and thinks that the world always existed, denies the very basis [of Judaism] and has no Torah at all.

RABBI MOSHE BEN NACHMAN (NACHMANIDES, RAMBAN) 1194–1270

Scholar, philosopher, author, and physician. Nachmanides was born in Spain and served as leader of Iberian Jewry. In 1263, he was summoned by King James of Aragon to a public disputation with Pablo Cristiani, a Jewish apostate. Though Nachmanides was the clear victor of the debate, he had to flee Spain because of the resulting persecution. He moved to Israel and helped reestablish communal life in Jerusalem. He authored a classic commentary on the Pentateuch and a commentary on the Talmud.

Initial word panel to the book of Genesis, in the *North French Miscellany*, an elaborately decorated thirteenth-century manuscript containing many Hebrew texts, illuminations, and miniatures of historical Jewish scenes. (British Library, London)

TEXT 7

Logical Proofs That the World Has a Beginning

Rabbi Saadia Gaon, *Beliefs and Opinions*, Chapter 1

אֱלֹקֵינוּ יִתְעַלֶּה הוֹדִיעָנוּ שֶׁכָּל הַדְּבָרִים מְחֻדָּשִׁים, וְשֶׁהוּא חִדְּשָׁם לֹא מִדָּבָר, כְּמוֹ שֶׁאָמַר: "בְּרֵאשִׁית בָּרָא אֱלֹקִים וְגוֹ'". וְאָמַר עוֹד: "אָנֹכִי ה' עֹשֶׂה כֹּל" . . . וְאִמֵּת לָנוּ אֶת זֶה בְּאוֹתוֹת וּבְמוֹפְתִים, וְלָכֵן קִבַּלְנוּהוּ.

וְאַחַר כָּךְ עִיַּנְתִּי עִנְיָן זֶה, הַאִם יִתְאַמֵּת עַל יְדֵי הָעִיּוּן כְּמוֹ שֶׁהִתְאַמֵּת עַל יְדֵי הַנְּבוּאָה? וּמְצָאתִיו כֵּן, מִכַּמָּה פָּנִים . . .

הָרִאשׁוֹנָה מֵהֶן מִן הַתַּכְלִיתוּת. וְהוּא שֶׁהַשָּׁמַיִם וְהָאָרֶץ, כֵּיוָן שֶׁהִתְבָּרֵר שֶׁיֵּשׁ לָהֶן תַּכְלִית . . . מֻכְרָח שֶׁיְּהֵא לְכוֹחָם תַּכְלִית, כִּי לֹא יִתָּכֵן שֶׁיְּהֵא כּוֹחַ לְלֹא תַּכְלִית בְּגוּף שֶׁיֵּשׁ לוֹ תַּכְלִית . . . וְכֵיוָן שֶׁיֵּשׁ תַּכְלִית לַכּוֹחַ הַמְקַיְּמָן, מֻכְרָח שֶׁיְּהֵא לָהֶם תְּחִלָּה וָסוֹף . . .

וְהָרְאָיָה הַשְּׁנִיָּה מִצֵּרוּף הַחֲלָקִים וְהַרְכָּבַת הַפְּרָקִים. וְהוּא, שֶׁרָאִיתִי הַגְּשָׁמִים חֲלָקִים מְחֻבָּרִים וּפְרָקִים מֻרְכָּבִים, וְהִתְבָּאֵר לִי בָּהֶם סִימָן מַעֲשֵׂה הָעוֹשֶׂה וְהַחִדּוּשׁ . . . וּמָצָאתִי הַכָּתוּב אוֹמֵר . . . "כִּי אֶרְאֶה שָׁמֶיךָ מַעֲשֵׂה אֶצְבְּעֹתֶיךָ, יָרֵחַ וְכוֹכָבִים אֲשֶׁר כּוֹנָנְתָּה" (תְּהִלִּים ח, ד).

G-d tells us [in the Torah] that all things were created from nothing, created by Him from a prior state of non-existence, as it is written, "In the beginning G-d created . . ." (GENESIS 1:1). It also says, "I am G-d, who makes everything . . ." (ISAIAH

RABBI SAADIA GA'ON (RASAG) 882–942 CE

Rabbinic scholar, philosopher, and exegete. Rabbi Saadia Ga'on was born in Egypt and came to the forefront of the rabbinic scene through his active opposition to Karaism, a divergent sect that denied the divinity of the Oral Law. In 928, the exilarch David ben Zakai invited him to head the illustrious yeshiva in Sura, Babylonia, thereby bestowing upon him the honorific title "Ga'on." He is renowned for his works on the Torah, Hebrew linguistics, and Jewish philosophy, and his redaction of a siddur.

44:24). This truth was corroborated for us with signs and miracles, and we therefore accepted it.

I then contemplated this truth, asking: Can this be verified by logic, as it is verified by prophecy? I found that it is, from a number of angles. . . .

The first proof is from the finiteness of the universe. Because we know that the heavens and the earth are of a limited size, . . . their potential must also be limited, as a finite object cannot possess an infinite potential. . . . Because the energy that sustains their existence is finite, they must have a beginning and an end. . . .

A second proof is from the particularization and complexity [of the universe]. I observe how every entity is comprised of interconnected parts and complex components, revealing to me the imprint of their Maker and Creator. . . . I found that this, too, is stated by the verse, . . . "When I see Your heavens, the work of Your fingers, the moon and stars which You arrayed" (PSALMS 8:4).

TEXT 8

A Universe of Choice

Maimonides, *Guide for the Perplexed* 2:25

אֱמוּנַת הַקַּדְמוּת, עַל הַצַּד אֲשֶׁר יִרְאֶה אוֹתוֹ אָרִיסְטוֹ שֶׁהוּא עַל צַד הַחִיּוּב, וְלֹא יִשְׁתַּנֶּה טֶבַע כְּלָל וְלֹא יֵצֵא דָבָר חוּץ מִמִּנְהָגוֹ – הִנֵּה הִיא סוֹתֶרֶת הַדָּת מֵעִקָּרָהּ, וּמְכַזֶּבֶת לְכָל אוֹת בְּהֶכְרֵחַ, וּמְבַטֶּלֶת כָּל מָה שֶׁתְּיַחֵל בּוֹ הַתּוֹרָה אוֹ תַּפְחִיד מִמֶּנּוּ . . .

וְדַע, כִּי עִם הַאֲמָנַת חִדּוּשׁ הָעוֹלָם יִהְיוּ הָאוֹתוֹת כּוּלָם אֶפְשָׁרִיּוֹת, וְתִהְיֶה הַתּוֹרָה אֶפְשָׁרִית, וְתִפֹּל כָּל שְׁאֵלָה שֶׁתִּשְׁאַל בְּזֶה הָעִנְיָן . . . לָמָּה שָׂם הָאֱלֹקַה נְבוּאָתוֹ בְּזֶה וְלֹא נְתָנָהּ לְזוּלָתוֹ? . . . וְלָמָּה צִוָּה בְּאֵלּוּ הַמִּצְווֹת וְהִזְהִיר בְּאֵלּוּ הָאַזְהָרוֹת? . . . וּמָה כַּוָּנַת הָאֱלֹקַה בְּאֵלּוּ הַתּוֹרוֹת? וְלָמָּה לֹא שָׂם אֵלּוּ הָעִנְיָנִים הַמְּצֻוֶּה בָּהֶם וְהַמֻּזְהָר מֵהֶם בְּטִבְעֵנוּ, אִם הָיָה זֶה כַּוָּנָתוֹ? יִהְיֶה מַעֲנֶה אֵלּוּ הַשְּׁאֵלוֹת כֻּלָּם שֶׁיֹּאמַר: כֵּן רָצָה אוֹ כֵּן גָּזְרָה חָכְמָתוֹ, כְּמוֹ שֶׁהִמְצִיא הָעוֹלָם כְּשֶׁרָצָה עַל זֹאת הַצּוּרָה . . . וְאִם יֹאמַר אוֹמֵר שֶׁהָעוֹלָם כֵּן הִתְחַיֵּב, יִתְחַיֵּב בְּהֶכְרֵחַ שֶׁיִּשְׁאֲלוּ הַשְּׁאֵלוֹת הָהֵם כֻּלָּם, וְאֵין לָצֵאת מֵהֶם כִּי אִם בְּמַעֲנִים מְגֻנִּים.

The belief in a preexisting world, as viewed by Aristotle, in which everything that is must be, nothing changes its nature, and nothing acts contrary to its custom—this view contradicts the very basis of our faith, denies every miracle, and negates all that the Torah strives for or warns against. . . .

Know that with the belief of a created world, all miracles are possible, the Torah is possible, and all challenges to these truths are answered. For should you ask . . . : Why did G-d communicate His prophecy to this one and not to the other . . . ? Why did He command these particular *mitzvot* and prohibitions . . . ? What is the Divine intent with these instructions? Why did G-d not inspire these actions and prohibitions in our nature, if this is [the behavior] that He desired? The answer to all these questions is: So G-d desired, and so His wisdom deemed, in the same way that it was desired by G-d to create the world in this particular manner. . . . But if we were to believe that the world is the way it is because it could not be any other way, then all these questions would necessarily arise, and they could only be answered with weak and unsatisfactory replies.

Full-page initial word panel of an introduction to Maimonides's *Guide for the Perplexed*, copied in Catalonia, Spain, in the fourteenth century. (British Library, London)

Rabbi Lord Jonathan Sacks on the controversy surrounding Maimonides and his teachings: **myjli.com/booksmart**

FIGURE 5.2

Two Worldviews and Their Implications

	ARISTOTELIAN VIEW *The world and the laws of nature always existed*	CREATIONISM *G-d created the world and the laws of nature*
MIRACLES	The laws of nature are immutable. Any "miracles" we experience have a natural explanation.	Nature is G-d's manner of running the world. A miracle is when G-d chooses to act on our reality in ways that disregard these conventions.
FREEDOM OF CHOICE	Our choices and actions are the products of our inborn nature.	G-d created us in His image, imbuing us with the ability to overrule our inborn nature. We fully own our moral choices and achievements.
HOPE AND CHANGE	The way things are is essentially the way things will be. All future states are the outgrowths of the present state of reality.	Prayer and our own actions have the power to change the way things are.

IV. SECOND TOPIC: *BITACHON*

Bitachon—trust in G-d—is a unique worldview that rejects both the hubris of self-reliance and the passivity of fatalism. Instead, it instills in us a confidence in G-d's goodness, an awareness of the purposefulness of every event and experience, and a proactive participation in the Divine providence of our lives.

TEXT 9

The Myth of the Self-Made Man

Deuteronomy 8:11–18

הִשָּׁמֶר לְךָ . . . פֶּן תֹּאכַל וְשָׂבָעְתָּ, וּבָתִּים טוֹבִים תִּבְנֶה וְיָשָׁבְתָּ. וּבְקָרְךָ וְצֹאנְךָ יִרְבְּיֻן, וְכֶסֶף וְזָהָב יִרְבֶּה לָּךְ, וְכֹל אֲשֶׁר לְךָ יִרְבֶּה. וְרָם לְבָבֶךָ; וְשָׁכַחְתָּ אֶת ה' אֱלֹקֶיךָ . . . וְאָמַרְתָּ בִּלְבָבֶךָ: כֹּחִי וְעֹצֶם יָדִי עָשָׂה לִי אֶת הַחַיִל הַזֶּה.

וְזָכַרְתָּ אֶת ה' אֱלֹקֶיךָ, כִּי הוּא הַנֹּתֵן לְךָ כֹּחַ לַעֲשׂוֹת חָיִל.

Beware . . . lest you eat and be sated, and you will build good houses and dwell therein; and your herds and your flocks will multiply, your silver and gold increase, and all that you have will increase. And your heart will grow haughty; and you will forget the L-rd your G-d. . . . And you will say in your heart: My ability and the might of my hand have accumulated this wealth for me.

Remember the L-rd your G-d, as it is He who gives you the ability to make wealth.

TEXT 10

In All That You Do

Sifrei, Deuteronomy 15:18

"וּבֵרַכְךָ ה' אֱלֹקֶיךָ", יָכוֹל אֲפִלּוּ עוֹמֵד וּבָטֵל?
תַּלְמוּד לוֹמַר, "בְּכָל אֲשֶׁר תַּעֲשֶׂה".

[Because it says,] "G-d will bless you,"
I might think that a person can sit idle.
So the Torah teaches us, "In all that you do."

SIFREI

An early rabbinic Midrash on the biblical books of Numbers and Deuteronomy. *Sifrei* focuses mostly on matters of law, as opposed to narratives and moral principles. According to Maimonides, this halachic Midrash was authored by Rav, a 3rd-century Babylonian Talmudic sage.

TEXT 11

Effort and Blessing

Rabbi Yosef Albo, *Sefer Ha'ikarim* 4:6

הַחֲרִיצוּת וְהַהִשְׁתַּדְלוּת מוֹעִיל וְהֶכְרֵחִי בְּכָל דָבָר מִן הַפְּעֻלּוֹת הָאֱנוֹשִׁיּוֹת . . . וְכֵן בַּפְּעֻלּוֹת שֶׁהֵן מְעֹרָבוֹת מִן הַהֶכְרֵחַ וְהַבְּחִירָה, הַהִשְׁתַּדְלוּת בָּהֶן מְבֹאָר שֶׁהוּא סִבָּה לְהַגָּעָתָן . . . כְּמוֹ הַתְּבוּאָה הַמַּגַּעַת מִפְּעֻלַּת עוֹבְדֵי הָאֲדָמָה וּמִן הַגְּשָׁמִים, שֶׁאֵין סָפֵק שֶׁעֲבוֹדַת הָעוֹבֵד וְהִשְׁתַּדְלוּתוֹ תְּנַאי בְּהַגָּעַת הַתְּבוּאָה כִּירִידַת הַמָּטָר, וְאִי אֶפְשָׁר שֶׁיַּגִּיעַ זוּלָתוֹ כְּלָל . . .

וּבַעֲבוּר זֶה הָיָה שְׁלֹמֹה מְשַׁבֵּחַ הַחֲרִיצוּת וְאוֹמֵר: "וְיַד חָרוּצִים תַּעֲשִׁיר" (מִשְׁלֵי י, ט), וּמְגַנֶּה הָעֲצֵלָה, לְהָעִיר הָאָדָם שֶׁיִּשְׁתַּדֵּל לְהַשִּׂיג מְבֻקָּשׁוֹ בְּכָל מַאֲמַצֵּי כּוֹחוֹ . . .

וְכֵן אָמַר הַמְשׁוֹרֵר: "אִם ה' לֹא יִשְׁמָר עִיר שָׁוְא שָׁקַד שׁוֹמֵר" (תְּהִלִּים קכז, א). אֲבָל אִם ה' יִשְׁמֹר עִיר, יָפֶה שָׁקַד שׁוֹמֵר, שֶׁעִם הַשְּׁמִירָה וְהַהִשְׁתַּדְלוּת הָאֱנוֹשִׁי יַגִּיעַ

RABBI YOSEF ALBO C. 1380–1444

Spanish rabbi and philosopher. A student of Rabbi Chasdai Crescas, Albo is renowned for his philosophical work *Sefer Ha'ikarim* (*Book of Fundamentals*). The work stresses three fundamental aspects of Jewish belief: the existence of G-d, the Divinity of the Torah, and reward and punishment.

הָעֵזֶר הָאֱלוֹקִי וְלֹא בְּזוּלָתוֹ . . . אֲבָל רָאוּי שֶׁנִּשְׁתַּדֵּל בְּכֻלָּן
כְּאִלּוּ הֵן בְּחִירִיּוֹת בְּחִירָה גְמוּרָה, וַה' הַטּוֹב בְּעֵינָיו יַעֲשֶׂה.

Diligence and effort are useful and necessary in all human actions. . . . This also applies to events in which both the [Divine] decree and [human] choice play a part, . . . like the grain that is produced by the work of the farmer and the rain. Certainly, the work and efforts of the farmer are as necessary a condition for the growth of the grain as the rain, as without them the grain would not grow. . . .

For this reason, King Solomon praises diligence and says, "The hand of the diligent makes rich" (PROVERBS 10:9), and condemns laziness—in order to urge a person to make all the efforts in their power to obtain their objectives. . . .

The Psalmist also states: "If G-d does not guard a city, the watchman's vigilance is in vain" (PSALMS 127:1). This implies that when G-d *does* guard the city, the watchman does well to be vigilant, for Divine help comes with human vigilance and effort, but not without it. . . . We should therefore exert our efforts in all things as though they were completely dependent on our choice, and G-d will do as He sees fit.

FIGURE 5.3

The Bitachon Triangle

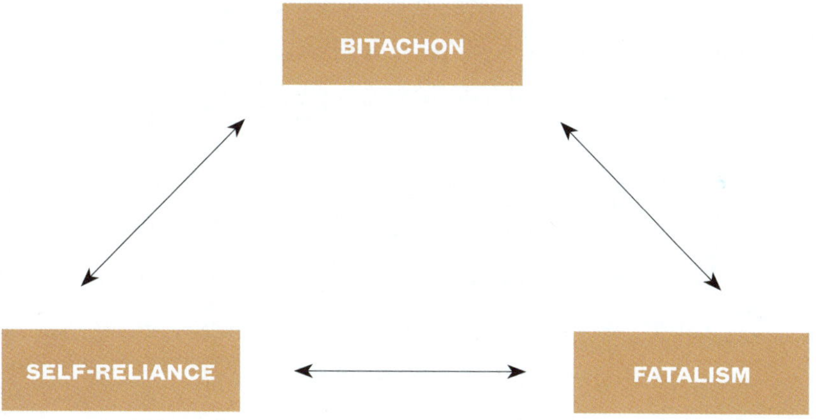

TEXT 12

The Vessel

Rabbi Eliyahu de Vidas, *Reshit Chochmah*, Portal of Love, chapter 12

וְלֹא יִבְטַח בְּשׁוּם דָּבָר מִבִּלְתִּי יְכֹלֶת ה' . . . שֶׁכָּל הֲסִבּוֹת הַמַּגִּיעוֹת אֵלָיו, כְּגוֹן הַמָּזוֹן אוֹ שְׁאָר קִנְיָנוֹ וּרְפוּאָתוֹ, כֻּלָּם הֵם סִבּוֹת מְסֻבָּבוֹת מֵאִתּוֹ יִתְבָּרֵךְ לְהַגִּיעַ הַדָּבָר הַהוּא אֵלָיו.

וּכְבָר הִמְשִׁיל הֶחָסִיד בַּעַל חוֹבוֹת הַלְּבָבוֹת הַדָּבָר בְּסִפְרוֹ אֶל גַּלְגַּל הַמַּיִם הַמּוֹצִיא מֵי הַבּוֹר עַל יְדֵי הַכֵּלִים הַמּוּכָנִים, שֶׁאִם יֶחְסַר אֶחָד מֵהֶם, יֵעָדֵר הוֹצָאַת מַיִם . . . כֵּן רָאוּי שֶׁיַּחֲשֹׁב הָאָדָם כִּי אֵין מַנְהִיג זוּלָתוֹ יִתְבָּרֵךְ, הַיִּחוּד הַמִּתְעַלֶּה עַל הַכֹּל, וּמִמֶּנּוּ מִסְתַּבְּבִים כָּל הַסִּבּוֹת וְהַמִּצּוּעִים לְהַגִּיעַ הַדָּבָר הַנִּרְצֶה אֵלָיו.

RABBI ELIYAHU DE VIDAS
1518–1587

Born in Safed; he is considered one of the prominent kabbalists of the 16th century. A student of Rabbi Moshe Cordovero and Rabbi Yitzchak Luria, he is best known as the author of *Reshit Chochmah*, a compendium of moral teachings culled from various sources in the Talmud, Midrash, and *Zohar*. He is buried in Hebron.

A person should trust in nothing save the ability of G-d, . . . for all the means by which a person acquires their food, their possessions, their health, and the like—these are all only the causations by which G-d causes these things to reach the person.

The author of *Duties of the Hearts* has an analogy for this: This is like a water wheel that raises water from a well by means of vessels that are affixed to it. If one of these vessels were missing, there would be a lack in the water supply. . . . This is how a person should think [about the sources of their livelihood]: the only source of sustenance is G-d, the Unity that transcends everything; and from Him extend all the means and avenues by which our needs are supplied to us.

ETERNALLY BONDED WITH G-D
Natalia Kadish

How Far Can *Bitachon* Take Us? **Rabbi Chaim Miller** answers: **myjli.com/booksmart**

FIGURE 5.4

The Waterwheel

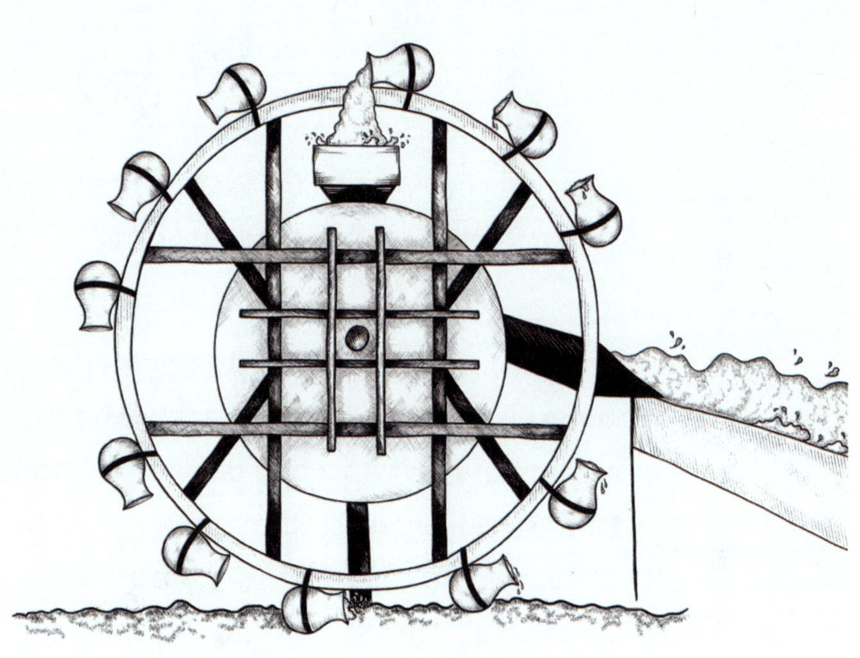

TEXT 13

The Bitachon Mindset

Rabbi Bachya ibn Pakudah, *Chovot Halevavot*, Portal of Trust

הַבִּטָּחוֹן עָלָיו [יִתְבָּרַךְ] בְּכָל דְּבָרָיו . . . שֶׁיֵּשׁ בּוֹ מִן הַתּוֹעָלִיּוֹת הַגְּדוֹלוֹת בְּעִנְיַן הַתּוֹרָה וּבְעִנְיַן הָעוֹלָם . . . מֵהֶן מְנוּחַת נַפְשׁוֹ וּבִטְחוֹנוֹ עַל אֱלוֹקָיו יִתְבָּרַךְ . . . מִפְּנֵי שֶׁאִם אֵינֶנּוּ בּוֹטֵחַ בֶּאֱלוֹקִים, בּוֹטֵחַ בְּזוּלָתוֹ . . .

שֶׁהַבּוֹטֵחַ בֶּאֱלוֹקִים יְבִיאֶנּוּ הַבְטָחָתוֹ עָלָיו שֶׁלֹּא יַעֲבֹד זוּלָתוֹ, וְשֶׁלֹּא יְקַוֶּה לְאִישׁ וְלֹא יְיַחֵל לִבְנֵי אָדָם, וְלֹא יַעַבְדֵם לְהִתְרַצּוֹת אֲלֵיהֶם, וְלֹא יַחְנִיף לָהֶם, וְלֹא יַסְכִּים עִמָּהֶם בְּבִלְתִּי עֲבוֹדַת הָאֱלוֹקִים, וְלֹא יַפְחִידֵהוּ עִנְיָנָם, וְלֹא יִירָא מִמַּחֲלוֹקְתָּם, אֲבָל יִתְפַּשֵּׁט מִבִּגְדֵי טוֹבָתָם וְטֹרַח הוֹדָאָתָם וְחוֹבַת תַּגְמוּלָם; וְאִם יוֹכִיחַ אוֹתָם לֹא יִזָּהֵר בִּכְבוֹדָם, וְאִם יַכְלִימֵם לֹא יֵבוֹשׁ מֵהֶם, וְלֹא יְיַפֶּה לָהֶם הַשֶּׁקֶר . . .

וּמִתּוֹעֶלֶת הַבִּטָּחוֹן בַּה' . . . אִם הוּא בַּעַל מָמוֹן, יְמַהֵר לְהוֹצִיא חוֹבוֹת הָאֱלוֹקִים וְחוֹבוֹת בְּנֵי אָדָם מִמָּמוֹנוֹ בְּנֶפֶשׁ חֲפֵצָה וְרוּחַ נְדִיבָה. וְאִם אֵינֶנּוּ בַּעַל מָמוֹן, יִרְאֶה כִּי חֶסְרוֹן הַמָּמוֹן טוֹבָה מִטּוֹבוֹת הַמָּקוֹם עָלָיו, מִפְּנֵי שֶׁנִּסְתַּלְּקוּ מֵעָלָיו הַחוֹבוֹת שֶׁהוּא חַיָּב בָּהֶם לֶאֱלֹקִים וְלִבְנֵי אָדָם בַּעֲבוּרוֹ, וּמִעוּט טִרְדַּת לִבּוֹ בִּשְׁמִירָתוֹ וְהַנְהָגָתוֹ . . . וְהַבּוֹטֵחַ בַּה' יַשִּׂיג תּוֹעֶלֶת הַמָּמוֹן – רְצוֹנִי לוֹמַר, פַּרְנָסָתוֹ – וְתִמָּנַע מִמֶּנּוּ טִרְדַּת הַמַּחֲשָׁבָה שֶׁל בַּעַל הַמָּמוֹן וְהַתְמָדַת דַּאֲגָתוֹ לוֹ . . . לֹא יִמְנָעֶנּוּ רֹב הַמָּמוֹן מִבְטֹחַ בַּה', מִפְּנֵי שֶׁאֵינֶנּוּ סוֹמֵךְ עַל הַמָּמוֹן, וְהוּא בְּעֵינָיו כְּפִקָּדוֹן צֻוָּה לְהִשְׁתַּמֵּשׁ בּוֹ עַל פָּנִים מְיֻחָדִים וּבְעִנְיָנִים מְיֻחָדִים לִזְמַן קָצוּב. וְאִם יַתְמִיד קִיּוּמוֹ

RABBI BACHYA IBN PAKUDAH, 11TH CENTURY

Moral philosopher and author. Ibn Pakudah lived in Muslim Spain, but little else is known about his life. *Chovot Halevavot* (*Duties of the Hearts*), his major work, was intended to be a guide for attaining spiritual perfection. Originally written in Judeo-Arabic and published in 1080, it was later translated into Hebrew and published in 1161 by Judah ibn Tibbon, a scion of the famous family of translators. Ibn Pakudah had a strong influence on Jewish pietistic literature.

אֶצְלוֹ, לֹא יַבִּיט בַּעֲבוּרוֹ, וְלֹא יַזְכִּיר טוֹבָתוֹ לְמִי שֶׁצִּוָּה לָתֵת לוֹ מִמֶּנּוּ וְלֹא יְבַקֵּשׁ עָלָיו גְּמוּל הוֹדָאָה וְשֶׁבַח, אֲבָל הוּא מוֹדֶה לְבוֹרְאוֹ יִתְבָּרַךְ אֲשֶׁר שָׂמוּהוּ סִבָּה לְטוֹבוֹת. וְאִם יֹאבַד הַמָּמוֹן מִמֶּנּוּ לֹא יִדְאַג וְלֹא יֶאֱבַל לְחֶסְרוֹנוֹ, אַךְ הוּא מוֹדֶה לֶאֱלוֹקָיו בְּקַחְתּוֹ פִּקְדוֹנוֹ מֵאִתּוֹ . . .

אַךְ תּוֹעֲלוֹת הַבִּטָּחוֹן בָּעוֹלָם . . . מְנוּחַת הַנֶּפֶשׁ וְהַגּוּף מִן הַמַּעֲשִׂים הַקָּשִׁים וְהַמְּלָאכוֹת הַמְיַגְּעוֹת אֶת הַגּוּפוֹת, וְעָזֹב עֲבוֹדַת הַמְּלָכִים וְחֻקֵּיהֶם וְחָמָס אַנְשֵׁיהֶם . . . וְהַבּוֹטֵחַ בַּה' הוּא תּוֹבֵעַ מִסִּבּוֹת הַטֶּרֶף מָה שֶׁיֵּשׁ בּוֹ יוֹתֵר מְנוּחָה לְגוּפוֹ וְשֵׁם טוֹב לוֹ וּפְנַאי לְלִבּוֹ, וּמָה שֶׁהוּא מֵפִיק יוֹתֵר לְחוֹבוֹת תּוֹרָתוֹ עִם יֶתֶר אֱמוּנָתוֹ, כִּי הַסִּבָּה לֹא תּוֹסִיף לוֹ בְּחֻקּוֹ וְלֹא תְּחַסְּרֵהוּ מִמֶּנּוּ מְאוּמָה אֶלָּא בִּגְזֵרַת הָאֱלוֹקִים יִתְבָּרַךְ . . . וּמֵהֶן מִעוּט צַעַר נַפְשׁוֹ בְּמִסְחָרוֹ, וְאִם תִּתְעַכֵּב אֶצְלוֹ פְּרַקְמַטְיָא, אוֹ אִם לֹא יוּכַל לִגְבּוֹת חוֹבוֹ, אוֹ אִם יִפְגָּעֵהוּ חֹלִי בְּגוּפוֹ. מִפְּנֵי שֶׁהוּא יוֹדֵעַ כִּי הַבּוֹרֵא יִתְבָּרַךְ מְתַקֵּן עִנְיָנוֹ יוֹתֵר מִמֶּנּוּ, וּבוֹחֵר לוֹ טוֹב יוֹתֵר מִמָּה שֶׁהוּא בּוֹחֵר לְעַצְמוֹ.

Bitachon (trust) in G-d in all of a person's affairs brings great advantages both religiously and materially. . . . [*Bitachon* engenders] absolute loyalty to one's Creator. . . . For one who does not rely on G-d is, by necessity, relying on something other than G-d. . . .

The person who trusts in the Almighty is freed of their subservience to other people. This person

Rabbi Bachya ibn Pakudah's "*Gate of Trust*" Is All the Rage
A panel discussion:
myjli.com/booksmart

will cease to pursue others, wait on them, flatter them, and bow to them, other than in the service of G-d. They will not fear animosity of others or be taken aback by their opposition, and will be unburdened of the debts incurred by their favors. They will be free to rebuke the guilty without fear or shame, and need not participate in the conspiracies of their falsehoods. . . .

Another advantage for the person who trusts in G-d . . . : If they are blessed with wealth, they will gladly and generously expedite their financial contributions toward Heaven and toward their fellows. And if they have no riches, they will see in their lack of wealth a kindness from the Almighty, in absolving them of the many obligations toward G-d and society it entails, and from the hassle of guarding and managing it. . . . Thus, the one who trusts in G-d enjoys the benefit of money—which is sustenance—but is free of the worries that the ownership of wealth brings. . . . Their money will not prevent them from trusting in G-d, as they do not rely on it, but rather see it as a deposit to be used for certain purposes for a certain limited time. If the money stays with them, it will not make them defiant, nor will they demand gratitude from those with whom they are obliged to share it, but will thank the Almighty for using them as a source of charity. And if the money is lost, they will not be pained by its loss, but will thank the Almighty for taking the deposit off their hands and relieving them of the responsibility. . . .

[These are all religious advantages.] Regarding worldly matters . . . , the person who trusts in G-d enjoys tranquility of both body and soul, and relief from difficult tasks and exhausting labor, from the service of kings and the exploitation of their subjects. They pursue a livelihood, but only in a manner that accords ultimate ease to their body, preserves their good name, provides leisure to their heart, and is most consistent with their religious needs and true beliefs. For this person knows that their choice of the material source of their livelihood will not add to their earnings nor subtract from them, save for their doing of G-d's will. . . . They have no worries when they are left with unsold merchandise, are unable to collect a debt, or illness befalls them; for they know that the Creator manages their affairs and chooses what is best for them, better than they could choose for themselves.

The Impact of Trust in G-d on Emotional Well-Being
Clinical psychologist **Dr. David Rosmarin** discusses:
myjli.com/booksmart

V. THIRD TOPIC: ANGER

In this section, we examine the Torah's perspective on negative emotions in general, and particularly the emotion of anger. We also discover how the ideological and psychological implications of the three topics we studied today—creation, *bitachon*, and anger—are intertwined. We conclude by tracing these ideas to their source in the biblical narrative of Joseph and his brothers.

TEXT 14

The Middle Road

Maimonides, *Mishneh Torah*, Laws of Character 1:4

הַדֶּרֶךְ הַיְשָׁרָה הִיא מִדָּה בֵּינוֹנִית שֶׁבְּכָל דֵּעָה וְדֵעָה מִכָּל הַדֵּעוֹת שֶׁיֵּשׁ לוֹ לָאָדָם . . . לְפִיכָךְ צִוּוּ חֲכָמִים הָרִאשׁוֹנִים שֶׁיְּהֵא אָדָם שָׁם דֵּעוֹתָיו תָּמִיד, וּמְשַׁעֵר אוֹתָם וּמְכַוֵּן אוֹתָם בַּדֶּרֶךְ הָאֶמְצָעִית, כְּדֵי שֶׁיְּהֵא שָׁלֵם בְּגוּפוֹ.

כֵּיצַד . . . לֹא יִקְפֹּץ יָדוֹ בְּיוֹתֵר וְלֹא יְפַזֵּר מָמוֹנוֹ, אֶלָּא נוֹתֵן צְדָקָה כְּפִי מִסַּת יָדוֹ וּמַלְוֶה כָּרָאוּי לְמִי שֶׁצָּרִיךְ. וְלֹא יְהֵא מְהוֹלֵל וְשׂוֹחֵק וְלֹא עָצֵב וְאוֹנֵן, אֶלָּא שָׂמֵחַ כָּל יָמָיו בְּנַחַת בְּסֵבֶר פָּנִים יָפוֹת, וְכֵן שְׁאָר דֵּעוֹתָיו. וְדֶרֶךְ זוֹ הִיא דֶּרֶךְ הַחֲכָמִים.

The correct path is the median temperament of each of the character traits that a person has. . . . The early sages therefore instructed that a person should evaluate their traits and direct them along the middle path, so as to achieve wholeness.

For example, . . . a person should not be overly stingy, nor squander their money, but should give charity according to their capacity and lend as is appropriate to one who is in need. A person should not be frivolous and jubilant, nor mournful and depressed, but should be tranquilly happy at all times and with a friendly demeanor. The same applies to all of a person's traits. This path is the path of the wise.

Decoration on a wimple—Torah scroll binder—used by Jews of Germanic origin. Painted on linen by Reuben M. Eschwege, New York, 1947. (Gross Family Collection, Tel Aviv)

TEXT 15

A Psychological Recipe

Orchot Tzadikim, Introduction

וְזֶה דוֹמֶה לְעֹשֶׂה תַּבְשִׁיל, וְצָרִיךְ יָרָק וּבָשָׂר וּמַיִם וּמֶלַח וּפִלְפְּלִין . . . אִם יְמַעֵט הַבָּשָׂר יִהְיֶה רָזֶה, אִם יַרְבֶּה מֶלַח לֹא יִהְיֶה נֶאֱכַל מֵחֲמַת מִלְחוֹ . . . אֲבָל הַבָּקִי אֲשֶׁר יִקַּח מִכָּל אֶחָד מִשְׁקָל הָרָאוּי, אָז יְהֵא הַמַּאֲכָל עָרֵב וּמָתוֹק לְאוֹכְלָיו.

וּכְעִנְיָן הַזֶּה בַּמִּדּוֹת: יֵשׁ מִדּוֹת שֶׁצָּרִיךְ לִקַּח מֵהֶן מַרְבֶּה, כְּגוֹן הָעֲנָוָה וְהַבֹּשֶׁת וְדוֹמֵיהֶן, וְיֵשׁ מִדּוֹת שֶׁצָּרִיךְ לִקַּח מֵהֶן מְעַט, כְּגוֹן הַגַּאֲוָה וְהָעַזּוּת וְהָאַכְזָרִיּוּת. לָכֵן בִּהְיוֹת הָאָדָם שׁוֹקֵל בְּפֶלֶס הַמֹּאזְנַיִם לִקַּח מִכָּל מִדָּה שִׁעוּרָהּ . . . בְּזֶה יַגִּיעַ לְתַכְלִית הַטּוֹבָה.

Building a character is like cooking a stew: You need greens and meat and water and salt and spices. . . . Too little meat and the broth is thin; too much salt and it is inedible. . . . But when the expert takes from each in the right measure, then the food will be tasty and pleasant for the one who eats it.

So, too, with the traits of the human character. There are traits of which one should avail oneself in a large measure, such as humility and bashfulness and the like; and traits that should be employed only minutely, such as pride and brazenness and cruelty. One who carefully weighs and measures the amount to be taken of each trait . . . will achieve goodness.

ORCHOT TZADIKIM

A classic work on Jewish ethics. The identity of the author is unknown, but it is believed to have been written by a French scholar, probably in the 14th century. Drawing much from earlier ethicists Solomon ibn Gabirol, Maimonides, and Bachya ibn Pakudah, *Orchot Tzadikim* ("The Ways of the Righteous") focuses on refining character traits and maintaining a balance in all matters.

TEXT 16

The Pitfalls of Anger

Maimonides, *Mishneh Torah*, Laws of Character 2:3

וְיֵשׁ דֵעוֹת שֶׁאָסוּר לוֹ לָאָדָם לִנְהֹג בָּהֶן בְּבֵינוֹנִית, אֶלָּא יִתְרַחֵק מִן הַקָּצֶה הָאֶחָד עַד הַקָּצֶה הָאַחֵר . . . וְכֵן הַכַּעַס מִדָּה רָעָה הִיא עַד לִמְאֹד, וְרָאוּי לָאָדָם שֶׁיִּתְרַחֵק מִמֶּנָּה עַד הַקָּצֶה הָאַחֵר, וִילַמֵּד עַצְמוֹ שֶׁלֹּא יִכְעֹס וַאֲפִלּוּ עַל דָּבָר שֶׁרָאוּי לִכְעֹס עָלָיו . . .

אָמְרוּ חֲכָמִים הָרִאשׁוֹנִים: "כָּל הַכּוֹעֵס, כְּאִלּוּ עוֹבֵד עֲבוֹדַת כּוֹכָבִים". וְאָמְרוּ, שֶׁ"כָּל הַכּוֹעֵס, אִם חָכָם הוּא חָכְמָתוֹ מִסְתַּלֶּקֶת מִמֶּנּוּ; וְאִם נָבִיא הוּא, נְבוּאָתוֹ מִסְתַּלֶּקֶת מִמֶּנּוּ". וּבַעֲלֵי כַּעַס, אֵין חַיֵּיהֶם חַיִּים. לְפִיכָךְ צִוּוּ לְהִתְרַחֵק מִן הַכַּעַס . . . וְזוֹ הִיא הַדֶּרֶךְ הַטּוֹבָה.

There are certain traits regarding which a person should not conduct themselves in an intermediate manner, but should distance themselves to the other extreme. . . . [For example,] anger is an extremely negative trait, from which a person should distance themselves in the extreme, and train themselves not to get angry even over things that are worthy of anger. . . .

The early sages said: "One who gets angry, it is as if they worshipped idols." They also said: "One who gets angry, if they are a wise person, their wisdom departs from them; and if they are a prophet, their prophecy departs from them." Those who are prone to anger—their life is not a life. The sages therefore instructed to distance oneself from anger. . . . This is the good path.

TEXT 17

The Paradox of Divine Providence and Free Choice

Rabbi Shneur Zalman of Liadi, *Tanya*, *Igeret Hakodesh* 25

מַאֲמַר רַבּוֹתֵינוּ זַ"ל: "כָּל הַכּוֹעֵס, כְּאִלּוּ עוֹבֵד עֲבוֹדַת כּוֹכָבִים וּמַזָּלוֹת וְכוּ'". וְהַטַּעַם מוּבָן לְיוֹדְעֵי בִינָה, לְפִי שֶׁבִּשְׁעַת כַּעֲסוֹ נִסְתַּלְּקָה מִמֶּנּוּ הָאֱמוּנָה. כִּי אִלּוּ הָיָה מַאֲמִין שֶׁמֵּאֵת ה' הָיְתָה זֹּאת לוֹ, לֹא הָיָה בְּכַעַס כְּלָל. וְאַף שֶׁבֶּן אָדָם שֶׁהוּא בַּעַל בְּחִירָה מְקַלְּלוֹ אוֹ מַכֵּהוּ אוֹ מַזִּיק מָמוֹנוֹ – וּמִתְחַיֵּב בְּדִינֵי אָדָם וּבְדִינֵי שָׁמַיִם עַל רֹעַ בְּחִירָתוֹ – אַף עַל פִּי כֵן, עַל הַנִּזָּק כְּבָר נִגְזַר מִן הַשָּׁמַיִם, וְהַרְבֵּה שְׁלוּחִים לַמָּקוֹם. וְלֹא עוֹד, אֶלָּא אֲפִלּוּ בְּשָׁעָה זוֹ מַמָּשׁ שֶׁמַּכֵּהוּ אוֹ מְקַלְּלוֹ, מִתְלַבֵּשׁ בּוֹ כֹּחַ ה' וְרוּחַ פִּיו יִתְבָּרֵךְ הַמְחַיֵּהוּ וּמְקַיְּמוֹ.

Our sages have said, "One who gets angry, it is as if they worshipped idols." The explanation of this statement is that a person will get angry only because, at the time of their anger, their faith has departed from them. For if they were to truly believe that what happened to them came from the Almighty, they would not be angered at all. Although a human being, possessed of free choice, has cursed them or struck them or damaged their property—and this perpetrator is indeed culpable for punishment, both by human courts of law and by the heavenly court, for the evil of their choice—nevertheless, the hurt that one has suffered had already been decreed from Above, and G-d has

RABBI SHNEUR ZALMAN OF LIADI (ALTER REBBE) 1745–1812

Chasidic rebbe, halachic authority, and founder of the Chabad movement. The Alter Rebbe was born in Liozna, Belarus, and was among the principal students of the Magid of Mezeritch. His numerous works include the *Tanya*, an early classic containing the fundamentals of Chabad Chasidism; and *Shulchan Aruch HaRav*, an expanded and reworked code of Jewish law.

many emissaries to carry out His will. Furthermore, even in the very moment that this person is striking them or cursing them, this person is being granted existence and life by the Divine utterance and vitality that is constantly being invested in them.

BELIEF
Nataly Grosman, 2014, acrylic on canvas.

Blessing G-d for the Bad? **Rabbi Adin Even-Israel Steinsaltz** explains: **myjli.com/booksmart**

TEXT 18

The Divine Emissary

Genesis 45:4–8

וַיֹּאמֶר יוֹסֵף אֶל אֶחָיו, "גְּשׁוּ נָא אֵלַי", וַיִּגָּשׁוּ. וַיֹּאמֶר, "אֲנִי יוֹסֵף אֲחִיכֶם, אֲשֶׁר מְכַרְתֶּם אֹתִי מִצְרָיְמָה".

"וְעַתָּה אַל תֵּעָצְבוּ, וְאַל יִחַר בְּעֵינֵיכֶם כִּי מְכַרְתֶּם אֹתִי הֵנָּה; כִּי לְמִחְיָה שְׁלָחַנִי אֱלֹקִים לִפְנֵיכֶם . . . וַיִּשְׁלָחֵנִי אֱלֹקִים לִפְנֵיכֶם לָשׂוּם לָכֶם שְׁאֵרִית בָּאָרֶץ, וּלְהַחֲיוֹת לָכֶם לִפְלֵיטָה גְּדֹלָה . . . לֹא אַתֶּם שְׁלַחְתֶּם אֹתִי הֵנָּה, כִּי הָאֱלֹקִים . . . "

Joseph said to his brothers, "Please come closer to me," and they drew near. And he said, "I am your brother Joseph, whom you sold into Egypt.

"And now, do not be distressed, and let it not trouble you that you sold me here; for it was to preserve life that G-d sent me before you. . . . G-d sent me before you to make for you a remnant in the land, and to keep you alive for a great refuge. . . . It is not you who sent me here, but G-d . . ."

KEY POINTS

1 *The Philosophy and Psychology of Judaism.* Notwithstanding its emphasis on action and behavior (Halachah), the Torah is a holistic guide to life that also aims to enlighten our mind, refine our character, and nourish the inner life of our soul. In fact, many of the *mitzvot* can be properly fulfilled only through an in-depth understanding of the principles of Judaism and a systematic program of character development. Hence, Torah literature includes the field of Musar, the psychology of Judaism; and the field of Chakirah, the philosophy and theology of Judaism.

2 *The Era of Specialization.* In the Bible, Talmud, and Midrashim, the philosophical and psychological teachings of Judaism are, for the most part, subsumed within the general Torah narrative. Other than a few notable exceptions, we do not find works dedicated to a specific "genre" of Torah. It is only in the post-Talmudic era that we see the development of specialized fields of study such as Musar and Chakirah.

3 *Major Works of Musar and Chakirah.* The first Torah work to systematically present a philosophy of Judaism was *The Book of Beliefs and Opinions*, authored by Rabbi Saadia Gaon in 933. In 1080, Rabbi Bachya ibn Pakudah wrote one of the most fundamental works of Jewish ethical philosophy, *Duties of the Hearts,* which is a classic of both Musar and Chakirah. Other classics of Jewish philosophy and theology are Rabbi Yehudah Halevi's *Kuzari* (1139) and Maimonides's *Guide for the Perplexed* (1190), as well as works by Ibn Gabirol (11th century), Ralbag (1288–1344), Rabbi Chisdai Crescas (early 15th century), Rabbi Yosef Albo (c. 1380–1444), Maharal (1520–1609), and Ramchal (1707–1746). Ibn Gabirol and Ramchal also composed works in the field of Musar, as did authors such as Rabbi Yonah Gerondi (d. 1263) and Rabbi Eliyahu de Vidas (1518–1587).

4 *The Modern Musar Movement.* In 1845, Rabbi Yisrael Salanter founded the modern Musar movement. The teachings of Rabbi Salanter and his disciples brought a new emphasis on ethical behavior, character refinement, and spiritual self-improvement to the *yeshivot* of eastern Europe, and to the Jewish world as a whole.

5 *Creation*. From the standpoint of Jewish philosophy, the statement "In the beginning G-d created the heavens and the earth" is fundamental to the Torah's view of reality. An eternally preexisting world—which was the prevailing scientific view until less than a century ago—negates the possibility of miracles, free choice, and hope for a better future. In contrast, the Torah asserts that G-d created all that exists, including the very laws of existence. This means that everything that is, is that way only because G-d desires that it should so be, and that G-d can obviously change the way it is—and empower us to do so.

6 *Bitachon*. The conception of G-d as absolute creator nourishes a mindset of *bitachon*, trust in G-d. *Bitachon* is a unique worldview that rejects both the hubris of self-reliance and the passivity of fatalism, in favor of proactive participation in Divine providence, confidence in G-d's goodness, and awareness of the purposefulness of every event and experience of our lives.

7 *Anger*. Most negative traits have certain positive applications. The emotion of anger, however, is seen by the masters of Musar as utterly irredeemable, and even as a subtle form of idolatry. This is because anger signifies a lapse of *bitachon*—of our trust in G-d's providence and in the Divine purpose of everything we experience.

8 *The Biblical Source*. Like everything in the Oral Torah, the ideas expounded in Chakirah and Musar are rooted in the Written Torah. The same is true of the principles of creationism, *bitachon*, and the psychology of anger, which can be discerned in the biblical narrative of how Joseph responded to the shame and guilt expressed by his brothers by saying, "It is not you who sent me here, but G-d."

The Thirteen Principles of Jewish Faith

As enumerated by Maimonides

1. Belief in G-d. G-d is perfect in every way, and is not dependent on any other existence for anything; whereas all other existences, phenomena, and realities were created by G-d, and are utterly dependent upon Him for their existence.

2. The absolute oneness of G-d. There are no composite parts or aspects within G-d's being.

3. G-d is not physical, nor does He possess any physical properties.

4. G-d is timeless, primordial (i.e., preceded all other existences), and eternal.

5. It is imperative to worship G-d and obey His commandments, and not worship any other power or entity.

6. G-d communicates to humanity through prophecy.

7 The primacy of the prophecy of Moses.

8 The Divinity of the Torah. The entire Torah now in our hands is the same Torah that was given to Moses by the Almighty.

9 The Torah—both the Written Torah and the Oral Torah—will never be changed, and nothing should be added to it or subtracted from it.

10 Divine providence. G-d knows and concerns Himself with everything that a person does.

11 G-d rewards those who fulfill the commandments of the Torah and punishes those who transgress them.

12 The coming of Mashiach (the Messiah) and the future messianic era of Divine goodness and perfection; to constantly await and anticipate its realization.

13 The resurrection of the dead. All who lived in the past will be brought back to life at a time of G-d's choosing.

Selected Teachings from Ethics of the Fathers

While all of the Talmud's sixty-three tractates include moral and ethical teachings, their primary focus is on a person's legal obligations under Torah law. The exception is the tractate Avot—"Fathers," commonly known as "Ethics of the Fathers"—which is wholly devoted to the cultivation of positive character traits and attitudes, imparting the Torah's guidance on how to approach our relationship with our Creator, with our fellows, and with the world in which we live.

SUMMER LEARNING

It is customary to study Ethics of the Fathers on Shabbat afternoons during the summer months. One chapter is studied each Shabbat, beginning on the Shabbat after Passover and ending on the Shabbat before Rosh Hashanah, thereby completing the six-chapter course of study four times each year.

SAY LITTLE AND DO MUCH.

1:15

Love work, loathe mastery over others, and avoid intimacy with the government.

1:10

The world stands on three things: Torah learning, service of G-d, and deeds of lovingkindness.

1:2

Hillel saw a skull floating on the water. He said to it: Because you drowned others, you were drowned; and those who drowned you will in the end be drowned.

2:6

It is not incumbent upon you to finish the job, but neither are you free to absolve yourself from it.

2:16

A bashful person cannot learn; a short-tempered person cannot teach.

2:5

Be of the disciples of Aaron: a lover of peace, a pursuer of peace, one who loves the creatures and draws them close to the Torah.

1:12

Any learning that is not accompanied by work is destined to fail and to cause sin.

2:2

All your deeds should be for the sake of Heaven.
2:12

The world endures by virtue of three things: justice, truth, and peace.
1:18

Your home should be open wide, and the poor should be members of your household.
1:5

Greet every person with a cheerful face.
1:15

Do not separate yourself from the community.
2:4

MORE POSSESSIONS, MORE WORRIES.
2:7

Do not be like servants who serve their master in order to receive a reward; rather, be like servants who serve their master not for the sake of receiving a reward.
1:3

Do not be wicked in your own eyes.
2:13

In a place where there are no men, strive to be a man.
2:5

Contemplate three things, and you will not fall into the hands of transgression. Know what is above you: an eye that sees, an ear that hears, and all your deeds are written in a book.
2:1

Which is the straight path that a person should choose for themselves? That which is harmonious for the one who does it and harmonious for humankind.
2:1

Do not judge your fellow until you have stood in their place.
2:4

If I am not for myself, who will be for me? And when I am only for myself, what am I? And if not now, when?
1:14

Do not scorn any person, and do not discount any thing. For there is no person that does not have their hour, and no thing that does not have its place.

4:3

Delve and delve into [the Torah], for all is in it; see with it; grow old and worn in it; do not budge from it, for there is nothing better.

5:21

Envy, lust, and honor drive a person from the world.

4:21

According to the pain is the reward.

5:21

One who shames a fellow in public has no share in the World to Come.

3:11

BE HUMBLE BEFORE EVERY PERSON.

4:10

One mitzvah brings another mitzvah; one transgression brings another transgression.

4:2

Against your will you are formed, against your will you are born, against your will you live, against your will you die.

4:22

Be a tail to lions rather than a head to foxes.

4:15

Do not look at the vessel, but at what it contains.

4:20

If there is no Torah, there is no common decency; if there is no common decency, there is no Torah. If there is no wisdom, there is no fear of G-d; if there is no fear of G-d, there is no wisdom. If there is no knowledge, there is no understanding; if there is no understanding, there is no knowledge. If there is no flour, there is no Torah; if there is no Torah, there is no flour.

3:17

Do not judge alone, for there is none qualified to judge alone, save for the One.

4:8

Do not appease your friend at the height of their anger; do not comfort them while their dead still lies before them.

4:18

SILENCE IS THE SAFEGUARD OF WISDOM.

3:13

There are seven things that characterize a boor, and seven that characterize a wise person. A wise person does not speak before one who is greater than himself in wisdom or age. He does not interrupt his fellow's words. He does not hasten to answer. His questions are on the subject and his answers to the point. He responds to first things first and to latter things later. Concerning what he did not hear, he says, "I did not hear it." He concedes to the truth. With the boor, the reverse of all these is the case.

5:7

Be bold as a leopard, light as an eagle, fleet as a deer, and strong as a lion to do the will of your Father in heaven.

5:20

A person who learns something from their fellow, whether it is a single chapter, a single law, a single verse, a single word, or even a single letter, is obligated to act respectfully toward them.

6:3

There are four types of temperaments. One who is easily angered and easily appeased — their virtue cancels their flaw. One whom it is difficult to anger and difficult to appease — their flaw cancels their virtue. One who it is difficult to anger and is easily appeased is a pious person. One who is easily angered and is difficult to appease is a wicked person.

5:11

Pray for the well-being of the government, for were it not for their fear of it, people would swallow each other alive.

3:2

**Who is wise?
The one who learns from every person.**

**Who is strong?
The one who conquers their desires.**

**Who is rich?
The one who is satisfied with their lot.**

**Who is honored?
The one who honors others.**

4:1

Any love that is dependent on something — when the thing ceases, the love also ceases. But a love that is not dependent on anything never ceases.

5:16

The Life and Works of Maimonides

GROUNDBREAKING AUTHOR AND AUTHORITY IN MULTIPLE GENRES OF TORAH

FIELDS OF LEARNING

 Talmudic commentary

 Halachah (Torah law)

 Philosophy & theology

1135
CORDOBA, SPAIN
MAIMONIDES BORN
Rabbi Moshe ben Maimon, known by the acronym "Rambam" and the patronymic "Maimonides," was born on the 14th of Nisan of the Jewish year 4895 (1135), in Cordoba, Spain. His father, Rabbi Maimon, served as *dayan* (rabbinical magistrate) of the city. His primary teachers in Torah were his father, Maimon, and his father's teacher, Rabbi Yehosef ibn Migash. The young prodigy also studied mathematics, philosophy, and medicine.

1148–1158
SOUTHERN SPAIN
WANDERING AND PERSECUTION
The conquest of Cordoba by the Almohads, a fanatical Muslim sect that sought to convert all Jews at the point of the sword, forced Maimonides's family to flee their native city, and to spend the next ten years wandering from place to place in southern Spain, evading the Almohads' persecution.

1158–1168
COMMENTARY ON THE MISHNAH
At the young age of 23, under conditions of wandering and persecution, Maimonides began writing his monumental commentary on the Mishnah, which he completed in 1168. In addition to elucidating the text of the Mishnah, the work includes many important philosophical and ethical treatises, such as Maimonides's famed "Eight Chapters" of ethical philosophy, written as an introduction to the tractate *Avot*, and his introduction to the chapter *Chelek*, in which he famously formulated the "Thirteen Principles" of the Jewish faith.

1159–1165
FEZ, MOROCCO
After ten years of homelessness and wandering, Maimonides's family settled in Fez, Morocco, where Maimonides studied with the great Torah sages of that city.

1162
FEZ, MOROCCO
IGERET HASHMAD
While still in his 20s, the young scholar was already emerging as an influential voice in the Jewish world. In 1162, Maimonides authored an epistle in defense of the Jews who were forced to ostensibly convert to Islam, while continuing to practice Judaism in secret. In this treatise, he outlined many of the fundamental principles of Judaism, including the particular conditions under which a Jew is obligated to sacrifice their life for their faith, as well as the imperative to judge others favorably.

1165
ACRE, JERUSALEM, AND HEBRON
IN THE HOLY LAND
Religious intolerance once again forced Maimonides's family to flee for their lives. Escaping Almohad-ruled Morocco in the dead of night, the family set sail for the Holy Land, where they hoped to settle. This plan, however, proved untenable, due to the harsh conditions under Crusader rule. After several months in Acre and brief visits to Jerusalem and Hebron, Maimonides reluctantly left the Holy Land for Egypt, where a more tolerant regime allowed Jews to freely practice their religion.

1166
ALEXANDRIA AND FUSTAT (OLD CAIRO), EGYPT
COMMUNAL LEADER
After a brief sojourn in Alexandria, Maimonides settled in Fustat (Old Cairo), where he was appointed as rabbi and leader of the Jewish community.

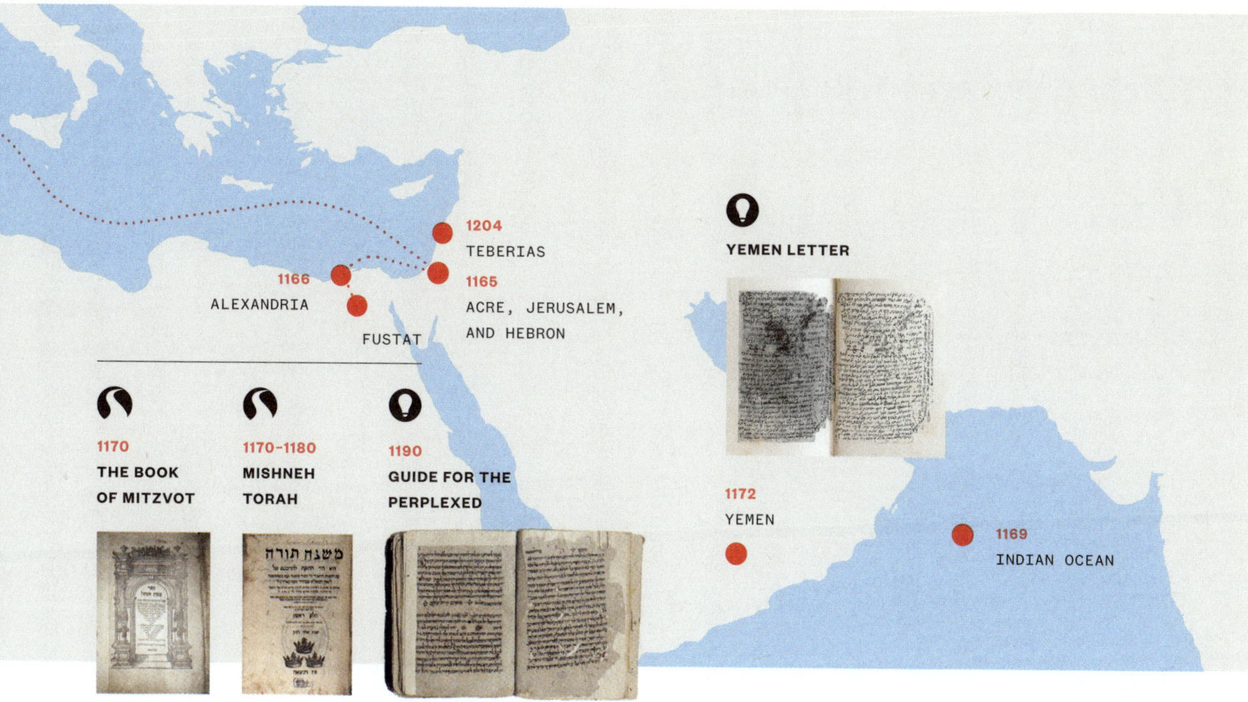

1169
INDIAN OCEAN
TRAGEDY AT SEA; MEDICAL CAREER

Three years after his arrival in Egypt, a tragedy occurred that would significantly impact the course of Maimonides's life.

Up until that point, the family was supported by Maimonides's beloved younger brother David, a dealer in precious stones, allowing Maimonides to devote himself entirely to Torah learning. But then, a storm in the Indian Ocean sank the ship on which David was travelling; David drowned, and all his merchandise and money, including funds entrusted to him by other merchants, were lost at sea, leaving the family penniless and in debt.

To support himself and his family, including his brother's widow and orphaned daughter, Maimonides took up the practice of medicine. His fame as a physician spread, and he was subsequently appointed court physician to the royal palace in Cairo. He also authored a number of important works on medicine.

In a letter to one of his disciples, Maimonides described how his duties as a physician and communal leader consumed the bulk of his days and nights, leaving him little time for his studies. Amazingly, he nevertheless succeeded in producing the voluminous and foundational works that dominate the fields of Torah scholarship, law, and philosophy to this day.

1170
FUSTAT
THE BOOK OF MITZVOT

A work that lists and describes all 613 *mitzvot* (Divine commandments) of the Torah, and identifies the biblical source of each.

1170–1180
FUSTAT
MISHNEH TORAH

Maimonides's magnum opus. A comprehensive codification of Halachah (Torah law) spanning 14 books, 83 sections, and 1,000 chapters. *Mishneh Torah* is the first and only Halachic work to distill and systematically codify all the laws of the Torah.

1172
YEMEN
YEMEN LETTER

An epistle addressing the challenges facing the Jews of Yemen. Among the themes discussed are the uniqueness of Judaism, the miracle of Jewish survival, and the timing of the messianic redemption.

1190
FUSTAT
GUIDE FOR THE PERPLEXED

The work that established Maimonides as the philosopher par excellence of Judaism. The "Guide" employs the language and methodology of classical philosophy to present Judaism's understanding of G-d, creation, and the purposes of the *mitzvot*.

1191
LETTER ON THE RESURRECTION OF THE DEAD

A treatise in which Maimonides defends and explains his understanding of the messianic redemption, the World to Come, and the future resurrection of the dead.

1204
PASSING AND BURIAL

Maimonides passed away in Egypt, and was buried in Tiberias, Israel. His headstone bears the epitaph, "From Moses to Moses none arose like Moses."

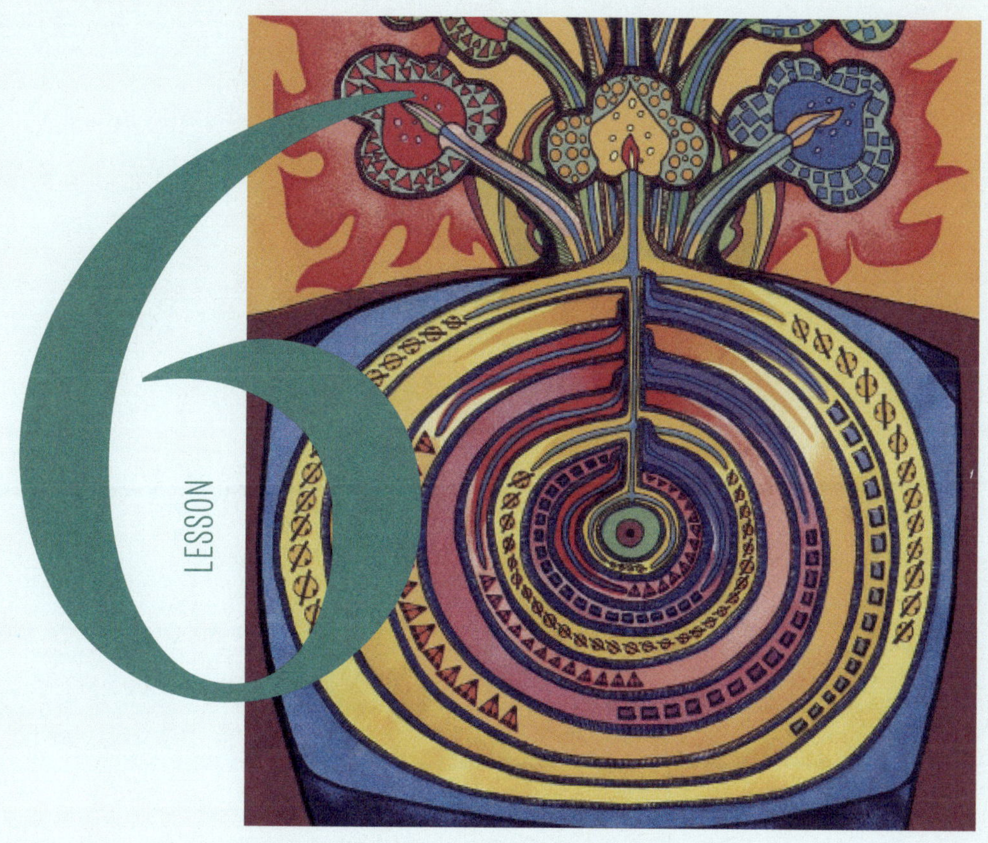

LESSON 6

KABBALAH AND CHASIDISM

Kabbalah is the Torah's mystical dimension, containing its most powerful and empowering ideas. Chasidism is both an extension of Kabbalah as well as a field of Torah in its own right, revealing the inner "soul" that unites the Torah's various components and applying its most abstract spiritual teachings in personally meaningful ways. In addition to surveying the history of Jewish mysticism, we will also uncover some of its most closely guarded secrets by studying an esoteric passage in the Zohar *and the Kabbalistic and Chasidic texts that decipher its meaning.*

THE TREE OF LIFE
(Detail), David Friedman

I. WHAT IS KABBALAH?

Kabbalah is the Torah's inner, spiritual dimension, containing its most powerful and empowering ideas. But these esoteric teachings are also extremely subtle, and can easily be misunderstood and corrupted. As a result, the history of Kabbalah is driven by two paradoxical aims: to transmit and to conceal.

FIGURE 6.1

Two Names, Opposite Meanings

	HEBREW NAME	MEANING
קַבָּלָה	*Kabbalah*	"that which is received"
סוֹד	*Sod*	"secret"

TEXT 1

Hidden Kernels

Maimonides, *Guide for the Perplexed* 1:71

וּכְבָר יָדַעְתָּ שֶׁאֲפִלּוּ הַתַּלְמוּד הַמְקֻבָּל לֹא הָיָה מְחֻבָּר בְּסֵפֶר מִקֹּדֶם לְעִנְיָן הַמִּתְפַּשֵּׁט בָּאֻמָּה . . . וְאִם הַתּוֹרָה שֶׁבְּעַל פֶּה נָפְלָה בָּהּ הַקְפָּדָה מֵהַשְׁאִירָה לָעַד בְּחִבּוּר מְפֻרְסָם לִבְנֵי אָדָם כֻּלָּם, לָמָּה שֶׁיַּגִּיעַ בָּזֶה מִן הַהֶפְסֵד, כָּל שֶׁכֵּן שֶׁיְּחֻבַּר דָּבָר מֵאֵלּוּ סִתְרֵי הַתּוֹרָה וִיפֻרְסַם לִבְנֵי אָדָם כֻּלָּם.

אֲבָל הָיוּ נִמְסָרִים מִיְּחִידֵי סְגֻלּוֹת לִיחִידֵי סְגֻלּוֹת. כְּמוֹ שֶׁבֵּאַרְתִּי לְךָ מַאֲמָרָם, "אֵין מוֹסְרִים סִתְרֵי תּוֹרָה אֶלָּא

לְיוֹעֵץ חֲכַם חֲרָשִׁים וְכוּ'" . . . וְלֹא תִּמְצָא מֵהֶם אֶלָּא הֶעָרוֹת קְטַנּוֹת וּרְמִיזוֹת בָּאוּ בַּתַּלְמוּד וּבְמִדְרָשׁוֹת. וְהֵן גַּרְגִּירֵי לֵב מְעַטִּים עֲלֵיהֶם קְלִפּוֹת רַבּוֹת, עַד שֶׁהִתְעַסְּקוּ בְּנֵי אָדָם כֻּלָּם בַּקְּלִפּוֹת הַהֵם וְחָשְׁבוּ שֶׁאֵין תַּחְתָּם לֵב בְּשׁוּם פָּנִים.

As you are well aware, even the Talmud, which was received by tradition, was not originally committed to writing in a book that was disseminated to the people. . . . Now, if care was taken to avoid writing the Oral Torah in a book accessible to all because of the disadvantages in such a system, certainly, then, no portion of the esoteric teachings of Torah could be written, which would divulge these teachings to everyone.

Rather, these teachings were orally communicated by a few uniquely qualified individuals to other uniquely qualified individuals, as I earlier explained the saying (TALMUD, CHAGIGAH 13A), "The secrets of the Torah can only be entrusted to skilled sages. . . ." Nothing but a few remarks and allusions to these teachings are to be found in the Talmud and the Midrashim. They are like small kernels enveloped in many husks, so that the reader is generally occupied with the husk without thinking that it encloses a kernel.

RABBI MOSHE BEN MAIMON (MAIMONIDES, RAMBAM) 1135–1204

Halachist, philosopher, author, and physician. Maimonides was born in Córdoba, Spain. After the conquest of Córdoba by the Almohads, he fled Spain and eventually settled in Cairo, Egypt. There, he became the leader of the Jewish community and served as court physician to the vizier of Egypt. He is most noted for authoring the *Mishneh Torah*, an encyclopedic arrangement of Jewish law; and for his philosophical work, *Guide for the Perplexed*. His rulings on Jewish law are integral to the formation of halachic consensus.

Is Mysticism Biblical?
Rabbi Menashe Wolf responds:
myjli.com/booksmart

TEXT 2

Four Who Entered the Orchard

Talmud, Chagigah 14b

אַרְבָּעָה נִכְנְסוּ בַּפַּרְדֵס וְאֵלוּ הֵן: בֶּן עַזַאי, וּבֶן זוֹמָא, אַחֵר, וְרַבִּי עֲקִיבָא . . . בֶּן עַזַאי הֵצִיץ וָמֵת . . . בֶּן זוֹמָא הֵצִיץ וְנִפְגַע . . . אַחֵר קִיצֵץ בִּנְטִיעוֹת, רַבִּי עֲקִיבָא נִכְנַס בְּשָׁלוֹם וְיָצָא בְּשָׁלוֹם.

Four sages entered the orchard: Ben Azai, Ben Zoma, Acher, and Rabbi Akiva. . . . Ben Azai looked and died. . . . Ben Zoma looked and went mad. . . . Acher cut down the plantings [i.e., became a heretic]. Rabbi Akiva entered in wholeness and peace, and emerged in wholeness and peace.

BABYLONIAN TALMUD

A literary work of monumental proportions that draws upon the legal, spiritual, intellectual, ethical, and historical traditions of Judaism. The 37 tractates of the Babylonian Talmud contain the teachings of the Jewish sages from the period after the destruction of the 2nd Temple through the 5th century CE. It has served as the primary vehicle for the transmission of the Oral Law and the education of Jews over the centuries; it is the entry point for all subsequent legal, ethical, and theological Jewish scholarship.

FOUR WENT TO PARADISE
Shoshannah Brombacher, drawing, 1996.

An Esteemed Kabbalist Explains Kabbalah:
myjli.com/booksmart

II. A BRIEF HISTORY OF KABBALAH

In this section, we survey the history of Kabbalah, noting the primary teachers, works, and schools of Kabbalistic teaching through the centuries.

TZFAT-SAFED, CITY OF KABBALAH LIGHT
Alex Levin, oil on canvas.

Where Did the Teaching of Kabbalah Come From? **Rabbi Dr. Breitowitz** explains: **myjli.com/booksmart**

FIGURE 6.2

Milestones in the History of Kabbalah

423 BCE
VISION OF THE CHARIOT
The prophet Ezekiel's vision of the "Divine chariot" *(merkavah)*, recorded in the biblical book of Ezekiel, is the origin for many Kabbalistic principles and ideas.

40 CE
BAHIR
"Book of Brilliance." A mystical exposition on the opening chapters of the Book of Genesis, attributed to 1st-century sage Rabbi Nechunia ben Hakanah.

100 CE
SEFER YETZIRAH
"Book of Formation." Attributed to the patriarch Abraham; transcribed by 2nd-century sage Rabbi Akiva. The work describes how the Creator employed ten *sefirot* (Divine attributes) and combinations of the letters of the Hebrew *alef-bet* to create the world. Numerous commentaries were composed over the centuries to decipher its cryptic verses.

1150-1300
CHASIDIM OF ASHKENAZ
School of Jewish mystics active in the German Rhineland in the 12th and 13th centuries. Its leaders included Rabbi Yehudah heChasid (1150–1217) and Rabbi Elazar Roke'ach of Worms (1176–1238).

100 CE
HEICHALOT
"Chambers." A series of Kabbalistic Midrashim attributed to Rabbi Yishma'el ben Elisha, a colleague of Rabbi Akiva.

150 CE
ZOHAR
The most fundamental work of Kabbalah. Records the teachings of 2nd-century sage Rabbi Shimon bar Yocha'i ("Rashbi") and his disciples. Its manuscripts were first made public by the Kabbalist Rabbi Moshe de Leon toward the end of the 13th century, but its texts were known and are cited in classical Jewish works going back to the Talmudic period.

1200
RABBI YITZCHAK THE BLIND
c. 1160–1235, Provence, France. A preeminent Kabbalist who was the son of Raavad and Nachmanides's teacher in Kabbalah.

1165
RAAVAD
Rabbi Abraham ben David of Posquieres, c. 1125–1198, was a key link in the transmission of Kabbalah.

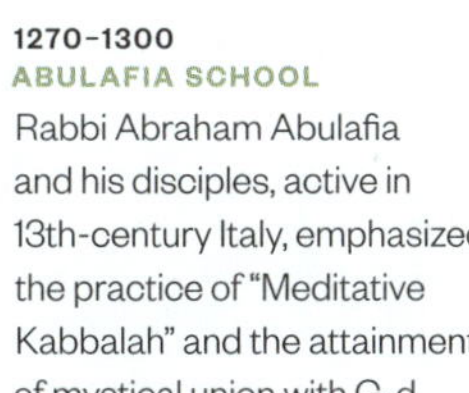

1270–1300
ABULAFIA SCHOOL
Rabbi Abraham Abulafia and his disciples, active in 13th-century Italy, emphasized the practice of "Meditative Kabbalah" and the attainment of mystical union with G-d.

1290
RECANATI
Rabbi Menachem Recanati (1223–1290, Italy) authored a Kabbalistic commentary on the Torah, which also explains many of the obscure Kabbalistic passages in Nachmanides's commentary.

1523
IBN GABBAI
Rabbi Meir ibn Gabbai (c. 1480–1540) lived in Spain and Egypt. Ibn Gabbai authored a number of foundational Kabbalistic works, including *Avodat Hakodesh* ("Holy Service").

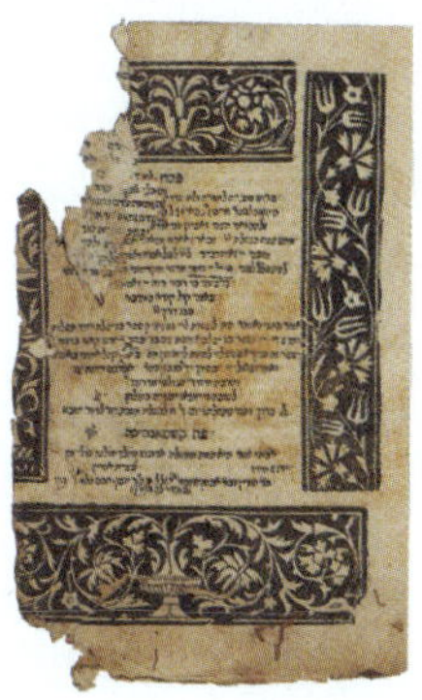

1300
5060

1400
5160

1500
5260

1264
NACHMANIDES
Rabbi Moshe ben Nachman, c. 1195–1270, of Girona, Catalonia and later Jerusalem, Israel. One of the preeminent sages of Spanish Jewry, Nachmanides authored prominent works in all areas of Torah scholarship: biblical commentary, Talmudic analysis, Torah law, Jewish philosophy, and ethics. Nachmanides was also a master Kabbalist, who incorporated many Kabbalistic ideas into his commentary on the Torah.

1350
MAARECHET HA'ELOKUT
"The Divine System." A foundational 14th-century Kabbalistic work of undetermined authorship. It was later published together with a commentary—essentially a work in its own right—by the Kabbalist Rabbi Yehudah Chayat (c. 1500; Spain and Italy).

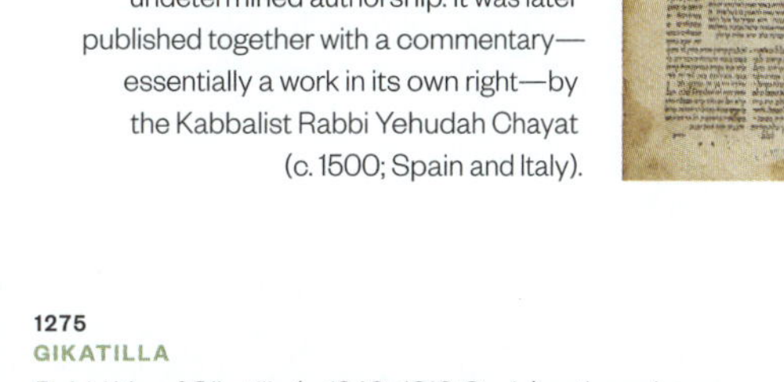

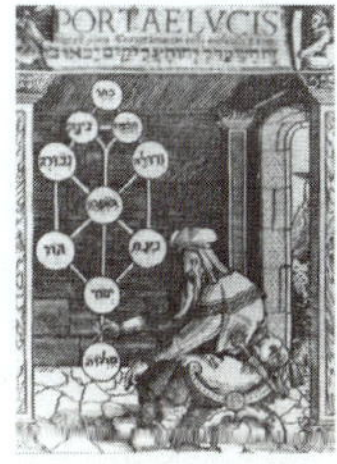

1275
GIKATILLA
Rabbi Yosef Gikatilla (c. 1248–1310, Spain) authored many important Kabbalistic works. His *Shaarei Orah* ("Gates of Light") discusses the relationship between the names of G-d and the *sefirot*, and other mystical topics. The Ari called it "the key to all esoteric knowledge."

1530
RABBI SHLOMO ALKABETZ
c. 1500–1580. One of the early teachers of Kabbalah in Safed, his students included Rabbi Yosef Caro and Rabbi Moshe Cordovero (although Alkabetz later considered Cordovero his teacher). Alkabetz is known as the author of the mystical poem *Lechah Dodi* ("Come, my beloved, to meet the bride . . ."), sung to welcome the Shabbat.

1560
RABBI ABRAHAM GALANTE
Disciple of Alkabetz and Ramak. Authored a number of important Kabbalistic works, including a commentary on *Zohar*.

1570
ARI
Rabbi Yitzchak Luria (1534–1572). Founder of the "Lurianic" School of Kabbalah, upon which almost all subsequent Jewish mystical teaching is predicated.

1588
RABBI ELAZAR AZIKRI
1533–1600. A disciple of Alkabetz. Authored *Charedim*, a Kabbalistic treatment of the 613 *mitzvot*. Composed the devotional poem *Yedid Nefesh* ("Soul Friend").

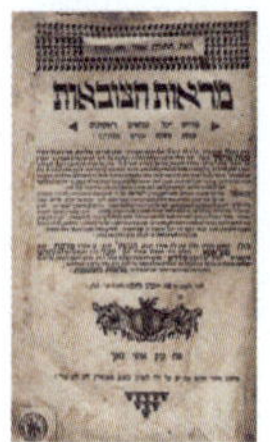

1593
ALSHICH
Rabbi Moshe Alshich (1508–1593) was a disciple of Caro, Ramak, and Ari. Alshich authored a popular commentary on the Torah.

THE SAFED KABBALISTS

1530 YEAR BCE
5290 YEAR ON JEWISH CALENDAR

1600
5360

POST-SAFEDIAN KABBALISTS & SCHOOLS

1533
RABBI YOSEF CARO
Known primarily as the author of the *Shulchan Aruch* (Code of Jewish Law), Caro was also an accomplished Kabbalist who recorded his mystical visions in his *Magid Mesharim*.

1550
RAMAK
Rabbi Moshe Cordovero (1522–1570), known by the acronym "Ramak," was the primary teacher of Kabbalah in Safed in the years 1550 to 1570.

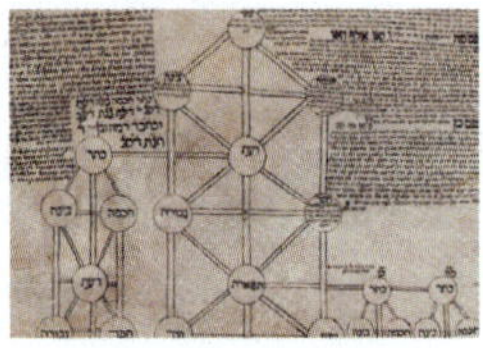

1572
RABBI CHAIM VITAL
1543–1620. Ari's leading disciple and the primary transcriber of his teachings.

1575
RABBI ELIYAHU DE VIDAS
1518–1587. A disciple of Ramak and Ari. Author of the moral-mystical work *Reshit Chochmah* ("Genesis of Wisdom").

1595
RABBI SHMUEL DE UCEDA
Died c. 1604. A disciple of Alkabetz, Ari, and Vital. De Uceda is most famous for his *Midrash Shmuel*, a comprehensive commentary on *Ethics of the Fathers*.

1600
RABBI YISRAEL NAJARA
c. 1555–1625. Najara's father was a disciple of Ari. His own works include poetry, Kabbalistic discourses, Torah law, ethics, and responsa. Known as the composer of the Shabbat song *Kah Ribon Olam*. Served as the rabbi of Gaza.

1600
RABBI MENACHEM AZARIAH DA FANO
1548–1620. A disciple of Rabbi Yisrael Sarug, who came to Da Fano's native Italy to spread the Lurianic Kabbalah. Author of *Asarah Maamarot* ("Ten Utterances"), a voluminous and fundamental Kabbalistic work.

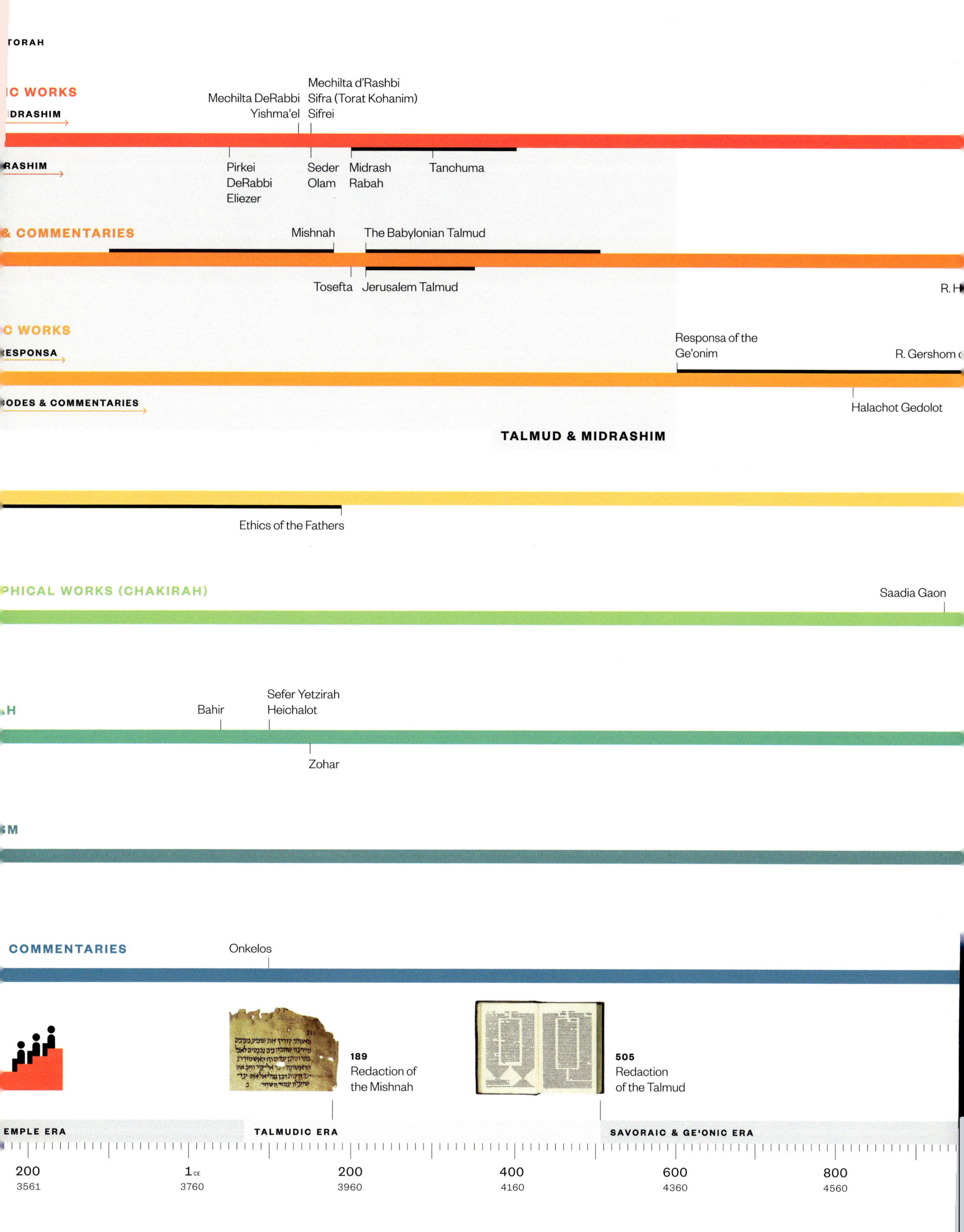
TORAH
IC WORKS
IDRASHIM
Mechilta d'Rashbi
Mechilta DeRabbi Yishma'el
Sifra (Torat Kohanim)
Sifrei
RASHIM
Pirkei DeRabbi Eliezer
Seder Olam
Midrash Rabah
Tanchuma
& COMMENTARIES
Mishnah
The Babylonian Talmud
Tosefta
Jerusalem Talmud
R. H
C WORKS
ESPONSA
Responsa of the Ge'onim
R. Gershom
ODES & COMMENTARIES
Halachot Gedolot
TALMUD & MIDRASHIM
Ethics of the Fathers
PHICAL WORKS (CHAKIRAH)
Saadia Gaon
H
Bahir
Sefer Yetzirah
Heichalot
Zohar
M
COMMENTARIES
Onkelos
189
Redaction of the Mishnah
505
Redaction of the Talmud
EMPLE ERA
TALMUDIC ERA
SAVORAIC & GE'ONIC ERA
200
3561
1 CE
3760
200
3960
400
4160
600
4360
800
4560

CONTENTS OF THE 24 BOOKS OF THE TANACH

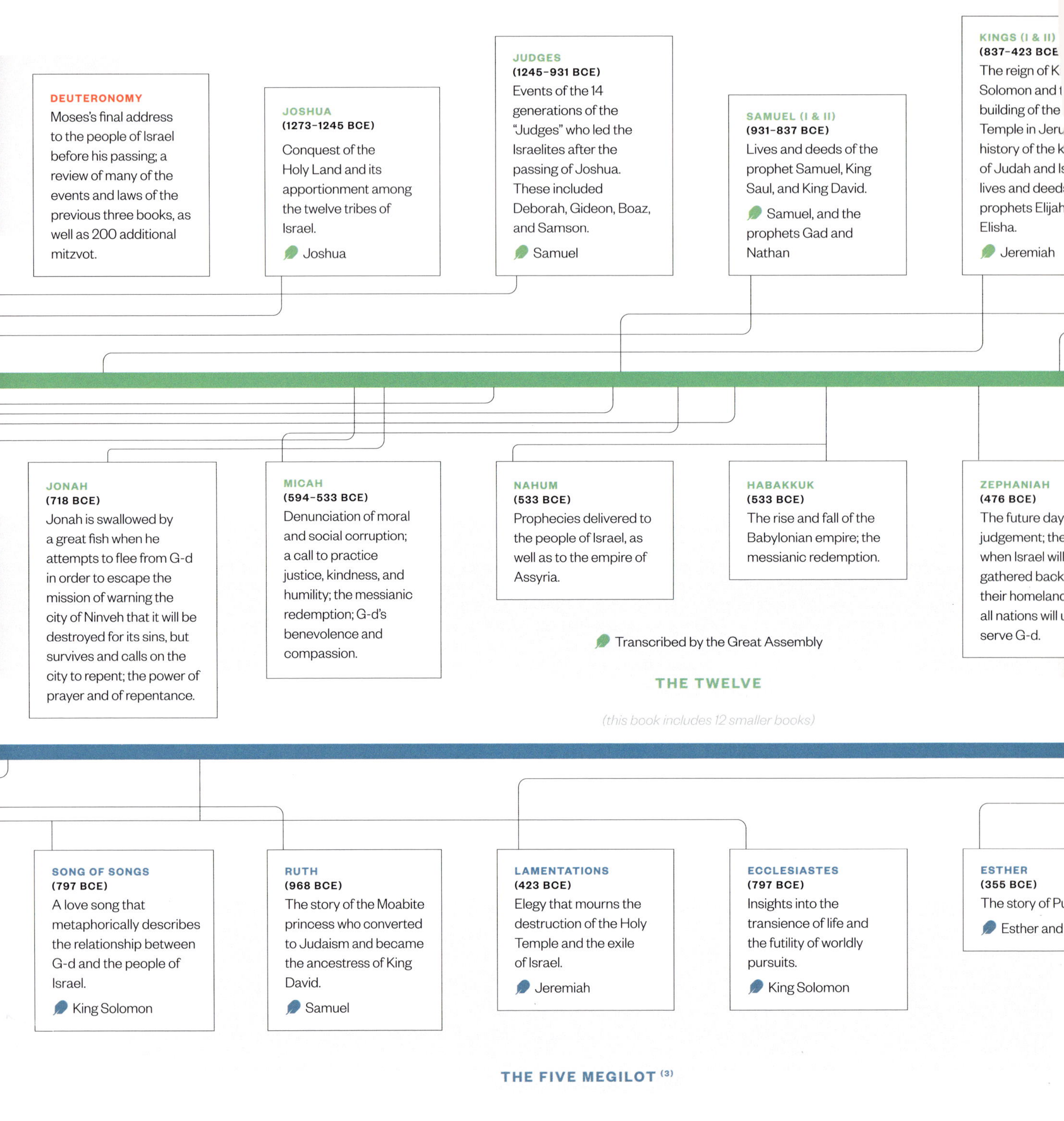

800	600
2961	3161

m;
oms
;
the
d

ISAIAH
(619–533 BCE)
Prophecies of consolation over the destruction of the Holy Temple and the Exile; the reconciliation between G-d and Israel; the coming of Mashiach and the future messianic age of peace, perfection, and Divine revelation.

authored by Isaiah; transcribed by Hezekiah and his court

JEREMIAH
(436–409 BCE)
Warnings of the destruction of Jerusalem and the Holy Temple because of the people's sins and injustices; the promise that the exiles to Babylon will return after 70 years.

Jeremiah

EZEKIEL
(429–409 BCE)
Vision of the "Divine chariot" that is the source for many of the mystical teachings of Kabbalah; prophecies of the future redemption, including a description of the third Holy Temple.

authored by Ezekiel; transcribed by the Great Assembly

e
d
e to

HAGGAI
(371 BCE)
Overcoming the difficulties in the return to Zion and the building of the second Holy Temple.

ZECHARIAH
(371 BCE)
Mystical visions of angels and celestial worlds; the peace, prosperity, and spiritual renaissance of the future redemption.

MALACHI
(371 BCE)
G-d's love for the people of Israel; rebuke of corrupt priests; Elijah's heralding of the future redemption, and the reconciliation of parents and children.

.
decai

DANIEL
(421–372 BCE)
Life and visions of Daniel, a Judean prince who served in the courts of Babylonian and Persian emperors; prophecies on the historical rise and fall of nations and of the timing of the messianic redemption.

authored by Daniel; transcribed by the Great Assembly

EZRA-NEHEMIAH
(348–313 BCE)
Describes the Jewish people's return from Babylon, the reestablishment of their commitment to the Torah, and the building of the second Holy Temple.

Ezra and Nehemiah

CHRONICLES (I & II)
(313 BCE)
Summary of the whole of Biblical history.

Ezra

400
3361

200
3561

Public readings from Tanach:

(1) THE WEEKLY PARSHAH

The custom for the community to gather each Shabbat to listen to the reading of the Torah dates back to the times of Moses. Each week, another section ("*parshah*") of the Torah is read, until the Five Books are completed. In order to complete the cycle in one year, the Torah is divided into 54 *parshiyot*. Each *parshah* is further divided into seven readings. During the Shabbat morning service in the synagogue, seven individuals are called up to the Torah scroll to recite the blessings on the Torah and read one section of the week's *parshah*. In addition to the public readings, each individual reviews the *parshah* of the week along with the *Targum* (the Aramaic translation/commentary by Onkelos) and, in the course of the week, studies it with Rashi's commentary, discovering in each day's reading a lesson that is relevant to that day of our lives.

(2) THE HAFTARAH

At the conclusion of the public reading of the *parshah*, an eighth person is called up to the Torah, and after a short segment of the *parshah* is repeated, that person reads a section from "Prophets" called the "*haftarah*." The topic of the *haftarah* reflects that of the week's *parshah*, or is otherwise connected with the time of year. This custom originated in a time when anti-Jewish decrees prevented the public reading of the Torah, so a passage from the Prophets was read in its place. Though initially prompted by negative circumstances, the custom was retained, and the poetry of the prophets is now a regular accompaniment to the Torah reading of the week.

(3) THE FIVE MEGILOT

These five books from the "Writings" section of Tanach, known as the "five scrolls" (*megilot* in Hebrew), are publicly read at special times of the year: the scroll of Esther on Purim, Song of Songs on Passover, Ruth on Shavuot, Lamentations on Tishah Be'Av, and Ecclesiastes on Sukkot.

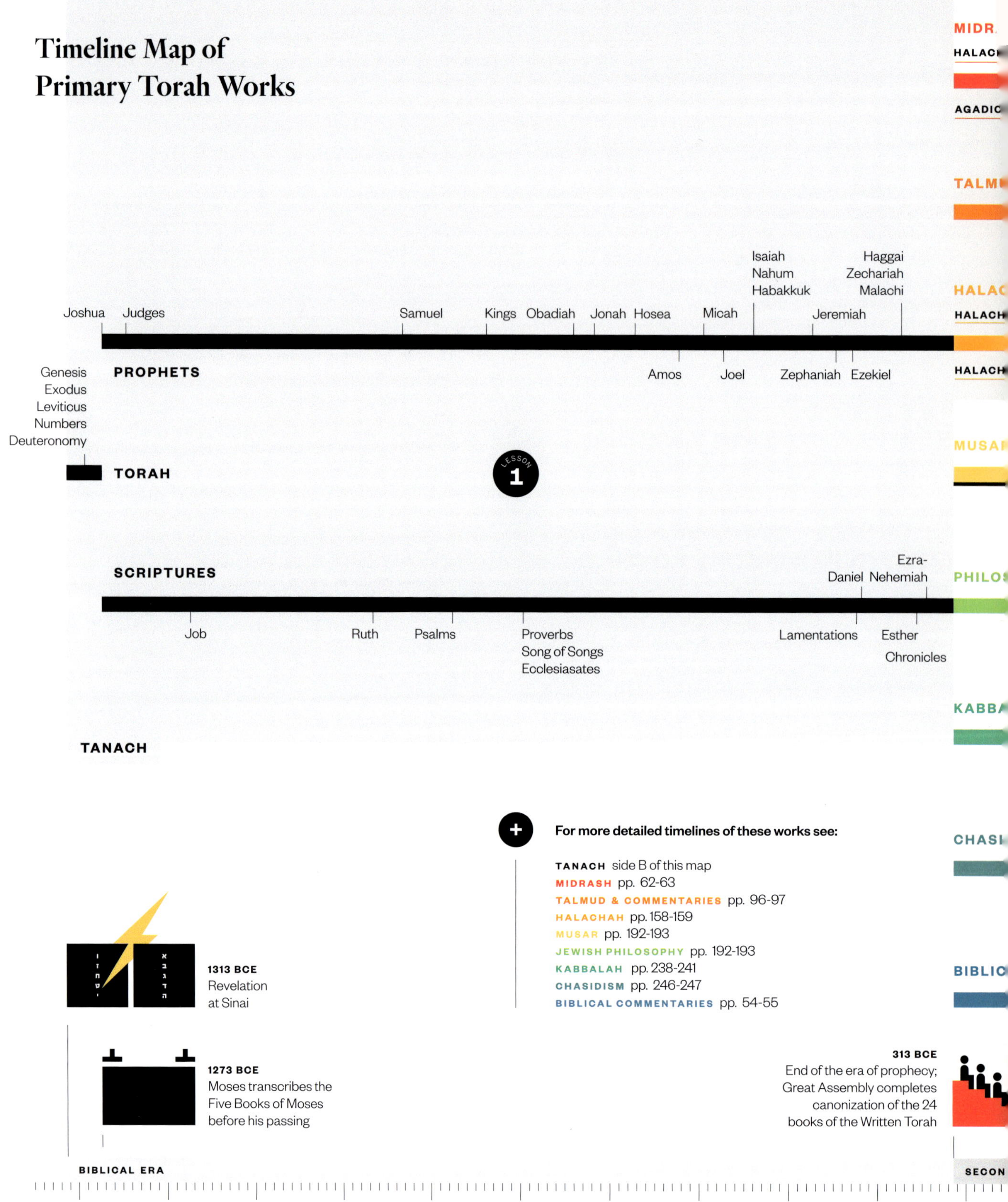

1300 YEAR BCE
2461 YEAR ON JEWISH CALENDAR

1300	1000	800	600	400
2461	2761	2961	3161	3361

TORAH [1]
(1313–1273 BCE)

GENESIS
Creation of the world; early human history (Adam & Eve, Cain & Abel, Noah's Flood, the Tower of Babel); and the lives and deeds of the founding fathers and mothers of the people of Israel—Abraham & Sarah, Isaac & Rebecca, Jacob, Rachel, Leah, and their children. Also includes the seven Noahide Laws and three of the 613 *mitzvot* of the Torah.

EXODUS
The Exodus from Egypt; the giving of the Torah at Mount Sinai; the construction of the Tabernacle. Includes the Ten Commandments and 101 other mitzvot.

LEVITICUS
Records 247 mitzvot commanded by G-d to Moses, pertaining to the Temple service, the kosher dietary laws, the festivals of the Jewish year, and a variety of ritualistic, social, and civil laws, including the maxim, "Love your fellow as yourself."

NUMBERS
Events of the Israelites' 40-year journey through the wilderness; also includes 52 mitzvot.

PROPHETS [2]

HOSEA
(671–646 BCE)
The prophet Hosea is told to marry an unfaithful woman in order to experience firsthand G-d's interminable love for His people despite their unfaithfulness.

JOEL
(571 BCE)
The future day of judgment of the nations who persecuted the people of Israel; the Divine enlightenment of the messianic era.

AMOS
(621 BCE)
Denunciation of the exploitation of the weak and poor by the rich and powerful; the hypocrisy in serving G-d while failing to practice justice and charity.

OBADIAH
(740 BCE)
Obadiah, an Edomite convert to Judaism, prophesizes the punishment of the enemies of Israel and the establishment of the Divine sovereignty in the world.

SCRIPTURES

PSALMS (TEHILIM)
(877 BCE)
Lyrical prayers and praises of G-d. Although composed in the Holy Land nearly 3000 years ago, the verses of Psalms express the yearnings, tribulations, and exultations of the Jewish soul in every land and century. They form an integral part of every Jewish prayer, and are read at every occasion from a birth to a funeral, and whenever a Jew has need to plead for divine assistance, celebrate a triumph, or simply talk to G-d.

composed by King David; includes psalms by Adam, Abraham, Moses, and other poets

PROVERBS
(797 BCE)
Aphorisms on the virtues of wisdom, hard work, and a moral life.

King Solomon

JOB
(1273 BCE)
Job and his three friends debate the question, "Why do the righteous suffer?"

Moses

ICON KEY

authored by

1300 YEAR BCE
2461 YEAR ON JEWISH CALENDAR

1000
2761

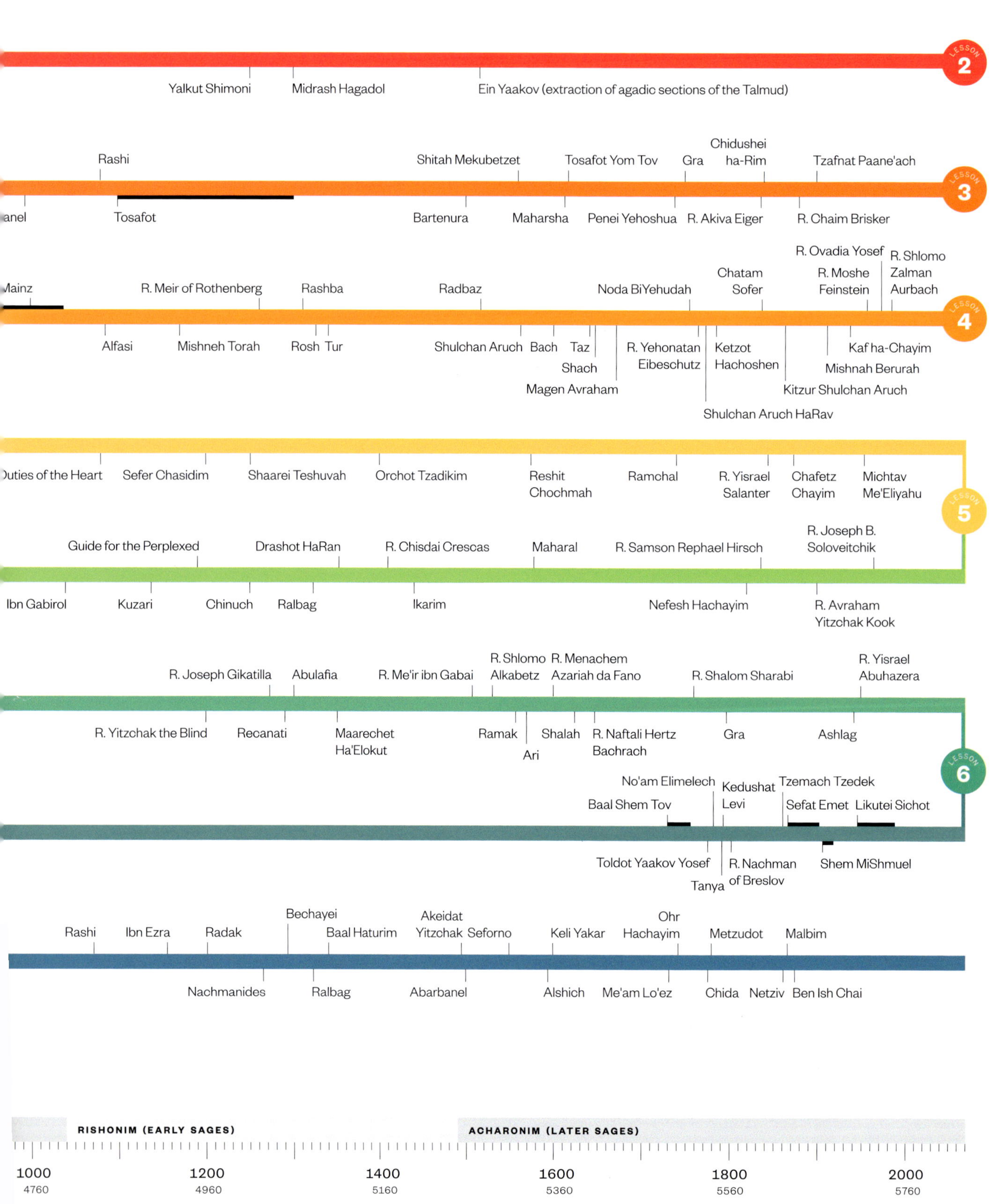

LESSON 2
Yalkut Shimoni
Midrash Hagadol
Ein Yaakov (extraction of agadic sections of the Talmud)
LESSON 3
Rashi
Shitah Mekubetzet
Tosafot Yom Tov
Gra
Chidushei ha-Rim
Tzafnat Paane'ach
anel
Tosafot
Bartenura
Maharsha
Penei Yehoshua
R. Akiva Eiger
R. Chaim Brisker
LESSON 4
Mainz
R. Meir of Rothenberg
Rashba
Radbaz
Noda BiYehudah
Chatam Sofer
R. Ovadia Yosef
R. Moshe Feinstein
R. Shlomo Zalman Aurbach
Alfasi
Mishneh Torah
Rosh
Tur
Shulchan Aruch
Bach
Taz
Shach
Magen Avraham
R. Yehonatan Eibeschutz
Ketzot Hachoshen
Shulchan Aruch HaRav
Kitzur Shulchan Aruch
Mishnah Berurah
Kaf ha-Chayim
LESSON 5
Duties of the Heart
Sefer Chasidim
Shaarei Teshuvah
Orchot Tzadikim
Reshit Chochmah
Ramchal
R. Yisrael Salanter
Chafetz Chayim
Michtav Me'Eliyahu
Guide for the Perplexed
Drashot HaRan
R. Chisdai Crescas
Maharal
R. Samson Rephael Hirsch
R. Joseph B. Soloveitchik
Ibn Gabirol
Kuzari
Chinuch
Ralbag
Ikarim
Nefesh Hachayim
R. Avraham Yitzchak Kook
LESSON 6
R. Joseph Gikatilla
Abulafia
R. Me'ir ibn Gabai
R. Shlomo Alkabetz
R. Menachem Azariah da Fano
R. Shalom Sharabi
R. Yisrael Abuhazera
R. Yitzchak the Blind
Recanati
Maarechet Ha'Elokut
Ramak
Ari
Shalah
R. Naftali Hertz Bachrach
Gra
Ashlag
No'am Elimelech
Baal Shem Tov
Kedushat Levi
Tzemach Tzedek
Sefat Emet
Likutei Sichot
Toldot Yaakov Yosef
Tanya
R. Nachman of Breslov
Shem MiShmuel
Rashi
Ibn Ezra
Radak
Bechayei
Baal Haturim
Akeidat Yitzchak
Seforno
Keli Yakar
Ohr Hachayim
Metzudot
Malbim
Nachmanides
Ralbag
Abarbanel
Alshich
Me'am Lo'ez
Chida
Netziv
Ben Ish Chai
RISHONIM (EARLY SAGES)
ACHARONIM (LATER SAGES)
1000 4760
1200 4960
1400 5160
1600 5360
1800 5560
2000 5760

1600
RABBI YISRAEL SARUG
A disciple of the Ari who for 20 years (1590–1610) traveled extensively to introduce the Lurianic Kabbalah in Italy, the Balkans, Germany, Poland, Turkey, Egypt, and elsewhere.

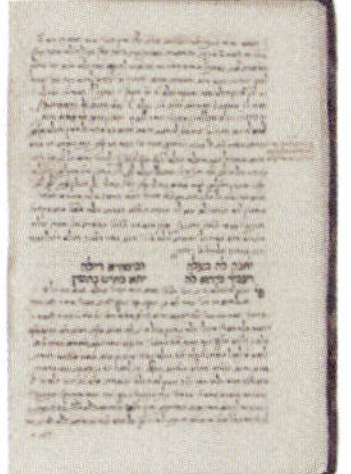

1600
MAHARAL
Rabbi Yehudah Loew (1520–1609) of Prague, known by the acronym "Maharal," was a mystic and philosopher who expressed Kabbalistic ideas in philosophical terms. There is a tradition that Maharal used Kabbalistic formulae to create a *golem* (humanoid) to save the Jewish community of Prague from the frequent blood libels of the time. Maharal's Kabbalah appears to derive from earlier sources, as the Safedian Kabbalah had not yet reached eastern Europe in his day.

1648
RABBI NAFTALI HERTZ BACHARACH
17th-century Germany. Author of *Emek Hamelech* ("King's Dale"), a comprehensive exposition of Lurianic Kabbalah.

1740
RAMCHAL
Rabbi Moshe Chaim Luzzatto (1707–1746), who lived in Italy and Holland, was a prodigious author in the areas of Kabbalah, philosophy, ethics, and poetry.

1750
THE GRA SCHOOL OF KABBALAH
The Kabbalistic teachings of Rabbi Eliyahu the Gaon of Vilna ("Gra") and his disciples. Kabbalists of the Gra School include Rabbi Chaim of Volozhin (1749–1821), Rabbi Menachem Mendel of Shklov (d. 1827), Rabbi Eizik Chaver (1789–1853), Rabbi David Luria (1798–1855), and Rabbi Shlomo Elyashiv (author of the *Leshem*, 1840–1926).

1700
5460

1800
5560

1624
SHALAH
Rabbi Yeshayahu Horowitz, 1560–1630. Served as a rabbi in numerous Jewish communities in both Europe and the Holy Land, including Dubna, Frankfurt, Prague, Jerusalem, Safed, and Tiberias. Known as "Shalah" after his magnum opus, *Shenei Luchot Haberit* ("Two Tablets of the Covenant"), which blends Kabbalah, Talmudic discourse, Torah law and customs, biblical commentary, and ethics. Shalah's works incorporate the teachings of Ramak and Ari and their disciples.

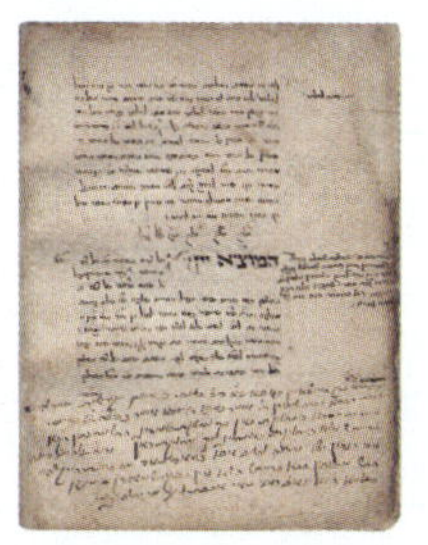

1734
CHASIDISM
Founded by Rabbi Yisrael Baal Shem Tov (1698–1760), predicated on the principles of Lurianic Kabbalah. In addition to revealing an entirely new dimension of Torah, Chasidism also popularized and made accessible the teachings of Kabbalah. See Figure 6.3 (pp. ###) for an overview of Chasidism's major works.

1742
RABBI CHAIM IBN ATTAR
1696–1743. Born in Morocco, in 1741 Ibn Attar actualized his life's dream to settle in the Holy Land, and in the following year he founded a yeshiva in Jerusalem. It is told that the Baal Shem Tov made a number of (unsuccessful) attempts to reach the Holy Land to meet with him, in the belief that together they could bring Mashiach. Known as "*Ohr Hachayim*" after his work by that name—a multifaceted commentary on Torah that incorporates Kabbalistic insights.

1760
BEIT-EL SCHOOL OF JERUSALEM
Served as a center of Kabbalah for 250 years. Its leaders included Rabbi Shalom Sharabi of Yemen (1720–1777), and Rabbi Chaim Yosef David Azulai ("Chida," 1724–1806).

III. WHAT IS CHASIDISM?

Chasidism is an extension of Kabbalah as well as a field of Torah in its own right. It is the inner "soul" that unites the various dimensions of Torah, and it represents the final phase of the Torah's unfolding revelation from Sinai to Mashiach.

TEXT 3

The Perpetual Voice

Rabbi Yeshayah Halevi Horowitz, *Shenei Luchot Haberit*, 1:25a–b

וְעִנְיַן "נוֹתֵן הַתּוֹרָה", בֶּאֱמֶת ה' יִתְבָּרַךְ כְּבָר נְתָנָהּ, אֲבָל עֲדַיִן נוֹתֵן הַתּוֹרָה וְלֹא יִפְסֹק. וְדָבָר זֶה צָרִיךְ בֵּאוּר רָחָב.

הַפָּסוּק אוֹמֵר: "אֶת הַדְּבָרִים הָאֵלֶּה דִּבֶּר ה' אֶל כָּל קְהַלְכֶם בָּהָר . . . קוֹל גָּדוֹל וְלֹא יָסָף" (דְּבָרִים ה, יט). פֵּרֵשׁ רַשִׁ"י: "וְלֹא יָסָף, מְתַרְגְּמִינָן 'וְלֹא פָּסַק', כִּי קוֹלוֹ חָזָק וְקַיָּם לְעוֹלָם. דָּבָר אַחֵר לֹא יָסָף, לֹא הוֹסִיף לְהֵרָאוֹת בְּאוֹתוֹ פֻּמְבֵּי", עַד כָּאן לְשׁוֹנוֹ.

יֵשׁ בָּזֶה הָעִנְיָן סוֹד כָּמוּס, וְהַשְּׁנֵי פֵּרוּשִׁים כֻּלָּם הֵם אֱמֶת. עִנְיָן "לֹא יָסָף – לֹא הוֹסִיף", הוּא מִצְוֹת דְּרַבָּנָן וְחֻמְרָתָן, הֵן וּסְיָגֵיהֶן, עֲדַיִן לֹא נִצְטַוּוּ מִפִּי הַגְּבוּרָה. וְעִנְיָן "לֹא פָּסַק", פֵּרוּשׁ שֶׁאַף זֶה לֹא פָּסַק מֵהַקּוֹל הַהוּא, כִּי הָיָה כָּלוּל בַּקּוֹל הַהוּא בְּכֹחַ, אֲבָל "לַכֹּל זְמַן וָעֵת", לֹא הִגִּיעַ עֲדַיִן עֵת שֶׁיֵּצֵא מִכֹּחַ אֶל הַפֹּעַל, כִּי הָיָה הַדָּבָר תָּלוּי לְפִי הִתְעוֹרְרוּת הַתַּחְתּוֹנִים, וּלְפִי מַהוּתָם וְאֵיכוּתָם, וּלְפִי מַדְרֵגוֹת נְשָׁמוֹת שֶׁבְּכָל דּוֹר וָדוֹר. וְאָז הוֹסִיפוּ הַחֲכָמִים לְהִתְעוֹרֵר [מִן] הַכֹּחַ הָעֶלְיוֹן, וְיָצָא לַפֹּעַל בִּזְמַנּוֹ וּבְעִתּוֹ; לֹא חַס וְשָׁלוֹם שֶׁחִדְּשׁוּ חֲכָמִים מִדַּעְתָּם, רַק כִּוְּנוּ דַּעַת עֶלְיוֹן.

RABBI YESHAYAH HALEVI HOROWITZ (*SHALAH*) 1565–1630

Kabbalist and author. Rabbi Horowitz was born in Prague and served as rabbi in several prominent Jewish communities, including Frankfurt am Main and his native Prague. After the passing of his wife in 1620, he moved to Israel. In Tiberias, he completed his *Shenei Luchot Haberit*, an encyclopedic compilation of kabbalistic ideas. He is buried in Tiberias, next to Maimonides.

[In the blessing recited before studying Torah, we say, "Blessed are you, G-d,] Who gives the Torah." In truth, G-d has already given us the Torah [at Mount Sinai]; yet He still "gives the Torah," perpetually. This matter requires some elaboration.

The Torah says (DEUTERONOMY 5:19): "These words G-d spoke to your entire assembly at the mountain . . . a great voice that did not cease." Rashi explains the meaning of the words "did not cease" (*velo yasaf*) in accordance with the translation by *Unkelos*—"it did not stop," for it is a powerful voice that endures forever. Rashi also offers a second interpretation of the words *velo yasaf*—"it did not any more," i.e., that G-d did not again speak so openly and publicly as He did at Sinai.

There is a profound significance in these two interpretations, as they are simultaneously true. The Divine voice spoke the Torah at Sinai and "did not any more," as all the subsequent laws and edicts instituted by the sages throughout the generations were not explicitly commanded by G-d at the time. At the same time, "it did not cease," for everything was included, in potential form, within that voice. It is only that "for everything there is a time and season" (ECCLESIASTES 3:1), and the time had not yet come for that potential to emerge into actuality, as that depends on the initiative of those down here below, in accordance with their nature and their abilities, and in accordance with the qualities of the souls of each generation. The sages of each generation were then roused to actualize from that potential in accordance with the time and season. Thus, the sages did not invent anything from their own minds, G-d forbid, but rather actualized the Divine intent.

ON THE WAY TO REBBI
Leon Zernitsky,
acrylic on canvas

What Is Chassidism and When Did It Start?
myjli.com/booksmart

TEXT 4

Spreading of the Wellsprings

Rabbi Yisrael Baal Shem Tov, *Keter Shem Tov*, Section 1

בְּרֹאשׁ הַשָּׁנָה שְׁנַת תק"ז עָשִׂיתִי הַשְׁבָּעַת עֲלִיַּת הַנְּשָׁמָה . . . וְעָלִיתִי מַדְרֵגָה אַחַר מַדְרֵגָה, עַד שֶׁנִּכְנַסְתִּי לְהֵיכַל מָשִׁיחַ . . . וְשָׁאַלְתִּי אֶת פִּי מָשִׁיחַ: "אֵימָת אָתֵי מַר?" וְהֵשִׁיב לִי: "בְּזֹאת תֵּדַע, בְּעֵת שֶׁיִּתְפַּרְסֵם לִמּוּדְךָ וְיִתְגַּלֶּה בָּעוֹלָם, וְיָפוּצוּ מַעְיְנוֹתֶיךָ חוּצָה".

On Rosh Hashanah of the year 5507 [1746], my soul ascended to the higher worlds. . . . I rose level after level until I reached the chamber of Mashiach. . . . I asked Mashiach: "When will the master come?" He answered, "By this you will know: when your teachings will become known and revealed throughout the world, and your wellsprings will be spread to the outside."

RABBI YISRAEL BAAL SHEM TOV (BESHT) 1698–1760

Founder of the Chasidic movement. Born in Slutsk, Belarus, the Baal Shem Tov was orphaned as a child. He served as a teacher's assistant and clay digger before founding the Chasidic movement and revolutionizing the Jewish world with his emphasis on prayer, joy, and love for every Jew, regardless of his or her level of Torah knowledge.

FIGURE 6.3

Timeline of Major Chasidic Works

First revealed by Rabbi Yisrael Baal Shem Tov (1698–1760), the teachings of Chasidism quickly spread throughout the Jewish world, energizing and revitalizing Jewish life. Deriving its core ideas from the *Zohar*, the teachings of Ari, and those of later mystics such as Maharal and Shalah, Chasidism stresses the mystical dimension of Torah, joyfulness in serving G-d, love of every Jew regardless of material or spiritual station, intellectual and emotional engagement in prayer, finding G-dliness in every aspect of one's existence, the elevation of the material universe, and the role of the *tzadik* (righteous leader) in guiding a person's relationship with the Almighty. The Chasidic masters made these previously esoteric concepts accessible to all, empowering every individual to form a personal relationship with G-d and find spirituality, meaningfulness, and joy in their everyday endeavors.

1700

1800

1734-1760
KETER SHEM TOV
Selected teachings of Chasidism's founder, Rabbi Yisrael Baal Shem Tov, transcribed by his disciples.

1780
TOLDOT YAAKOV YOSEF
The first printed work of Chasidic philosophy, by Rabbi Yaakov Yosef of Polonye (c. 1710–1784), a senior disciple of the Baal Shem Tov.

ספר
תולדות יעקב יוסף

1787
NO'AM ELIMELECH
Chasidic commentary on the Torah by Rabbi Elimelech of Lizensk (1717–1787), pioneer of Chasidism in Poland and Galicia.

נועם אלימלך

1798
TANYA
Called "the Bible of Chasidism," this work draws from a wide range of classical and mystical Torah works—including the Talmud, *Zohar*, and the teachings of Ari and Shalah—as well as the teachings of the Baal Shem Tov and the Magid of Mezeritch. Authored by the founder of the "Chabad" branch of Chasidism, Rabbi Shneur Zalman of Liadi (1745–1812).

1796
KEDUSHAT LEVI
("Holiness of Levi") Chasidic commentary on the Torah by Rabbi Levi Yitzchak of Berditchev (1740–1809), known for his all-encompassing love, compassion, and advocacy on behalf of the Jewish people.

1808
LIKUTEI MOHARAN
The collected teachings of Rabbi Nachman of Breslov (1772–1810), founder of the Breslov Chasidic movement, as recorded by his disciple Rabbi Natan Sternhartz. Rabbi Nachman also authored a series of esoteric tales and parables that are studied for the mystical ideas they contain.

1866
TZEMACH TZEDEK
("Sprouting of Righteousness") Collective name for the works of Rabbi Menachem Mendel Schneersohn of Lubavitch (1789–1866), which includes thousands of Chasidic discourses, Halachic responsa, and expositions of Jewish philosophy.

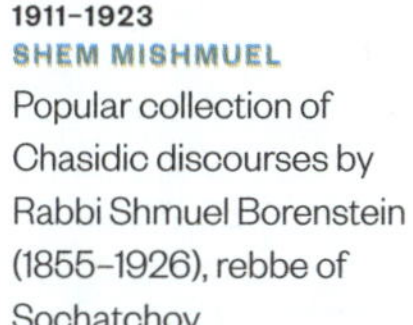

1911–1923
SHEM MISHMUEL
Popular collection of Chasidic discourses by Rabbi Shmuel Borenstein (1855–1926), rebbe of Sochatchov.

1900

2000

1845
PERI TZADIK
A series of innovative works by Chasidic master Rabbi Tzadok Hakohen of Lublin (1823–1900).

1871–1904
SEFAT EMET
("Edge of Truth") A classic of Chasidic teaching that includes commentaries on the Torah, Talmud, and Shulchan Aruch by Rabbi Yehudah Aryeh Leib Alter (1847–1905), the second leader of the Ger branch of Chasidism.

1950–1992
LIKUTEI SICHOT
("Collected Talks") A 40-volume compilation of scholarly essays based on the talks of Rabbi Menachem Mendel Schneerson, 1902–1994, the seventh Lubavitcher Rebbe, which he edited for publication. The essays demonstrate the "unity of Torah" by revealing the inner connecting essence behind its Talmudic, Halachic, mystical, philosophical, and ethical aspects.

IV. A TASTE OF KABBALAH

In this section, we read a mysterious Kabbalistic text and introduce a number of arcane Kabbalistic terms.

TEXT 5

Engravings in the Supernal Purity

Zohar, Vol. 1, p. 15a

בְּרֵישׁ הוּרְמְנוּתָא דְמַלְכָּא
גָּלִיף גְּלוּפֵי בִּטְהִירוּ עִלָּאָה בּוּצִינָא דְקַרְדִינוּתָא
וְנָפִיק גוֹ סָתִים דִסְתִימוּ
מֵרָזָא דְאֵין סוֹף
קוּטְרָא בְּגוּלְמָא נָעִיץ בְּעִזְקָא
לָא חִוָּור וְלָא אוּכָם וְלָא סוּמָק וְלָא יָרוֹק ולָא גָּוֶן כְּלָל.
כַּד מָדִיד מְשִׁיחָא
עָבִיד גַּוְנִין לְאַנְהָרָא
לְגוֹ בְּגוֹ בּוֹצִינָא נָפִיק חַד נְבִיעוּ
דְמִנֵּיהּ אִצְטַבְּעוּ גַּוְנִין לְתַתָּא.

At the beginning of the manifestation of the King's will,
the lamp of darkness engraved engravings in the supernal purity.
It emanated from the most concealed of all concealed things,
from the secret of endlessness.

ZOHAR

The seminal work of kabbalah, Jewish mysticism. The *Zohar* is a mystical commentary on the Torah, written in Aramaic and Hebrew. According to the Arizal, the *Zohar* contains the teachings of Rabbi Shimon bar Yocha'i, who lived in the Land of Israel during the 2nd century. The *Zohar* has become one of the indispensable texts of traditional Judaism, alongside and nearly equal in stature to the Mishnah and Talmud.

A formless vapor was inserted into a circle
that was neither white nor black nor red nor green,
nor any color at all.
When He began its measurements,
He created bright colors to shine forth.
From within the center of the lamp a fountain spouted,
from which the colors down below were painted.

Initial word decoration from fifteenth-century manuscript of the *Zohar* on Genesis. (British Library, London)

Hands-on science experiments that can help us understand the greatest Kabbalistic metaphors: **myjli.com/booksmart**

V. THE GREAT PARADOX

In this section, we introduce a "great paradox" that is one of the core subjects of Kabbalah. On the one hand, a principal belief of Judaism is that G-d cannot be defined or described in any way, shape, or form. But no less central to Judaism is the belief that G-d is intimately involved in His creation—an involvement described in the Torah in terms of Divine "attributes" such as wisdom, love, judgment, anger, joy, compassion, sovereignty, etc.

TEXT 6

The Soul of the Universe

Talmud, Berachot 10a

מָה הַקָדוֹשׁ בָּרוּךְ הוּא מָלֵא כָּל הָעוֹלָם,
אַף נְשָׁמָה מְלֵאָה אֶת כָּל הַגוּף.

G-d fills the world
like the soul fills the body.

ILLUMINATED CITY
Naomi Young, acrylic on canvas. Los Angeles.

TEXT 7

The Warning

Deuteronomy 4:15–19

וְנִשְׁמַרְתֶּם מְאֹד לְנַפְשֹׁתֵיכֶם, כִּי לֹא רְאִיתֶם כָּל
תְּמוּנָה בְּיוֹם דִּבֶּר ה' אֲלֵיכֶם בְּחֹרֵב מִתּוֹךְ הָאֵשׁ.
פֶּן תַּשְׁחִתוּן, וַעֲשִׂיתֶם לָכֶם פֶּסֶל תְּמוּנַת כָּל
סָמֶל . . . וְנִדַּחְתָּ וְהִשְׁתַּחֲוִיתָ לָהֶם וַעֲבַדְתָּם.

Guard your souls exceedingly, as you have not seen any form on the day that G-d spoke to you at Horeb from within the fire. Lest you be corrupted, and make for yourselves a graven image, the form of any symbol, . . . and be led astray to bow to it and worship it.

TEXT 8

The Third Principle

Maimonides, Commentary on the Mishnah, Introduction to Chapter *Chelek*

הַיְסוֹד הַשְּׁלִישִׁי: שְׁלִילַת הַגַּשְׁמוּת מִמֶּנּוּ.
וְזֶה שֶׁנַּאֲמִין כִּי הָאֶחָד הַזֶּה שֶׁזָּכַרְנוּ אֵינוֹ גוּף,
וְלֹא כֹּחַ בַּגּוּף, וְלֹא יַשִּׂיגוּהוּ מְאֹרְעוֹת הַגּוּפִים.

The third principle is the negation of any physical qualities in regard to G-d. Meaning, we believe that the One G-d is neither a physical entity nor a physical force, nor is He subject to any physical state.

TEXT 9

The Incomparable

Isaiah 40:25

וְאֶל מִי תְדַמְּיוּנִי וְאֶשְׁוֶה,
יֹאמַר קָדוֹשׁ.

Says the Holy One: To what can you liken me, that I would be compared?

TEXT 10

Divine Qualities

Exodus 34:6; and Chronicles 29:11

אֵ־ל רַחוּם וְחַנּוּן, אֶרֶךְ אַפַּיִם, וְרַב חֶסֶד וֶאֱמֶת.

A compassionate and gracious G-d, slow to anger, and abundant in lovingkindness and truth.

לְךָ ה' הַגְּדֻלָּה וְהַגְּבוּרָה וְהַתִּפְאֶרֶת וְהַנֵּצַח
וְהַהוֹד . . . לְךָ ה' הַמַּמְלָכָה.

Unto You, G-d, is greatness, and power, and beauty, and triumph, and splendor. . . .
Unto You, G-d, is kingship.

ISAIAH

Biblical book. The book of Isaiah contains the prophecies of Isaiah, who lived in the 7th–6th centuries BCE. Isaiah's prophecies contain stern rebukes for the personal failings of the contemporary people of Judea and the corruption of its government. The bulk of the prophecies, however, are stirring consolations and poetic visions of the future Redemption.

CHRONICLES

Biblical book. The book of Chronicles (Divrei Hayamim), commonly divided into two parts, is the concluding book of the Writings (*Ketuvim*) section of the Tanach. Chronicles contains a genealogical list from Creation until the establishment of the first Kingdom of Israel, and then it briefly surveys the history of the Davidic dynasty until the destruction of the First Temple. The book was written by Ezra the Scribe in the fourth century BCE. The book has been artificially divided into I Chronicles and II Chronicles, but it is essentially one book.

TEXT 11

The Source of All

Psalms 94:9

הֲנֹטַע אֹזֶן הֲלֹא יִשְׁמָע?
אִם יֹצֵר עַיִן הֲלֹא יַבִּיט?

Would the One who implants the ear not hear?
Would the One who forms the eye not see?

PSALMS

Biblical book. The book of Psalms contains 150 psalms expressing praise for G-d, faith in G-d, and laments over tragedies. The primary author of the psalms was King David, who lived in the 9th century BCE. Psalms also contains material from earlier figures. The feelings and circumstances expressed in the psalms resonate throughout the generations and they have become an important part of communal and personal prayer.

Decorated title page in the *De Pinto Psalter*. Produced in Amsterdam in 1728, the figures of Aaron and Joseph on the title page reference the name of the book's first patron, Aaron ben Joseph. (Braginsky Collection 62)

VI. THE TEN *SEFIROT*

Kabbalistic tradition describes a constellation of ten Divine "attributes"—the ten *sefirot*—which G-d generated within His infinite being in order to create and relate to our existence. According to the *Zohar*, this is the "Divine image" in which the human being was created. It is also the model that Kabbalah employs to explain the paradox of G-d's transcendence and immanence.

TEXT 12

The Divine Image

Genesis 1:26–27

וַיֹּאמֶר אֱלֹקִים: "נַעֲשֶׂה אָדָם בְּצַלְמֵנוּ כִּדְמוּתֵנוּ . . . "

וַיִּבְרָא אֱלֹקִים אֶת הָאָדָם בְּצַלְמוֹ, בְּצֶלֶם אֱלֹקִים בָּרָא אֹתוֹ, זָכָר וּנְקֵבָה בָּרָא אֹתָם.

G-d said: "Let us make a human being in our image, after our likeness. . . ."

And G-d created the human in His image,
in the Divine image He created him;
male and female He created them.

FIGURE 6.4

The *Sefirot*

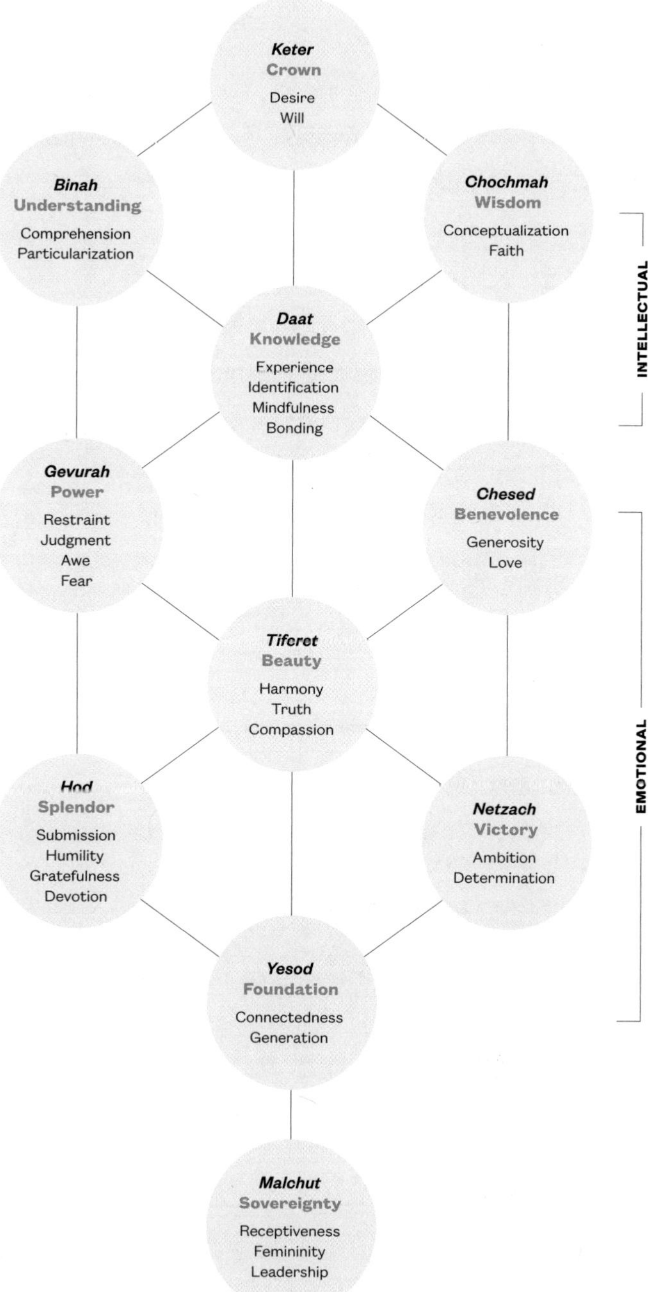

TEXT 13

The Analogue

Rabbeinu Bechaye, Genesis 1:26

וְיֵשׁ בַּכָּתוּב הַזֶּה עִנְיָן עָמֹק, חָתוּם בְּאוֹצְרוֹת הַמְקֻבָּלִים מְבַקְשֵׁי ה׳. כִּי הוּא סוֹד בִּנְיַן עֶשֶׂר סְפִירוֹת, אֲשֶׁר הָאָדָם כָּלוּל בָּהֶם וְתַבְנִיתוֹ דֻגְמָא לָהֶם. אָמַר ״בְּצַלְמֵנוּ״, בַּצֶּלֶם הֶעָשׂוּי לָנוּ.

This verse contains a very deep idea, which is sealed away in the treasure-houses of the Kabbalists who seek out G-d. It holds the secret of the structure of the ten *sefirot*, which the human being incorporates in themselves and for which the human form is an analogue. G-d therefore says, “in our image,” meaning: in the image we made for ourselves.

RABBI BACHYA BEN ASHER IBN HALAWA (RABBEINU BECHAYE) C. 1255–1340

Biblical commentator. Rabbeinu Bechaye lived in Spain and was a disciple of Rabbi Shlomo ben Aderet, known as Rashba. He is best known for his multifaceted commentary on the Torah, which interprets the text on literal, Midrashic, philosophical, and kabbalistic levels. Rabbeinu Bechaye also wrote *Kad Hakemach*, a work on philosophy and ethics.

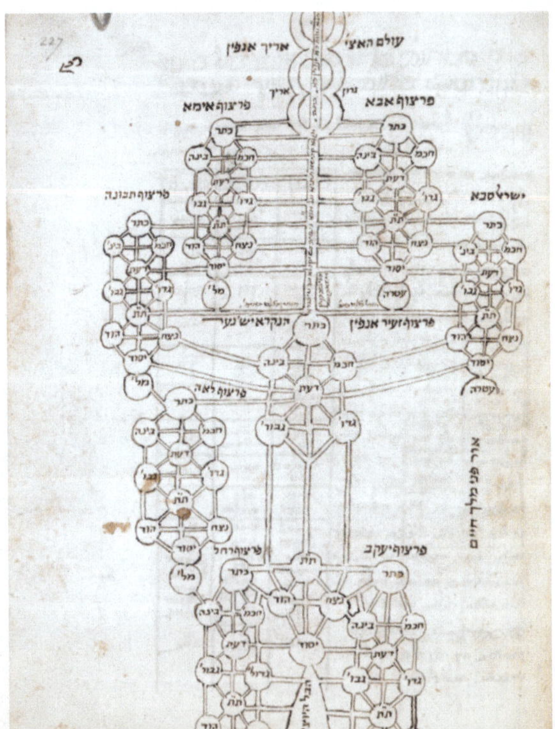

Diagram of the *sefirot* in a seventeenth-century codex of Rabbi Chaim Vital's *Otzrot Chayim.* (British Library, London)

Ten Mystical *Sefirot* Explained in this animated video: **myjli.com/booksmart**

TEXT 14

The Ten-Part Human

Tikunei Zohar, 116a

"נַעֲשֶׂה אָדָם בְּצַלְמֵנוּ כִּדְמוּתֵינוּ": כָּל סְפִירָה יָהִיב בֵּיהּ חוּלְקֵיהּ, מִלְּגָאו וּמִלְּבָר. וְאִם חָסֵר חַד מֵעֶשֶׂר סְפִירָן דְלָא הֲוָה יָהִיב בֵּיהּ חוּלְקֵיהּ, לָא הֲוָה אִשְׁתַּלִים בִּנְיָינָא דְאָדָם.

"Let us make a human being in our image, after our likeness": Each *sefirah* imparted its portion to the human being, internally and externally. Had even one of the ten *sefirot* not imparted its portion, the structure of the human being would have been incomplete.

TIKUNEI ZOHAR

An appendix to the *Zohar*, the seminal work of kabbalah (Jewish mysticism). *Tikunei Zohar* consists mostly of seventy kabbalistic expositions on the opening verse of the Torah. It was first printed in Mantua in 1558.

TEXT 15

The Colored Vessels Analogy

Rabbi Moshe Cordovero, *Pardes Rimonim*, 4:4

אֱמֶת כִּי יוֹצְרֵנוּ יוֹצֵר הַכֹּל אֵין סוֹף . . . וּבוֹ אֵין אָנוּ יְכוֹלִין לְדַבֵּר וְלֹא לְצַיֵּר וְלֹא לְחַיֵּב לֹא דִין וְלֹא רַחֲמִים לֹא רֹגֶז וְלֹא כַּעַס לֹא שִׁנּוּי וְלֹא גְבוּל וְלֹא שׁוּם מִדָּה, לֹא קֹדֶם הָאֲצִילוּת לֹא עַתָּה אַחַר הָאֲצִילוּת.

אָמְנָם מָה שֶׁרָאוּי שֶׁנֵּדַע הוּא, כִּי בִּתְחִלַּת הָאֲצִילוּת הֶאֱצִיל הָאֵין סוֹף מֶלֶךְ מַלְכֵי הַמְּלָכִים הַקָּדוֹשׁ בָּרוּךְ הוּא עֶשֶׂר סְפִירוֹת . . . וְנוּכַל לְהַמְשִׁיל מָשָׁל נָאֶה כְּדֵי שֶׁיִּתְקַבֵּל דָבָר הַזֶּה בְּדַעַת הַמַּשְׂכִּיל.

RABBI MOSHE CORDOVERO (RAMAK) 1522–1570

Prominent kabbalist. Ramak belonged to the circle of Jewish mystical thinkers who flourished in 16th-century Safed. The name Cordovero indicates that his family originated in Córdoba, Spain. His most famous kabbalistic work is *Pardes Rimonim*.

הַמָּשָׁל אֶל הַמַּיִם אֲשֶׁר הֵם מִתְחַלְּקִים אֶל הַכֵּלִים, וְהַכֵּלִים מְשֻׁנִּים בְּגְוָנָם, זֶה לָבָן וְזֶה אָדֹם וְזֶה יָרֹק, וְכֵן כֻּלָּם. הִנֵּה, כַּאֲשֶׁר יִתְפַּשֵּׁט הַמַּיִם אֶל הַכֵּלִים הָהֵם, עִם הֱיוֹת הַמַּיִם פְּשׁוּטִים מִכָּל גָּוֶן, הִנֵּה יִתְרָאוּ בְּגְוָנֵי הַכֵּלִים הָהֵם וְיִשְׁתַּנּוּ אֶל גַּוְנָם. וְהִנֵּה לְפִי הָאֱמֶת אֵין שִׁנּוּי הַגָּוֶן הַהוּא קָנוּי בַּמַּיִם, אֲבָל עַל יְדֵי הַכֵּלִים הַמְשֻׁנִּים יִשְׁתַּנּוּ אֶל הַגָּוֶן הַהוּא בְּמִקְרֶה, לֹא בְּעֶצֶם, וְהַמִּקְרֶה הַהוּא בְּעֵרֶךְ הָרוֹאִים, לֹא בְּעֵרֶךְ הַמַּיִם בְּעַצְמָם.

וְכֵן הַדָּבָר בַּסְּפִירוֹת. הַכֵּלִים הֵם הַסְּפִירוֹת הַמְכֻנִּים אֵלֵינוּ "חֶסֶד", "גְּבוּרָה", "תִּפְאֶרֶת", וְלָהֶן גָּוֶן לְפִי פְּעֻלָּתָם, לָבָן אָדֹם וְיָרֹק. וְאוֹר הַמַּאֲצִיל, שֶׁהוּא עַצְמוּת הָעֶשֶׂר אוֹרוֹת הַמִּתְפַּשֵּׁט בְּעֶשֶׂר סְפִירוֹת, הֵם הַמַּיִם אֲשֶׁר אֵין לָהֶם גָּוֶן כְּלָל, כִּי הֵם פְּשׁוּטִים מִכָּל שִׁנּוּי וּמִכָּל פְּעֻלָּה, וְלֹא יִפְעֲלוּ הַשִּׁנּוּי אֶלָּא עַל יְדֵי הַכֵּלִים הַמִּשְׁתַּנִּים בִּפְעֻלָּתָם.

In truth, in regard to our Creator, the Infinite Creator of all, . . . we cannot speak, nor describe, nor require neither judgment nor compassion, neither anger nor wrath, neither variation nor limitation, nor any properties whatsoever—not before the emanation [of the ten *sefirot*], nor now, after they were emanated.

What we should know, however, is that at the very beginning G-d emanated ten *sefirot*. . . . And we can provide a nice analogy to make the matter understood by the mind of the wise thinker.

The analogy is of water that is distributed among various vessels. These vessels are of different colors: one is white, another is red, another is green, and so on with the rest of them. Now, when the water is channeled in these vessels, although the water itself is colorless, it will be seen in the colors of the respective vessels, and appear to have changed to its vessel's color. In truth, however, the water did not acquire any new color. The variously colored vessels have imposed their colors on the water, but this imposition is only in relation to how the water appears to those who see it, not in relation to the water itself.

So it is with the *sefirot*. The "vessels" in the analogy are the Divine attributes that we call "Lovingkindness," "Power," "Beauty," [and so on]. Each is "colored" in accordance with its function: white, red, green. The light of the Emanator, which is the essence of the ten Divine energies that flow into the ten *sefirot*, are like the "colorless water," as they transcend all variation and functions. The variation in their effect [on the world] is only due to the differences in function of their vessels.

VII. THE CONTRACTION

While Kabbalah provides "technical" explanations for the paradox of G-d's relationship with our existence, Chasidic teaching uses an analogy from our own experience that makes this truth relatable on the human level.

TEXT 16

The Game

Rabbi Dov Ber of Mezeritch, *Magid Devarav LeYaakov*, sections 202 and 177

וְגָדְלוֹ וְעוֹצֶם יְכָלְתּוֹ לֹא הָיוּ יְכוֹלִים לְהַשִּׂיג כָּל הָעוֹלָמוֹת. לְפִיכָךְ עָשָׂה צִמְצוּם אַחַר צִמְצוּם, עַד שֶׁיְּכוֹלִים לְסָבְלוֹ יִתְבָּרֵךְ. . .

כְּמוֹ הָאָב שֶׁרוֹאֶה אֶת בְּנוֹ מְשַׂחֵק בֶּאֱגוֹזִים, אָז מֵחֲמַת אַהֲבָתוֹ מְשַׂחֵק גַם הוּא עִמּוֹ. הֲגַם שֶׁאֵצֶל אָבִיו נִרְאֶה זֶה מַעֲשֵׂה נַעֲרוּת וְקַטְנוּת, אַף עַל פִּי כֵן, מֵחֲמַת אַהֲבָתוֹ לִבְנוֹ שֶׁיְּקַבֵּל תַּעֲנוּג מִמֶּנּוּ, מְצַמְצֵם אֶת שִׂכְלוֹ הַגָּדוֹל וְשׁוֹרֶה בְּקַטְנוּת שֶׁיּוּכַל הַקָּטָן לִסְבֹּל. אֲבָל אִם הָיָה מִתְנַהֵג עִמּוֹ לְפִי שִׂכְלוֹ, לֹא הָיָה הַבֵּן יָכוֹל לְסָבְלוֹ, וְלֹא הָיָה הָאָב מְקַבֵּל תַּעֲנוּג מִמֶּנּוּ.

All the worlds cannot apprehend G-d's greatness and power. G-d therefore performed many "contractions" to enable the worlds to relate with Him. . . .

RABBI DOV BER "THE MAGID" OF MEZERITCH D. 1772

Primary disciple and eventual successor of the Baal Shem Tov. Among his disciples were the founders of various Chasidic dynasties, including Rabbi Nachum of Chernobyl, Rabbi Levi Yitzchak of Berditchev, and Rabbi Shne'ur Zalman of Liadi. His teachings, recorded by his students, appear in various volumes, including *Magid Devarav LeYaakov*.

This is like a father who sees his child playing a game, and out of his love for his child, the father plays along with the child. Although for the father this is a childish and petty activity, nevertheless, out of his love for his child, and in order to derive pleasure from the child, the father "contracts" his adult mind and inserts himself in this childish mentality, so that the child can relate to him. On the other hand, if the father were to conduct himself in accordance with his own mentality, the child would not be able to relate to the father, and the father would not derive pleasure from the child.

DREIDEL I
Elena Flerova, oil on canvas.

Five Most Frequently Asked Questions on Kabbalah
myjli.com/booksmart

VIII. IN CHASIDISM: THE "GREAT PARADOX" PERSONALIZED

In this section, we see how Chasidism explores the inner spiritual meaning of a legalistic Torah passage, and applies the "great paradox" to our everyday lives.

TEXT 17

The Roadside Assistance Law

Exodus 23:5

כִּי תִרְאֶה חֲמוֹר שֹׂנַאֲךָ רֹבֵץ תַּחַת מַשָּׂאוֹ
וְחָדַלְתָּ מֵעֲזֹב לוֹ, עָזֹב תַּעֲזֹב עִמּוֹ.

When you see the donkey of your enemy collapsing under its burden, and you are inclined to desist from assisting him, assist must you assist with him.

TEXT 18

The Body's Burden

Rabbi Yisrael Baal Shem Tov, cited in *Hayom Yom*, Shevat 28

"כִּי תִרְאֶה חֲמוֹר" – כַּאֲשֶׁר תִּסְתַּכֵּל בְּעִיּוּן טוֹב בְּהַחֹמֶר שֶׁלְּךָ שֶׁהוּא הַגּוּף, תִּרְאֶה,

"שׂוֹנַאֲךָ" – שֶׁהוּא שׂוֹנֵא אֶת הַנְּשָׁמָה הַמִּתְגַּעְגַּעַת לֶאֱלוֹקוּת וְרוּחָנִיּוּת. וְעוֹד תִּרְאֶה שֶׁהוּא,

RABBI YISRAEL BAAL SHEM TOV 1698–1760

Founder of the Chasidic movement. Born in Slutsk, Belarus, the Baal Shem Tov was orphaned as a child. He served as a teacher's assistant and clay digger before founding the Chasidic movement and revolutionizing the Jewish world with his emphasis on prayer, joy, and love for every Jew, regardless of his or her level of Torah knowledge.

"רוֹבֵץ תַּחַת מַשָּׂאוֹ" – שֶׁנָּתַן הַקָּדוֹשׁ בָּרוּךְ הוּא לְהַגּוּף שֶׁיִּזְדַּכֵּךְ עַל יְדֵי תּוֹרָה וּמִצְוֹת, וְהַגּוּף מִתְעַצֵּל בְּקִיּוּמָם. וְאוּלַי יַעֲלֶה בִּלְבָבְךָ,

"וְחָדַלְתָּ מֵעֲזֹב לוֹ" – שֶׁיּוּכַל לְקַיֵּם שְׁלִיחוּתוֹ, כִּי אִם תַּתְחִיל בְּסִגּוּפִים לִשְׁבֹּר אֶת הַחָמְרִיּוּת. הִנֵּה לֹא בְּזוֹ הַדֶּרֶךְ יִשְׁכֹּן אוֹר הַתּוֹרָה, כִּי אִם,

"עָזֹב תַּעֲזֹב עִמּוֹ" – לְבָרֵר אֶת הַגּוּף וּלְזַכְּכוֹ.

"When you see the *chamor*"—When you contemplate your material self, which is your body, you will see that it is,

"Of your enemy"—The material self is antagonistic to the soul, which yearns for G-dliness and spirituality. You will further see that it is,

"Collapsing under its burden"—G-d gave the Torah and its commandments to sanctify our physical existence, but the body regards them as a burden and is loath to fulfill them. Your inclination may therefore be,

"And you are inclined to desist from assisting him"—You may be inclined to deprive the body, in order to break its materialistic nature. This approach, however, is not the way by which the light of Torah will come to dwell in us. Rather,

"Assist must you assist with him"—Lift up the body by refining and elevating it.

IX. COURSE CONCLUSION: WHAT SHALL WE LEARN TODAY?

Because the truths of the Torah find expression in so many different genres, every person can discover a field of Torah learning that resonates with their distinct personality and inclinations.

JEWISH WOMAN READING TSENO URENO ON THE SABBATH
Yehudah Moiseyevitch Pen, oil on canvas laid onto card, Belarus, c. 1920

TEXT 19

The Torah of Your Desire

Talmud, Avodah Zarah 19a

לֵוִי וְרַבִּי שִׁמְעוֹן בְּרֶבִּי יַתְבִי קַמֵּיה דְרֶבִּי וְקָא פַּסְקֵי סִדְרָא. סָלִיק סִפְרָא. לֵוִי אָמַר: "לֵייתוּ [לָן] מִשְׁלֵי". רַבִּי שִׁמְעוֹן בְּרֶבִּי אָמַר: "לֵייתוּ [לָן] תִּלִים". כַּפְיֵיה לְלֵוִי וְאַייתוּ תִּלִים.

כִּי מָטוּ הָכָא, "כִּי אִם בְּתוֹרַת ה' חֶפְצוֹ", פָּרִישׁ רֶבִּי וְאָמַר: "אֵין אָדָם לוֹמֵד תּוֹרָה אֶלָּא מִמָּקוֹם שֶׁלִּבּוֹ חָפֵץ". אָמַר לֵוִי: "רֶבִּי! נָתַתָּ לָנוּ רְשׁוּת לַעֲמֹד . . . "

Levi and Rabbi Shimon the son of Rebbi [Rabbi Yehudah Hanasi] were sitting before Rebbi, and they were studying the Torah portion. When the book was concluded, Levi said, "Let the book of Proverbs be brought to us." Rabbi Shimon said, "Let the book of Psalms be brought to us." Levi was compelled [to agree], and the book of Psalms was brought.

When they came to this verse, "But only in G-d's Torah is his desire" (PSALMS 1:2), Rebbi expounded its meaning and said: "A person can only learn Torah in the area that their heart desires." Said Levi: "Rebbi! You have given me permission to get up [and leave]!"

Class Exercise

If you were able to devote one full year to studying one of the fields of Torah we explored in this course, which field would you choose? Check one box only:

- Tanach
- Midrash
- Talmud
- Halachah
- Musar
- Chakirah
- Kabbalah
- Chasidut

Explain your choice. Why did you choose this field?

List one or more topics that you would like to explore in your chosen field:

KEY POINTS

1 *Transmitted Secrets.* Kabbalah is the Torah's inner, spiritual dimension, containing its most powerful and empowering ideas. But these esoteric teachings are also extremely subtle, and can easily be misunderstood and corrupted. As a result, the history of Kabbalah is driven by two paradoxical aims: to transmit and to conceal. For many centuries, the teachings of Kabbalah were carefully guarded secrets, transcribed only in the guise of esoteric terminology and metaphors, and taught only to a small exclusive circle of mystics in each generation.

2 *A Brief History of Kabbalah.* The history of the transmission and revelation of Kabbalah can be divided into five stages: (1) The esoteric texts of the Talmudic era. (2) The increased Kabbalistic activity in southern Europe beginning in the 12th century, prompted by the publication of the *Zohar* and by Kabbalists such as the Raavad, Rabbi Yitzchak the Blind, Nachmanides, Abulafia, Gikatilla, Recanati, Ibn Gabbai, and others. (3) The flourishing of Kabbalah in 16th-century Safed under the tutelage of Rabbi Moshe Cordovero ("Ramak") and Rabbi Yitzchak Luria ("Ari") and their disciples. (4) The spread of Kabbalistic learning throughout the Jewish world in the generations following the Safedian period; Kabbalists of this period include Maharal, Da Fano, Shalah, Ramchal, and Gra. (5) The revelation of Chasidism in 1734, which disseminated the "soul of Torah" beyond the circle of sages and mystics in a manner accessible to all.

3 *The Revelation of Chasidism.* Chasidism is an extension of Kabbalah as well as a field of Torah in its own right. The teachings of Chasidism take the Torah's innermost truths beyond the specialized language of Kabbalah, employing metaphors and explanations that make them accessible to all. Chasidism also reveals the inner "soul" element that unites the various dimensions of Torah, and it represents the final phase of the Torah's unfolding revelation from Sinai to Mashiach.

4 *The Great Paradox.* A major subject in Kabbalah is the "great paradox" that underlies G-d's relationship with our existence. On the one hand, a principal belief of Judaism is that G-d cannot be defined or described in any way, shape, or form. Idolatry, which ascribes human traits to G-d, is categorically condemned in the Torah as a cardinal transgression and as a harbinger of moral corruption. But no less central to Judaism is the belief that G-d is intimately involved in His creation—an involvement described in the Torah in terms of Divine "attributes" such as wisdom, love, judgment, anger, joy, compassion, sovereignty, etc. Indeed, a central idea in Kabbalah is that we can understand G-d's relationship with His creation by contemplating our own soul's relationship with our body.

5 *The Ten Sefirot.* The teachings of Kabbalah describe a constellation of ten Divine "attributes"—the ten *sefirot*—which G-d generated within His infinite being in order to create and relate to our existence. According to the *Zohar*, this is the "Divine image" in which the human being was created. The ten *sefirot* also provide the formula that explains the "great paradox" of G-d's transcendence and immanence. Ramak uses an analogy of colorless water being channeled through colored vessels to illustrate the manner in which the "featureless" Divine effluence, being channeled through the *sefirot*, retains its transcendence even as we experience it as a manifestation of Divine wisdom, Divine love, Divine sovereignty, etc.

6 *The Contraction.* Complementing Kabbalah's "colored vessels" analogy for the *sefirot*, Chasidic teaching employs an analogy of a parent "contracting" their adult personality in order to engage in play with their young child. The adult self is fully present within the child-persona they have isolated within themselves, with the result that their interaction with their child is both genuine and fully relatable by the child. In the same way, G-d is fully present within the "attributes" He assumes in order to relate to us.

7 *The Great Paradox Personalized.* Chasidism seeks to not only understand the spiritual cosmos, but also to unite spirit with matter. In the teachings of Kabbalah, the "great paradox" informs the spiritual infrastructure of Creation; in Chasidism, it also describes our own soul's relationship with our physical self. Guidance comes in the form of a passage in the Torah instructing us to offer roadside assistance to an enemy's overburdened animal, whose inner meaning is revealed by a Chasidic teaching to address the challenge of reconciling our material nature with our spiritual goals.

Dimensions of Meaning in Modeh Ani

FOUR LAYERS OF MEANING

According to the *Zohar*, there are four general dimensions of Torah: *peshat*, or plain meaning; *remez*, allegory; *derush*, legal and homiletic exposition; and *sod*, the mystical (expressed by the four letters of the acronym ***pardes***, "orchard"). Chasidic teaching endeavors to uncover the "soul," or inner essence, of all four dimensions, revealing new depths in each and showing how all four aspects complement and fulfill each other.

In an essay titled *On the Essence of Chassidus*, the Lubavitcher Rebbe, Rabbi Menachem M. Schneerson, presents one example of this dynamic. The Modeh Ani prayer, recited each morning upon awakening, has a plain meaning, alludes to a futuristic event, expresses a legal principle, and represents a mystical formula; and Chasidic teaching opens a window into the "soul" of each of these four dimensions.

מוֹדֶה אֲנִי לְפָנֶיךָ
מֶלֶךְ חַי וְקַיָּם
שֶׁהֶחֱזַרְתָּ בִּי
נִשְׁמָתִי בְּחֶמְלָה,
רַבָּה אֱמוּנָתֶךָ.

I submit thanks before You, living and ever-enduring king, that You have restored my soul within me with compassion; great is Your faithfulness.

Rooster (poster detail),
Paul Rand, United States, 1988

FOUR LEVELS OF INTERPRETATION | **CHASIDIC TEACHING**

PLAIN MEANING

Every time we partake of one of the gifts of life (eat a food, smell a flower, etc.), we first recite a blessing expressing our gratitude to the Creator. Certainly, then, the gift of a new day of life calls for a blessing. A proper blessing, however, contains the sacred name of G-d, whereas in the Modeh Ani prayer we address G-d simply as "You."

The reason for this is that Modeh Ani is said immediately upon awakening, even before we have washed our hands and performed our morning ablutions, and it is forbidden to mention the Divine name when one is not in a state of cleanliness.

A "name" is a representation, a projected self that is extrinsic to the core self. When we address G-d by one of His names, we are relating to a specific projection of G-d's relationship with us. But when we relate to G-d as "You," we relate to G-d's essence.

To invoke a Divine name requires a standard of holiness commensurate to the expression of G-dliness that it represents. But in Modeh Ani, our very "I" addresses the very "You" of G-d. Modeh Ani can therefore be said in any state, as no impurity in the world can taint the Modeh Ani of the soul.

ALLEGORY

One of the fundamental beliefs in Judaism is the resurrection of the dead, prophesied to occur in the messianic World to Come.

The Talmud (*Berachot* 57b) describes sleep as "one-sixtieth of death." So the Modeh Ani prayer, in which we thank the Almighty for "restoring my soul within me" after the minor death of sleep, is an allusion to the future resurrection.

Chasidic teaching elaborates on the principle of "perpetual creation": in every moment of time, the entirety of Creation is brought into being from a state of utter nothingness, as G-d continually imparts existence and life to everything that is.

This gives us a deeper appreciation of the gratitude to G-d we express in Modeh Ani. Not only is our soul restored to our body each morning, but our body is also regenerated, as it will be in the future resurrection. Indeed, this occurs each and every moment of the day; our moment of awakening is simply a daily opportunity to tangibly experience and acknowledge this truth.

LEGAL EXPOSITION

One of the 613 *mitzvot* of the Torah is the obligation to return an object that has been entrusted to us for safekeeping. This obligation is categorical: even in the case that the owner of the object has an outstanding financial obligation to us, this does not absolve us from the duty to return their property to them.

This law is implicit in the Modeh Ani prayer. Every night, we entrust our soul to G-d. Often we are deficient in our obligations toward our Creator; yet, as we confirm in Modeh Ani, "great is Your faithfulness"—G-d returns the trust, regardless of our outstanding debts to Him.

To understand this law, we need to understand what a mitzvah is. There are logical *mitzvot* and suprarational *mitzvot*; social *mitzvot* and "religious" *mitzvot*. But these differentiations all pertain to a mitzvah's "garments," its outer packaging. At its core, every mitzvah is the infinite will of G-d. Thus, if the Torah commands us to return the property of a fellow that has been placed in our trust, the logic of this mitzvah does not constitute its essence, which lies in the act itself.

MYSTICAL

In the terminology of Kabbalah, "king" refers to G-d's involvement within the time and space of Creation, whereas "living and ever-enduring" describes G-d as He transcends time and space. In Modeh Ani, we attribute the restoration of our soul to the "living and ever-enduring king," implying that it is a product of the union of these two Divine modalities.

There are no greater opposites than spirit and matter. Spirit expresses its subservience to a higher truth; matter proclaims its own being. The marriage of body and soul is thus an impossible union of opposites. Every breath of life is an expression of the infinite power of G-d, who both transcends and permeates existence.

The Baal Shem Tov's Early Years

Excerpted and translated from *Sefer Hatoldot Rabbi Yisrael Baal Shem Tov*, pp. 31–33

When I was five years old, I was orphaned from both my father and mother. The last words spoken to me by my holy father before his passing were, "Yisrolik, fear nothing but G-d alone."

In keeping with my father's words, I was drawn to walk the fields and the great, deep forest near our village, where I would review by heart what I had learned in cheder. Often, I would sleep over the night in the field or the forest. My guardians, who looked after me and several other orphan boys and girls, did not tolerate this behavior of mine, and dealt severely with me.

So passed two years. One morning, I heard in the forest the sound of a human voice, and came upon the figure of a Jew enveloped in *talit* and *tefilin*, praying with a fervor such as I had never before witnessed.

I hid myself behind the trees and derived great pleasure from listening to the man praying. I decided that this holy man must be one of the thirty-six hidden *tzadikim* [righteous and saintly people] that are in the world. The *tzadik* concluded his prayers and began to read from the Book of Psalms in a melodious voice, following which he spent some time in ecstatic Torah study. He then gathered his books and his *talit* and *tefilin* and placed them in a sack. At this point, I stepped out from my hiding place and walked toward him.

When the man saw me, he asked, "What is a small child doing all alone in the forest? Are you not afraid to be in the forest all by yourself?"

I answered him, "I like the field and the forest, because there are no people—the great majority of whom are arrogant and dishonest. I am an orphan without father or mother. My father, peace be to him, said to me before his passing: 'Yisrolik, fear nothing but G-d alone.' So, I'm not afraid of anything."

The man asked me if I was Reb Eliezer's son. When I replied that my father was indeed called by that name, the man took a volume of Talmud—the tractate Pesachim—from his sack, and studied with me for a while. I then joined him on his way, without knowing where we were going or the purpose of our journey.

In our wanderings, we would stop for different periods of time in various cities, towns, villages, and hamlets—sometimes for a few days, sometimes for a week or longer. I never learned the man's name. I would study with him each day. He never accepted alms from anyone, yet he fed and clothed me and looked after my needs all the time. Three years passed in this manner.

One day we stopped in a small settlement and the man said to me, "Not far from here, in the forest, lives a learned and G-d-fearing Jew. I will leave you with him for a while." I lived in Reb Meir's hut for four years, during which time he learned with me with great diligence. Each day, we would go to the village for the daily prayers, where people knew him only as a simple workman, a charcoal smelter.

In Reb Meir's home, I became familiar with the ways of the hidden *tzadikim* and their leader, the great sage and *tzadik* Rabbi Adam Baal Shem. I was accepted into their society, and began journeying from town to town and from settlement to settlement on various missions that the society's leadership placed upon me. Before having attained sixteen years, I had gained a significant knowledge of the teaching of kabbalah and would occasionally pray with the mystical meditations of the Lurianic kabbalistic tradition.

On my sixteenth birthday, Elul 18, 5474 (1714), I was in a small village. The local innkeeper was a simple Jew who could barely read the prayers and was completely ignorant of the meaning of their words. Yet he was an extremely devout Jew whose custom it was to say, regarding everything and on every occasion, "Blessed be He forever and ever." His wife, the innkeeperess, would constantly avow, "Praised be His holy name."

That day, I went to meditate alone in the field in accordance with the practice, instituted by the early sages, to set aside time on one's birthday for private contemplation. I recited chapters of Psalms, and meditated upon the unifications of the Divine names as prescribed in the teachings of kabbalah.

Suddenly, I beheld Elijah the prophet standing before me, a smile on his lips. In Reb Meir's home, and in the company of other hidden *tzadikim*, I had, on occasion, merited a revelation of Elijah the prophet, but never on my own, so I wondered at the reason for this unexpected vision. I also could not understand the significance of the prophet's smile.

Elijah said to me, "You are toiling mightily, investing great effort and concentration to meditate upon the unifications of the holy names implicit in the verses compiled by King David. On the other hand, Aaron Shlomo the innkeeper and Zlateh Rivkah the innkeeperess are completely unaware of the unifications that emerge from their utterances, 'Blessed be He forever and ever,' and 'Praised be His holy name.' Yet these words resonate through all the worlds, causing a greater stir than the unifications configured by the greatest *tzadikim*."

Elijah went on to explain to me the great pleasure that G-d derives from these words of gratitude and praise, especially by simple folk, reflecting a pure faith, wholesome heart, and a state of perpetual attachment to G-d.

From that point on, I embarked upon a new method of serving G-d. Wherever I went, I would talk to people, inquiring after their health, their children, and their livelihood, and they would all reply with expressions of praise to the Almighty—"Thanks to G-d," "Blessed be His name," and the like—each after his or her manner.

At a conference of the fellowship of hidden *tzadikim*, it was resolved to adopt this method of Divine service, which in turn became the beginning of an approach that stressed the importance of brotherly love toward every Jew, regardless of their degree of Torah knowledge or spiritual attainment.

Acknowledgments

We are grateful to the following individuals for their contributions to this course.

Flagship Director
RABBI SHMULY KARP

Curriculum Coordinator
RIVKI MOCKIN

Flagship Administrator
NAOMI HEBER

Author
RABBI YANKI TAUBER

Instructors Advisory Committee
RABBI LEVI DUBOV
RABBI DOVID FLINKENSTEIN
RABBI MENDY LEWIS
RABBI SHOLOM RAICHIK
RABBI ARI SOLLISH

Copywriters
RABBI ELI BLOCK
RABBI YAAKOV PALEY

Proofreading
RACHEL MUSICANTE
YA'AKOVAH WEBER

Hebrew Punctuation
RABBI MOSHE WOLFF

Instructor Support
RABBI ISAAC ABELSKY
RABBI LEVI GOLDSHMID

Design and Layout Administrator
SARA OSDOBA

Textbook and Marketing Design
CHAYA MUSHKA KANNER
ESTIE RAVNOY
RABBI LEVI WEINGARTEN

Textbook Layout
SHAYNA GROSH
RABBI MOTTI KLEIN
RABBI ZALMAN KORF

Infographics
RABBI LEVI WEINGARTEN

Imagery
SARA ROSENBLUM

Permissions
SHULAMIS NADLER

Publication and Distribution
RABBI LEVI GOLDSHMID
RABBI MENDEL SIROTA

PowerPoint Presentations
CHANIE SHEMTOV

Course Videos
GETZY RASKIN
MOSHE RASKIN

Key Points Videos
RABBI MOTTI KLEIN

We are immensely grateful for the encouragement of JLI's visionary chairman, and vice-chairman of *Merkos L'Inyonei Chinuch*—Lubavitch World Headquarters, **Rabbi Moshe Kotlarsky**. Rabbi Kotlarsky has been highly instrumental in building the infrastructure for the expansion of Chabad's international network and is also the architect of scores of initiatives and services to help Chabad representatives across the globe succeed in their mission. We are blessed to have the unwavering support of JLI's principal benefactor, **Mr. George Rohr**, who is fully invested in our work, continues to be instrumental in JLI's monumental growth and expansion, and is largely responsible for the Jewish renaissance that is being spearheaded by JLI and its affiliates across the globe.

The commitment and sage direction of JLI's dedicated Executive Board—**Rabbis Chaim Block**, **Hesh Epstein**, **Ronnie Fine**, **Yosef Gansburg**, **Shmuel Kaplan**, **Yisrael Rice**, and **Avrohom Sternberg**—and the countless hours they devote to the development of JLI are what drive the vision, growth, and tremendous success of the organization.

Finally, JLI represents an incredible partnership of more than 1,600 *shluchim* and *shluchot* in more than 1,000 locations across the globe, who contribute their time and talent to further Jewish adult education. We thank them for generously sharing feedback and making suggestions that steer JLI's development and growth. They are our most valuable critics and our most cherished contributors.

Inspired by the call of the **Lubavitcher Rebbe**, of righteous memory, it is the mandate of the Rohr JLI to provide a community of learning for all Jews throughout the world where they can participate in their precious heritage of Torah learning and experience its rewards. May this course succeed in fulfilling this sacred charge!

On behalf of the Rohr Jewish Learning Institute,

RABBI EFRAIM MINTZ
Executive Director

RABBI YISRAEL RICE
Chairman, Editorial Board

Rosh Chodesh Kislev, 5783

The Rohr Jewish Learning Institute

AN AFFILIATE OF MERKOS L'INYONEI CHINUCH,
THE EDUCATIONAL ARM OF THE CHABAD-LUBAVITCH MOVEMENT
832 EASTERN PARKWAY, BROOKLYN, NY 11213

CURRICULUM DEVELOPMENT

Rabbi Mordechai Dinerman
Rabbi Naftali Silberberg
EDITORS IN CHIEF

Rabbi Shmuel Klatzkin, PhD
ACADEMIC CONSULTANT

Rabbi Yanki Tauber
SENIOR EDITOR

Rabbi Levi Bendet
Rabbi Eli Block
Rabbi Yoni Brown
Rabbi Eliezer Gurkow
Rabbi Berel Polityko
Rabbi Levi Shmotkin
Rabbi Shmuel Super
Rabbi Menashe Wolf
CURRICULUM AUTHORS

Rabbi Ahrele Loschak
EDITOR, TORAH STUDIES

Rabbi Yaakov Paley
Rabbi Boruch Werdiger
WRITERS

Rabbi Mendel Glazman
Mrs. Chanie Shemtov
Rabbi Moshe Wolff
EDITORIAL SUPPORT

Rabbi Yakov Gershon
RESEARCH

Rabbi Michoel Lipskier
Rabbi Mendel Rubin
EXPERIENTIAL LEARNING

Mrs. Rivki Mockin
CONTENT COORDINATOR

MARKETING AND BRANDING

Mr. David Kaplan
CHIEF MARKETING OFFICER

Mendel Backman
Lazer Cohen
Tova Farro
Yosef Feigelstock
Tzivi Gorowitz
Menachem Klein
Basya Stevenson
Baila Vogel
MARKETING AND SOCIAL MEDIA

Mendel Jacobson
Avi Webb
BRAND COPYWRITERS

Ms. Sara Osdoba
DESIGN ADMINISTRATOR

Mrs. Chaya Mushka Kanner
Ms. Chaya Mintz
Ms. Estie Ravnoy
Mrs. Shifra Tauber
Rabbi Levi Weingarten
GRAPHIC DESIGN

Mrs. Rivky Fieldsteel
Mrs. Shayna Grosh
Rabbi Motti Klein
Rabbi Zalman Korf
Rabbi Moshe Wolff
PUBLICATION DESIGN

Rabbi Yaakov Paley
COPYWRITER

Rabbi Yossi Grossbaum
Rabbi Mendel Lifshitz
Rabbi Shraga Sherman
Rabbi Ari Sollish
Rabbi Mendel Teldon
MARKETING COMMITTEE

MARKETING CONSULTANTS

Alan Rosenspan
ALAN ROSENSPAN & ASSOCIATES
Sharon, MA

Gary Wexler
PASSION MARKETING
Los Angeles, CA

JLI CENTRAL

Rabbi Isaac Abelsky
Rabbi Levi Goldshmid
Ms. Mushka Majeski
Ms. Mimi Rabinowitz
Mrs. Aliza Scheinfeld
Mrs. Orah Smith
Rabbi Menashe Treitel
ADMINISTRATION

Ms. Liba Leah Gutnick
Rabbi Motti Klein
Mrs. Sara Rosenblum
Rabbi Shlomie Tenenbaum
PROJECT MANAGERS

Mrs. Mindy Wallach
AFFILIATE ORIENTATION

Rabbi Mendel Backman
Ms. Tova Farro
Mrs. Esty Geisinsky
Rabbi Motti Klein
Getzy Raskin
Moshe Raskin
Mrs. Chanie Shemtov
MULTIMEDIA DEVELOPMENT

Rabbi Mendel Ashkenazi
Yoni Ben-Oni
Rabbi Mendy Elishevitz
Mendel Grossbaum
Ms. Dani Hess
Ms. Mushkie Osdoba
Rabbi Aron Liberow
Mrs. Chana Weinbaum
ONLINE DIVISION

Mrs. Ya'akovah Weber
LEAD PROOFREADER

Mrs. Rachel Musicante
Mrs. Pamela Russ
PROOFREADERS

Rabbi Levi Goldshmid
Rabbi Mendel Sirota
PRINTING AND DISTRIBUTION

Mrs. Musie Liberow
Mrs. Shaina B. Mintz
Mrs. Shulamis Nadler
ACCOUNTING

Ms. Chaya Mintz
Mrs. Shulamis Nadler
Mrs. Mindy Wallach
CONTINUING EDUCATION

JLI FLAGSHIP

Rabbi Yisrael Rice
CHAIRMAN

Rabbi Shmuly Karp
DIRECTOR

Mrs. Naomi Heber
PROJECT MANAGER

PAST FLAGSHIP AUTHORS

Rabbi Yitzchak M. Kagan
of blessed memory

Rabbi Zalman Abraham
Brooklyn, NY

Rabbi Berel Bell
Montreal, QC

Rabbi Nissan D. Dubov
London, UK

Rabbi Tzvi Freeman
Atlanta, GA

Rabbi Eliezer Gurkow
London, ON

Rabbi Aaron Herman
Pittsburgh, PA

Rabbi Simon Jacobson
New York, NY

Rabbi Chaim D. Kagan, PhD
Monsey, NY

Rabbi Shmuel Klatzkin, PhD
Dayton, OH

Rabbi Nochum Mangel
Dayton, OH

Rabbi Moshe Miller
Chicago, IL

Rabbi Yosef Paltiel
Brooklyn, NY

Rabbi Yehuda Pink
Solihull, UK

Rabbi Yisrael Rice
S. Rafael, CA

Rabbi Eli Silberstein
Ithaca, NY

Mrs. Rivkah Slonim
Binghamton, NY

Rabbi Avrohom Sternberg
New London, CT

Rabbi Shais Taub
Cedarhurst, NY

Rabbi Shlomo Yaffe
Longmeadow, MA

ROSH CHODESH SOCIETY

Rabbi Shmuel Kaplan
CHAIRMAN

Mrs. Shaindy Jacobson
DIRECTOR

Mrs. Chana Dechter
ADMINISTRATOR

Mrs. Malky Bitton
Mrs. Shula Bryski
Mrs. Rochel Holzkenner
Mrs. Leah Rosenfeld
Mrs. Yehudis Wolvovsky
EDITORIAL BOARD

JLI TEENS

In Partnership with CTeen: Chabad Teen Network

Rabbi Chaim Block
CHAIRMAN

Rabbi Shlomie Tenenbaum
DIRECTOR

TORAH STUDIES

Rabbi Yosef Gansburg
CHAIRMAN

Rabbi Shlomie Tenenbaum
PROJECT MANAGER

Rabbi Ahrele Loschak
EDITOR

Rabbi Levi Fogelman
Rabbi Yaacov Halperin
Rabbi Nechemia Schusterman
Rabbi Ari Sollish
STEERING COMMITTEE

SINAI SCHOLARS SOCIETY

In Partnership with Chabad on Campus

Rabbi Menachem Schmidt
CHAIRMAN

Rabbi Dubi Rabinowitz
DIRECTOR

Ms. Chanie Chesney
PROJECT MANAGER

Ms. Mussi Rabinowitz
Mrs. Miriam Rapoport
Ms. Miriam Spalter
Mrs. Manya Sperlin
Mrs. Devorah Zlatopolsky
ADMINISTRATION

Rabbi Yossy Gordon
Rabbi Efraim Mintz
Rabbi Menachem Schmidt
Rabbi Avi Weinstein
EXECUTIVE COMMITTEE

Rabbi Chaim Leib Hilel
Rabbi Yossi Lazaroff
Rabbi Levi Raichik
Rabbi Shmuel Tiechtel
Rabbi Shmuly Weiss
STEERING COMMITTEE

THE WELLNESS INSTITUTE

Rabbi Menachem Klein
ADMINISTRATOR

Rabbi Zalman Abraham
VISION AND STRATEGIC PLANNING

Pamela Dubin
IMPACT ANALYSIS

Mindy Wallach
ADMINISTRATIVE SPECIALIST

Mushky Lipskier
PROJECT MANAGERS

Dina Zarchi
NETWORKING AND DEVELOPMENT

Raizy Lifshitz
COMMUNICATIONS

Matti Feigelstock
PROJECT L'CHAIM COORDINATOR

Rivka Mogilevsky
TWI TORONTO COORDINATOR

Orah Smith
NETWORKING AND DEVELOPMENT

CLINICAL ADVISORY BOARD

Sigrid Frandsen-Pechenik, PSY.D.
CLINICAL DIRECTOR

David A. Brent, M.D.
Randal M. Erenst, Ed.D
Gittel Francis, LMSW
Jill Harkavy-Friedman, PhD
Kenneth Ginsburg, M.D., M.S. Ed
Madelyn S. Gould, PhD, M.P.H.

Lisa A. Horowitz, PhD, MPH
Lisa Jacobs, M.D., MBA
Thomas Joiner, PhD
E. David Klonsky, PhD
Laura H. Mufson, PhD
Tayyab Rashid, PhD
Sylvia J. Sandler, LMFT
Bella Schanzer, M.D.
Andrew Shatte, PHD
Arielle H. Sheftall PhD
Jonathan Singer, PhD, LCSW
Casey Skvorc, PhD, JD
Darcy Wallen, LCSW, PC

JLI INTERNATIONAL

Rabbi Avrohom Sternberg
CHAIRMAN

Rabbi Dubi Rabinowitz
DIRECTOR

Rabbi Mendel Glazman
ADMINISTRATOR

Rabbi Eli Wolf
ADMINISTRATOR, JLI IN THE CIS

In Partnership with the Federation of Jewish Communities of the CIS

Flor Setton
COORDINATOR,
CHABAD OF ARGENTINA

Rabbi Nochum Schapiro
REGIONAL REPRESENTATIVE, AUSTRALIA

Rabbi Avrohom Steinmetz
REGIONAL REPRESENTATIVE, BRAZIL

Rabbi Shevach Zlatopolsky
EDITOR, JLI IN THE CIS

Rabbi Shlomo Cohen
FRENCH COORDINATOR,
REGIONAL REPRESENTATIVE

Rabbi Avraham Golovacheov
REGIONAL REPRESENTATIVE, GERMANY

Rabbi Shlomo Koves
REGIONAL REPRESENTATIVE, HUNGARY

Rabbi Shmuel Katzman
REGIONAL REPRESENTATIVE,
NETHERLANDS

Rabbi Bentzi Sudak
REGIONAL REPRESENTATIVE,
UNITED KINGDOM

NATIONAL JEWISH RETREAT

Rabbi Hesh Epstein
CHAIRMAN

Mrs. Shaina B. Mintz
DIRECTOR

Bruce Backman
HOTEL LIAISON

Rabbi Menachem Klein
PROGRAM COORDINATOR

Rabbi Isaac Mintz
SHLUCHIM LIAISON

Rabbi Mendel Rosenfeld
LOGISTICS COORDINATOR

Ms. Mushka Majeski
Mrs. Aliza Scheinfeld
SERVICE AND SUPPORT

JLI LAND & SPIRIT
Israel Experience

Rabbi Shmuly Karp
DIRECTOR

Rabbi Levi Goldshmid
Rabbi Isaac Mintz
SHLUCHIM LIAISONS

Mrs. Shaina B. Mintz
ADMINISTRATOR

Rabbi Yechiel Baitelman
Rabbi Dovid Flinkenstein
Rabbi Chanoch Kaplan
Rabbi Levi Klein
Rabbi Mendy Mangel
Rabbi Sholom Raichik
STEERING COMMITTEE

SHABBAT IN THE HEIGHTS

Rabbi Shmuly Karp
DIRECTOR

Mrs. Shulamis Nadler
SERVICE AND SUPPORT

Rabbi Chaim Hanoka
CHAIRMAN

Rabbi Mordechai Dinerman
Rabbi Zalman Marcus
STEERING COMMITTEE

MYSHIUR
Advanced Learning Initiative

Rabbi Shmuel Kaplan
CHAIRMAN

Rabbi Shlomie Tenenbaum
ADMINISTRATOR

TORAHCAFE.COM

ONLINE LEARNING

Rabbi Mendy Elishevitz
WEBSITE DEVELOPMENT

Moshe Levin
CONTENT MANAGER

Mendel Laine
FILMING

MACHON SHMUEL
The Sami Rohr Research Institute

Rabbi Zalman Korf
ADMINISTRATOR

Rabbi Moshe Miller
Rabbi Gedalya Oberlander
Rabbi Chaim Rapoport
Rabbi Levi Yitzchak Raskin
Rabbi Chaim Schapiro
RABBINIC ADVISORY BOARD

Rabbi Yakov Gershon
RESEARCH FELLOW

FOUNDING DEPARTMENT HEADS

Rabbi Mendel Bell
Rabbi Zalman Charytan
Rabbi Mendel Druk
Rabbi Menachem Gansburg
Rabbi Meir Hecht
Rabbi Levi Kaplan
Rabbi Yoni Katz
Rabbi Chaim Zalman Levy
Rabbi Benny Rapoport
Dr. Chana Silberstein
Rabbi Elchonon Tenenbaum
Rabbi Mendy Weg

JLI Chapter Directory

ALABAMA

BIRMINGHAM
Rabbi Yossi Friedman 205.970.0100

MOBILE
Rabbi Yosef Goldwasser 251.265.1213

ALASKA

ANCHORAGE
Rabbi Yosef Greenberg
Rabbi Mendy Greenberg 907.357.8770

ARIZONA

CHANDLER
Rabbi Mendy Deitsch 480.855.4333

FLAGSTAFF
Rabbi Dovie Shapiro 928.255.5756

FOUNTAIN HILLS
Rabbi Mendy Lipskier 480.776.4763

ORO VALLEY
Rabbi Ephraim Zimmerman 520.477.8672

PARADISE VALLEY
Rabbi Shlomo Levertov 480.788.9310

PHOENIX
Rabbi Dovber Dechter 347.410.0785
Rabbi Zalman Levertov
Rabbi Yossi Friedman 602.944.2753

SCOTTSDALE
Rabbi Yossi Levertov 480.998.1410

SEDONA
Rabbi Mendel Kessler 928.985.0667

TUCSON
Rabbi Yehuda Ceitlin 520.881.7956

ARKANSAS

LITTLE ROCK
Rabbi Pinchus Ciment 501.217.0053

CALIFORNIA

AGOURA HILLS
Rabbi Moshe Bryski 818.516.0444

ALAMEDA
Rabbi Meir Shmotkin 510.640.2590

BAKERSFIELD
Rabbi Shmuli Schlanger 661.834.1512

BEL AIR
Rabbi Chaim Mentz 310.475.5311

BEVERLY HILLS
Rabbi Dovid Begun 310.242.7750

BURBANK
Rabbi Shmuly Kornfeld 818.954.0070

CARLSBAD
Rabbi Yeruchem Eilfort
Mrs. Nechama Eilfort 760.943.8891

CHATSWORTH
Rabbi Yossi Spritzer 818.307.9907

CONCORD
Rabbi Berel Kesselman 925.326.1613

CONTRA COSTA
Rabbi Dovber Berkowitz 925.937.4101

DANA POINT
Rabbi Eli Goorevitch 949.290.0628

DANVILLE
Rabbi Shmuli Raitman 213.447.6694

EMERYVILLE
Rabbi Menachem Blank 510.859.8808

ENCINO
Rabbi Aryeh Herzog 818.784.9986
Chapter founded by Rabbi Joshua Gordon, OBM

FOLSOM
Rabbi Yossi Grossbaum 916.608.9811

FREMONT
Rabbi Moshe Fuss 510.300.4090

GLENDALE

Rabbi Simcha Backman 818.240.2750

HOLLYWOOD

Rabbi Zalman Partouche 818.964.9428

HUNTINGTON BEACH

Rabbi Aron David Berkowitz 714.846.2285

LAGUNA NIGUEL

Rabbi Mendy Paltiel 949.831.7701

LA JOLLA

Rabbi Baruch Shalom Ezagui 858.455.5433

LAKE BALBOA

Rabbi Eli Gurary 347.403.6734

LOMITA

Rabbi Sholom Pinson 310.326.8234

LONG BEACH

Rabbi Abba Perelmuter 562.773.1350

LOS ANGELES

Rabbi Yossi Elifort 310.515.5310
Rabbi Leibel Korf 323.660.5177
Rabbi Zalmy Labkowsky 213.618.9486
Rabbi Mendel Zajac 310.770.9051

MALIBU

Rabbi Levi Cunin 310.456.6588

MARINA DEL REY

Rabbi Danny Yiftach-Hashem
Rabbi Dovid Yiftach 310.859.0770

MAR VISTA

Rabbi Shimon Simpson 646.401.2354

NEWHALL

Rabbi Choni Marosov 661.254.3434

NORTHRIDGE

Rabbi Eli Rivkin 818.368.3937

OJAI

Rabbi Mordechai Nemtzov 805.613.7181

PACIFIC PALISADES

Rabbi Zushe Cunin 310.454.7783

PALO ALTO

Rabbi Menachem Landa 415.418.4768
Rabbi Yosef Levin
Rabbi Ber Rosenblatt 650.424.9800

PASADENA

Rabbi Zushe Rivkin 626.788.3343

PLEASANTON

Rabbi Josh Zebberman 925.846.0700

PORTOLA VALLEY

Rabbi Mayer Brook 650.304.2098

POWAY

Rabbi Mendel Goldstein 858.208.6613

RANCHO CUCAMONGA

Rabbi Sholom Ber Harlig 909.949.4553

RANCHO MIRAGE

Rabbi Shimon H. Posner 760.770.7785

RANCHO PALOS VERDES

Rabbi Yitzchok Magalnic 310.544.5544

RANCHO S. FE

Rabbi Levi Raskin 858.756.7571

REDONDO BEACH

Rabbi Yossi Mintz
Rabbi Zalman Gordon 310.214.4999

RIVERSIDE

Rabbi Shmuel Fuss 951.329.2747

S. CLEMENTE

Rabbi Menachem M. Slavin 949.489.0723

S. CRUZ

Rabbi Yochanan Friedman 831.454.0101

S. DIEGO

Rabbi Rafi Andrusier 619.387.8770
Rabbi Yechiel Cagen 832.216.1534

S. FRANCISCO

Rebbetzin Mattie Pil 415.933.4310
Rabbi Gedalia Potash 415.648.8000
Rabbi Shlomo Zarchi 415.752.2866

S. LUIS OBISPO

Rabbi Meir Gordon 347.675.3383

S. MATEO
Rabbi Yossi Marcus 650.341.4510

S. RAFAEL
Rabbi Yisrael Rice 415.492.1666

SHERMAN OAKS
Rabbi Nachman Abend 818.989.9539

SONOMA
Rabbi Mendel Wolvovsky 707.292.6221

SOUTH LAKE TAHOE
Rabbi Mordechai Richler 530.539.4363

SUNNYVALE
Rabbi Yisroel Hecht 408.720.0553

TEMECULA
Rabbi Yonason Abrams 951.234.4196

TIBURON
Rabbi Levi Mintz 415.378.9364

TUSTIN
Rabbi Yehoshua Eliezrie 714.508.2150

VACAVILLE
Rabbi Chaim Zaklos 707.592.5300

VAIL
Rabbi Yisroel Shemtov 347.372.3092

WEST HILLS
Rabbi Avi Rabin 818.337.4544

WEST HOLLYWOOD
Rabbi Mordechai Kirschenbaum 310.691.9988

WEST LOS ANGELES
Rabbi Mordechai Zaetz 424.652.8742

YORBA LINDA
Rabbi Dovid Eliezrie 714.693.0770

COLORADO

ASPEN
Rabbi Mendel Mintz 970.544.3770

DENVER
Rabbi Yossi Serebryanski 303.744.9699
Rabbi Mendel Popack 720.515.4337
Rabbi Mendy Sirota 720.940.3716

FORT COLLINS
Rabbi Yerachmiel Gorelik 970.407.1613

HIGHLANDS RANCH
Rabbi Avraham Mintz 303.694.9119

LONGMONT
Rabbi Yakov Borenstein 303.678.7595

VAIL
Rabbi Dovid Mintz 970.476.7887

WESTMINSTER
Rabbi Benjy Brackman 303.429.5177

VALENCIA
Rabbi Choni Marozov 661.644.5735

CONNECTICUT

FAIRFIELD
Rabbi Shlame Landa 203.373.7551

GREENWICH
Rabbi Yossi Deren
Rabbi Menachem Feldman 203.629.9059

GUILFORD
Rabbi Yossi Yaffe 203.645.4635

HAMDEN
Rabbi Moshe Hecht 203.635.7268

MILFORD
Rabbi Schneur Wilhelm 203.887.7603

NEW HAVEN
Rabbi Mendy Hecht 203.589.5375
Rabbi Chanoch Wineberg 203.479.0313

NEW LONDON
Rabbi Avrohom Sternberg 860.437.8000

STAMFORD
Rabbi Yisrael Deren
Rabbi Levi Mendelow 203.3.CHABAD

WESTPORT
Rabbi Yehuda Kantor 561.460.3758

WEST HARTFORD
Rabbi Shaya Gopin 860.232.1116

SHELTON
Rabbi Schneur Brook 203.364.4149

DELAWARE

WILMINGTON

Rabbi Chuni Vogel 302.529.9900

DISTRICT OF COLUMBIA

Rabbi Levi Shemtov
Rabbi Yitzy Ceitlin 202.332.5600

FLORIDA

ALTAMONTE SPRINGS

Rabbi Mendy Bronstein 407.280.0535

BAL HARBOUR

Rabbi Dov Schochet 305.868.1411

BOCA RATON

Rabbi Zalman Bukiet 561.487.2934
Rabbi Arele Gopin 561.994.6257
Rabbi Moishe Denburg 561.526.5760
Rabbi Ruvi New 561.394.9770

BONITA SPRINGS

Rabbi Mendy Greenberg 239.949.6900

BOYNTON BEACH

Rabbi Yosef Yitzchok Raichik 561.732.4633

BRADENTON

Rabbi Menachem Bukiet 941.388.9656

CAPE CORAL

Rabbi Yossi Labkowski 239.963.4770

CORAL GABLES

Rabbi Avrohom Stolik 305.490.7572

CORAL SPRINGS

Rabbi Hershy Bronstein 954.798.6023
Rabbi Yankie Denburg 954.471.8646

CUTLER BAY

Rabbi Yossi Wolff 305.975.6680

DAVIE

Rabbi Aryeh Schwartz 954.376.9973

DELRAY BEACH

Rabbi Yaakov Perman 561.666.2770

FISHER ISLAND

Rabbi Efraim Brody 347.325.1913

FLEMING ISLAND

Rabbi Shmuly Feldman 904.290.1017

FORT LAUDERDALE

Rabbi Yitzchok Naparstek 954.568.1190

HALLANDALE BEACH

Rabbi Mordy Feiner 954.458.1877

HOLLYWOOD

Rabbi Leibel Kudan 954.801.3367

JUPITER

Rabbi Berel Barash 561.317.0968

KENDALL

Rabbi Yossi Harlig 305.234.5654

KEY BISCAYNE

Rabbi Avremel Caroline 305.365.6744

LAUDERHILL

Rabbi Shmuel Heidingsfeld 323.877.7703

LONGWOOD

Rabbi Yanky Majesky 407.636.5994

MAITLAND

Rabbi Sholom Dubov
Rabbi Levik Dubov 470.644.2500

MARION COUNTY

Rabbi Yossi Hecht 352.330.4466

MIAMI

Rabbi Mendy Cheruty 305.219.3353
Rabbi Yakov Fellig 305.445.5444
Rabbi Chaim Lipskar 305.373.8303

MIAMI BEACH

Rabbi Yisroel Frankforter 305.534.3895
Rabbi Sholom Korf 786.423.6483
Rabbi Shmuel Mann 305.674.8400

N. MIAMI BEACH

Rabbi Eli Laufer 305.770.4412

NAPLES

Rabbi Fishel Zaklos 239.404.6993

ORLANDO

Rabbi Yosef Konikov 407.354.3660

ORMOND BEACH

Rabbi Asher Farkash 386.672.9300

PALM CITY
Rabbi Shlomo Uminer 772.485.5501

PALM BEACH
Rabbi Zalman Levitin 561.659.3884

PALM BEACH GARDENS
Rabbi Dovid Vigler 561.624.2223

PALM HARBOR
Rabbi Pinchas Adler 727.789.0408

PARKLAND
Rabbi Mendy Gutnick 954.600.6991

PEMBROKE PINES
Rabbi Mordechai Andrusier 954.874.2280

PENSACOLA
Rabbi Mendel Danow 850.291.9600

PLANTATION
Rabbi Pinchas Taylor 954.644.9177

PONTE VEDRA BEACH
Rabbi Nochum Kurinsky 904.543.9301

ROYAL PALM BEACH
Rabbi Nachmen Zeev Schtroks 561.714.1692

S. AUGUSTINE
Rabbi Levi Vogel 904.521.8664

S. JOHNS
Rabbi Mendel Sharfstein 347.461.3765

SARASOTA
Rabbi Chaim Shaul Steinmetz 941.925.0770
Rabbi Levi Steinmetz 941.928.9267

SATELLITE BEACH
Rabbi Zvi Konikov 321.777.2770

SINGER ISLAND
Rabbi Berel Namdar 347.276.6985

SOUTH PALM BEACH
Rabbi Leibel Stolik 561.889.3499

SOUTH TAMPA
Rabbi Mendy Dubrowski 813.922.1723

SOUTHWEST BROWARD COUNTY
Rabbi Aryeh Schwartz 954.252.1770

SUNNY ISLES BEACH
Rabbi Alexander Kaller 305.803.5315

SURFSIDE
Rabbi Dov Schochet 305.790.8294

TAMARAC
Rabbi Kopel Silberberg 954.882.7434

VENICE
Rabbi Sholom Ber Schmerling 941.330.4477

VERO BEACH
Rabbi Motty Rosenfeld 772.245.6712

WESLEY CHAPEL
Rabbi Mendy Yarmush
Rabbi Mendel Friedman 813.731.2977

WEST PALM BEACH
Rabbi Yoel Gancz 561.659.7770

WESTON
Rabbi Yisroel Spalter 954.349.6565

GEORGIA

ALPHARETTA
Rabbi Hirshy Minkowicz 770.410.9000

ATLANTA
Rabbi Yossi New
Rabbi Isser New 404.843.2464
Rabbi Alexander Piekarski 678.267.6418

ATLANTA: INTOWN
Rabbi Eliyahu Schusterman
Rabbi Ari Sollish 404.898.0434

CUMMING
Rabbi Levi Mentz 310.666.2218

GAINESVILLE
Rabbi Nechemia Gurevitz 770.906.4970

GWINNETT
Rabbi Yossi Lerman 678.595.0196

MARIETTA
Rabbi Ephraim Silverman 770.565.4412

HAWAII

KAPA'A
Rabbi Michoel Goldman 808.647.4293

IDAHO

BOISE
Rabbi Mendel Lifshitz 208.853.9200

ILLINOIS

ARLINGTON HEIGHTS
Rabbi Yaakov Kotlarsky 224.357.7002

CHAMPAIGN
Rabbi Dovid Tiechtel 217.355.8672

CHICAGO
Rabbi Mendy Benhiyoun 312.498.7704
Rabbi Meir Hecht 312.714.4655
Rabbi Dovid Kotlarsky 773.495.7127
Rabbi Mordechai Gershon 773.412.5189
Rabbi Yosef Moscowitz 773.772.3770
Rabbi Levi Notik 773.274.5123

DES PLAINES
Rabbi Lazer Hershkovich 224.392.4442

ELGIN
Rabbi Mendel Shemtov 847.440.4486

GLENVIEW
Rabbi Yishaya Benjaminson 847.910.1738

GURNEE
Rabbi Sholom Tenenbaum 847.782.1800

HIGHLAND PARK
Mrs. Michla Schanowitz 847.266.0770

NAPERVILLE
Rabbi Mendy Goldstein 630.957.8122

NORTHBROOK
Rabbi Meir Moscowitz 847.564.8770

NORWOOD PARK
Rabbi Mendel Perlstein 312.752.8894

OAK PARK
Rabbi Yitzchok Bergstein 708.524.1530

PEORIA
Rabbi Eli Langsam 309.370.7701

SKOKIE
Rabbi Yochanan Posner 847.677.1770

VERNON HILLS
Rabbi Shimmy Susskind 718.755.5356

WILMETTE
Rabbi Dovid Flinkenstein 847.251.7707

INDIANA

INDIANAPOLIS
Rabbi Avraham Grossbaum
Rabbi Dr. Shmuel Klatzkin 317.251.5573

IOWA

BETTENDORF
Rabbi Shneur Cadaner 563.355.1065

KANSAS

OVERLAND PARK
Rabbi Mendy Wineberg 913.649.4852

KENTUCKY

LOUISVILLE
Rabbi Avrohom Litvin 502.459.1770

LOUISIANA

BATON ROUGE
Rabbi Peretz Kazen 225.267.7047

METAIRIE
Rabbi Yossie Nemes
Rabbi Mendel Ceitlin 504.454.2910

NEW ORLEANS
Rabbi Mendel Rivkin 504.302.1830

MAINE

BANGOR
Rabbi Chaim Wilansky 207.650.7223

PORTLAND

Rabbi Levi Wilansky 207.650.1783

MARYLAND

BALTIMORE

Rabbi Velvel Belinsky 410.764.5000
Classes in Russian

Rabbi Dovid Reyder 781.796.4204

BEL AIR

Rabbi Kushi Schusterman 443.353.9718

BETHESDA

Rabbi Sender Geisinsky 301.913.9777

CHEVY CHASE

Rabbi Zalman Minkowitz 301.260.5000

COLUMBIA

Rabbi Hillel Baron
Rabbi Yosef Chaim Sufrin 410.740.2424

FREDERICK

Rabbi Boruch Labkowski 301.996.3659

GAITHERSBURG

Rabbi Sholom Raichik 301.926.3632

OLNEY

Rabbi Bentzy Stolik 301.660.6770

OWINGS MILLS

Rabbi Nochum Katsenelenbogen 410.356.5156

POTOMAC

Rabbi Mendel Bluming 301.983.4200
Rabbi Mendel Kaplan 301.983.1485

ROCKVILLE

Rabbi Shlomo Beitsh 646.773.2675
Rabbi Moishe Kavka 301.836.1242

MASSACHUSETTS

ANDOVER

Rabbi Asher Bronstein 978.470.2288

ARLINGTON

Rabbi Avi Bukiet 617.909.8653

BOSTON

Rabbi Yosef Zaklos 617.297.7282

BRIGHTON

Rabbi Dan Rodkin 617.787.2200

CAPE COD

Rabbi Yekusiel Alperowitz 508.775.2324

CHESTNUT HILL

Rabbi Mendy Uminer 617.738.9770

LEXINGTON

Rabbi Yisroel New 646.248.9053

LONGMEADOW

Rabbi Yakov Wolff 413.567.8665

NEWTON

Rabbi Shalom Ber Prus 617.244.1200

PEABODY

Rabbi Nechemia Schusterman 978.977.9111

SUDBURY

Rabbi Yisroel Freeman 978.443.0110

SWAMPSCOTT

Rabbi Yossi Lipsker 781.581.3833

MICHIGAN

ANN ARBOR

Rabbi Aharon Goldstein 734.995.3276

BLOOMFIELD HILLS

Rabbi Levi Dubov 248.949.6210

GRAND RAPIDS

Rabbi Mordechai Haller 616.957.0770

TROY

Rabbi Menachem Caytak 248.873.5851

WEST BLOOMFIELD

Rabbi Shneur Silberberg 248.855.6170

MINNESOTA

MINNETONKA

Rabbi Mordechai Grossbaum
Rabbi Shmuel Silberstein 952.929.9922

S. PAUL

Rabbi Shneur Zalman Bendet 651.998.9298

MISSOURI

CHESTERFIELD
Rabbi Avi Rubenfeld 314.258.3401

S. LOUIS
Rabbi Yosef Landa 314.725.0400
Rabbi Yosef Abenson 314.448.0927

MONTANA

BOZEMAN
Rabbi Chaim Shaul Bruk 406.600.4934

NEVADA

LAS VEGAS
Rabbi Yosef Rivkin 702.217.2170

SUMMERLIN
Rabbi Yisroel Schanowitz
Rabbi Tzvi Bronchtain 702.855.0770

TRUCKEE
Rabbi Levi Sputz 347.262.4531

NEW JERSEY

BASKING RIDGE
Rabbi Mendy Herson
Rabbi Mendel Shemtov 908.604.8844

CHERRY HILL
Rabbi Mendel Mangel 856.874.1500

CLINTON
Rabbi Eli Kornfeld 908.623.7000

ENGLEWOOD
Rabbi Shmuel Konikov 201.519.7343

FAIR LAWN
Rabbi Avrohom Bergstein 201.794.3770

FARNWOOD
Rabbi Avrohom Blesofsky 908.790.0008

GREATER MERCER COUNTY
Rabbi Dovid Dubov
Rabbi Yaakov Chaiton 609.213.4136

HASKELL
Rabbi Mendy Gurkov 201.696.7609

HOLMDEL
Rabbi Shmaya Galperin 732.772.1998

JACKSON
Rabbi Shmuel Naparstek 732.668.7702

MADISON
Rabbi Shalom Lubin 973.377.0707

MANALAPAN
Rabbi Boruch Chazanow
Rabbi Levi Wolosow 732.972.3687

MEDFORD
Rabbi Yitzchok Kahan 609.451.3522

MOUNTAIN LAKES
Rabbi Levi Dubinsky 973.551.1898

MULLICA HILL
Rabbi Avrohom Richler 856.733.0770

OLD TAPPAN
Rabbi Mendy Lewis 201.767.4008

RED BANK
Rabbi Dovid Harrison 718.915.8748

ROCKAWAY
Rabbi Asher Herson
Rabbi Mordechai Baumgarten 973.625.1525

RUTHERFORD
Rabbi Yitzchok Lerman 347.834.7500

SCOTCH PLAINS
Rabbi Avrohom Blesofsky 908.790.0008

SHORT HILLS
Rabbi Mendel Solomon
Rabbi Avrohom Levin 973.725.7008

SOUTH BRUNSWICK
Rabbi Levi Azimov 732.398.9492

TENAFLY
Rabbi Mordechai Shain 201.871.1152

TOMS RIVER
Rabbi Moshe Gourarie 732.349.4199

WEST ORANGE
Rabbi Mendy Kasowitz 973.325.6311

WOODCLIFF LAKE
Rabbi Dov Drizin 201.476.0157

NEW MEXICO

LAS CRUCES
Rabbi Bery Schmukler 575.524.1330

NEW YORK

ALBANY
Rabbi Mordechai Rubin 518.368.7886

BAY SHORE
Rabbi Shimon Stillerman 631.913.8770

BEDFORD
Rabbi Arik Wolf 914.666.6065

BENSONHURST
Rabbi Avrohom Hertz 718.753.7768

BINGHAMTON
Mrs. Rivkah Slonim 607.797.0015

BRIGHTON BEACH
Rabbi Dovid Okonov 718.368.4490
Rabbi Moshe Winner 718.946.9833

BRONXVILLE
Rabbi Sruli Deitsch 917.755.0078

BROOKLYN
Rabbi Nissi Eber 347.677.2276
Rabbi Dovid Okonov 917.754.6942

BROOKVILLE
Rabbi Mendy Heber 516.626.0600

CEDARHURST
Rabbi Zalman Wolowik 516.295.2478

COMMACK
Rabbi Mendel Teldon 631.543.3343

DELMAR
Rabbi Zalman Simon 518.866.7658

DOBBS FERRY
Rabbi Benjy Silverman 914.693.6100

EAST HAMPTON
Rabbi Leibel Baumgarten
Rabbi Mendy Goldberg 631.329.5800

ELLENVILLE
Rabbi Shlomie Deren 845.647.4450

FOREST HILLS
Rabbi Yossi Mendelson 917.861.9726

GLEN OAKS
Rabbi Shmuel Nadler 347.388.7064

GREAT NECK
Rabbi Yoseph Geisinsky 516.487.4554

KINGSTON
Rabbi Yitzchok Hecht 845.334.9044

LARCHMONT
Rabbi Mendel Silberstein 914.834.4321

LITTLE NECK
Rabbi Eli Shifrin 718.423.1235

LONG BEACH
Rabbi Eli Goodman 516.574.3905

LONG ISLAND CITY
Rabbi Zev Wineberg 347.218.2927

MANHASSET
Rabbi Mendel Paltiel 516.984.0701

MINEOLA
Rabbi Anchelle Perl 516.739.3636

MONTEBELLO
Rabbi Shmuel Gancz 845.746.1927

MELVILLE
Rabbi Yosef Raskin 631.276.4453

NEW HARTFORD
Rabbi Levi Charitonow 716.322.8692

NEW YORK
Rabbi Yakov Bankhalter 917.613.1678
Rabbi Berel Gurevitch 212.518.3122
Rabbi Daniel Kraus 917.294.5567
Rabbi Shmuel Metzger 212.758.3770

NYC TRIBECA
Rabbi Zalman Paris 212.566.6764

NYC UPPER EAST SIDE
Rabbi Uriel Vigler 212.369.7310

NYC WEST SIDE
Rabbi Shlomo Kugel 212.864.5010

OCEANSIDE
Rabbi Levi Gurkow 516.764.7385

OSSINING

Rabbi Dovid Labkowski 914.923.2522

OYSTER BAY

Rabbi Shmuel Lipszyc
Rabbi Shalom Lipszyc 347.853.9992

PARK SLOPE

Rabbi Menashe Wolf 347.957.1291

PORT WASHINGTON

Rabbi Shalom Paltiel 516.767.8672

PROSPECT HEIGHTS

Rabbi Mendy Hecht 347.622.3599

ROCHESTER

Rabbi Nechemia Vogel 585.271.0330

ROSLYN HEIGHTS

Rabbi Aaron Konikov 516.484.3500

SOUTHAMPTON

Rabbi Chaim Pape 917.627.4865

STATEN ISLAND

Rabbi Mendy Katzman 718.370.8953

STONY BROOK

Rabbi Shalom Ber Cohen 631.585.0521

SUFFERN

Rabbi Shmuel Gancz 845.368.1889

YORKTOWN HEIGHTS

Rabbi Yehuda Heber 914.962.1111

NORTH CAROLINA

CARY

Rabbi Yisroel Cotlar 919.651.9710

CHAPEL HILL

Rabbi Zalman Bluming 919.357.5904

CHARLOTTE

Rabbi Yossi Groner
Rabbi Shlomo Cohen 704.366.3984

GREENSBORO

Rabbi Yosef Plotkin 336.617.8120

RALEIGH

Rabbi Pinchas Herman
Rabbi Lev Cotlar 919.637.6950

WINSTON-SALEM

Rabbi Levi Gurevitz 336.756.9069

OHIO

BEACHWOOD

Rabbi Moshe Gancz 216.647.4884

CINCINNATI

Rabbi Yisroel Mangel 513.793.5200

COLUMBUS

Rabbi Yitzi Kaltmann 614.294.3296

DAYTON

Rabbi Nochum Mangel
Rabbi Shmuel Klatzkin 937.643.0770

OKLAHOMA

OKLAHOMA CITY

Rabbi Ovadia Goldman 405.524.4800

TULSA

Rabbi Yehuda Weg 918.492.4499

OREGON

PORTLAND

Rabbi Mordechai Wilhelm 503.977.9947

SALEM

Rabbi Avrohom Yitzchok Perlstein 503.383.9569

TIGARD

Rabbi Menachem Orenstein 971.329.6661

WEST LINN

Rabbi Shimon Wilhelm 503.753.4744

PENNSYLVANIA

AMBLER

Rabbi Shaya Deitsch 215.591.9310

BALA CYNWYD

Rabbi Shraga Sherman 610.660.9192

CLARKS SUMMIT

Rabbi Benny Rapoport 570.587.3300

DOYLESTOWN
Rabbi Mendel Prus 215.340.1303

GLEN MILLS
Rabbi Yehuda Gerber 484.620.4162

LAFAYETTE HILL
Rabbi Yisroel Kotlarsky 484.533.7009

LANCASTER
Rabbi Elazar Green 717.723.8783

LEWISBURG
Rabbi Yisroel Baumgarten 631.880.2801

MONROEVILLE
Rabbi Mendy Schapiro 412.372.1000

NEWTOWN
Rabbi Aryeh Weinstein 215.497.9925

PHILADELPHIA: CENTER CITY
Rabbi Yochonon Goldman 215.238.2100

PITTSBURGH
Rabbi Yisroel Altein 412.422.7300 EXT. 269

PITTSBURGH: SOUTH HILLS
Rabbi Mendy Rosenblum 412.278.3693

READING
Rabbi Yosef Lipsker 610.334.3218

RYDAL
Rabbi Zushe Gurevitz 267.536.5757

UNIVERSITY PARK
Rabbi Nosson Meretsky 814.863.4929

WYNNEWOOD
Rabbi Moishe Brennan 610.529.9011

PUERTO RICO

CAROLINA
Rabbi Mendel Zarchi 787.253.0894

RHODE ISLAND

WARWICK
Rabbi Yossi Laufer 401.884.7888

SOUTH CAROLINA

BLUFFTON
Rabbi Menachem Hertz 843.301.1819

COLUMBIA
Rabbi Hesh Epstein
Rabbi Levi Marrus 803.782.1831

GREENVILLE
Rabbi Leibel Kesselman 864.534.7739

TENNESSEE

KNOXVILLE
Rabbi Yossi Wilhelm 865.588.8584

MEMPHIS
Rabbi Levi Klein 901.754.0404

TEXAS

AUSTIN
Rabbi Mendy Levertov 512.905.2778

BELLAIRE
Rabbi Yossi Zaklikofsky 713.839.8887

CYPRESS
Rabbi Levi Marinovsky 832.651.6964

DALLAS
Rabbi Mendel Dubrawsky
Rabbi Moshe Naparstek 972.818.0770

EL PASO
Rabbi Levi Greenberg 347.678.9762

FORT WORTH
Rabbi Dov Mandel 817.263.7701

HOUSTON
Rabbi Dovid Goldstein
Rabbi Zally Lazarus 281.589.7188
Rabbi Moishe Traxler 713.774.0300

HOUSTON: RICE UNIVERSITY AREA
Rabbi Eliezer Lazaroff 713.522.2004

LEAGUE CITY
Rabbi Yitzchok Schmukler 281.724.1554

PLANO

Rabbi Eli Block 214.620.4083
Rabbi Mendel Block 972.596.8270

ROCKWALL

Rabbi Moshe Kalmenson 469.350.5735

ROUND ROCK

Rabbi Mendel Marasow 512.387.3171

S. ANTONIO

Rabbi Chaim Block
Rabbi Levi Teldon 210.492.1085
Rabbi Tal Shaul 210.877.4218

SOUTHLAKE

Rabbi Levi Gurevitch 817.451.1171

SUGAR LAND

Rabbi Mendel Feigenson 832.758.0685

THE WOODLANDS

Rabbi Mendel Blecher 281.865.7242

UTAH

PARK CITY

Rabbi Yehuda Steiger 435.714.8590

SALT LAKE CITY

Rabbi Benny Zippel 801.467.7777

S. GEORGE

Rabbi Mendy Cohen 862.812.6224

VERMONT

BURLINGTON

Rabbi Yitzchok Raskin 802.658.5770

VIRGINIA

ALEXANDRIA/ARLINGTON

Rabbi Mordechai Newman 703.370.2774

FAIRFAX

Rabbi Leibel Fajnland 703.426.1980

GAINESVILLE

Rabbi Shmuel Perlstein 571.445.0342

LOUDOUN COUNTY

Rabbi Chaim Cohen 248.298.9279

NORFOLK

Rabbi Aaron Margolin
Rabbi Levi Brashevitzky 757.616.0770

RICHMOND

Rabbi Shlomo Pereira 804.740.2000

WINCHESTER

Rabbi Yishai Dinerman 540.324.9879

WASHINGTON

BAINBRIDGE ISLAND

Rabbi Mendy Goldshmid 206.397.7679

BELLINGHAM

Rabbi Yosef Truxton 360.224.9919

MERCER ISLAND

Rabbi Elazar Bogomilsky 206.527.1411
Rabbi Nissan Kornfeld 206.851.2324

OLYMPIA

Rabbi Yosef Schtroks 360.867.8804

SEATTLE

Rabbi Yoni Levitin 206.851.9831
Rabbi Shnai Levitin 347.342.2259

SPOKANE COUNTY

Rabbi Yisroel Hahn 509.443.0770

WISCONSIN

BAYSIDE

Rabbi Cheski Edelman 414.439.5041

BROOKFIELD

Rabbi Levi Brook 925.708.4203

KENOSHA

Rabbi Tzali Wilschanski 262.359.0770

MADISON

Rabbi Avremel Matusof 608.335.3777

MEQUON

Rabbi Menachem Rapoport 262.242.2235

MILWAUKEE

Rabbi Levi Emmer 414.277.8839
Rabbi Mendel Shmotkin 414.961.6100

ARGENTINA

BAHIA BLANCA

Rabbi Shmuel Freedman 347.300.2779

BUENOS AIRES

Rabbi Abraham Benchimol 54.11.6048.5333
Rabbi Yossi Birman 54.11.5334.6606
Mrs. Chani Gorowitz 54.11.4865.0445
Rabbi Menachem M. Grunblatt 54.911.3574.0037
Rabbi Mendy Gurevitch 55.11.4545.7771
Rabbi Mendel Levy 54.11.3687.8258
Rabbi Shlomo Levy 54.11.4807.2223
Rabbi Yosef Levy 54.11.4504.1908
Rabbi Yosef Yitzjok Levy 54.11.6292.4125
Rabbi Yossi Ludman 54.11.3935.0214
Rabbi Yoel Migdal 54.11.4963.1221
Rabbi Mendi Mizrahi 54.11.4963.1221
Rabbi Shiele Plotka 54.11.4634.3111
Rabbi Itzjak Safranchik 54.11.3699.3977
Rabbi Shniur Zalmen Schvetz 54.11.3552.5208
Rabbi Shloimi Setton 54.11.4982.8637
Rabbi Pinhas Sudry 54.1.4822.2285

CORDOBA

Rabbi Menajem Turk 54.351.233.8250

SALTA

Rabbi Rafael Tawil 54.387.421.4947

S. MIGUEL DE TUCUMÁN

Rabbi Ariel Levy 54.381.473.6944

AUSTRALIA

NEW SOUTH WALES

BELLEVUE HILL

Mrs. Chaya Kaye 614.3342.2755

DOUBLE BAY

Rabbi Yanky Berger 612.9327.1644

DOVER HEIGHTS

Rabbi Motti Feldman 614.0400.8572

MAROUBRA

Rabbi Schneur Goldstein 614.3476.0722

NEWTOWN

Rabbi Eli Feldman 614.0077.0613

NORTH SHORE

Rabbi Nochum Schapiro
Rebbetzin Fruma Schapiro 612.9488.9548

TASMANIA

SOUTH LAUNCESTON

Mrs. Rochel Gordon 614.2055.0405

QUEENSLAND

BRISBANE

Rabbi Levi Jaffe 617.3843.6770

VICTORIA

EAST S. KILDA

Rabbi Sholem Gorelik 614.5244.8770

MOORABBIN

Rabbi Elisha Greenbaum 614.0349.0434

WESTERN AUSTRALIA

PERTH

Rabbi Shalom White 618.9275.2106

AZERBAIJAN

BAKU

Mrs. Chavi Segal 994.12.597.91.90

BELARUS

BOBRUISK

Mrs. Mina Hababo 375.29.104.3230

MINSK

Rabbi Shneur Deitsch
Mrs. Bassie Deitsch 375.29.330.6675

BELGIUM

ANTWERP

Rabbi Mendel Gurary 32.48.656.9878

BRUSSELS

Rabbi Shmuel Pinson 375.29.330.6675

BRAZIL

CURITIBA

Rabbi Mendy Labkowski 55.41.3079.1338

S. PAULO

Rabbi Avraham Steinmetz 55.11.3081.3081

CANADA

ALBERTA

CALGARY

Rabbi Mordechai Groner 403.281.3770

EDMONTON

Rabbi Ari Drelich
Rabbi Mendy Blachman 780.200.5770

BRITISH COLUMBIA

NANAIMO

Rabbi Benzti Shemtov 250.797.7877

RICHMOND

Rabbi Yechiel Baitelman 604.277.6427

VANCOUVER

Rabbi Dovid Rosenfeld 604.266.1313
Rabbi Shmuel Yeshayahu 604.738.7060

VICTORIA

Rabbi Meir Kaplan 250.595.7656

MANITOBA

WINNIPEG

Rabbi Shmuel Altein 204.339.8737

ONTARIO

BAYVIEW

Rabbi Levi Gansburg 416.551.9391

MAPLE

Rabbi Yechezkel Deren 647.883.6372

MISSISSAUGA

Rabbi Yitzchok Slavin 905.820.4432

NORTH YORK

Rabbi Sruli Steiner 647.501.5618

OTTAWA

Rabbi Menachem M. Blum 613.843.7770

RICHMOND HILL

Rabbi Mendel Bernstein 905.303.1880

THORNHILL

Rabbi Yisroel Landa 416.897.3338

GREATER TORONTO REGIONAL OFFICE & THORNHILL

Rabbi Yossi Gansburg 905.731.7000

TORONTO

Rabbi Shmuel Neft 647.966.7105
Rabbi Moshe Steiner 416.635.9606

WATERLOO

Rabbi Moshe Goldman 226.338.7770

WHITBY

Rabbi Tzali Borenstein 905.447.8215

QUEBEC

CÔTE S.-LUC

Rabbi Levi Naparstek 438.409.6770

DOLLARD-DES ORMEAUX

Rabbi Leibel Fine 514.777.4675

HAMPSTEAD

Rabbi Moshe New
Rabbi Berel Bell 514.739.0770

MONTREAL

Rabbi Ronnie Fine
Pesach Nussbaum 514.738.3434

OLD MONTREAL/GRIFFINTOWN

Rabbi Nissan Gansbourg
Rabbi Berel Bell 514.800.6966

S. LAZARE

Rabbi Nochum Labkowski 514.436.7426

TOWN OF MOUNT ROYAL

Rabbi Moshe Krasnanski
Rabbi Shneur Zalman Rader 514.342.1770

SASKATCHEWAN

SASKATOON

Rabbi Raphael Kats 306.384.4370

CAYMAN ISLANDS

GEORGE TOWN

Rabbi Berel Pewzner 717.798.1040

COLOMBIA

BOGOTA

Rabbi Chanoch Piekarski 57.1.635.8251

COSTA RICA

S. JOSÉ

Rabbi Hershel Spalter

Rabbi Moshe Bitton 506.4010.1515

CROATIA

ZAGREB

Rabbi Pinchas Zaklas 385.1.4812227

DENMARK

COPENHAGEN

Rabbi Yitzchok Loewenthal 45.3316.1850

DOMINICAN REPUBLIC

S. DOMINGO

Rabbi Shimon Pelman 829.341.2770

ESTONIA

TALLINN

Rabbi Shmuel Kot 372.662.30.50

FRANCE

BOULOGNE

Rabbi Michael Sojcher 33.1.46.99.87.85

DIJON

Rabbi Chaim Slonim 33.6.52.05.26.65

LA VARENNE-S.-HILAIRE

Rabbi Mena'hem Mendel Benelbaz 33.6.17.81.57.47

MARSEILLE

Rabbi Eliahou Altabe 33.6.11.60.03.05

Rabbi Mena'hem Mendel Assouline 33.6.64.88.25.04

Rabbi Emmanuel Taubenblatt 33.4.88.00.94.85

PARIS

Rabbi Yona Hasky 33.1.53.75.36.01

Rabbi Acher Marciano 33.6.15.15.01.02

Rabbi Avraham Barou'h Pevzner 33.6.99.64.07.70

PONTAULT-COMBAULT

Rabbi Yossi Amar 33.6.61.36.07.70

VILLIERS-SUR-MARNE

Rabbi Mena'hem Mendel Mergui 33.1.49.30.89.66

GEORGIA

TBILISI

Rabbi Meir Kozlovsky 995.32.2429770

GERMANY

BERLIN

Rabbi Yehuda Tiechtel 49.30.2128.0830

DUSSELDORF

Rabbi Chaim Barkahn 49.173.2871.770

HAMBURG

Rabbi Shlomo Bistritzky 49.40.4142.4190

HANNOVER 49.511.811.2822

Chapter founded by Rabbi Binyamin Wolff, OBM

GREECE

ATHENS

Rabbi Mendel Hendel 30.210.323.3825

GUATEMALA

GUATEMALA CITY

Rabbi Shalom Pelman 502.2485.0770

ISRAEL

ASHKELON

Rabbi Shneor Lieberman 054.977.0512

BALFURYA

Rabbi Noam Bar-Tov 054.580.4770

CAESAREA

Rabbi Chaim Meir Lieberman 054.621.2586

EVEN YEHUDA

Rabbi Menachem Noyman 054.777.0707

GANEI TIKVA

Rabbi Gershon Shnur 054.524.2358

GIV'ATAYIM

Rabbi Pinchus Bitton 052.643.8770

JERUSALEM

Rabbi Levi Diamond 055.665.7702

Rabbi Avraham Hendel 054.830.5799

KARMIEL

Rabbi Mendy Elishevitz 054.521.3073

KFAR SABA

Rabbi Yossi Baitch 054.445.5020

KIRYAT BIALIK

Rabbi Pinny Marton 050.661.1768

KIRYAT MOTZKIN

Rabbi Shimon Eizenbach 050.902.0770

KOCHAV YAIR

Rabbi Dovi Greenberg 054.332.6244

MACCABIM-RE'UT

Rabbi Yosef Yitzchak Noiman 054.977.0549

NES ZIYONA

Rabbi Menachem Feldman 054.497.7092

NETANYA

Rabbi Schneur Brod 054.579.7572

RAMAT GAN-KRINITZI

Rabbi Yisroel Gurevitz 052.743.2814

RAMAT GAN-MAROM NAVE

Rabbi Binyamin Meir Kali 050.476.0770

RAMAT YISHAI

Rabbi Shneor Zalman Wolosow 052.324.5475

RISHON LEZION

Rabbi Uri Keshet 050.722.4593

ROSH PINA

Rabbi Sholom Ber Hertzel 052.458.7600

TEL AVIV

Rabbi Shneur Piekarski 054.971.5568

JAMAICA

MONTEGO BAY

Rabbi Yaakov Raskin 876.452.3223

JAPAN

TOKYO

Rabbi Mendi Sudakevich 81.3.5789.2846

KAZAKHSTAN

ALMATY

Rabbi Shevach Zlatopolsky 7.7272.77.59.49

KYRGYZSTAN

BISHKEK

Rabbi Arye Raichman 996.312.68.19.66

LATVIA

RIGA

Rabbi Shneur Zalman Kot

Mrs. Rivka Glazman 371.6720.40.22

LITHUANIA

VILNIUS

Rabbi Sholom Ber Krinsky 370.6817.1367

LUXEMBOURG

LUXEMBOURG

Rabbi Mendel Edelman 352.2877.7079

MEXICO

S. MIGUEL DE ALLENDE

Rabbi Daniel Huebner 52.41.5181.8092

PUERTO VALLARTA

Rabbi Shneur Hecht 52.32.2141.7279

NETHERLANDS

ALMERE

Rabbi Moshe Stiefel 31.36.744.0509

AMSTERDAM

Rabbi Yanki Jacobs 31.644.988.627
Rabbi Jaacov Zwi Spiero 31.652.328.065

EINDHOVEN

Rabbi Simcha Steinberg 31.63.635.7593

HAGUE

Rabbi Shmuel Katzman 31.70.347.0222

HEEMSTEDE-HAARLEM

Rabbi Shmuel Spiero 31.23.532.0707

MAASTRICHT

Rabbi Avrohom Cohen 32.48.549.6766

NIJMEGEN

Rabbi Menachem Mendel Levine 31.621.586.575

ROTTERDAM

Rabbi Yehuda Vorst 31.10.265.5530

PANAMA

PANAMA CITY

Rabbi Ari Laine
Rabbi Gabriel Benayon 507.223.3383

RUSSIA

ASTRAKHAN

Rabbi Yisroel Melamed 7.851.239.28.24

BRYANSK

Rabbi Menachem Mendel Zaklas 7.483.264.55.15

CHELYABINSK

Rabbi Meir Kirsh 7.351.263.24.68

MOSCOW

Rabbi Aizik Rosenfeld 7.906.762.88.81
Rabbi Mordechai Weisberg 7.495.645.50.00

NIZHNY NOVGOROD

Rabbi Shimon Bergman 7.920.253.47.70

NOVOSIBIRSK

Rabbi Shneur Zalmen Zaklos 7.903.900.43.22

OMSK

Rabbi Osher Krichevsky 7.381.231.33.07

PERM

Rabbi Zalman Deutch 7.342.212.47.32

ROSTOV

Rabbi Chaim Danzinger 7.8632.99.02.68

S. PETERSBURG

Rabbi Shalom Pewzner 7.911.726.21.19
Rabbi Zvi Pinsky 7.812.713.62.09

SAMARA

Rabbi Shlomo Deutch 7.846.333.40.64

SARATOV

Rabbi Yaakov Kubitshek 7.8452.21.58.00

TOGLIATTI

Rabbi Meier Fischer 7.848.273.02.84

UFA

Rabbi Dan Krichevsky 7.347.244.55.33

VORONEZH

Rabbi Levi Stiefel 7.473.252.96.99

SINGAPORE

SINGAPORE

Rabbi Mordechai Abergel 656.337.2189
Rabbi Netanel Rivni 656.336.2127
Classes in Hebrew

SOUTH AFRICA

JOHANNESBURG

Rabbi Dovid Masinter
Rabbi Ari Kievman 27.11.440.6600

SWEDEN

STOCKHOLM

Rabbi Chaim Greisman 46.70.790.8994

SWITZERLAND

LUZERN

Rabbi Chaim Drukman 41.41.361.1770

THAILAND

BANGKOK

Rabbi Yosef C. Kantor 6681.837.7618

UKRAINE

BERDITCHEV

Mrs. Chana Thaler 380.637.70.37.70

DNEPROPETROVSK

Rabbi Dan Makagon 380.504.51.13.18

NIKOLAYEV

Rabbi Sholom Gotlieb 380.512.37.37.71

ODESSA

Rabbi Avraham Wolf
Rabbi Yaakov Neiman 38.048.728.0770 EXT. 280

ZAPOROZHYE

Mrs. Nechama Dina Ehrentreu 380.957.19.96.08

ZHITOMIR

Rabbi Shlomo Wilhelm 380.504.63.01.32

UNITED KINGDOM

BOURNEMOUTH

Rabbi Bentzion Alperowitz 44.749.456.7177

CHEADLE

Rabbi Peretz Chein 44.161.428.1818

ESSEX

EPPING

Rabbi Yossi Posen 44.749.650.4345

LEEDS

Rabbi Eli Pink 44.113.266.3311

LONDON

Rabbi Moshe Adler 44.771.052.4460
Rabbi Boruch Altein 44.749.612.3342
Rabbi Mendel Cohen 44.736.640.8244
Rabbi Mechel Gancz 44.758.332.3074
Rabbi Chaim Hoch 44.753.879.9524
Rabbi Dovid Katz 44.207.625.2682
Mrs. Esther Kesselman 44.794.432.4829
Rabbi Mendy Korer 44.794.632.5444
Rabbi Eli Levin 44.754.046.1568
Mrs. Chanie Simon 44.208.458.0416
Rabbi Bentzi Sudak 44.781.211.1890
Rabbi Shneur Wineberg 44.745.628.6538

MANCHESTER

Rabbi Levi Cohen 44.161.792.6335
Rabbi Shmuli Jaffe 44.161.766.1812

RADLETT, HERTFORDSHIRE

Rabbi Alexander Sender Dubrawsky 44.794.380.8965

The Jewish Learning Multiplex

Brought to you by the Rohr Jewish Learning Institute

In fulfillment of the mandate of the Lubavitcher Rebbe, of blessed memory, whose leadership guides every step of our work, the mission of the Rohr Jewish Learning Institute is to transform Jewish life and the greater community through the study of Torah, connecting each Jew to our shared heritage of Jewish learning.

While our flagship program remains the cornerstone of our organization, JLI is proud to feature additional divisions catering to specific populations, in order to meet a wide array of educational needs.

THE ROHR JEWISH LEARNING INSTITUTE

A subsidiary of Merkos L'Inyonei Chinuch,
the adult educational arm of the Chabad-Lubavitch movement

Torah Studies provides a rich and nuanced encounter with the weekly Torah reading.

Jewish teens forge their identity as they engage in Torah study, social interaction, and serious fun.

The Rosh Chodesh Society gathers Jewish women together once a month for intensive textual study.

TorahCafe.com provides an exclusive selection of top-rated Jewish educational videos.

Participants delve into our nation's past while exploring the Holy Land's relevance and meaning today.

This yearly event rejuvenates mind, body, and spirit with a powerful synthesis of Jewish learning and community.

Equips youths facing adulthood with education and resources to address youth mental health.

Select affiliates are invited to partner with peers and noted professionals, as leaders of innovation and excellence.

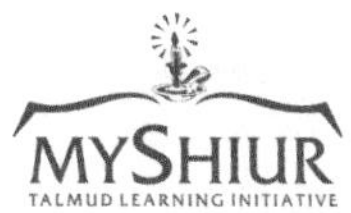

MyShiur courses are designed to assist students in developing the skills needed to study Talmud independently.

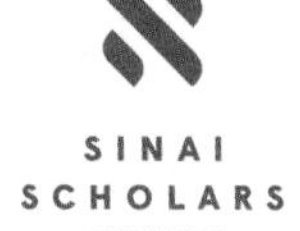

This rigorous fellowship program invites select college students to explore the fundamentals of Judaism.

A crash course that teaches adults to read Hebrew in just five sessions.

Machon Shmuel is an institute providing Torah research in the service of educators worldwide.

Notes

Notes

Notes

Notes

Notes

Notes